HAROLD LLOYD
MAGIC IN A PAIR OF HORN-RIMMED GLASSES

AND OTHER TURNING POINTS
IN THE LIFE AND CAREER OF A COMEDY LEGEND

BY ANNETTE D'AGOSTINO LLOYD

Harold Lloyd
Magic in a Pair of Horn-Rimmed Glasses
and Other Turning Points in the Life and Career of a Comedy Legend
©2009 Annette D'Agostino Lloyd

All rights reserved.

No part of this book may be reproduced in any form or by any means, electronic, mechanical, digital, photocopying, or recording, except for in the inclusion of a review, without permission in writing from the publisher.

Published in the USA by:

BearManor Media
P.O. Box 71426
Albany, Georgia 31708
www.BearManorMedia.com

ISBN: 1-59393-332-0 (alk. paper)

Edited by Lon Davis

Book design and layout by Valerie Thompson

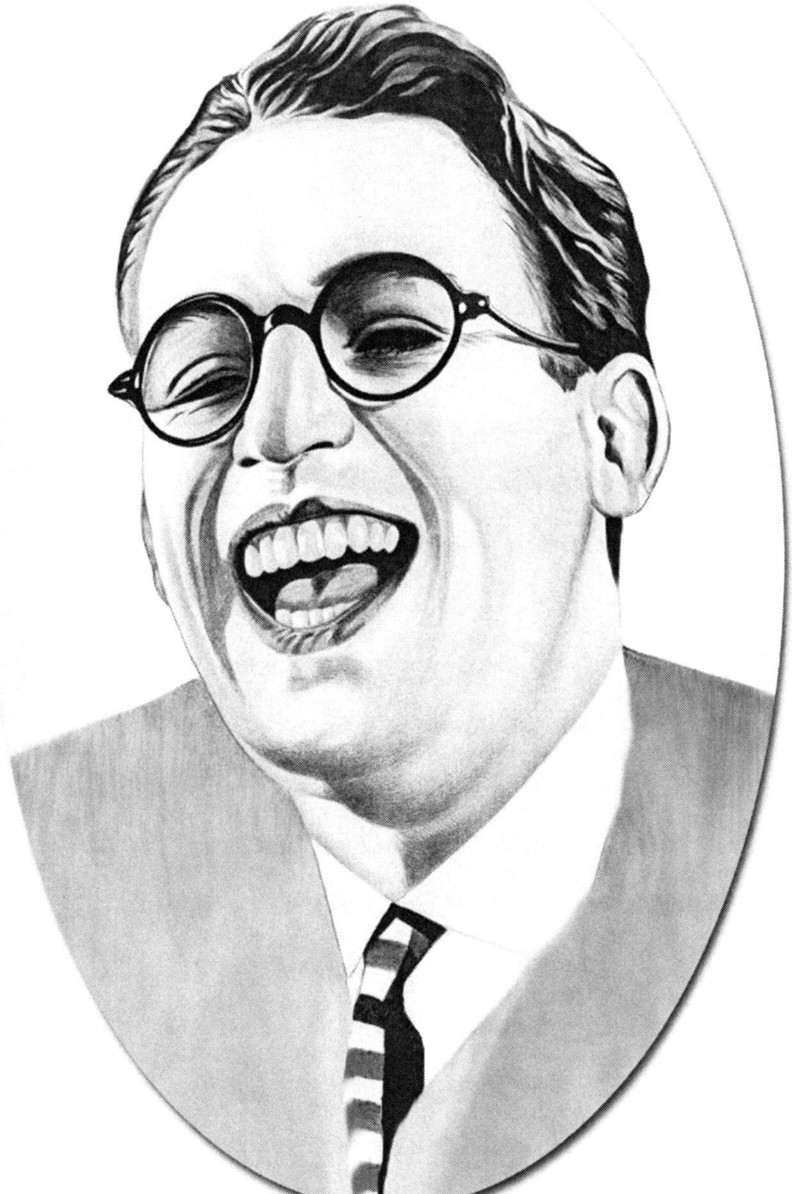

TABLE OF CONTENTS

ACKNOWLEDGMENTS . . . 1

INTRODUCTION . . . 6

HAROLD LLOYD 101 . . . 12

FACTS IN SUMMARY: HAROLD CLAYTON LLOYD . . . 17

NOTES ON THE WORDS OF HAROLD LLOYD . . . 31

THE DAWN OF HAROLD LLOYD . . . 34

THE EARLY INFLUENCE OF THE THEATRE . . . 40

MEETING JOHN LANE CONNOR . . . 44

THE SERENDIPITOUS FLIP OF A COIN . . . 51

HAROLD LLOYD'S FOUR-SECOND FILM DEBUT . . . 55

HAROLD LLOYD AND HAL ROACH CONNECT AT UNIVERSAL . . . 59

JUST NUTS IMPRESSES PATHÉ . . . 65

LONESOME LUKE . . . 73

THE GLASS CHARACTER . . . 83

HAROLD LLOYD'S USE OF THE PREVIEW . . . 109

THE GLASS CHARACTER GOES MULTIPLE REEL . . . 115

HAROLD LLOYD'S BOMB ACCIDENT . . . 125

Harold Lloyd's Entry into Features . . . 138

Harold Lloyd Releases *Grandma's Boy* . . . 145

The Harold Lloyd Thrill Comedies . . . 152

Harold Lloyd Corporation Makes Harold His Own Boss . . . 170

Marriage and Fatherhood . . . 183

Harold Lloyd Releases *The Freshman* . . . 195

Harold Lloyd's Rise with the Shriners . . . 206

Harold Lloyd Releases *The Kid Brother* . . . 212

Building Greenacres . . . 224

Harold Lloyd Releases *Speedy* . . . 240

Harold Lloyd Writes His Autobiography . . . 253

The Sunrise of Sound, and *Welcome Danger* . . . 259

Harold Lloyd Releases *The Cat's-Paw* . . . 271

Harold Lloyd Retains Control of His Pathé Output . . . 281

A Curious Human Being Turns Interested Hobbyist . . . 287

Harold Lloyd Releases His Final Film . . . 312

Granddaughter Suzanne Enters Harold's Life . . . 324

Harold Lloyd Is Recognized with Awards . . . 332

The Crafting of Two Film Compilations . . . 345

Harold Lloyd Succumbs to Cancer . . . 351

Harold Lloyd Lives On . . . 356

The Complete Chronological Filmography of Harold Lloyd . . . 367

Bibliography . . . 375

Index . . . 401

*Dedicated to
Fans of Harold Lloyd
Worldwide*

Harold is lucky to have each of you on his side.
You inspire me, and I thank you.

*"Children are the easiest of audiences, business men the most difficult,
and it is our particular pride that we draw both extremes
as well as the middle."*
— *Harold Lloyd, 1928*

ACKNOWLEDGMENTS
Among Those Present . . .

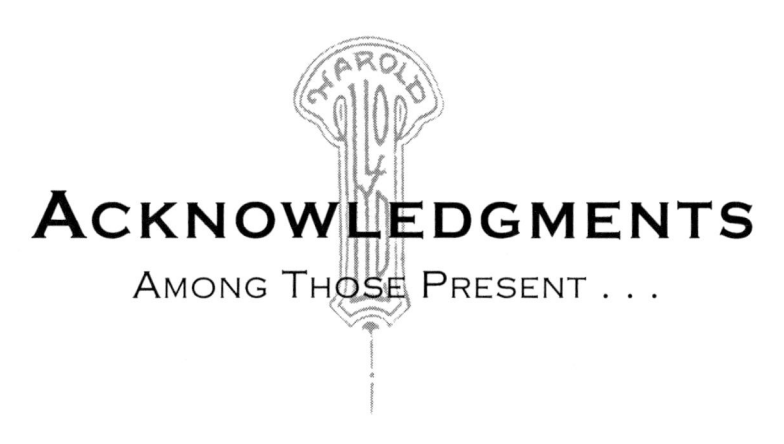

"We were able to work hand and glove, and figure out ideas together, and it was wonderful . . . it was a wonderful relationship." [1]

Much in the same spirit in which Harold Lloyd recognized the importance of his work with Hal Roach, I, too, am filled with gratitude for the throngs of friends, colleagues, acquaintances, and mentors who have made my years of work on this man infinitely easier and more joyous.

No author works alone. Collaboration is the life breath of research, and because of those who have helped me along the way, my contribution to film scholarship has been stronger, my resolve more unyielding, and my belief in Harold Lloyd more unwavering. I am a better person, and a better chronicler, because of those around me.

First, I have to thank those friends and colleagues who did not live to see this work, but who aided me greatly, either directly or circuitously. Among those I will miss all my days, and who I thank profusely, yet posthumously: Richard A. Braff, Gaylord Carter, Peggy Cartwright, Harold "Rusty" Castleton, Constance Cummings, Critt Davis, Sally A. Dumaux, William K. Everson, David Gill, Herb Graff, Bernice LaPorta, Ted Larson, Robert Nudleman, Phil Serling, Gene Vazzana, and Constance Williams.

I am blessed with a wonderful family, from New York to California to Florida, and points in between, filled with supportive and patient people who not only put up with my passion for all things Harold, but who genuinely seem to share in it. At the top of that list is my darling husband, Scott Lloyd, who I met on my haroldlloyd.us website in 1996, and who remains the veritable other half of me: Harold might have been my *first* Mr. Lloyd, but Scott is my *last*, and my *finest*. Our son Matthew was "in the oven" when my *Harold Lloyd Encyclopedia* was published in 2003 — he now asks me daily how my work on Uncle Harold is coming along. Being Matt's Mama is my life's greatest gift: Mattman, always run with what you believe in, and most of all, believe in yourself. My parents, Michael and Annette D'Agostino, have remained a source of strength and inspiration for me, and always will be: they raised me to believe in myself, and my every accomplishment in life will root from them. Finally, one of my greatest sources of pride is my beautiful stepdaughter Jessica Lloyd Cannistraci, her husband Anthony, and their beautiful daughter — our first grandchild — Gianna: you will always have Nana Annie's love, support, gratitude and respect. What a dynamite family I have.

To Ben Ohmart, the head of BearManor Media — thank you, so very much, for your belief in me and in Harold Lloyd.

To the many people who made significant contributions to this book, I thank you in alphabetical order. You might have sent me an anecdotal e-mail, or a mass mailing, or a photocopy; you might have watched Matt for me, or otherwise gave me time to write — it *all* helped, and I am grateful to you. Here's hoping that you enjoy the part you played in the realization of this addition to the Lloyd library: Joseph Adamson, Brian Anthony, Robert Arkus, Richard W. Bann, Jane Bartholomew, John Bengtson, Floyd C. Bennett, Jr., Bo Berglund, Robert S. Birchard, Bernadette Bowman, Dorothy Bradley, Kelly Brown, Gary Browning, Kevin Brownlow, Bruce Calvert, Diana Serra Cary, Lynn Clarke, John Cocchi, Ned Comstock (University of Southern California, Special Collections), Richard Correll, Susan Dalton, The Daughters of Naldi, Gerald N. Davis, Lon Davis, Anthony DiFlorio, Diana Doyle, Tim Dunleavy, William D. Eggert, Rob Farr, Richard Finegan, George Fisher, Cal Francis, Joe Franklin, Loretta Gentes, Dennis Gibson, Paul E. Gierucki, Sam Gill, Stella Grace, Dave Greim, Jere Guldin, Ron Hall, Rosemary Hanes and Madeline Matz (Library of Congress, Motion Picture, Broadcasting, and Recorded Sound Division), Patricia Hanson

ACKNOWLEDGMENTS: AMONG THOSE PRESENT

From 1995: Your author beside a life-sized cardboard cutout of Harold Lloyd — he's just one of the people she's grateful to.

The late Peggy Cartwright, co-star with HL in From Hand to Mouth, *understood the mission: Remembering Harold.*

(American Film Institute), Bob Henderson, Eugene Hilchey (Century Archives), Donna Hill, Caroline Hodge, Daniel W. Horton, Tracy Houston, Will Hutchins, the Island Trees Public Library, Martha Jett, Cole Johnson, Mark Johnson, Henry Joncas, David Kalat, Marton Kurutz, J.B. Kaufman, Marty Kearns, Bob King, Peter Langs, Steve Langs, Rick Levinson, Philip Leibfried, Paul Lisy, Duane Lloyd, Gloria Lloyd, Suzanne Lloyd, Bruce Long, Tim Lussier, Leonard Maltin, Jeffery Masino, Laura Mazzuca, Donald W. McCaffrey, Don McCormick, Agnes McFadden, Diane McIntyre, Hooman Mehran, Glenn Mitchell, Joseph D. Moore, the Museum of Modern Art Film Library, Joan Myers, Jeff Paris, James Robert Parish, Christine Patterson, David B. Pearson, Steve Ramsey, Joe Rinaudo, Richard Roberts, Ben Robinson, David Lloyd Ross, Ulrich Ruedel, Rod Searcey, Michael Schlesinger, Jerry Schwartz, Andrew Sholl, Richard Simonton, Randy Skretvedt, Christopher Snowden, Bill Sprague, L. Joe Stehlik, Ed Stratmann, Doug Swarthout, Terry Swindol, Stan Taffel, Olwen Terris (British Film Institute), Karl Tiedemann, Patricia Eliot Tobias, the

Tournament of Roses Public Relations Department, Greg Travis, Sarah Treanor, George Tselos (Thomas A. Edison Archive), Steve Vaught, Anthony Walker, Marc Wanamaker (Bison Archives), Edward C. Watz, Brent Walker, Wendy Warwick White, Dell Wolfensparger, Valerie Yaros, and Tonie Zwaneveld. Please, if I forgot anybody, forgive me. Sixteen years' worth of good people can overwhelm even the most grateful of minds.

To the many fans of Harold Lloyd — his best friends in this new generation — I extend my heartfelt thanks and admiration. You are a strong lot, a faithful bunch, and your loyalty towards him and his work has always been a source of inspiration to me. Your years' worth of questions and comments have expanded my mind and my drive. I hope you enjoy this work — and I am grateful for your example of fortitude and enthusiasm.

Finally, to Harold Clayton Lloyd: my most heartfelt thanks of all go to you. I owe you every energy I have given you, and more — finding you was one of the most glorious turning points of my life.

INTRODUCTION

A TURNING POINT LLOYD STILL LIVES WITH
"There are so many things, when you think of them, that are actual turning points." [A]

A first date . . . an initial job promotion . . . a marriage proposal . . . a big move. These, and many others, are typical *turning points* in one's life — the moments, the events, the occurrences that change us, better us, ruin us, shape who we ultimately are. They are the episodes that spur you on to further successes, push you to fix mistakes, help you to know yourself better, define *you*.

In my continuing journey through the statement, "Harold Lloyd is an undiscovered country," I have felt it vital to ponder, identify, research, and thoroughly nitpick the happenings in Lloyd's life that shaped his personal and professional evolution. Through three books on Lloyd (*Harold Lloyd: A Bio-Bibliography* was published in 1994, and *The Harold Lloyd Encyclopedia* in 2003; a third book was privately commissioned in 2005 and had a run of *one* copy), I touched the surface of the major turning points in his life and career. Still, however, I was unable, either for space or time reasons, to delve deeply enough into his motivations, his challenges, his obstacles and his victories — the actual happenings and events that changed him, for better or worse. Harold, himself, actually realized the importance of these events: "There are so many things, when you think of them, that are *actual* turning points." [A] This book will, as no other of my books could, present the existence-altering finds in my Lloyd dig — a nearly 30-year archaeological expedition filled with dirt, dust, some bones, yet lots of exhilaration and discovery. And, utilizing scores of quotes and excerpts from personally transcribed interviews with the man himself, Harold Lloyd will help me tell his amazing tales.

In his day, Harold Lloyd was one of the most popular and successful film comedians in the world, a true shining star in the cinematic galaxy. His popularity can be measured somewhat in terms of polls and questionnaires, but is most effectively demonstrated in terms of cold, hard box office numbers. Lloyd's eleven silent features, from 1921–1928, grossed more than $19 million; unlike any filmmaker or star today, Lloyd got 80% of the profits, according to his contract. Thus, he personally made more than $15 million in that seven-year span. If we translate 1920s money into contemporary terms by, say, analyzing the relative share of the Gross Domestic Product, one 1928 dollar is worth $142.16 today. Using those same calculations, by the end of 2007, $15 million from 1928 was worth $2,132,388,554.03 — today, at the level of his popularity in his day, Harold Lloyd would have made over $2.1 billion in just seven years.

> **FUN FACT**
>
> HAROLD LLOYD WAS SERIOUS ABOUT NOT WANTING HIS FILMS SHOWN ON TELEVISION. ON FEBRUARY 11, 1952, HAROLD LLOYD CORPORATION FILED SUIT AGAINST NBC AND LOS ANGELES AFFILIATES KTTV AND KNBH FOR BROADCASTING CLIPS OF *SAFETY LAST!* ON JULY 5, 1951 AND FEBRUARY 7, 1952. THE DAMAGES REQUESTED WERE $300,000 — ALSO MENTIONED WAS THAT ALL POSITIVE AND NEGATIVE FILMS OF THE TELECASTS BE IMPOUNDED AND DESTROYED.

Given just that one arena of facts, why is his name not more widely recognized, or his films better known and appreciated? It's easily explained, when you think of *the most* far-reaching and ultimately damaging turning point of his life and career . . .

Harold Lloyd didn't allow his films to be aired in the infancy of television.

Television was commercially introduced to US consumers in 1941. In its earliest days, TV stations were hungry for programming, so in

HL put himself into quite the perilous pickle by keeping his films off the small screen.

many cases they turned to classic films: shorts and features, sound and silent. This was a golden opportunity for new generations to be introduced to the film luminaries who entertained early-20th century audiences. Laurel & Hardy, Our Gang, Chaplin, Keaton, even Conway Tearle and Mabel Normand, were given fresh life via this new medium of television. Interest in their careers, and discussion of their "legacies" (strange, because most of them were still alive at the time) abounded, and old names quickly became new yet familiar friends.

One name glaringly missing from the programming rundown was Harold Lloyd. He flatly refused to allow his films to be aired on television — as the sole owner of his films, he had every right to do so — yet his simple reasoning has, to this day, grave and complex consequences.

Pre-cable television had very stringent time restraints — programs were normally aired in 15, 30, or 60-minute intervals, with frequent (and necessary) commercial breaks. To Lloyd, this translated to a less-than-ideal venue for the screening of his pictures. It meant interruption of story flow (". . . as Harold holds onto that clock hand, let's take a break from the action and hear from our good friends at Joe's Pizzeria . . ."); it meant editing for program length (60 minutes of air time typically resulted in 51 minutes of programming with an average of five commercial breaks — the "cutting room floor" ramifications for the 82-minute-long *Girl Shy* seem rather obvious). His reasoning was sound — he respected his films, and didn't want them edited down or interrupted — to him, the flow of the story and the development of the character would have suffered, and the impact of his films, as a result, would have been diminished.

But what Lloyd *didn't* consider was the long-term impact of his absence from television screens. While his contemporaries were being thrown into the mainstream anew, Harold wasn't. While new generations were being born — some growing to become today's film scholars, critics, and image movers — Lloyd wasn't there to entertain them. And his name and career legacy suffered — relegated to a veritable footnote, compared with some of his friendly rivals, whose names and works remain much better known, and more celebrated.

I dare speculate that, had television *then* been like television *now*, with many movies shown, uninterrupted and in their entirety, Lloyd would have embraced the medium wholeheartedly — he'd have loved it. And it would have done wonders for his visibility and his name recognition quotient.

Back in 1979, when I first stumbled upon the Time-Life PBS series *Harold Lloyd's World of Comedy*, my excitement and curiosity knew no bounds. Having watched only a handful of silent films to that time, and with cursory classic-film knowledge of only Laurel & Hardy and Our Gang, I knew little to nothing about 1920s cinema, and had never heard the name Harold Lloyd before — thus, my mind was a rather clean palate to start painting upon. I eagerly shared my discovery with my parents, born during the FDR administration — they had no idea who I was talking about.

From *Why Worry?* (1923) — formerly mired in invisibility, HL and his fans can smile increasingly more.

My friends in high school looked at me like I had three heads (imagine a 17-year-old actually watching something black and white *and* with no dialogue!). On the other hand, my grandparents, Italian immigrants who became US citizens in the 1920s, knew *exactly* who I was talking about, and totally understood my enthusiasm; they loved him, and never missed a new Lloyd film.

However, when I contracted to write my first book on Lloyd in late 1992, my grandparents' understanding didn't help me out much. These were pre-Internet-in-every-home-and-on-every-phone days. DVD players hadn't been introduced yet. What VHS tapes I could get were fuzzy copy-of-a-copy-of-a-copy collections of, mostly, Blackhawk 8mm dupes. He was never on television (by that time, the Time-Life series was long off the air), and hardly ever in the theatres. Of the roughly six books written on him to that date, only four remotely satisfied me. The blank stares I got when I spoke of my initial book subject both irritated and strangely inspired me. Many, many of his fans have told me the same tales of having glimpsed the genius, but being denied a further look. It was, for a very long time, a great challenge to be a Lloyd fan, simply because it was so hard to find him.

During the year that I worked on my first book, things changed — his centennial year of 1993 saw his name propelled into newspapers and magazines, and his films popped up on movie screens the world over. He was put on a US postage stamp in 1994. Websites emerged on the Internet, dedicated to his life and work (and I am proud that my own, www.haroldlloyd.us, founded in 1995, has the distinction of being *the first*). From 1995–1999, I ran H.E.L.L.O.! (Harold, Everyman, Lloyd Lives On!), and published its quarterly newsletter, *The Lloyd Herald*, and that helped broaden his worldwide fan base significantly. Lloyd books became reachable via Internet and mail vendors, as did memorabilia and collectibles. In 2005, *The Harold Lloyd Comedy Collection* DVD set, sanctioned by the Harold Lloyd Estate and Film Trust, offered 15 features and 13 shorts; their international counterparts have been issued worldwide, and more such releases are planned. And, largely due to increased accessibility of his films, Lloyd frequently airs on classic movie channels. New generations are finally, at long last, easily discovering this comic genius and his wonderful films.

It's not as hard to find him anymore — this Harold Lloyd country is slowly being discovered — but there is still so much unearthing yet to be done. It is my hope that this book will help shed new light on not only an appreciation and understanding of Harold Lloyd's life-changing turning points, but help towards a general celebration of just *how* they changed both him and the film industry. There are many stories that comprise the dash between his dates, and it's my honor to share them with you — *Let's Go!*

HAROLD LLOYD 101

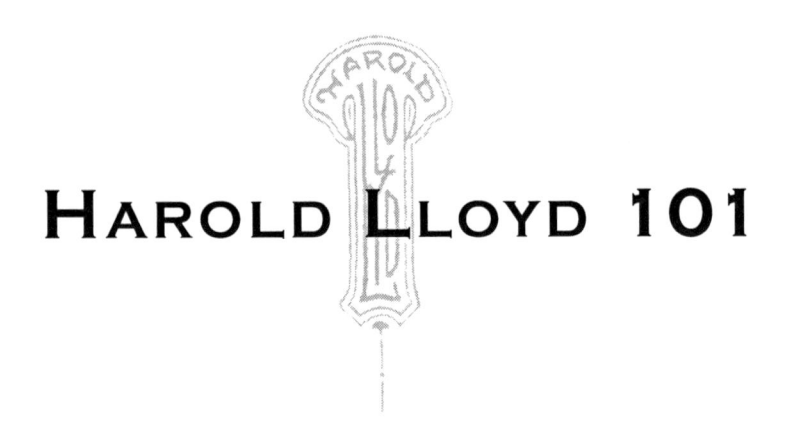

The Magic Behind the Glasses
"I want to leave something worthwhile on the screen."

"A lot of people have said would you discourage or encourage youngsters wanting a histrionic career? You certainly can't discourage them; I couldn't, because from the background I've had, I didn't have anything that pointed that I should be an actor, nothing particularly." [E]

He is mainly remembered today for his antics on a skyscraper clock, but the life and career of Harold Lloyd remain much more diverse and exciting than any single image. This man lived, indeed, *the* American Success story, and the tales that comprise his life reveal a dazzling array of turning points.

Harold Clayton Lloyd was born in Burchard, Nebraska, on April 20, 1893, the second son of James Darsie and Elizabeth Fraser Lloyd. During his childhood, they lived, at various times, in the towns of Pawnee City, Humboldt, Beatrice, and Omaha, Nebraska, and Fort Collins, Durango, and Denver, Colorado. The reason for this nomadic existence was his father's difficulty in keeping a job; it was this inconsistency that led Elizabeth to divorce her husband, nicknamed "Foxy," in 1910. The two boys (elder brother Gaylord Fraser Lloyd was born in 1888, and died in 1943) shuffled between mother and father for a time, before making permanent home with Foxy.

Throughout Harold's childhood, he shared with his mother a passion for the theatre, and engaged in amateur theatrics for most of his adolescence. In 1906, young Harold met the single greatest influence on his histrionic art, actor and mentor John Lane Connor: "Point by point he went over my performance as a mechanic goes over a motor, pointed out bad timing, wrong emphasis, and other A B C errors of technic." [1]

In 1912, Foxy, now working for the Singer Sewing Machine Company, had an accident, which produced a monetary settlement of three thousand dollars. With this money, the Lloyd men could really live, but the question was: where? The flip of a coin sent the men to San Diego, California, where Connor had established a dramatic school, which Harold joined immediately, as both a student and an instructor.

It wasn't long, however, before Harold bowed to the lure of "cellu-Lloyd" — a 1913 film debut led to sporadic extra work for Edison, Keystone, and Universal. While at Universal City, Lloyd met a fellow extra, Hal Roach, who would later establish his own production house, The Rolin Film Company, and take on Lloyd as principal talent. Together, the young men would learn how to make films, and would grow to virtually define film comedy in the process.

Harold Lloyd's first comedy character was *Willie Work*, whose appearance was directly patterned after Charles Chaplin's Tramp. With this character, at least two films were released, though many more were made. The next character, *Lonesome Luke*, varied the Tramp theme somewhat, by employing tight clothes, two-dot mustache, and wide smile. Lloyd was never happy with this persona ("Wide, heavy slapstick on the simplest theme . . . eight hundred feet of so-called plot . . . I loathed the get-up and the character. . ."), though sixty-seven films were released to very good reviews and popular acclaim. A newer, better, and more unique character was in Lloyd's mind, as early as 1916, but it was a year later, after threatening to quit, that Harold was allowed to try out the new persona, dubbed *The Glass Character*. This role, which put a normal-looking boy onto the screen, with the single defining characteristic being a pair of lens-less horn-rimmed glasses, came to change the standard definition of comedy at the time, and reflected the very audience it was entertaining. No more did a character have to be quirky, grotesque, or out-of-the-ordinary in order to be funny: Lloyd proved that.

On the beach in Santa Monica, **HL** (WITH RIGHT HAND IN THE SAND) **smiles at author Ethel Sands, who was profiling him for a 1922 *Picture Play* magazine article. Flanking them are Roy Brooks and Mildred Davis.**

From the beginning, the new character found favor with audiences. With each film, reviews got more and more favorable. In April 1919, Lloyd signed a contract for a series of longer, and more sophisticated, two-reel comedies, at a greater salary and wider distribution. Life seemed to be just starting for the comic.

Then came August 24, 1919. This day found Harold posing for publicity stills at Witzel Photographers, Los Angeles. One shot called for Lloyd to light a cigarette from a prop bomb, striking a sassy, devil-may-care pose. The prop, though, so resembled a real bomb that an actual real bomb got mistakenly mixed in with the fakes — the real bomb was handed to Lloyd. He lit an already-lit cigarette onto the wick, but found that the excessive smoke prohibited a good picture. As he signaled for a new wick, the bomb exploded. The force of the blast temporarily blinded Lloyd, ripped the thumb and forefinger from his right hand, and kept him out of the studio for almost five months. Thanks to the input of former glove salesman Sam Goldwyn, Lloyd's impairment was covered within a prosthetic glove. At no time did Lloyd ever publicly discuss the loss of the fingers — he would acknowledge the accident, even mentioned an "injury" to his hand, but never the disability. Lloyd did not want his audiences to come to see his films out of pity or curiosity. He wanted people, simply, to laugh with him.

And that they did . . . popularity grew with each release, and so did his coverage in the magazines. Author Ethel Sands interviewed Lloyd in 1922, and had this to report: "Really, I think he is *the* favorite comedian with the girl fans, because he never seems like a clown . . . he is different . . . instead of that sort of self-assured, rather 'nervy' manner he affects on screen, he has a shy modest way about him that is the biggest surprise of all."

The films kept on coming. Two-reelers grew to three-reelers, then to feature length with *A Sailor-Made Man* in 1921. Eleven silent features were released between 1921 and 1928. Seven sound features followed from 1929 through 1947. All the films took The Glass Character to new heights, exploring a wide array of situations and lifestyles, but all featuring the optimistic go-getter whose enthusiasm got him out of scrape after scrape. Obstacles were laughed at, while the audiences rolled in the aisles. Lloyd once claimed that the toughest part of a screen comic's life was "fresh invention, to think up gags," noting that he took in the "comedies every season to find out what gags to avoid." The sound age saw a decline in Lloyd's popularity, mainly because Depression-era audiences lost their association with the optimism of his character.

A staggering number of hobbies and interests filled Lloyd's life outside of his cinematic pursuits — Harold was always a curious being. His penchants for photography, bowling, magic, painting, microscopy, handball, etc., were met with investigation and mastery. His passions — legendary romantic trysts with his leading ladies, and photo sessions with nude models — reveal a very human being with superhuman tastes. A red-blooded American boy.

Lloyd married his leading lady, Mildred Davis, on February 10, 1923, and together they raised three children at Greenacres, their spectacular 16-acre Beverly Hills estate. Gloria, born in 1923, still lives in Los Angeles. Peggy, adopted in 1930, died in 1986. Harold, Jr., born in 1931, died three months after his father in 1971. Mildred, Lloyd's wife of forty-six years, died on August 18, 1969, at 68.

Harold Lloyd's final public appearance found him in London, at the Cinema City Exhibition celebrating the seventy-fifth anniversary of film. He showed his classic, *The Kid Brother*, to the cheers of appreciative audiences and, four months before his death, waxed career nostalgic: "My humor was never cruel or cynical. I just took life and poked fun at it. We made it so it could be understood the world over, without language barriers. We seem to have conquered the time barrier, too."

Harold Clayton Lloyd succumbed to prostate cancer on March 8, 1971, at 77. He died in bed, at his beloved Greenacres, the exquisite estate built upon every laugh that his films produced.

As new generations are introduced to Harold Lloyd's work and legend, the magic behind the glasses will continue to conjure the quintessential American Success Story. He cared about his work, and understood his legacy: "I want to leave something worthwhile on the screen . . . Something with guts, not just the froth of old." Truth be told: every time we enjoy his films, we see that he met his goal.

Facts in Summary
Harold Clayton Lloyd

Biographical Facts

BIRTH: Thursday, April 20, 1893, Burchard, Nebraska

ANCESTRY: Welsh

FATHER: JAMES DARSIE LLOYD, born June 21, 1864, Ebensberg, Pennsylvania, to James and Helen Lloyd; died December 17, 1947, Los Angeles, California

MOTHER: ELIZABETH FRASER LLOYD, born January 10, 1869, Toulon, Illinois, to James and Sarah Fraser; died August 17, 1941, Beverly Hills, California

BROTHER: GAYLORD FRASER LLOYD, born March 29, 1888, Burchard, Nebraska; died September 1, 1943, Los Angeles, California

WIFE: MILDRED HILLARY DAVIS LLOYD, born February 22, 1901, Philadelphia, Pennsylvania, to Howard Beckett and Caroline Boileau Davis; died August 18, 1969, Santa Monica, California

CHILDREN: MILDRED GLORIA LLOYD GUASTI ROBERTS, born May 22, 1923, Los Angeles, California; MARJORIE ELIZABETH "PEGGY" LLOYD ROSS

PATTEN, born Gloria Gabrielle Freeman on April 15, 1925, Hermosa Beach, California, adopted by Lloyds December 5, 1930, died November 18, 1986, Newport Beach, California; HAROLD CLAYTON LLOYD, JR., born January 25, 1931, Hollywood, California, died June 8, 1971, North Hollywood, California

RELIGIOUS AFFILIATION: Episcopalian

POLITICAL PARTY: Republican

HONORS: Grauman's Chinese Theatre Ceremony #4, November 21, 1927; Academy Award nomination (Best Comedy Direction, *Speedy*), 1927-28; Imperial Potentate, Ancient Arabic Order of the Nobles of the Mystic Shrine, July 1949; named Head of California Delegation at 1952 Republican National Convention; Honorary Academy Award, March 19, 1953; George Eastman Awards ("For distinguished contribution to the art of motion pictures"), for 1915-1925, awarded on November 19, 1955, and 1926-1930, given on October 26, 1957; Cannes Film Festival plaque ("To the Grand Prince of Cinema"), May 13, 1962; Harold Lloyd's World of Comedy Week, Los Angeles, July 22-29, 1962; Man of the Year, The Masquers, January 18, 1963; Beverly Hills Man of the Year, February 11, 1963; Thalian Award ("Mr. Wonderful"), October 7, 1967; American Film Institute Inaugural Master Seminar (eventually named for him), September 23, 1969; Memorialization Resolution #252, Assembly Rules Committee – California Legislature, April 1, 1971; National Register of Historic Places (The Harold Lloyd Estate), February 9, 1984; The Harold Lloyd Motion Picture Scoring Sound Stage founded at the University of Southern California, 1984; National Register of Historic Places (The Harold Lloyd Birthplace), December 22, 1993; "Silent Screen Stars," United States 29-cent postage stamp, April 27, 1994

DEATH: Monday, March 8, 1971, 3:45pm, Greenacres, Beverly Hills, California

BURIAL: Thursday, March 11, 1971, Great Mausoleum, Begonia Terrace, Crypt 771, Forest Lawn Memorial Park, Glendale, CA (also in the family crypt: James Darsie Lloyd, Elizabeth Fraser Lloyd, Gaylord Fraser Lloyd, Maye Belle [Mrs. Gaylord] Lloyd, Mildred Davis Lloyd, Harold Lloyd, Jr.)

CHRONOLOGY

1864   Father, James Darsie Lloyd born, June 21

1869   Mother, Elizabeth Fraser born, January 10

1874   John Lane Connor born, May 21

1888   Brother, Gaylord Fraser born, March 29

1889   Harry "Snub" Pollard born, November 9

1890   Unnamed Sister born to James and Elizabeth, and then dies, either stillborn or in infancy

1892   Harry Eugene "Hal" Roach born, January 14

1893   Harold Clayton Lloyd born, April 20

1894   Lloyd family moves to Pawnee City, Nebraska

1895   Lloyd family moves to Humboldt, Nebraska

1896   Lloyd family moves to Denver, Colorado

1900   Jobyna Ralston born, November 21

1901   Virginia "Bebe" Daniels born, January 14
                 Mildred Hillary Davis born, February 22

1903   Harold Lloyd's stage debut, as Fleance in *Macbeth*

1906   Harold Lloyd meets John Lane Connor

1907   Lloyd family moves to Omaha, Nebraska
                 Harold Lloyd's first major stage role, as Abraham in *Tess of the d'Urbervilles*, January 10

1910   James and Elizabeth Lloyd divorce

1912   James, Gaylord and Harold Lloyd move to San Diego, California

1913   Harold Lloyd's film debut, as a Yaqui Indian in *The Old Monk's Tale*, February 15
                 James, Gaylord and Harold Lloyd move to Los Angeles, California
                 Harold Lloyd appears in four known released films

1914   Harold Lloyd joins Hal Roach's new Rolin Film Company
                 Harold Lloyd appears in three known released films

1915   Harold Lloyd appears in 24 known released films
                 Willie Runs the Park, the first known Willie Work release, issued, February 2
                 Just Nuts, the final Willie Work comedy, released, April 19
                 Harold Lloyd leaves Keystone and rejoins Rolin Film Company, June

Spitball Sadie, the first Lonesome Luke comedy, released, July 26
Harold Lloyd's weekly salary, $5, February 1
Harold Lloyd's weekly salary, $50, June 19

1916 Harold Lloyd appears in 34 films, all in one-reel length
Harold Lloyd's weekly salary, $100, August 5

1917 Harold Lloyd appears in 29 films, in one- and two-reel lengths
Lonesome Luke's Lively Life, the first two-reel Lonesome Luke comedy, released, March 18
Over the Fence, the first Glass Character comedy, released, September 9
Lonesome Luke in We Never Sleep, the final Lonesome Luke comedy, released, December 2
Harold Lloyd's weekly salary, $125, February 3
Harold Lloyd's weekly salary, $175, February 10
Harold Lloyd's weekly salary, $150, March 10

1918 Harold Lloyd appears in 34 films, all in one-reel length
James, Gaylord and Harold Lloyd move to 369 S. Hoover Street
Harold Lloyd's weekly salary, $200, February 9
Harold Lloyd's weekly salary, $300, February 16

1919 Harold Lloyd appears in 40 films, in one- and two-reel lengths
Look Out Below, the first of Lloyd's legendary thrill comedies, released, March 16
Harold Lloyd's weekly salary, $400, April 5
Rolin Film Company and Pathé Distributors contract for two-reel Glass Character shorts, April 12
Just Neighbors, the final Glass Character one-reeler, released, July 13
Final day of shooting on *Haunted Spooks* before

Lloyd's bomb accident, August 23
Harold Lloyd's bomb accident, August 24
Harold Lloyd released from hospital, September 9
Harold Lloyd's weekly salary, $500, October 18
Bumping Into Broadway, the first two-reel Glass Character comedy, released November 2
Bebe Daniels' final film with Harold Lloyd, *Captain Kidd's Kids*, released, November 30
Mildred Davis' first film with Harold Lloyd, *From Hand to Mouth*, released, December 28

1920
Harold Lloyd appears in six films, in two- and three-reel lengths
Shooting resumes on *Haunted Spooks*, January 5
Harold Lloyd's weekly salary, $750, January 10
Snub Pollard's final film with Harold Lloyd, *His Royal Slyness*, released, February 8

1921
Harold Lloyd appears in five films in two-, three- and four-reel lengths
Harold Lloyd's weekly salary, $1000, January 8
Now or Never, the first Glass Character three-reeler, released, May 5
Never Weaken, the final Glass Character short subject, released, October 22
A Sailor-Made Man, the first Glass Character feature, released, December 25

1922
Grandma's Boy released, September 3
Dr. Jack released, December 19
Harold Lloyd Corporation established, April 24
Building climb sequence in *Safety Last!* shot, August

1923
Marriage of Harold Lloyd and Mildred Davis, February 10
Mildred Davis' final film with Harold Lloyd, *Safety Last!*, released, April 1

Daughter Mildred Gloria Lloyd born, May 22
Jobyna Ralston's first film with Harold Lloyd, *Why Worry?*, released, September 16
Harold Lloyd Corporation purchases 40 acres for his Westwood Location Ranch, October 16

1924 Harold and Mildred Lloyd move to 502 S. Irving Boulevard
Girl Shy released, April 20
Harold Lloyd signs distribution deal with Paramount Pictures, October 1
Hot Water released, November 2
On-location shooting for *The Freshman* during Stanford/UC-Berkeley game, November 22

1925 James and Harold Lloyd join Ancient Arabic Order of the Nobles of the Mystic Shrine
Daughter Marjorie Elizabeth "Peggy" Lloyd born, April 15
The Freshman released, September 20

1926 *For Heaven's Sake* released, April 5
Harold Lloyd initiated into Shriners' Al Malaikah Temple, July 10
Harold Lloyd named "life member" of Al Malaikah Temple, October 25

1927 Jobyna Ralston's final film with Harold Lloyd, *The Kid Brother*, released, January 22
Harold Lloyd and crew arrive in New York for location shooting on *Speedy*, August 18
Harold Lloyd's Grauman's Chinese Theatre ceremony, November 21

1928 *An American Comedy*, Lloyd's autobiography, published by Longmans, Green & Co., September 12
Speedy, the final Glass Character silent film, released, April 7

1929	H.C. Witwer sues Harold Lloyd Corporation for copyright infringement over *The Freshman*, April 11 Harold, Mildred and Gloria Lloyd move to 1225 Benedict Canyon Drive (Greenacres), August *Welcome Danger*, the first Glass Character sound film, released, October 12
1930	Harold Lloyd and crew aboard the S.S. Malolo for location shooting on *Feet First*, June 5 H.C. Witwer's widow wins infringment lawsuit, July 9 Gloria Freeman joins Lloyd household, renamed Marjorie Elizabeth "Peggy," September 2 *Feet First* released, November 8 Peggy Lloyd's adoption legalized, December 5
1931	Son Harold Clayton Lloyd, Jr., born, January 25 Harold Lloyd has appendectomy, April 9
1932	*Movie Crazy* released, September 23 Remarriage of James Darsie Lloyd to Helen Marshall, October 27
1933	Witwer infringement lawsuit result reversed after appeal, April 10
1934	*The Cat's-Paw* released, August 7
1936	*The Milky Way* released, February 7
1938	Explosion and fire at Pathé's New Jersey storage facility, destroying many Lloyd shorts, January 17 *Professor Beware* released, July 29
1939	Harold Lloyd elected Potentate of Al Malaikah Temple

1940	Harold Lloyd announced as one of the new Board of Directors of KMPC radio, Los Angeles, January 14
1941	Harold Lloyd-produced *A Girl, a Guy and a Gob* released, March 14 Elizabeth Fraser Lloyd dies, August 17 John Lane Connor dies, September 10
1942	Harold Lloyd-produced *My Favorite Spy* released, June 12
1943	Nitrate explosion and fire at Greenacres film vault, destroying many Lloyd shorts, August 5 Gaylord Fraser Lloyd dies, September 1
1944	Harold Lloyd debuts as host of *Old Gold Comedy Theatre* radio series, October 29
1945	Final episode of *Old Gold Comedy Theatre* airs, June 10
1947	*The Sin of Harold Diddlebock* released, April 4 James Darsie Lloyd dies, December 17
1948	Marriage of Peggy Lloyd and Almon Bartlett Ross, April 17 Harold Lloyd serves as Delegate from California at Republican National Convention, Philadelphia, June 21 Harold Lloyd appears on *NBC-Life Magazine* TV program, June 23
1949	Harold Lloyd appears on *Mary Margaret McBride* radio show, June 6 Harold Lloyd makes cameo appearance on *Toast of the Town*, June 8 Harold Lloyd appears on *Howdy Doody*, June 9

Harold Lloyd appears on *Hi! Jinx* radio show, July 10
Harold Lloyd elected Imperial Potentate of the Shriners, July 21

1950 Harold Lloyd appears on *Welcome Travelers* radio show, January 27
Grandson David Lloyd Ross born, May 26
Marriage of Gloria Lloyd and William Orcutt Guasti, September 16
Mad Wednesday, the Diddlebock reissue, released, October 28

1952 Harold Lloyd is introduced to stereo photography
Harold Lloyd serves as Delegate from California at Republican National Convention, Chicago, July 7
Granddaughter Suzanne Gloria Lloyd Guasti born, July 28

1953 Gloria and William Guasti divorce, January 5
Harold Lloyd hosts exhibition of his paintings, Los Angeles, January 16-February 14
Harold Lloyd receives Honorary Academy Award, inscribed to "Master Comedian and Good Citizen", March 19
Harold Lloyd joins Stereo Division of the Photographic Society of America, April
Harold Lloyd appears on *What's My Line?*, April 26
Peggy Lloyd and Almon Ross divorce, May 5

1954 Harold Lloyd guests on *This Is Your Life*, honoring Mack Sennett, March 10
Harold Lloyd guests on *This Is Your Life*, honoring Bebe Daniels, September 29

1955 UCLA Oral History of Harold Lloyd, conducted by Arthur Friedman
Harold Lloyd awarded Medal of Honor at George

Eastman House, November 19
Harold Lloyd honored on *This Is Your Life*, December 14

1956 Harold Lloyd appears on *The Sunday Spectacular*, January 29
Marriage of Peggy Lloyd and Robert Patten, March 3
Grandson Robert Patten born
Peggy Lloyd and Robert Patten divorce, November (they would remarry, and divorce again in 1962)

1957 Harold Lloyd, Jr., and Sr., appear together on *Tonight! America After Dark*, February 20
Harold Lloyd awarded Medal of Honor at George Eastman House, October 26

1958 Harold Lloyd awarded star on Hollywood's Walk of Fame, for motion picture acting, at 1501 Vine Street, August

1959 Columbia Oral History of Harold Lloyd, conducted by Robert and Joan Franklin, January

1960 Harold Lloyd appears on *Hedda Hopper's Hollywood*, September 10

1961 Harold Lloyd appears on *Venture* radio show (Canada), July 9
Harold Lloyd appears on *The Mitch Miller Show* (radio), July 29

1962 Harry "Snub" Pollard dies, January 19
Harold Lloyd appears on *Calendar*, April 16
Harold Lloyd appears on *Today*, April 19
Cannes Film Festival, France, screens and honors *Harold Lloyd's World of Comedy*, May 13
Harold Lloyd's World of Comedy released, June 4

Harold Lloyd appears on *Here's Hollywood*, August 16

1964 *Harold Lloyd's World of Comedy*, book by William Cahn, published
Harold Lloyd, Jr., and Sr., appear together on *The Tonight Show Starring Johnny Carson*, October 2

1965 Harold Lloyd, Jr., suffers brain hemorrhage, May 19

1966 University of Michigan Film Seminar, conducted by Hubert I. Cohen, November
Harold Lloyd's Funny Side of Life released, November 9

1967 Jobyna Ralston dies, January 22

1969 Harold Lloyd awarded star on Hollywood's Walk of Fame, for motion picture producing, at 6840 Hollywood Boulevard, June 5
Mildred Davis Lloyd dies, August 18
American Film Institute Seminar with Harold Lloyd, inaugural session, September 23

1970 Harold Lloyd makes final public appearance at the Cinema City exhibition, London, September 22

1971 Sylmar Earthquake, magnitude 6.6, rocks Southern California, February 9
Harold Lloyd's Last Will and Testament signed and finalized, March 2
Harold Clayton Lloyd dies, March 8
Harold Lloyd's funeral held at Scottish Rite Temple, with entombment following at Forest Lawn Memorial Park, March 11
Bebe Daniels dies, March 16
Harold Clayton Lloyd, Jr. dies, June 9

1974	*Harold Lloyd: The Shape of Laughter*, book by Richard Schickel, published
1976	*Three Classic Silent Screen Comedies Starring Harold Lloyd*, book by Donald W. McCaffrey, published
1977	Time-Life 26-episode series *Harold Lloyd's World of Comedy* airs on public television *Harold Lloyd: The King of Daredevil Comedy*, book by Adam Reilly, published
1983	*Harold Lloyd: The Man on the Clock*, book by Tom Dardis, published
1984	Harold Lloyd Motion Picture Scoring Sound Stage dedicated at the University of Southern California Harold Lloyd Estate (Greenacres) named to National Register of Historic Places, February 9
1985	Great-grandson Christopher Lloyd Hayes born, August 4
1986	Peggy Lloyd dies, November 18
1988	Great-granddaughter Jacqueline Gates Hayes born, December 28
1989	*Harold Lloyd: The Third Genius* airs on PBS' American Masters series, November 15
1992	Hal Roach dies, November 2 *3-D Hollywood*, book by Suzanne Lloyd Hayes, published
1993	Harold Lloyd's birth centennial is celebrated with worldwide screenings and retrospectives

Harold Lloyd Birthplace named to National Register of Historic Places, December 22

1994 *Harold Lloyd: A Bio-Bibliography*, book by Annette D'Agostino, published
Harold Lloyd appears on 29c USPS postage stamp in "Stars of the Silent Screen" series, April 27

1995 World Wide Web goes Harold with debut of www.haroldlloyd.us, December 18

2002 *Harold Lloyd: Master Comedian*, book by Jeffrey Vance and Suzanne Lloyd, published

2003 *The Harold Lloyd Encyclopedia*, book by Annette D'Agostino Lloyd, published

2004 *Harold Lloyd's Hollywood Nudes in 3D!*, book by Suzanne Lloyd, published

2005 The Harold Lloyd Comedy Collection DVD box set released, November 15

Notes on the Words of Harold Lloyd

On the Jump
"Such comedy as there will be here – and there should be plenty of it – will lie in the humor of events, not in any conscious effort of the author to be cute." [1]

There is, indeed, something to be said for being a collector, a saver and an appreciator. In my case, my collecting, saving and appreciating what made up Harold Lloyd's world – films, photos, writings, interviews, etc. — has always come quite in handy in the execution of my own research into his life and career. In the unique case of this book, I am sincerely grateful that I've kept everything — this doesn't necessarily make for the sharpest home office, but it does ensure that, literally, when I need Harold, he's there — and, for this book, he's been both needed *and* there.

Harold Lloyd died in 1971. I hadn't even heard his name until 1979. I never had the privilege of personally interviewing him. However, many (not all, but most) of the questions I would have asked him were already answered in the bounty of interviews and writings he shared throughout his lifetime. Couple that with the joy of befriending and interviewing Lloyd's family — most notably daughter Gloria and granddaughter Suzanne — and I can honestly profess growing into a good working knowledge and understanding of this underappreciated and gloriously worthy man.

Having had the good fortune of being a fan of Harold Lloyd for close to 30 years, and a focused chronicler of his life since 1992, I have had the time to digest (and personally transcribe, verbatim) all of his major oral histories, as well as scores of minor and casual interviews, and to read just about everything written by and about him. Every note I've made, I've kept, and I've inventoried. This gives me the unique opportunity, at this juncture, to *allow Lloyd to help me* tell the stories behind the major turning points in his life. In a sense, this book affords Harold a fresh chance to voice his story anew — in a way that only he could — and gives us a peek into what really made him tick, both personally and professionally. Lloyd could be verbose or pithy; that is to say, he could go on at length or say it in one sentence — in any case, his insights, however brief or long, will help you understand his work and life ethics better. It's a veritable feast for a fan of his . . . think of this book as a freshly baked pizza, with his words the sauce that flavors and defines it.

You're going to want to know the sources of the passages you will read, to know where they came from, and when they were voiced. Quotes from Harold himself date from 1928 to 1969 — and each major extract by Lloyd, or an associate or family member, will be followed by a letter code in brackets. Other incidental quotes, from newspaper or magazine articles, will have their date and citation noted alongside. Below is the guide which will assist you in identifying how, where or when the words were spoken. It is my hope that, in so doing, you will seek out available sources, and be inspired to do what I've always endeavored to do: learn even more about Harold Lloyd.

CODE	QUOTE SOURCE
A	"INTERVIEW WITH HAROLD LLOYD" UCLA, 1955, ARTHUR FRIEDMAN
B	*HI! JINX*, NBC RADIO PROGRAM, JULY 10, 1949, JINX FALKENBURG AND TEX MCCRARY
C	INTERVIEW PROMOTING *HAROLD LLOYD'S WORLD OF COMEDY*, SAN FRANCISCO RADIO, 1962

Code	Quote Source
D	*Here's Hollywood*, NBC television program, August 16, 1962 (filmed at Greenacres August 2), Jack Linkletter
E	"Oral History Project" Columbia University, January 1959, Robert and Joan Franklin
F	*Calendar*, CBS television program, April 16, 1962, Harry Reasoner and Mary Fickett
G	Author Interview with Gloria Lloyd, at home of Suzanne Lloyd, Wednesday, July 27, 2005
H	Author Interview with Suzanne Lloyd, at her home, Wednesday, July 27, 2005
I	*An American Comedy*, autobiography by Harold Lloyd with Wesley W. Stout. New York: Longmans, Green & Co., 1928
J	"The American Film Institute Seminar with Harold Lloyd" September 23, 1969
K	Interview with HL for his book *Harold Lloyd's World of Comedy*, by William Cahn. New York: Duell, Sloan and Pearce, 1964
L	"The Serious Business of Being Funny" University of Michigan, November 1966, Hubert I. Cohen
M	Comments by friend Richard Simonton, Tuesday, July 19, 2005
N	Interview, April 1958, George C. Pratt

The Dawn of Harold Lloyd

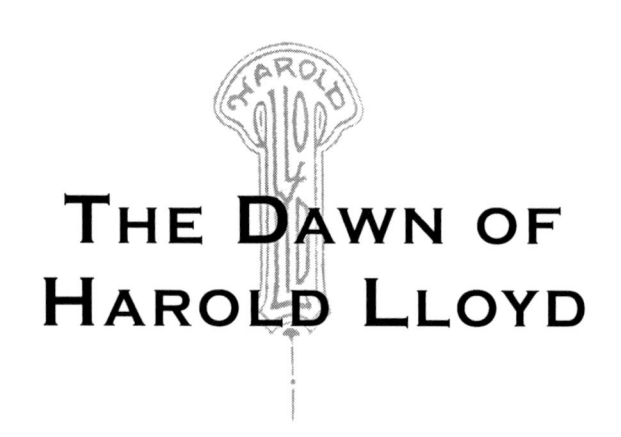

We Never Sleep . . .
"I was average and typical of the time and place."

"Birth was one of the least interesting things that ever happened to me," [I] wrote Harold Lloyd as he began his autobiography. Most people would probably say the same thing in commencing their own life stories. However, he was born, and on that day began a very important and, yes, interesting life. There is no way a compilation of his life's turning points could be possible without citing his birth. And, compared to the dusk of his life — complete with fame, fortune and dreams realized — the dawn of Lloyd's life was a mighty stark contrast indeed.

Born on Thursday, April 20, 1893, Harold Clayton Lloyd was the second son of James Darsie (known as "Foxy") and Elizabeth Fraser Lloyd. Elder brother Gaylord Fraser Lloyd was born on March 29, 1888; an unnamed daughter was either stillborn or died in infancy in 1890 (Harold never spoke of a sister, and it is possible he never knew about her; records of her death and interment were located through Nebraska ancestral research microfilm).

Many people live in the same house they grew up in, or at least in the same town. Such was not the case for Harold. "The journeying of the Lloyds began when I was a year old," [I] and it virtually never stopped. His birth home, at 24 Pawnee Street, on the northwest corner of 4th Street, Burchard, Nebraska, still stands, and was named to the National Register of Historic Places on December 22, 1993 (interestingly, Harold's first *and* last homes each earned a spot on the National Register). But Harold and his young family stayed

The house where HL was born on April 20, 1893. It has since been fully restored.

there only a brief time. Foxy's inability to hold a steady job meant that he had to frequently search for work where he could get it, and this meant perpetual uprooting for himself, Elizabeth, and their sons. During his first seventeen years, Harold lived, at one time or another, in Beatrice, Burchard, Humboldt, Omaha and Pawnee City, Nebraska, and Denver, Durango and Fort Collins, Colorado. He went to many different schools, but sheer numbers of schools didn't produce any pigskin: Harold Lloyd never graduated from high school.

The nomadic nature of his upbringing caused continual pressure within the family — one sad consequence of their inconsistency was the 1910 divorce of Elizabeth and Foxy. For the balance of his teen years, Harold alternated living with mother and father — wherever they were, and however they were living — and such turmoil could have severely damaged the youngster's sense of security and peace. However, the frequent moving, the inevitable struggles and the constant state of the unknown actually strengthened Harold's view of himself, as well as his burgeoning ambitions to do better.

HL at age three, taken at his father's photography studio in Humboldt, Nebraska.

He knew he was poor, but was not ashamed of his situation. "I was average and typical of the time and place. Supposing Atlantic City had been holding Average American Boy contests, with beauty waived, I might have been Master America most any year between 1893 and 1910. This is assuming that the average boy before the war was moderately poor, that his folks moved a great deal and that he worked for his spending money at any job that offered." [I] It

In 1894, at age one and a half: little Harold doesn't look too happy about wearing a puffy dress.

The Lloyd family strikes a serious pose, circa 1894: mother Elizabeth and father Foxy flank sons Gaylord (MIDDLE LEFT) and Harold.

was at this important time in his life that he amazingly developed the enthusiasm, the zest for life and the self-respect that would serve him well, later on, as a pioneering and industry-leading filmmaker.

Much as he would later as an adult, young Harold immersed himself in hobbies and avocations to pass the time and keep life interesting — magic, hypnotism and boxing prime among them. He took odd jobs at a very early age, much younger than the norm, in such varied forms as a telegraph messenger boy, a stock room boy, a paper route boy and a popcorn salesman (this bright youngster sold his own homemade popcorn at local train stations, public libraries, and saloons — and netted between $12-$15 weekly). The constant thread, however, throughout his earliest years was his passion for, and ambition towards, the theatre. More on that later. "I had a family reputation of being fickle. For instance, I had a succession of hobbies, each ridden furiously for a time, then abruptly tossed aside forever; but through all I played actor, and at the first opportunity became one." [I]

Oh, by the way: in his earliest years, it was the *live* theatre that captured the imagination and beckoned Harold as an actor — NOT the movies. He did recall that the first film he ever went to see was *The Great Train Robbery*, released in December 1903. He enjoyed the novelty of the medium of cinema: "Much of my money went to nickelodeons, where two pictures make a show and the usual picture was half a reel — never more than one reel. If I had a quarter I went to five shows in an afternoon . . . Pictures, however, were just another form of something to do, falling somewhere between the Sunday comic sections and running to a fire. They had no reality. I never associated them with so romantic a place as the theater." [I]

> **FUN FACT**
>
> According to an article written by Harold for *Playboy* magazine — but which was never published: "When I was a boy growing up in my home town in Nebraska, interstate passenger trains used to stop at the local station. Since there was no dining car on it, the candy and sandwich 'butcher' used to get on at one end of the train and work his way to the other end before the train pulled out. At thirteen years of age, I needed extra money for all those things thirteen year old boys need extra money for. I decided to sell something the 'butcher' didn't sell — popcorn.
>
> "I bought the raw stock and had my mother make it up for me. Then I appeared at the train. The 'butcher' refused to let me get on. I then devised a plan: I would get on at the opposite end of the train, and I always sold a great deal of popcorn by the time I met him coming in the opposite direction. We would meet in the middle and that's where he would throw me off. I made quite a bit of money for a youngster who only had half a train. But half a train was better than none, and more than most."

THE EARLY INFLUENCE OF THE THEATRE

Bumping Into Broadway . . .
"I was stage crazy."

"I cannot remember ever of wanting to be an engineer, fireman, policeman, bakery-wagon driver or any of the other pre-Lindbergh goals of boys. As far back as memory goes, and to the exclusion of all else, I was stage crazy." [I]

The passion that Harold had for the live theatre — known in his day as "the legitimate stage" — began quite early for the youngster. In fact, "I've been interested in the theatre pretty much since my incipiency. We were not in a theatrical family; I don't think any of them did anything in the theatre that you might call professional until I came on the horizon." [E] His interest grew, most likely, from a need for something to do in those late-19th-century days when there was little for a youngster to do but use his imagination. His brother Gaylord and he did just that.

"Gaylord was bitten by the same bug less severely, but long before he got his first job backstage I already was playing theater, with the loose hats and caps in the house as my actors. We lived in a duplex apartment, an aunt living across the hall. She owned a large couch, probably one of those trick furnitures that double by day as a davenport and by night as a bed. It was my stage. Taking off my shoes, which was required by my aunt, I would sit tailor fashion on the couch with the hats ranged in front of me. I invented and spoke their lines and moved them about. This was a regular diversion, they tell me." [I]

Teenaged Harold, a young dandy, even then endeavoring towards a career in the histrionic arts.

Moving from town to town, as the Lloyd family frequently did, meant both economic instability and the continual establishment of roots — the need for some semblance of normalcy — and young Harold soon discovered that there were jobs in the theatre for those eager to work. He was an usher, a stage hand, and a call boy — yelling "Curtain!", "Overture!", "Fifteen minutes!" In return for opening and closing the doors of the Pawnee hall that served as the Opera House, for instance, Harold would get to see the shows. "Plays differed from one another only as pies. There were many kinds of pies and all were good." [1] He loved all of them.

Eventually, however, the performer inside had to come to the surface, and did in 1903 — the first defining moment of this turning point in young Harold's life. "The first real theatrical work that I did was when I was about 10 years old. It was in the little town of Beatrice. My brother was trying to make extra money in the theatre; this was a Shakespearean play, *Macbeth*. In each city, they needed a

> **FUN FACT**
>
> "YEARS BEFORE THE VITAPHONE AND MOVIETONE I SAW AND HEARD TALKING PICTURES IN OMAHA. STATIONED BEHIND THE SCREEN, WHERE THEY WERE INVISIBLE YET COULD FOLLOW THE ACTION OF THE FILM, WERE A MAN AND A WOMAN. THE MAN MADE UP LINES FOR ALL THE MALE CHARACTERS, THE WOMAN FOR HER SEX. BOTH CHANGED THEIR VOICES TO SUIT, RATTLED DISHES, SLAMMED DOORS, ANSWERED THE TELEPHONE AND WERE AS BUSY AS A JAZZ-BAND TRAP DRUMMER IN FLANNEL UNDERWEAR. THE EFFECT WAS MORE NOVEL THAN ELECTRIFYING." [I]

youngster to play the son of [Banquo] — he was murdered, and the child comes out with his father, and the assassins attack him, and then he runs screaming across the stage. I got this part, of course, because my brother, who was five years older than me, suggested that I might be very good for it. The prescribed time came, and I went out with my father, and he was grabbed by the assailants — of course, I was told to yell, 'Help, Help' — as I went screaming back across the stage, which was fine. I worked beautifully there. But the moment when I got off and was to continue yelling, I became embarrassed with all the stage hands around. So someone had to take up my voice and yell help for me, and finish it out. So that was my initial introduction to the stage." [E]

Throughout the early teen years that followed, the youngster developed a greater sense of confidence — bordering on cockiness — by performing slapstick shows in his Nebraska and Colorado neighborhoods. While teens typically will be shy, Harold and his pals were safely nestled in costume and makeup, which helped them overcome any nerves or self-consciousness. Harold saw how beneficial such neighborhood shows were: "Without raising a finger or leaving our front yard, we were the cocks of the walk before nightfall," and was accurate when he noted, "The fact that we gave the act in the front yard rather than the back indicates that we hoped for an audience." [I]

Eventually, Harold developed his own mock repertory company, and garnered many of the neighborhood kids as cast and crew. The company put on many shows, and Harold wore many hats, behind the scenes, on stage, directing, applying makeup, designing, and always learning, practicing, and remembering. He always chose to stretch himself and his abilities, and continually cast himself in the more challenging and intricate roles.

Makeup, truly, took on a whole new meaning for Harold, as his theatrical apprenticeship ensued. He realized that his acting options could be endless: he could be a few years older, a few decades older, or downright ancient — all he had to do was learn how. He also realized that, for the stage, how one sounds is just as important as how one looks, so Harold became a student of dialect. He mastered the English language with variations in Irish, German, Swedish, and Jewish, by studying the vocal habits of his immigrant neighbors. Harold Lloyd was a consummate study.

He often noted that the Beatrice performance as Fleance in *Macbeth* back in 1903 was a mere incident . . . that his theatre jobs and neighborhood shows were great experience, but were minimal apprenticeships. However, Lloyd forever acknowledged that the curtain really rose for him in 1906, when he met the man who would be one of the single greatest influences on his career and life: John Lane Connor.

Meeting John Lane Connor

Fresh From the Farm . . .
"I have many reasons to be grateful to Connor."

Each of us, hopefully, has a favorite teacher, a prized relative, or a special friend who can be looked back upon as a mentor, an influence, a guide in life. You can remember singular moments with that person, and understand, with hindsight, how that person helped to shape the individual you became.

In the life of Harold Lloyd, there are a handful of people who could be said to have guided him — Harold definitely marched to the beat of his own drummer, in many respects, and was the chief architect of his success. His parents, despite their own instabilities, provided amazingly strong roots for the youngster to grab hold of: "My parents encouraged me by not discouraging me. My mother had a great desire to go on the stage, but hadn't, but I think she had a great talent — she had a beautiful voice. My father was a natural actor — he never pursued that, but he could have." [A]

However, besides his folks, there was one man who single-handedly changed the course of the entire life of Harold Lloyd, who truly excited the youngster about acting, and who was the single strongest influence on Lloyd's development and evolution in the histrionics. His name was John Lane Connor, and he is owed a debt of gratitude by every fan of Harold Lloyd.

The initial meeting of the mentor and the pupil: "I was going to school, to public school, in Omaha, Nebraska. There was one of these street vendors selling horoscopes — he was selling these horoscopes and he had his charts set up by the curb, and he had

The youthful students of the Connor School of Expression: HL is in the front row, second from right.

quite an audience around, and his chart was up on this stand, and he was explaining about how this controlled someone's life. I was entranced with the idea of what it might do with mine. And, just at this time, a fire engine went by. It went by, not on the street that we were on, but about a half a block up. So, practically everyone ran to see this fire engine — at that time, they were pulled by horses, and they were very spectacular, because out of the hoofs of the horses, you'd see the sparks fly — so everyone ran, but I didn't. I stood there, and of course the man didn't want to lose his audience. He tried very hard, and so he kept right on talking. And the only other person who stayed was another gentleman, an adult, who proved, later on, to be the leading man in one of the local stock companies. This was John Connor. He was so amazed that, here was a kid that didn't run to see the fire engines, but stayed and listened to the man talking about astrology. So when I started to leave, he introduced himself — well, of course, the moment he said he was connected with the theatre — and I was theatrically minded, and had been practically all the time up to that tender age — in the conversation, I found out that he was looking for some place to live. So, I said,

John Lane Connor, in *propria persona*. He was one of a handful of people who deeply affected and influenced the growth and evolution of Harold Lloyd.

'well, we take in borders,' well, we'd never taken in a border in our lives. But, of course, he said, fine, and gave me the number how to get in touch with him. Of course, I talked my mother into it. So we finally made a room available, and he came to live with us. So the first part came up in what was known as the Burwood Stock Company, he suggested me for it, and it was a very big part. It was little Abraham in a play called *Tess of the D'Urbervilles*." [A] The show opened on January 10, 1907; Harold was 13; the show played for a week, with three matinees, at the Burwood Stock Company's theatre. "It was something like about 40 sides — sides are pages — and so he coached me in it. And it was a wonderful training he gave me from that standpoint. And I received exceptionally good notices — 'Master Harold Lloyd, who will go on in this histrionic art,' — and I still remember some of the reviews. Then he got me several different parts — in *Nell Gwynn*, in *Private Secretary*, and I think I had about four or five parts that year. I got excuses to be out of school, and take a little extra tutoring." [A]

A rare shot of John Lane Connor, in character as Parsifal, as he appeared in 1906, right around the time he first met thirteen-year-old Harold.
COURTESY UNIVERSITY OF WASHINGTON LIBRARIES, SPECIAL COLLECTIONS, UW 28042z.

The experience Harold got at this juncture was immense. "I did a lot of kid parts in those times — of course, then, I got too old to play boy parts, and I wasn't old enough to play a young man, a juvenile. Then I did everything else in the theatre; practically everything you could think of; I really ran the gamut." [C]

"The experience that I gained on the stage was a tremendous asset. I was just Harold Lloyd the character. No, the comic didn't develop until quite a while afterward. Although, in the dramatic school that I was assistant in, and I would take part in the different plays that we put in with the students, there was a bent that there would always come along a comedy part, and we tried to get the students to do it, and it seemed to be a flair with me. So when they came along with a comedy part, it seemed to be something I dropped into readily. Although, to tell you the truth, I really wanted to be a villain to start with; I wanted to be the heavy. In fact, in all the kid shows I put on in the neighborhood, I always took the part of the villain, the heavy; it seemed to have more bite to it." [E]

Connor became Harold's mentor, his model, and his friend — caring, yet demanding at the same time. Harold studied under Connor at the Burwood Stock Company in Nebraska, and later at the Connor School of Expression in San Diego, California. As exhaustive a teacher as Connor was, Lloyd grew to be an even more thorough and absorbing learner. Connor insisted that his young charge never grow complacent, and always stretch himself, attempting to glean more from his talents, and expect self-improvement with each performance. Connor was not shy about cutting down an overly confident Harold, when he felt the youngster needed the guidance.

Through the years, Harold recognized this as a stark benefit. "I had so enormous an advantage over schoolboy amateurs, moreover, that the leading parts fell to me without question, and I came nearer to losing my head here than ever before or after. I have many reasons to be grateful to Connor, but the greatest service he did me was to reduce this swelling at the psychological moment.

"We gave *Going Some*, a collegiate farce, in the school auditorium on December 6 and 7, 1912 — and I was J. Wallingford Speed, head yeller. By contrast I should have been pretty good. Furthermore, in the training-quarters scene, where the trainer and I held the stage and exhorted the team, the trainer's amateur nose began to bleed copiously. He walked off the stage, leaving me to conduct a monologue, and I got away with it.

"The next morning I drifted into the dramatic school with my brow bared for the laurel wreath. Connor said hello and went about his business. I stood about waiting for it and when it failed to come I asked for it.

"'Not so bad last night, was I?' — or something like that was the prefatory remark.

"Connor hesitated as if reluctant to be drawn into so painful a discussion, then said quietly:

"'Harold, I was very much disappointed in you. After all, you're not an amateur in his first play — not that I would have known it at times last night. You pulled yourself out of a hole in the training-quarters scene very well, and why shouldn't you? You've been working at the trade for years. On the other hand, how many times have I told you how to get the full value out of a laugh? Of course you got laughs. The laughs were in the lines and the situations. Half the time, though, you choked them to death before they were well started.'" [I]

"As I remember it, Connor went over my performance point by point, as a mechanic goes over a motor, pointing out bad timing, wrong emphasis, and other errors in technique. I have never forgotten this incident. Not only was I brought down out of the clouds with a thud which I deserved, but I was taught important techniques of comedy, of spacing, of timing,

> **FUN FACT**
>
> THE NEVER-MARRIED JOHN LANE CONNOR WAS A VERY HANDSOME IRISHMAN, WITH A SHOCK OF THICK LIGHT BROWN HAIR AND EXTREMELY PIERCING EYES. HE WAS POPULAR, AND SOUGHT-AFTER, AMONG THE FEMALE THEATREGOERS IN SAN DIEGO. HOWEVER, CONNOR MOVED BACK TO CHICAGO IN THE MID-TEENS, AND IN 1918, HE WAS ARRESTED FOR HOMOSEXUALITY, AND WAS JAILED. HAROLD, BY THEN MAKING MUCH MORE MONEY THAN HIS FORMER TEACHER, SPENT A SMALL FORTUNE GETTING HIM OUT OF THIS PREDICAMENT.

which have remained a permanent part of my comic vocabulary throughout my career." [K]

The influence of this man, John Connor, on Harold Lloyd was immense, but more than anything, Connor enhanced Lloyd's enjoyment of his endeavors. "I had interest in life. But I was one-track, as far as the theatre was concerned. That was my one great love. I didn't have any desire to do anything but work in the theatre." [A]

John Lane Connor was born on May 21, 1874, in Chicago, Illinois, and died on September 10, 1941, at age 67, in Santa Monica, from the effects of what is now known as Parkinson's Disease. Years after their initial meeting on that street in Omaha, after the student became richer and more successful than the teacher, their mutual admiration never waned with the passage of time. Among the pictures on the wall of Harold's corporate office was a framed photograph of John Lane Connor. The lessons taught by this man, to a future cinematic legend, should be recognized as having been a prime guiding force behind film history itself.

The Serendipitous Flip of a Coin

Why Worry? . . .
"We flipped the coin and it came up for the Coast."

Question: How *did* Harold and his family wind up in California after nearly two decades in the heart of the Midwest? Answer: The flip of a coin. It sounds almost too silly to believe, but it *is* true.

In the fall of 1912, two years after the divorce of Foxy and Elizabeth Lloyd, father and sons were living in Omaha, Nebraska, and it was during this autumn that the direction of the entire family, mother included, took a daring turn. Foxy was working, at that time, for the Singer Sewing Machine Company. As a salesman, then as a supervisor, Foxy was part of a growing organization at a time when virtually all clothes were being made in the home. Part of his responsibilities included confiscating unpaid-for machines, and returning them, via buggy, to the warehouse. During one such jaunt, a brewery truck, driven by a crew of over-indulgent employees fresh from a few cold ones, ran down Foxy's buggy, severely injuring the elder Lloyd. A lengthy hospital stay, and a lawsuit, ensued.

"Here's another turning point — father had an accident, and had received some money, I think around $3000, which was a tremendous amount of money to us in those days.

"And we were living in Omaha, and at that time, he did encourage me. Here's where the turning point comes in. He said, 'Harold, do you think it would be better for you to go to New York, or to go to the Coast, where you know Mr. Connor,' who was then playing the leading man in one of the San Diego stock companies. I had always corresponded with him, and he said that if I came out, he would

It was this style of nickel that Foxy and Harold flipped — the wreath flanking the Roman numeral V sent the men westward.

give me a position in one of the stock companies he worked with. So it was a question of whether New York would be better for me, or San Diego. We couldn't quite decide, so we hit upon the idea of flipping a coin. And it came up heads or tails, whichever we chose, we'd go to New York or we'd go to the Coast. And we abided by it. We flipped the coin and it came up for the Coast." [A]

What is crucial to the tale is that, at the time, the prospects for aspiring thespian Harold in the West Coast cities were especially boundless. The legitimate stage was a definite draw, particularly considering Harold's experience and talent and, at the time, there was continual stock company work to be had.

Moreover, the motion picture industry was, at this point, seeing the left coast as a superior venue for production, particularly from a weather standpoint. Scores of US film companies were leaving New York and New Jersey, the first real headquarters of filmdom, and moving west in search of better conditions for outdoor shooting, as well as an escape from brutal winters which, in the days before mass indoor studios, necessitated frequent shutdowns of outdoor lots. This was an exceptionally good time for Harold to go west — the timing of that coin flip was mighty fine.

But what *if* it had fallen the other way? "The possibilities are infinite; the probabilities are that we would have gone to New York and I would have become a Broadway actor — I hope a good one. Had we turned Eastward rather than West, certainly the odds are long that it wouldn't have been pictures, for I went into pictures only because they were on hand in California when nothing else offered." [I]

Harold's early days in San Diego, California, were hectic, thrilling yet scary, and tested his mettle as had no other time. Father Foxy was busy running the lunch counter and pool hall he had invested his money in, and brother Gaylord was toiling at back stage jobs in the theatre. Harold stuck by his histrionic ambitions — but it was a challenge at times.

> **FUN FACT**
>
> ALONG WITH THE IMAGE OF A 1912 COIN, THIS IS HOW WE CAN BE SURE (AS SURE AS WE CAN BE) THAT HL'S MENTION OF THE WREATH SAID THAT THE COIN CAME UP TAILS: "THE COIN WENT UP, HIT THE CEILING, DROPPED AND ROLLED UNDER A BED. IT WAS A PRE-BUFFALO NICKEL AND IT STOPPED WREATH SIDE UP. HAD IT FALLEN HEADS, THIS STORY WOULD NOT HAVE BEEN WRITTEN." [I]

"I went to the Coast and went into the stock company out there. I played in about three different stock companies there. Then, later, all the stock companies had closed. By that time, my father had come on up to Los Angeles, but I stayed in San Diego, and I came down to one nickel. It's kind of nice to look back on that. I had five cents. I remember I bought some doughnuts with that, and I was living up on a roof, in some kind of little tent house upon the roof of a hotel, and we got it for practically nothing. And I was down to this five cents piece, and I was able to go over to the Spreckels Theatre, and help the electricians. This was with May Robson's company — I got to meet Miss Robson — I was always good at meeting people. She was very kind to me; she was a grand lady, one of the grand ladies of the theatre.

"All the stock companies had closed down. There were a number of us who needed work — our funds were getting rather low — and I had worked for Connor, he had a dramatic school down there, and I had worked for him as an assistant in this dramatic school. I'd help the fencing master, and I became his assistant — I became assistant to everybody. We were all out of money, so we got up what we called the Kerosene Circuit, and we chose six little towns like Escondido and Oceanside, little towns down the coast, and we made a contract with them in the different opera houses. In Oceanside, we'd play every Monday. Say, Escondido, we'd play every Tuesday. We were like a traveling stock company — we'd get up these little shows, and while we'd be going around we'd take the weekend to really do our dress rehearsal and learn our parts. So that, each week, we would change it. This was great training, of course." [A]

However, it was inconsistent work, and money was extremely tight. Soon, very soon, it would be time for Harold to leave San Diego, and head north 120 miles to Los Angeles. But, one of his seemingly minor experiences with the Connor School of Expression, from late 1912, would prove that his relocation to Los Angeles, his time in San Diego, and the flip of that coin, were all part of an integral turning point in the gradual creation of a superstar.

HAROLD LLOYD'S FOUR-SECOND FILM DEBUT

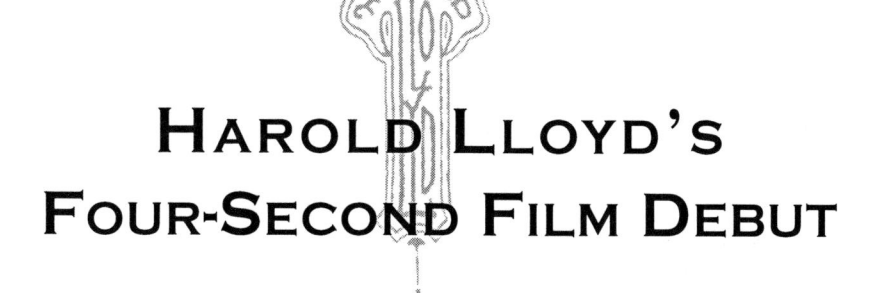

The Old Monk's Tale . . .
"The three dollars pay, however, was more significant at the moment."

The students and instructors at the Connor School of Expression lived an interesting, if unsure, existence. Theatrical work came and went, and funds were perennially tight. And what work they got was not relegated solely to the "legitimate stage," either.

"The old Edison Company came out from New York on temporary location in the winter of 1912-13 to do a half a dozen pictures. They settled in Balboa, just below Long Beach, and one day they made an excursion to San Diego to shoot an atmospheric scene requiring a number of extras as Indian background." [I] The film in question was *The Old Monk's Tale*, and shooting began on December 19, 1912.

"The Edison Company came down there, and they came to Mr. Connor's dramatic school, to get some of his pupils to use as extras. And, so, I thought that, while I was above the pupil stage, I was very anxious to go out and work as an extra, and I became a Yaqui Indian: I had this wig on, and passed a tray around through the scene." [A]

His part was small, unglamorous, and barely noticeable — he earned a whopping $3 for his four seconds on the screen, in his film debut, released on February 15, 1913. "The three dollars pay, however, was more significant at the moment." [I]

HL in his film debut, in *The Old Monk's Tale* — he is the white-shirted Yaqui Indian, screen center, with long flowing wig, tight headdress, cummerbund, and a tray of drinks for the thirsty party goers. Audience members who blinked slowly would have missed him.

As Summer 1913 approached, Harold found that San Diego's theatrical life had come to a virtual standstill, as theatre attendance waned in the warm months. He began to look at film in a bit of a different way. "I couldn't sit in my roof tent and wait for fall. Los Angeles, a much larger city, was a hundred and twenty miles away, dad was there, the theatres there did not shut down in summer and there were picture companies knocking about. If I couldn't find work on the Los Angeles stage, perhaps I could piece out the summer as an extra to this poor relation of the stage and eat until the San Diego season should revive. So I went to Los Angeles." [I]

Upon arrival in the City of Angels, Harold moved into a theatrical hotel, The Belmont, on Main Street in the downtown section of Los Angeles; Foxy had moved there following the collapse of his lunch counter/pool hall business. Gaylord lived there, too, working as the Belmont's night clerk, and Harold toiled as bell boy and relief clerk while also looking for theatrical work.

The home of the Lloyd men from 1913-1915: the Hotel Belmont, at 326 S. Main Street. A parking lot now graces HL's first Los Angeles address.

Main Street as it looked around the time HL began in films.

> **FUN FACT**
>
> THE ORIGINAL WORKING TITLE OF *THE OLD MONK'S TALE* WAS "THAT LOST PEARL OF LORETTO." ACCORDING TO RECORDS FROM THE EDISON KINETOGRAPH DEPARTMENT LOG BOOK, PROVIDED BY THE EDISON NATIONAL HISTORIC SITE, FILMING BEGAN ON DECEMBER 19, 1912, AND WRAPPED JUST TEN DAYS LATER. THE EAST COAST HEADQUARTERS IN ORANGE, NEW JERSEY, GAVE FINAL APPROVAL TO THE FOOTAGE ON JANUARY 16, 1913; EDITING AND DISTRIBUTION TOOK LESS THAN A MONTH.

"When I came to Los Angeles afterwards, the first place I went to was the old Edison company, and I went out there and did a couple of little short films. I remember I was a little Dutch boy. And I got the chance to see it — I was so disappointed — I looked and I was gone." [A]

Imagine seeing yourself on a moving picture screen for the first time. Harold wasn't just dismayed at the duration of his cameo: "Vanity never took a worse wallop. None of us photographs as he imagines himself, and of the two likenesses, the camera's is not the flattering one.

"Disgusted as I was with the movies, nothing else offered." [I] And for that, Harold's fans can be most grateful.

Harold Lloyd & Hal Roach Connect at Universal

Them Was the Happy Days . . .
"We got to be known as kind of the regular extras."

It is not hard to imagine the draw that the big movie studios had in the early days of motion pictures: inside the gates, the world was a forgotten entity, and in its stead, glamour and imagination reigned. Anything was possible. Life was fun. For a man of twenty, a man with enthusiasm, will and drive, a man like Harold Lloyd, there soon was no other environment that could compare.

Not one to mince words or intentions, Harold began his search for extra work at the top, at the granddaddy of all movie studios: "Universal was at its original California lot at Sunset Boulevard and Gower Street, Hollywood, and there I went." [I] He went, but he didn't exactly find the gates easy to enter.

"I had a hard time getting into Universal. They had to go through what they called the Bullpen. That was a name given to a room where the aspirants would go and sit down and then the assistant directors, as they needed atmosphere, they would go into this room, and they'd look over to see what atmosphere they wanted, and not knowing your name, they'd point at you, and then you were to follow them, and you got the required work for the day. Well, that didn't suit me. I was too proud to go into a bullpen. I'd had too much stage experience. I'd had lots of very fine parts on the stage and in the stock companies, little road companies, and for me to resort to that, my pride was plucked there. So, I had to find a way to get into the studio to contact the assistant directors there or someone else in the company in a different manner." [E]

Hal Roach, partner and friend of Harold Lloyd when they both were in their cinematic infancies, and beyond.
COURTESY SAM GILL.

Here's where his ingenuity, craftiness and pluck come into play in true turning point fashion. "I noticed that anyone with makeup on could get through that gate. The actors would come out of there and go across at lunch time to a little restaurant and eat, and then go back in — they all had makeup on. So, I conceived the idea, the next day, to bring some makeup — I slipped around the corner, and put some makeup on my face, and when I saw them coming out of the restaurant, I slid right in with them. And, of course with the makeup on, they didn't challenge me. So I got in. And then, coming out, I made it a point — I had to do that for about three days — I made it a point to talk to the old gate man, so that he'd know that I'd been inside and must belong.

"At that time, I was hoping to get a job to get $3 a day. Then, you would follow around the assistant director, and he would have a picture, and maybe if you were lucky you would get to work that day and earn $3. And if you could get about four days a week, that was a big week — so you'd get $12 you'd live on." [B]

"That's determination. And, I think later on maybe that came through in something I added to a character later." [E]

What *character* was he referring to? Well, that's another of the questions I would have asked him — but one can surmise what he meant...

He could have been talking about his Glass Character in *Hey There!*, released on April 28, 1918. This one-reeler, made when Harold was in his fifth year as a professional film actor, has The Boy following a moving picture Girl (Bebe Daniels) to the studios of the Near Famous Film Company, where he encounters no end of trouble trying to get near her. In the picture, Lloyd not only replicates his own challenges simply trying to enter the studio gate (as at Universal), but also dons a costume to give the appearance that he belongs on the lot (a variation of the makeup he had to apply to look like a regular, and finally get in the gate).

Or, Harold could have been making a blanket reference to his famed Glass Character, the screen persona that he debuted in 1917, his veritable screen self for the rest of his filmmaking days. "In a great many instances, he did belie his appearance. In other words, you thought he could be pushed around, but he was resourceful, and had great fortitude, beyond what you would expect." [A] As we will discuss later, there was no *one* Glass Character — the Boy and his challenges changed with each film — but at each Boy's core, from picture to picture, was an inner strength and determination needed to overcome what obstacles he encountered. Most likely, the experience he had in merely gaining entry into Universal — the cleverness mustered and the benefits he drew from it — was a supreme influence on the inner workings of his later Glass Character and its films.

Harold was not the only future legend toiling at the Universal lot. Hal Roach "got on at the Universal ranch in the San Fernando Valley as a cowboy in Westerns by virtue of being able to stick on a horse." [I]

A pivotal scene in the 1914 biblical extravaganza *Samson*: the three interested hooded men in the rear, from left, are Hal Roach, HL, and Frank Borzage.

"We got to be known as kind of the regular extras — in other words, whenever they had anything to do, they gave them to us. And then they began to give us the opportunity to play different small parts. And this one small part was in one of the plays with an actor, J. Warren Kerrigan, and they gave it to Hal, and Hal couldn't do it. And, remember, Hal had never had experience in acting before. And, so I got the opportunity to do it, and of course I carried it off, and Hal always had a little bit of reverence and respect for me, because I had done the scene that he had been denied because he hadn't had enough experience. So we became fast friends." [E]

The two young men — Roach was one year older than Lloyd, and lived to be 100 — worked on many films together. One extant example of their acting talents was *The Patchwork Girl of Oz*, released on September 28, 1914, in which Roach and Lloyd "clowned as Hottentots and similar savages in breechclouts and bolomania, a heavy but easily removed body paint." [I] At Universal, they also collaborated on an elaborate four-reeler, *Samson*, released on April 30, 1914 — in it, Lloyd, Roach and future director Frank Borzage were unbilled in their appearances as Philistines. On this film, Harold worked for two straight weeks, at $5 a day, and also served as makeup man, specializing in application of crêpe paper beards on the Philistines.

Eventually, work at Universal was less steady, and Harold began to shop himself around in his off-lot hours. It was at this time that he visited Christy Cabanne, then in charge of casting at one of the industry's leading studios — that Lloyd brand of determination he had built up came in quite handy that day. "I remember one time going to the old Biograph, to the casting director there, and at that

> **FUN FACT**
>
> ONE OF THE FILMS THAT WE KNOW HAROLD APPEARED IN AT UNIVERSAL — AND IT MAY BE THE KERRIGAN FILM THAT HAROLD REFERRED TO FOR WHICH ROACH HAD TO RELINQUISH HIS ROLE TO THE MORE EXPERIENCED LLOYD — WAS *RORY O' THE BOGS*, RELEASED IN THREE REELS ON DECEMBER 22, 1913. THIS FILM IS NOT KNOWN TO SURVIVE. HOWEVER, HAROLD'S PARTICIPATION IN IT IS ASSURED, BASED ON A SURVIVING STILL, TAKEN WITH J. WARREN KERRIGAN. IN IT, LLOYD, WHO APPEARS TO THE RIGHT OF THE PHOTO, SEEMS TO BE POINTING AT KERRIGAN, WITH TWO POSSE MEMBERS (AFTER RORY) LOOKING ON. THIS PHOTOGRAPH, BEFORE NOW, HAD NEVER BEEN CORRECTLY IDENTIFIED IN ANY PRIOR LLOYD BOOKS.

time, I had what I considered then, still do, some very fine character makeups, things that I had done in the theatre. I took out this little portfolio of mine, and he looked them over, and even looking at these he said, 'Lloyd, you're not the picture type.' So, of course, if I had listened to him, I would never have followed through in this industry." [E]

Good thing he stuck to his guns, because his pal Hal Roach surprised him one day by announcing that he had come into several thousand dollars. With it, "he decided to form his own company, and he asked me if I would go with him, which I was very happy to do. I got a little better than a couple of days a week then. So he started making two reel dramas, at that time, and in those I played all sorts of parts, I played character parts, fathers, juvenile parts. So, from 12 on, mine was really quite an evolution. Then he decided to do comedy, and said, 'Let's let Lloyd do it.' So, Roy Stewart played the lead in the drama, and I played various characters, and then I was the comedian in the comedy and Roy Stewart played the big overpowering villain." [E]

Of these earliest comedies and dramas made by Roach's new company, called Rolin (a merging of some letters from the surnames of original partners ROach and Dan LINthecum), only one is known to exist to this day. They called it *Just Nuts*.

Just Nuts Impresses Pathé

Just Nuts . . .
"We'd make up our comedies as we went along."

For Harold Lloyd and Hal Roach, this film game was just about to start getting interesting. Very interesting. To begin their new production venture, Rolin would produce two-reel dramas, and alternate the releases with one-reel short comedies.

Harold was the leading comedian for this new troupe (which also included drama leading man Roy Stewart, and all-around leading lady Jane Novak); after months of important comedy research, Lloyd developed his initial screen persona. "I experimented with dress and make-up and about the fifth picture settled on a character we christened Willie Work." [I] The name was a hint to the personality of the character: *willie work, or won't he?* "The name wrongly suggests a tramp; it was, instead, a hash of different low-comedy get-ups, with a much-padded coat, a battered silk hat and a cat's-whisker mustache as its distinguishing marks." [I] The lessons Lloyd learned from this period of his development were crucial, for this taught him, inherently, that he would not want to be this kind of actor for long.

Hal Roach called Willie "a definite imitation of Chaplin." At that time, as Harold often noted, ". . . exhibitors would hear of no departures from the Chaplin track," [I] meaning that no matter how Harold disliked following the leader at the time, *he had to*, for the comedy standards were too strong and unmovable at that point in cinema.

A lovely — and most fashionably wardrobed — portrait of HL's first regular female lead. The autograph reads, "Kindest Wishes to My Friends, Sincerely, Jane Novak." COURTESY SAM GILL.

The chief protagonist in *Just Nuts*, Willie Work (HL), lands on his posterior outside of the watering hole — he earned the seat, too.

Interestingly, through Willie Work, Harold began, for the first time, to think of himself as a comedian, and not just an actor — this was a thought-provoking early distinction, and in later years Lloyd preferred to call himself a comic actor. Truth be told, though Willie Work was his first major screen character, Lloyd would later be quite embarrassed by these early imitative days. That being noted, it was probably a relief for Harold that only one of the Willie Work comedies, *Just Nuts*, survived the ravages of time. Yet, its very being remains an important early turning point in his comedy career.

Released on April 19, 1915, *Just Nuts* is a typical knockabout farce, surrounding Willie and his attempts to woo a pretty girl (Novak). His advances are thwarted by a fellow admirer (Stewart), and the film ends with a brawl in a restaurant, chiefly instigated by Willie and his annoying habits.

"As I look back, it looks terrible now — but as I look back, we had a lot of cute business in it, at that time. Of course, remember, at that time, we'd just go out in a park, we'd build a set or two;

Roy Stewart — he played the heavy in the Willie Work comedies, and the lead in the dramatic pictures, both opposite HL. COURTESY SAM GILL.

but we'd go out to a park like Echo Park or Hollenbeck Park, parks around there, with no script, no ideas, just characters, and we'd make up our comedies as we went along. It always ended up generally in a chase or a fight or something of that kind. For instance, we'd say that we'd have the girl sitting there, and the comedian comes along, and through some circumstance, he flirts with the girl or gets acquainted with her, and then her sweetheart would come along and then altercations would start. That was just one type. You ad-libbed and worked it out in those days. You'd work up your ideas right where you are, with all the people around, maybe sometimes you'd have more than a hundred people standing around looking at you." [E]

In contemporary terms, *Just Nuts* is nothing special at all. However, based on this single reel, Rolin was approached by an interested Pathé Exchange, which distributed the single reeler. So happy were they with the film — typical for the times yet somehow unique — that Pathé decided to offer Rolin a contract as sole distributor of the Lloyd product. Per an agreement signed on November 2, 1916, Pathé agreed to pay Rolin $500 per single reel film provided to them for distribution. This began a Lloyd-Pathé affiliation that continued, and thrived, for over a decade — but its start was not as clear cut as one might imagine.

True, Rolin was making dramatic pictures as well as comedies — but behind the scenes, there was no absence of *actual* drama. The good times were about to come to a screeching halt:

"A program was mapped out calling for a one-reel comedy one week and a two-reel drama the next, Stewart to play the leads in the dramas and I the second business — sometimes as many as three parts. In the comedies I was to have the lead. Then came the discovery that Stewart was getting ten dollars a day. The following exchange of verbal notes took place between Roach and Lloyd:

LLOYD: How come you are paying Stewart ten dollars and me only five?

ROACH: Well, Harold, you see, it is this way: Stewart won't work for less than ten dollars and I simply can't pay two men that much. Now if you will be patient and wait until we are on our feet —

LLOYD: As I understand it, Stewart is getting ten dollars because he asked for it. If that is the way to get ten dollars I ask for it too.

ROACH: I'm sorry. You know that I'd like to pay you ten dollars and more if I could, but we can't afford it.

LLOYD: I'm sorry, too, and I guess that I shall have to try to get it somewhere else.

ROACH: Well, good luck, Harold.

LLOYD: So long, Hal." [1]

At this juncture, in late 1914, Harold left Rolin, and found work at the famed Keystone studios, headed by Mack Sennett. Lloyd worked on at least six Keystone films from February to July 1915.

"I branched out with Ford Sterling into being the juvenile of the company. And of course Sterling always had a prop plot: stealing the pearls. It was a rubber plot, more or less, and they stretched it into different directions, but somehow, somebody always stole the pearls. And, Ford liked me because he had very little trouble with me — some of the boys he'd try to have do certain parts, he'd have to work with them quite a bit, but Ford used to come around and say, 'I tell Lloyd what I want and he gives it to me.' But it was right at that time, and I was doing very well, and I was headed towards getting one of the principal parts. Then, my termination with Sennett came — Roach and I had made a picture that I had been the comedian in, that we had made in alternation with the dramatic picture, and we called it *Just Nuts*. I played the lead in it, a funny little character with screwball comedy clothes and a cat's mustache. And, they were offered this contract if Roach could get the principals back — there was Jane Novak, Roy Stewart, and myself. And they said, 'if you could get those three people back we'll give you a contract just on the strength of that one comedy.' So, I was at Sennett and Roach had been offered this contract. It seemed that Stewart had been tied up with someone and they couldn't get him, and he couldn't find Jane Novak — I was the only one of the trio that he could get. So, they said, 'all right, you get Lloyd, the comic, and so we'll give you this contract.' Of course, then Roach came out and approached me. And I said, 'Well, I'm doing pretty well out here at Sennett.' And he offered me $50 a week. That was a lot of money — it was to me." [E]

Money was an important consideration for Harold, to be sure. However, his thinking at this juncture of his career was very mature, and in the following exchange, Lloyd reveals the defining moment *within* this turning point in his professional life: "I remember one time, the last picture I did with Sterling, we were working by a little alley way. Ford liked me very well. I told him I was leaving and I was going with Roach, and he said, 'Oh, my God, Lloyd, why do you want to go with a little one-horse independent company like that for; you're with a big company here with Keystone. You've got places to go. Besides, you've worked with me, and I put you in the juvenile parts,' and he said, 'I don't think you should go in for this comedy stuff. You're the kind of an actor like Bobby Harron,' that was the juvenile with D.W. Griffith. He said, 'I think you're just as good as Bobby. I think you'll really go places if you'll get into that category. Don't go with Roach.' I said, 'No, I think I'm going to go there; I'm going to be the comedian, and I've got confidence in him. Besides, if I go there, I'll be the big fish in the little pond, rather than the little fish here, in the bigger pond.' That was the gist of that — I went with Roach, and that was when Roach and I became fast friends." [E]

HL's first regular character, Willie Work, bearing the costume, makeup and gesture characterizations that were expected of comic actors of the day.

> **FUN FACT**
>
> How many Willie Work comedies were made? That question may never be answered, for the Rolin office records were not very carefully maintained in its earliest days, and a great number of the films produced were not sold, or even released. In addition, a large number of the films that were sold and released were not copyrighted; coupled with the fact that most are not extant, and there is little way to definitively say exactly how many Willie Work shorts were made and released. Amongst the un-copyrighted Rolin films that are not known to have survived to this day for reappraisal, but which were released, are the 1915 single reelers *Beyond His Fondest Hopes*, *Close-Cropped Clippings*, and *Pete the Pedal Polisher*. These three shorts were probably directed by Hal Roach. Of the two unquestionable Willie Work releases, *Willie Runs the Park* (released in February 1915) and *Just Nuts*, only the latter survives to this day.

Very smart thinking — that big fish in the little pond theory — for it not only shows smarts in the short term, but it shows Harold's eye towards his future — a future to be later characterized as Harold Lloyd's World of *Comedy*. For now, juvenile parts would be a thing of the past for Lloyd, and smooth comedy sailing lay ahead.

LONESOME LUKE

Luke Laughs Last . . .
"He wasn't a believable character . . ."

"Comedy is very difficult to make. It's sort of hazardous. I'll qualify that by saying that a lot of pictures might start out to be comedies but they don't always end up that way." [C]

Harold Lloyd's second major film series character, following Willie Work, and preceding the Glass Character, was a major turning point in his career, purely because it assisted him in creating his ideal screen persona. Yes, Lonesome Luke, for all his quirks and strangeness, is important.

"I wore a little hat with the brim cut off of it, and his big shoes, and he had a black striped shirt — he was purely a comedy character. Before that I did a character called Willie Work. He was a strange individual too — I used to have great big wide shoulders, tremendous shoulders, long Prince Albert coat and a crushed hat with a kind of a cat mustache. That preceded Lonesome Luke. Well, I never cared for them — they *were* a great training ground for me." [C]

The character of Lonesome Luke was developed upon the regeneration of the Rolin Film Company in June 1915, following the period in which the company paused production (after Lloyd quit over the $5 versus $10 per day saga; during this hiatus, Lloyd worked at Keystone, and Roach at Essanay). As had been the case with Willie Work, Lloyd developed Lonesome Luke in response to the film comedy standards of the day.

A trade ad for the Rolin Phunphilms, the trade name used for the Lonesome Luke comedies from August 1915 through April 1916.

"Chaplin was going great guns, his success such that unless you wore funny clothes and otherwise aped him you were not a comedian. Exhibitors who could not get the original demanded imitations — and were given them in numbers from brazen counterfeits to coy skirtings about the Chaplin manner. Had I had the Glass Character then, and had I been allowed to try it out, I have no doubt that it would have sold on its merits, but these are two large ifs. On the one hand, I had only vague yearnings to do something different; on the other, the distributors and exhibitors would hear of no departures from the Chaplin track.

"I told Roach that I had something that was an improvement on Willie Work, at least. When he saw it he approved. Later it was tagged with the name of Lonesome Luke. For it my father had found a worn pair of Number 12AA last shoes in a repair shop on Los Angeles Street, where they had been left for resoling by an Englishman on his uppers. Dad asked the cobbler if he thought five dollars would compensate the owner. The cobbler was sure of it — five dollars bought a good pair of shoes. In a haberdashery dad found a black-and-white vertical-striped shirt and bought out the stock. The coat of a woman's tailored suit, a pair of very tight and

The Lloyd brothers, Gaylord (left) and Harold, appeared in *Luke's Double* together in June 1916 — Gaylord would play a Harold double again, three years later, in *His Royal Slyness*

short trousers, a vest too short, a cut-down collar, a cut-down hat and two dots of a mustache completed the original version of Lonesome Luke. The cunning behind all this, you will observe, was to reverse the Chaplin outfit. All his clothes were too large, mine all too small. My shoes were funny, but different; my mustache funny, but different.

"Nevertheless, the idea was purely imitative and was recognized as such by audiences, though I painstakingly avoided copying the well-known Chaplin mannerisms . . . Not only was the get-up imitative but it was an offense to the eye originally. I cleaned it up as time went on until it was self-respecting before it died, but I do not like to recall it and I am sorry that it is necessary to exhume it for this autopsy." [I]

Interestingly, on October 14, 1915, a memo was passed around, proposing renaming the series, still in is infancy, to "Handsome Luke." That idea went nowhere, fast.

Lonesome Luke as he looked in the spring of 1916. Note the black striped shirt, the triangular eyebrows and the two-dot mustache — it was this sort of eccentric costuming that rendered HL increasingly weary of "purely imitative" acting.

Lloyd was a pure comic actor, at this point — he was learning valuable lessons, and was always studying. "I think that for a man to achieve really strong success or popularity he has got to have a bent for it, to start with. Then, the studying of it, and the observing and the trail and error, will bring him out and make him either great or just ordinary. But I can envision a great many individuals who just do not seem to have a funny bone in their body. With those men, I think they could study forever, and they would find that they have chosen the wrong profession. I think you could probably get someone with a fair knowledge of comedy, and with a great deal of diligent work, and effort, concentration, they might make themselves a very fine comedian. But I think that they should have a feeling for it. But underneath it all, I do think that to rise above the ordinary strata of comedy, you've got to be a student of comedy, and know what basic ideas you're trying to project in the comedy line and the humorous end. You've got to make a study. People like to express themselves in different ways. Actors are expressing themselves and being someone else all the time." [A]

No matter how deeply Lloyd loathed being Lonesome Luke, and the imitative qualities inherent in the expression of the character, the series was very well received, both critically and popularly. In April 1917, *The New York Dramatic Mirror* reported, "To have become in less than eighteen months a comedian so popular as to

Bebe Daniels and HL, circa 1915: the two shared a love that evolved into a lifelong friendship. They died within eight days of each other in 1971.

be ranked with the leaders in that line and one who is an advertised attraction in many theaters, is the story of Harold Lloyd's achievements in the Pathé Lonesome Luke comedies." Add to that this quote by Andrew L. Stone, a San Francisco theatre owner: "Of all the shows I ran, the Lonesome Lukes with Harold Lloyd seemed to be the most popular, even more popular than Chaplin's. He seemed to have more gags than Chaplin."

A poster for the 30th Lonesome Luke comedy, released on July 3, 1916: the influence of the Chinese laundry is most evident. Note the rooster in the upper left of the sheet — it was the mascot of Pathé Distributors.

The trio that anchored the earliest Harold Lloyd comedies: Harry "Snub" Pollard, Bebe Daniels, and HL, circa 1915.

The series, for all the moderate acclaim, *can* be seen today as a mere training ground for Harold's future greatness. Nothing spectacular was done in any of the Lonesome Luke years; the greatest thing that can be said about the period at all was Lloyd's growing dissatisfaction with the character, and the concurrent development of a desire for comedy independence. No longer did he wish to follow the comedy standard — he wanted to lead a new pack. "The comedy should be better for not depending upon a putty nose or its equivalent and the situations should be better for not being tied to low-comedy coat tails; funnier things happen in life to an ordinary boy than to a Lonesome Luke." [I] It was this sentiment, and almost two years of persuasion, that sealed the fate of Lonesome Luke, and brought to eventual life Lloyd's Glass Character.

"I had a hard time dropping Luke, because they were making a quite a bit of money, the company was, and they weren't even using my name — it was Lonesome Luke at the time — but he wasn't a believable character; he was purely a comic that served his purpose.

The Rolin Film Company actors and officials, 1915. Bebe Daniels is in the front row, center; above her, HL; to his left, Snub Pollard; to his left, Earl Mohan; above HL, Hal Roach; to his left, Dwight Whiting, Roach's partner. In the top row, to the right of the lighting fixture, Charles Stevenson.

But, with the Glasses, you became an individual in reality. Lonesome Luke was not related to Chaplin's Tramp. In fact, you try to get something entirely different — Charlie's was all baggy clothes, loose, and mine were just the opposite; they were tight and so forth. But, comedy characters, regardless of what you do to make them different, they can all fall into the same slot very easily. We all had our own characters, but I was never proud of my Lonesome Luke character, because he restricted me and so many of the things I wanted to do. For instance, with the glasses — when I say restricted, wearing the glasses, and no comedy clothes, unless the picture called for it — he was like any boy you'd see or pass on the street." [C]

There were, in total, 67 Lonesome Luke comedies released from 1915-1917, 53 in one-reel length, 14 in two reels. Only fourteen of them are known to survive to this day — a large chunk of the Luke series was lost in a pair of nitrate explosions in 1938 and 1943. The first Luke scenarios were submitted by rather well-known journalists of the day: the initial four were written by Tad Dorgan, a sports cartoonist, and another half a dozen were offered by Dolly Twist, who received $20 per scenario, whether the story was used or not. The first Lonesome Luke film produced and released was *Spitball Sadie*, and the final was *We Never Sleep*. An attempt to revive the shell of the character of Lonesome Luke was made in March 1921 by, of all people, Harold's elder brother, Gaylord Lloyd. The experiment was an utter failure — of the 26 one-reel comedies contracted for, only five were released before the series was canceled.

Back to what Harold said about comedy being "hazardous." In the arena of Lonesome Luke, the hazard was in the execution for the young actor. "To tell you the truth, I tried very hard to get away from the Chaplin end of it. Because, where Charlie had loose baggy pants, I went the opposite direction and I wore them very tight. And I wore an old black and white striped shirt all the time, and a little kind of a felt hat. Charles had the corner on big shoes and comedy clothes and somebody using a cane — Charlie was so good at it that he had cornered that market. Consequently, anybody who was in that field at all — and of course we all probably had a little tendency to use some of Chaplin's characteristics — in fact, he did so many of them that he really had a corner on that, too — but in that field, that's where people got the idea that you were trying to imitate Chaplin. But I never did really, even in the slightest sense, try to imitate Charlie, in that others did who took his character. The only thing that I did was that it was a comedy character with big shoes and probably some mannerisms that I used were probably borrowed, ill-advisedly, from Charlie. But I was never happy with that at all. Because, even though the company was making quite a bit of money from these Lonesome Luke comedies, still, at the same time, I felt that, even though I had gone from one-reelers to two-reelers, and Pathé was very contented with them, I had the feeling, and rightly so, that I would never get any farther with

> **FUN FACT**
>
> "On location one day a boy called to me, 'Say, we had a contest at our theater last week and you beat Sterling.' For just an instant I was flattered, then I realized that he had taken me for Chaplin." [1]

Lonesome Luke than I had. Because, underneath it all, he was a comedy character that couldn't possibly rise to the heights that Chaplin had, and in some ways, while you didn't directly try to imitate Chaplin, he was a character that dropped into that category." [E]

In the midst of the inner turmoil that Harold was experiencing at his time — inner, in that audiences had not a clue of his dissatisfaction with the character (not that they, or Pathé or Roach for that matter, were asking) — Lloyd went to the cinema one night. The film he saw changed his life.

THE GLASS CHARACTER

That's Him...
"The basic ideas of comedy, there, seemed unending."

"Now, a lot of people used to say that Lloyd's character was a brash character; someone said he was an introverted character; well they're both wrong, because I was both. A lot of them said that Lloyd never used pathos; well, that's wrong too, because The Freshman *had a lot of pathos in it, so did* Grandma's Boy, *so did* Kid Brother. *But I made different types of pictures. Now,* Safety Last! *didn't have pathos in it — it was made purely for a laugh picture and a thrill on the side of a building. Now you may recall when I hung from the hands of a clock — now that wasn't made with pathos. So I broke them up, and did different things, the same as I played my character differently. Also, a lot of them thought that the Lloyd character wasn't exactly a comedy character. Well, that was wrong, because comedians in those days not only had to learn to time and space but they worked with their body as well as their facial expression. And when we ran, we had our own individual way of running; when I got into a situation, I'd create an attitude towards life."* [C]

"Lonesome Luke had funny clothes — they were very tight clothes — and he had a little mustache, they were like two little dots on either side of his lip. I did that character for a great many years, and Pathé, that I did it for, were doing very well from a monetary standpoint. But, from my standpoint, I felt that it was not getting me anyplace. It wasn't individual enough; it just fell into the slot of all the rest. And Charlie Chaplin, at that time, I would say, he had the monopoly, from comedy clothes, and mustaches, he was the undisputable king. And so naturally I was striving for an individuality, and I wanted something that would allow me to carry on with the broad comedy but would still make me a very believable character. Now the broad comedy characters, you never believed any real romance in them. So, I wanted something we could believe in as the boy next door. So the Glass Character seemed to kind of be sent to me out of the blue, as it were." [A]

In early 1916, Harold hit upon an idea for this new character, totally unlike any comedy persona on the screen at that time. The standard of grotesqueness, quirk, and unusualness was a must for laugh makers on screen in the mid-1910s: the more unlike real people you appeared, the funnier you were perceived to be. The laughs, chiefly, were found in the way a comic looked, not necessarily in the character. Harold wanted to change that, reasoning that funnier things happen to real people than to an eccentric comedy persona. Lloyd desperately wanted to present the humor to be found in life, reflecting his audience on screen, and allowing them to see themselves in the hilarious process. An evening at the Alhambra Theatre on Hill Street began, for Harold, an up-and-down ride towards making that dream character a reality.

"I was attending a feature picture — it was a *dramatic* picture — and the main character, who was a minister, wore horn-rimmed glasses. But his particular type of character appealed to me, at that time, because he belied his appearance. You thought that he was one way, because of the glasses, and because of his attitude, but he turned out to be a regular virile he-man, which belied the whole thing. And I thought, well, here's an idea — and I was going to do it as a college boy, and I thought that with the glasses that you would imagine he was very studious, and expect certain things of him, and then the character would be entirely opposite from what they anticipated. Well, that struck me as a good character." [A]

"I was *looking* for a different character. A unique character is very difficult to establish." [L]

The glasses were the key to the concept — they were the needed trademark that each comic had to have — but the frames were used in a unique fashion. The trademark wasn't the crux of the humor: the character wearing the specs was. At that time, those who needed optical aids were characterized as milquetoast, erudite, and studious. For Lloyd, reversing this trend started a magical cycle of comedy: an average, recognizable youth with everyday appeal, believable in romantic situations, physically ready for any obstacle, laughing at adversity, who just happened to wear glasses. And, most importantly for Harold, he would now be able to act, not hide behind (and be defined by) the restraints of elaborate costuming and makeup. He could wear normal clothes, do normal things, and appear psychologically and physically normal — a silent film comedy first. Roach and Pathé, however, were reluctant factors in the equation.

"Of course they were horrified to think that I was going to change a going character, and start all over again — that was just ridiculous! I mean, here is a character that was making money for them, was established and had been exploited. And, now I wanted to start again — they wouldn't listen to it. I guess it was nearly a year later, when I had reached the breaking point where I knew that Lonesome Luke was nothing that I was proud of, it was a character that I was getting great experience from, it was a stepping stone, but it was nothing original, nothing creative. I told Roach that I was very dissatisfied, that I was going to leave, and was going to try something else. And, of course, when he found out that there was no changing me, rather than lose me, well, he'd better join me. So, he conceded." [E]

Hal may have conceded, but "Roach didn't believe in the character." [C] However, "when he found out that I was determined to do this character with the glasses, and not knowing anything about it himself or what I wanted or what I intended, he said, 'all right, Lloyd, I'm going to turn it over to you. You pick whoever you want to direct you and how you want to do it.' And of course, he assumed I was going to go on with two-reelers — but I told him, no, I wanted to make one-reelers. Of course, he thought I was a little out of my mind then — because for a person to advance to two-reelers from one-reelers and wanting to go back to one-reelers, it didn't make sense. But, I think my logic, in wanting to do that, was sound, in that I said, 'Look, we only make about one two-reeler a month. Now, I'm getting started in a new character and you want people to get used to the character, you want them to see the

One of the earliest Glass Character studies, from 1917. The glasses changed little over the years, but the hinges and temples decreased in size over time, as did the width of the rims. Note the checkered suit and flowing black tie, a Lloyd wardrobe staple until 1920.

character; and besides, if you make a poor, or mediocre, or moderately good, or even a bad picture in a two-reeler, it'll kind of tend to sour the people on you because they won't see another one for a month. But if I make one-reelers, we'll get one out every week, so if a couple of them are not so good, and the third one is, it will cover up the other two, and besides it will keep you in front of the public.' So, he said, 'All right, if that's what you want,' and I started in." [E]

Through his Glass Character, Harold Lloyd is generally recognized as the man who single-handedly made eyeglass wearing fashionable in America. According to the *Journal of the American Optometric Association*, "For optometrists in the 1920s he was the man who popularized the use of glasses, especially horn-rimmed glasses, to a population who resisted the use of spectacles. Suddenly, there he was on the silent screen demonstrating for all to see that the wearing of eyeglasses added to one's personality."

The Glass Character wore *lens-less* horn-rimmed glasses — minus lenses to eliminate the glare from studio lights which would obscure expression. And, the glasses themselves were designed, specifically, to separate actor from role. "When I came to choose a pair of my own the vogue of horn-rims was new and it was youth, principally, that was adopting them. The novelty was a picture asset and the suggestion of youth fitted perfectly with the character I had in mind." [I]

To find spectacles that were just right, Harold shopped around. He tried two sets of frames — the first pair was too heavy, the second too large. Finally, in a tiny optical shop on Spring Street in Los Angeles, he hit upon the perfect pair. They were thin enough as to not be overwhelming; they were diametrically perfect for expressiveness. The first pair of horn-rims, which cost him seventy-five cents, lasted him a year and a half. Then, when the time came to order a new pair, he sent a check for seventy-five cents to the manufacturer, Optical Products Corporation; the company promptly sent Lloyd the check back, and included in the package *twenty* pairs of frames. "The advertising we had given tortoise-shell rims, they wrote, still left them in our debt." [I]

"The character that I finally devised was a character that I think could be your next door neighbor. He was just a young man that wore glasses. He was sort of out of the normal group. He was a character in a great many of the stories that we devised who looked like he never had a chance to succeed. Or that he couldn't overcome certain, what appeared to be insurmountable, obstacles. But he had great concentration, and determination, and regardless of how hopeless a situation looked, he just seemed to keep going ahead, and eventually succeeded in the end. Now, with that all, he had to be a character that you kind of liked. So you kind of had a sympathy for him. But at the same time, he struck you as a kind of an odd, amusing kind of a pathetic type of a character. And, so, the whole summation was that you not only laughed at him, but you kind of laughed *with* him. The basic ideas of comedy, there, seemed unending." [A]

"I symbolized the struggling little average man, who got himself into difficulties and had trouble getting out but finally rose above it, surmounting the whole thing and came out in the end. But I changed my character — that's different from what the other boys did — one time I might be very shy character, timid like in *Grandma's Boy*, another one I might be an extravert, I might be a hypochondriac, one of these brash ones, or I might be very normal, or a cowardly kind of character. But, always, he was the little character who was always in trouble." [D]

"I think he is a fellow that you see walking down the street that you pass all the time. He wears ordinary clothes; he wears glasses as his only distinguishing mark. His attitude towards things — it's the difficulties he gets into and how he surmounts them that I think makes the comedy out of it. But, otherwise, he isn't really what you might call a comedy character. And I didn't try to devise a lot of eccentricities, like so many other comedians had scored upon, and wonderfully so. But he was just an ordinary boy that you liked, that could have been living next door to you, and you were interested in his problems, because his problems were ones that you might have gotten into yourself." [A]

"The main idea was to get away from the funny clothes; have a trademark — we all should have a trademark in those days, somebody had funny chin pieces, someone else had a big mustache, another one had sideburns — but they were all funny comedy characters. This boy with the glasses would be a boy next door, someone human, someone that you knew, someone that you believed could happen. You could have romance with him, and still you could do the broad type of comedy. So the first five, I had to write them, and direct them, and work in them. By that time, they found out that the Glass Character was going to work, so they came piling back and they gave me two directors, and by that time I was really in trouble. I had to do them so fast. It was a nightmare, every night, going to bed trying to dream up gags to do in the next one." [B]

> ## Fun Fact
>
> THE VERY FIRST GLASS CHARACTER ONE-REELER, *OVER THE FENCE*, FEATURES A CAMEO BY HAROLD'S DAD, JAMES DARSIE "FOXY" LLOYD, AS THE UMPIRE AT THE BASEBALL PARK. HIS APPEARANCE WAS FILMED ON JUNE 18, 1917, AT WASHINGTON PARK — HE RECEIVED $3 FOR THE DAY'S WORK.
>
> WASHINGTON PARK WAS PRIMARILY USED FOR BASEBALL AND WAS THE HOME OF THE LOS ANGELES ANGELS MINOR LEAGUE TEAM FROM 1912 UNTIL THEY MOVED TO THE FORMER WRIGLEY FIELD IN LOS ANGELES LATE IN THE 1925 SEASON. THE ROLIN COMPANY WAS BILLED BY THE VERNON ATHLETIC ASSOCIATION, INC., $12 FOR UNIFORM RENTALS, AND $50 PER DAY FOR THE TWO DAYS (JUNE 13 AND 18) THEY SHOT *OVER THE FENCE* AT WASHINGTON PARK. IN RESPONSE TO THIS, ROLIN OFFICIAL DWIGHT WHITING SENT THE FOLLOWING NOTE:
>
> "AT VERNON, WE HAVE ALWAYS BEEN WELCOME TO THE GROUNDS GRATIS, AND WE HAVE USED WASHINGTON PARK IN PREVIOUS PICTURES GRATIS AND WITH WELCOME. I FEEL SURE THAT YOU KNOW HOW OFTEN THE PICTURE PEOPLE SEE THE GAMES AND THAT THE ABOVE IS WITHOUT YOUR KNOWLEDGE OR SANCTION. WILL YOU PLEASE SEE THAT MR. JACKSON GETS THE ENCLOSED CHECK FOR $12.00 FOR UNIFORM CHARGES AND INSTRUCT HIM TO CROSS OFF THE OTHER CHARGE. I SURMISE THAT WALTER S. JOHNSON KNOWS NOTHING OF THE ABOVE AND THAT IT WAS THE SPONTANEOUS IDEA OF HIS EVIDENT YOUNGER BROTHER."

"The first one, I wrote and directed and played in myself. The first one I did was one that had to do with a tailor shop. I was a tailor in it, and the boy who was playing with me, a boy by the name of Harry Pollard, he was also one of the tailors, and we were sort of rivals for the girl's hand. It had to do with a baseball picture — the title of the picture was *Over the Fence* [released on September 9, 1917]. The idea was that the count, with his frock coat on, had come in to get some tailoring work done, and in cutting some cloth, I had cut off one of the coat tails, and in the coat tail was two tickets to the baseball game. So, I invited the girl to go with me.

The beautiful Bradbury Mansion, at 406 Court Street in Los Angeles; it was here that Rolin had offices and shot films, off and on, from 1914-1920.

But, in the meantime, Pollard, my rival, got the tickets away from me without my knowing it. And, of course, when I showed up at the baseball park with my girl, and went to go in, I had no tickets — and, of course, he just inadvertently happened to be there, and happened to have a couple of tickets. Of course, they were my tickets. And so he took the girl in, leaving me with no girl and no admission — and then the comedy revolved around how I got into the baseball park. And that was the first Glass Character, and I never followed through on the college boy idea." [E]

Having had more than a year to conceptualize and, literally, dream about this new persona, Harold thoroughly understood it and consistently enjoyed its diversity and its flexibility — he was truly, now, a rubber band that could be stretched in an infinite number of directions. "I think it represented, pretty well, a group of young men, mostly American youth. My character was so very different from the other boys in a certain phase, in that I played an introvert, or an extrovert, or a hypochondriac, or just a normal boy. Now, most of the other comedians, they had their set character and that character went through all the pictures they did. Now, I had glasses and about 2/3 of the time, if the picture called for it, I wore a straw hat, but still my attitude towards life changed. One of the things, when I was going to get the picture together, not only was the idea, whether it was going to be a college picture, or a baseball picture, or something to do with a coward, et cetera: I would say, what kind of a character, what *attitude* is this character going to be. I changed the character and the other boys went blissfully on in their own way — which was fine — it's just this other fitted mine and that's where it was entirely different." [C]

"I like the Glass Character because it allowed you to be a human being. It allowed you to be the boy next door, anyone you could see. While they weren't wearing horn-rimmed glasses too much, and they were just coming into being, still they were a definite trademark and they gave the feeling of being studious, and they filled in for me what a mustache or a chin piece would be, but still a natural one. At the same time, you could still be a milquetoast if you want to be — you can be anything you want to be. My glasses not only served me to give me the kind of characterization I wanted, but it served as my trademark. They referred to me as the man with the glasses — until of course my name was thoroughly established; I don't think it was too far established in Lonesome Luke; I think they thought of me as Lonesome Luke rather than as Harold Lloyd. In Europe, you have different names — this was before the name Lloyd became established — in London, it was Winkle, and the name Lloyd meant nothing; in Germany, it was Herr, which means He, and in France it was Lui, which also means He. It's better than having them point at you." [E]

The Glass Character debuted (at Harold's suggestion) in single-reel length, alternating with two-reel Lonesome Luke Comedies, for three months, from September through December 1917. By the time the final Luke short, *We Never Sleep*, was released (on December 2, 1917), the new Harold Lloyd Comedies had taken flight, and were increasing in appeal with each weekly release. Of interesting note is the change of focus in early reviews of the new character. Now, instead of focusing on gags and "business," as was commonplace, early Glass Character film reviews were now commenting on "...The Lloyd personality and the extremely novel way the comedy has been presented..." (*Exhibitor's Trade Review* for *All Aboard*,

> **Pathé**
>
> # You don't have to be "on the fence"
>
> when it comes to picking the BEST one reel comedies made!
>
> Pick out at random any half dozen
>
> # HAROLD LLOYD
>
> comedies from the Pathé program. Ask your Pathé exchange to screen them for you. Weigh them carefully for humorous situations, acting and quality of production. You'll no longer be "on the fence" as to what are the best one reel comedies made. Your own judgment will point unerringly to the Lloyd!
>
> Produced by Rolin

A 1918 trade ad for the Lloyd one-reelers: in the original picture this ad used, Snub Pollard was seated to HL's left.

December 1, 1917), ". . .The Lloyd originality . . ." (*Exhibitor's Trade Review* for *Bashful*, December 22, 1917), and ". . .Plenty of original and entertaining humor . . . the usual Lloyd originality" (*Exhibitor's Trade Review* for *The Lamb*, February 2, 1918). Such high praise, centering on the very heart of what Harold desired — to do something unique and singular. This certainly proved that Lloyd was now ready to lead, not follow, in the comedy film arena. "I was looking for something individual. I was looking for a character who would be my own. I would rather have been a serious actor than continue as an imitation." [K]

Harold was fiercely proud and protective of his character: "Some critic one time said that Lloyd's character was a brazen type of character, that if he fell from a first floor and lit on his head why he'd get up and he wouldn't even have a headache — well, he couldn't have been more wrong on my character. That was just the opposite way from what I tried to do. And one of the things was that I didn't try to clown as much and ad lib in a lot of the clowning, because it would spoil a certain reality in the character and I didn't want to do that." [C]

"There is more magic in a pair of horn-rimmed glasses than the opticians dream of, nor did I guess the half of it when I put them on in 1917.

"With them, I am Harold Lloyd; without them, a private citizen. I can stroll unrecognized down any street in the land at any time without the glasses, a boon granted no other picture actor and one which some of them would pay well for." [I]

This anonymity served Harold well during his Summer 1927 location shoot in New York City for *Speedy*. Ted Wilde, the film's director, was incredulous as to Lloyd's ability to mingle, unnoticed, in the big city crowds. Harold went one further: "I bet him that I could walk down any two blocks of Fifth Avenue in daylight and in make-up, and go unrecognized, and won the bet, though he chose the most difficult stretch of the Avenue — Forty-first to Forty-third streets. I fixed the time at 4pm and Wilde and others followed in a car. Two tricks account for my escape. The first is to lower the eyes. Once you catch the eye of any one, he may start in sudden recognition. The other trick is the time of day. At four o'clock there are no promenaders or idlers on the Avenue. As the business day nears its close every one is bound somewhere in a hurry and preoccupied with his business." [I]

GLASS CHARACTER ONE-REEL FILMS THAT MAP LLOYD'S COMIC EVOLUTION

The Glass Character, which debuted in September 1917 in *Over the Fence* (one of only two times that Lloyd took on-screen credit for the direction of his films; the other was *Just Neighbors*, in 1919), looked very different from Lonesome Luke. No more clothing that emphasized the differences between the audience and the character — now, the adornment of the on-screen persona *mirrored* the audience; now, the look of the character was representative of the very people it was entertaining. Truth be told, though normal in appearance, the earliest Glass films can hardly be seen as any real change from the Lonesome Luke character. Lloyd didn't become brilliant overnight.

Yet, throughout the first two years of the Glass Character — when Lloyd made only single-reel pictures, released practically every seven days — Harold's growth as an intelligent comic, his story depth and his creative ingenuity, are evident. His was an evolution, charted weekly, on screen, before millions.

In *Pinched* (9/23/1917), Lloyd's character, whose identity has been mixed with that of a drunk, is in jail, and watches as two fellow cellmates endeavor to break out, by tearing away at the wall, cinder block by cinder block. Finally, when they are almost through, Lloyd knocks each over their heads with a block, and breaks through the hole in the wall — only to find himself not out in the free, but inside the main office of the police station. *Pinched* is an important film to seek out (and it is extant), because it offers viewers a rare opportunity to see costar Harry "Snub" Pollard without his famed mustache. In addition, this film marks the final time Harold Lloyd could be seen in a non-Luke acting role without his glasses on (note that, in 1938's *Professor Beware*, he did take off his glasses, but with his back to the camera): both Lloyd and Pollard strayed, in just the second Glass Character short, from the appearance formula that each would adhere to for the balance of their careers. This was necessary, however, from a plot point of view, and the mixed-identity scenario between Pollard and Lloyd worked splendidly in this, a most delightful and entertaining reel.

Bud Jamison ready to do bodily harm to HL in the first Glass Character short, *Over the Fence* (1917): Harold looks less than worried.

Look Pleasant, Please (3/10/1918), was called by *Exhibitor's Trade Review*, in its 3/9/18 review, "…something unusual to laugh at," and it was just that. Lloyd really hit upon some great ideas in this film, in which he plays a vegetable vendor who gets suckered into managing a photography studio. Its prior manager (William Gillespie), with his roving eyes (and hands and mouth!), fell out of favor with a female pose (Bebe Daniels), who summoned her hubby — "My husband will be over to murder you shortly," reads one of the titles. What fun work, with the most eccentric persons coming in for photos — three drunks (led by James Parrott, brother of Charley Chase), a scantily-clad bathing beauty, and the loquacious Patsy O'Byrne, who only stops talking when Lloyd forces her mouth shut. Some object-throwing is resorted to, but the cleverness of the titles (Harley M. "Beanie" Walker was hitting his stride as a top-notch title writer by

HL laughing at Snub Pollard in *Look Pleasant, Please* (1918), one of the best HL shorts.

A production still for *The City Slicker* (1918) featuring Helen Gilmore at the front desk of the Punkville Hotel managed by HL. From the look of the signs, someone needs a spelling lesson.

this time), and the wonderful character work make this a stellar example of a great short. This film survives, and is a must-see.

In *Pipe the Whiskers* (4/14/1918), Lloyd plays an attendant at the "Old Boys' Muditorium," a gymnasium of sorts for men. This one-reeler definitely has sparks of the Lloyd ingenuity to come: Lloyd is encouraging his charges to give the active life a try — Harold slowed down his own actions, the other men in the room moved normally, yet when the film, cranked slower, is run at normal speed, Lloyd looks normal, and the men are frenetic in their speed — the sight of James "Slim Jim" Fitzgerald, at over seven feet tall, Sammy Brooks, at 4 feet 6 inches, and Gus Leonard, then 62 years old, zooming around the exercise equipment at break-neck speed is utterly hilarious. That having been said, the film also has the time-worn look of the era: one resident has the gout (evident in the big, wrapped foot), and, of course, it is somehow set on fire. The Lloyd solution? Dip the foot in the Muditorium fountain.

Lloyd and Bebe Daniels exhibit their grace and execution as a dance team in *It's a Wild Life* (4/21/1918) — they won, in private life, a bevy of cups for their dancing acumen. Yet, while this was reviewed in *Motion Picture News*, on 4/20/18, as ". . .perhaps, Harold Lloyd's funniest single reel comedy," the standard is still an influence. Three men are vying for Bebe's hand — Lloyd, the Baron de Muss and the Duke of Approcot (nobility characters were extremely prevalent then, and are continued signs of the pull of the standard of comedy on Lloyd). Harold, in an attempt to escape them, disguises himself as a cigar store Indian. There are, by this time, glimpses of originality (using his own personal strengths to enhance his comedies) present in the Lloyd comedies, but not quite full focus. This film is extant, and should be sought out: it is an important personal and professional relic in the life and career of Harold Lloyd.

In *An Ozark Romance* (7/7/1918), Bebe Daniels has one of her best roles in any Lloyd comedy — she plays a daughter in probably the most nutty back country family ever. When she encounters Harold, who is simply in the country doing a little fishing, she is wearing two different socks, kicks Lloyd in the shin as a sign of affection, and invites him to her house. Harold arrives at her shack in a top hat and tails — meanwhile, her little and big siblings are *everywhere*, and bootleg whiskey flows from a wall faucet. One of the children is a gun-toting smartie — shoots Harold's hat to the wall three times, reducing Harold to frantic prayers for his life. Here is slapstick with a purpose - a really fun film.

Harold Lloyd never functioned, actively, in the military — however, through his filmmaking efforts, he did serve his country. Within the 1914-1919 span of World War I, for example, Lloyd released such films as *Kicking the Germ Out of Germany* (7/21/1918), which kept the world smiling through the horrors of the global altercation. In this non-extant offering, Army man Harold had a dream while in the trenches, during which he went to Berlin to rescue a Red Cross girl (Daniels) from the Kaiser. This film, and other similarly plotted shorts, established Lloyd as a star who could better help his country during wartime through laughter than in active trenches. This short was frequently used in all-war programs in theatres nationwide.

A most deliberately posed still for *Kicking the Germ Out of Germany* (1918). Notice the Rolin Film Co. sign on the stand behind HL, as well as the make-shift nature of the stage construction.

Hear 'Em Rave (12/1/1918) showcased the full-blast ingenuity that Lloyd became known for in gag-land. Harold plays a "freckle remover" at a beauty parlor, and has a machine that *really* works miracles, turning overweight women into svelte dolls. Clever editing accomplished this: Helen Gilmore, frequent heavy-weight co-star dating back to the Lonesome Luke days, sits in Lloyd's chair. The "machine" is placed over her head, her back to the camera. As each stays perfectly still, "Cut!" When action resumes, the lady is suddenly sweet, thin, and played by a slender extra. Neat and innovative.

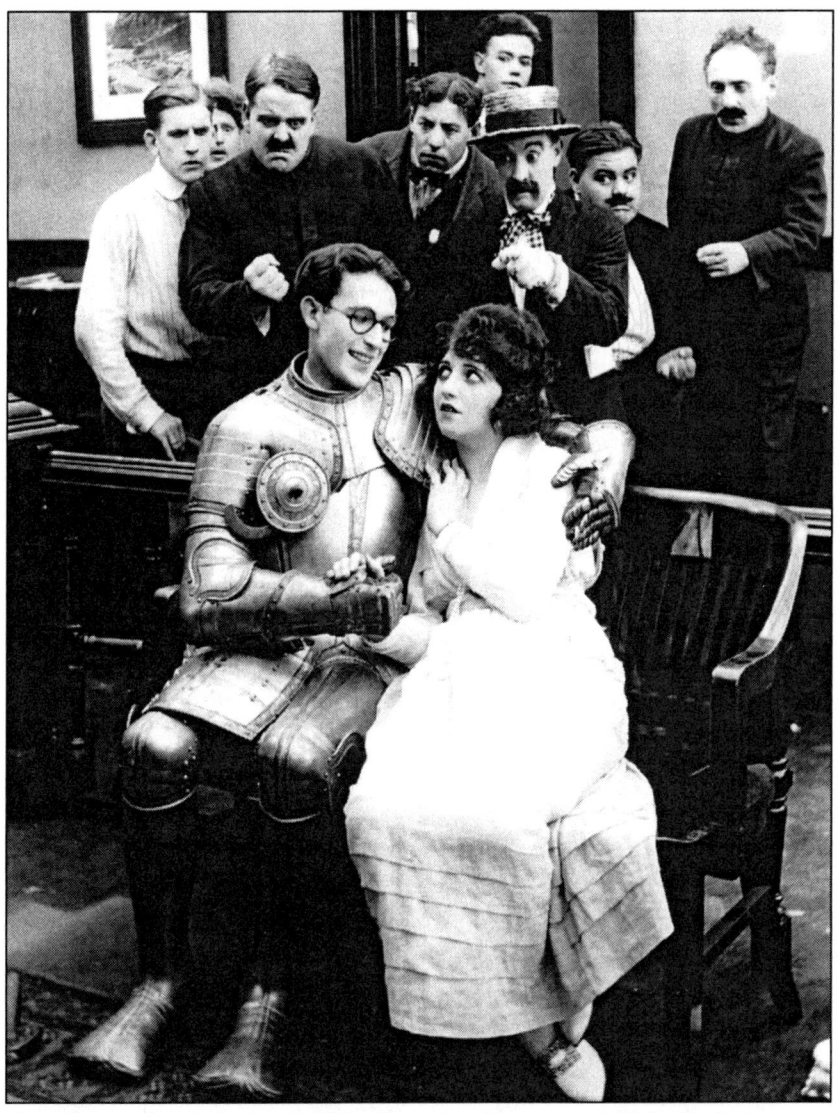

The climax of *Ask Father* (1919). HL and Bebe are seated; behind them, from left, Jimmy Parrott, unknown, Bud Jamison, Noah Young, James "Slim" Fitzgerald, Snub Pollard, Dee Lampton and Sammy Brooks.

With *Ask Father* (2/9/1919), we have probably the first example of romance in which the audience can fully believe. Lloyd wants to marry the daughter (Marie Mosquini) of the busiest man in town (Wallace Howe) — in response to his proposal, she says, "Ask Father," but Harold has the hardest time getting in to ask the father. He tries via many methods, throughout the reel, to get into the man's office, yet, each time, is kicked out on his anterior — the only thing saving him from a "frail tail" is the fair Bebe, office receptionist, who saves him each time by tossing her pillow right where he falls. We, the audience, notice her *way* before Harold does; thus, in the course of the reel, we are rooting for Harold and *Bebe* to get together. And, by the end, they do: this is perhaps the first case of Lloyd film romance made believable — Lloyd's and Daniels' characters are not just thrown together for the sake of plot. It is grown into and, thus, is made more satisfying for the audience. This film also conjures a question: Was *this* the unofficial first thrill picture in Harold Lloyd's film repertoire? Could be. In the midst of Harold's attempts to ask the father for his daughter's hand, he is unceremoniously shuffled out of the office by a trap door, which sends him flying out of the building, onto the street. Harold climbs the building to regain access to the office via a window. Lloyd's building climb in this film was a sure influence on another such thrill sequence in the 1923 feature *Safety Last!* His ascent, the first of the famed thrills he became so well known for, was quickly accomplished, and was not exploited for time and effect, as in later thrill shorts *Look Out Below!* (1919), *High and Dizzy* (1920), and *Never Weaken* (1921).

In *I'm On My Way* (3/9/1919), flash *forward* is used in fabulous fashion. Harold and Bebe are on the verge of marriage — he's awaiting her arrival at a neighbor's house — Snub's place. He (Snub Pollard) is married (to Margaret Joslyn Todd), and is father to at least seven children, ranging from six feet tall to infant. The kids make Harold's stay *miserable* — so much so that he seeks refuge in the dining room, where he fantasizes about *his* future married life, complete with rolling pins about the head and broken china. Tumult galore. Harold decides that married life is not for him — "No wedding bells for me! I'm cured!" A very imaginative story, with very creative plot development — a year and a half after the dawn of the Glass Character, Lloyd is finally defining his range as a crafty comic. When one considers that, at the time this film was shot, Harold Lloyd and Bebe Daniels were in love, and planning to marry, the vision his character had in the film takes on a more ironic significance. Mercy, they must have had such fun filming that short.

Ring Up the Curtain (1919) features a true rarity in Lloyd land: Bebe choosing Snub over Harold.

Look Out Below! (3/16/1919) was truly the first time that the *illusion* of peril would be used to such marvelous advantage in a Lloyd film. In it, Harold and Bebe have eyes only for each other — sitting on a girder near a building under construction, they are unaware when it starts to rise, seemingly towards the clouds. The key to its success was a set, comprising the building, with girders actually made of wood painted to look like steel. The mock edifice, appearing on screen as two stories, was built upon the Hill Street tunnel, close to a terrace fence, with downtown Los Angeles laying in the background. Shot on film by Roach cameraman Walter Lundin, the marriage of the girder set and the city scape in the distance gave the appearance of a much taller building, hence the danger element for the audience. A hoisted girder, seen dangling next to the top of the shell, looked as if it were miles from the ground. A magician could not have crafted this visual film trick any better.

A Sammy in Siberia (4/6/1919) introduces Harold as a member of the Squad of Sammies who undertakes the rescue of a fair damsel

A Sammy in Siberia (1919) was shot on location in Bear Valley, California — the snow in this Russian burlesque was real.

in distress (Daniels) from a gang of Bolsheviki. This, without question, was a reel with appeal, according to Rolin. It was filmed in late January 1919, copyrighted the next month, and released on April 6 — a total turnaround of about two and a half months. This was far from the ordinary for the Lloyd company — the average film was shot seven or eight months prior to release — and shows that Lloyd and Roach felt very strongly about this particular reel, to rush it to the theatres as they did.

In *Ring Up the Curtain* (4/27/1919), Harold plays a stage hand in an Opera House — he is infatuated with prima donna Bebe, who hardly notices him. Harold and Snub Pollard struggle over her — *on* stage, disrupting the ongoing performance — and Bebe winds up leaving the Opera House on Snub's arm. A dejected Harold is left all alone, thinking, "There's a sucker born every minute, and I must've been twins." This film, along with the later *Number, Please?* (1920), mark the only fully unhappy endings in the Lloyd film repertoire. Harold's films almost always ended on an upbeat note, but this film — which closed with Harold beginning suicide by gas — broke the spell. Even if, as happened in some instances, Harold wound up behind bars at the close of a picture, we always had some kind of clue that things would work out for his character. These two unhappily ending films are important examples of total dejection at the close of pictures that saw him work hard for a goal, only to be truly defeated in the end: rare instances indeed.

Young Mr. Jazz (5/4/1919) contains some exceptional sequences, all occurring in a dance hall. In an attempt to retrieve stolen money, Harold hung from a ceiling fan to attack the thieving thugs, jumped off an entertainment stand to overpower his foes, and generally used sincerely excellent acrobatics and skill in creating a faction of physical fun. In addition, the team of Bebe Daniels and Harold Lloyd executed some fun dance moves, in costumed disguise to ward off her father — the two strutted around the dance floor like ballroom gangsters, stooped yet graceful, and looked just beautiful together.

In *Spring Fever* (6/29/1919), Harold was tired of working, and longed to go outside and play (what office worker doesn't?). His supervising co-worker (Noah Young), would not hear of it, and

Hal Roach directing HL, Sammy Brooks and Snub Pollard in *Spring Fever* (1919). Seated at right are Pathé official Paul Brunet and his son, along with an attentive Bebe Daniels.

demanded that Harold sit back down. Harold proceeded to grab his hat from the rack; Noah took it off his head and placed it back on the rack. Again, Harold got up and put his hat on, only to have it snatched from his scalp and back onto the rack. Finally, our boy got smart. He grabbed another man's hat, and put it on his head, while hiding his own hat behind his back. When Noah grabbed the hat from Harold's head, Harold kept on walking, and as he exited the office, he put on his own hat, whilst sporting *the* most satisfying smirk on his face. Beautiful. It is at this point in his filmmaking career that Harold developed a continuing facet in his character: resourcefulness in a pinch. The ability to find a way out of adversity, in creative and tricky ways (inevitably building the comedy) will be seen in virtually all of the Lloyd films that followed. Harold was continuing to learn what worked, and what did not, about comedy bits, and perennially absorbed lessons from his own failures and successes, which helped subsequent efforts. Case in point is *Spring Fever*, which has many splendid examples of ingenious pieces of business — the Lloyd/Roach camp obviously saw the strengths in this film early on, for it was rushed to release in front of no less than 13 films shot before it. This was not exclusive to *Spring Fever*: in similar fashion, the release of *A Sammy in Siberia* was pushed ahead of 17 films produced before it, and *Just Neighbors* was released before 13 previously completed films.

Billy Blazes, Esq. (7/6/1919) is one of Harold's finest single-reelers, perhaps *the* best. The gag work in this, without question, is superb, particularly a sequence in the town restaurant, where Noah Young, as the town villain, had taken Bebe Daniels hostage. Lloyd overpowered Young through rapid-fire gun work (with *two* pistols), and had Young seeing stars within moments. At one point, Harold looked to be pointing his gun again, only to be merely whipping out his handkerchief, with which he wiped his brow. Eventually, Lloyd had Young squatting on the floor, Harold using Noah's back as a chair. This singular sequence, as no other, shows Harold Lloyd at his crafty and physical best. In a June 6, 1919 telegraph from Hal Roach to Paul Brunet of Pathé, an interesting fact was raised: "I advise that you release *Billy Blazes, Esq.* as soon as possible. Arbuckle is working on same idea and we should have ours out first." Companies were very aware of what rival film concerns were

One of HL's best one-reelers, the shoot-'em-up romp *Billy Blazes, Esq.* (1919). HL and Bebe are front and center, with HL's foot on Fred Newmeyer's back; Noah Young stands, hands up and boots knee-high, second from right.

producing, and always looked out for their own interests. Incidentally — the Arbuckle film in question was *The Hayseed*, released in October 1919, some three months after *Billy Blazes, Esq.* hit theatres.

Just Neighbors (7/13/1919) was called, by *Motion Picture News*, ". . . as clever a skit on suburban life as ever was fashioned." It really was, too. Suburban and married life, as pictured in *Just Neighbors*, was not exploited to as extreme a degree as in *I'm On My Way*, four months earlier. This was a reasonable, and realistic, look at neighborhood life, complete with marital devotion, domestic rifts, and friendly squabbles. It was not a farce, or a knockabout, attempt to show neighborly situations: everything that happened in this film *could* happen in life, showing Lloyd's influence (as co-director) in making his films a mirror of his audiences' lives. This, without question, was one of the keys to Harold Lloyd's success. Though 13 more would be released, *Just Neighbors* was the 81st and final Glass Character short produced in one-reel length.

Filming Just Neighbors (1919), the final Glass Character one-reeler produced. As Fred Guiol films HL, Bebe and Snub, Pathé vice-president and general manager Paul Brunet looks on, joined by his two sons.

Count the Votes (10/5/1919) was a burlesque on politics. The film, itself, is not known to be available for reappraisal, but in its praise of the film and its star, *Motion Picture News* dubbed Lloyd ". . . effective and clean." This cleanliness issue — not at all related to the Boy Scouts or the use of soap — was a growing one amongst film reviewers and social groups as the 1910s came to a close. Uniformly, Harold Lloyd's films were praised for being generally wholesome and suitable for all members of the family — this was certainly not the case during the Lonesome Luke and early Glass Character era, when random acts of violence were often used for a laugh's sake. But as the Glass Character evolved, so did Lloyd's realization that the humor to be found in real life was, ultimately, funnier and meatier than ferocity for a chuckle. This point is an important and enduring one — that Harold Lloyd's films remain excellent choices for family viewing. They knew it then, and we still know it today.

A beautiful fake thrill sequence was presented in *Pay Your Dues* (10/12/1919), during Harold's unwitting initiation into the Ancient Order of Simps, Young Turks Lodge #13. The fraternity

Harry "Snub" Pollard appeared in 149 Lloyd films. In 1924, he told *The Albertan*, "My association with Harold Lloyd has left me many pleasant memories . . . this was one of the best times of my career at the studio."
COURTESY SAM GILL.

tricked a blindfolded Harold (who was so masked because he thought he was playing Pin the Tail on the Donkey at Bebe's party) into thinking that he was climbing a building ladder onto a high ledge, on which Harold had to struggle to escape injury. An electric fan simulates an outdoor breeze; Simps lay on the floor to make their voices seem far below — here, Harold shows the fright that he never showed during his *actual* thrill pictures. Fun stuff.

"The comedy we did then, I think, was basic. We took things that would happen to people in every day life, then, the same as it happens right now, and we just enlarged upon them, we stretched them a bit, but they're just as funny today as they were then." [C]

Harold Lloyd's Use of the Preview

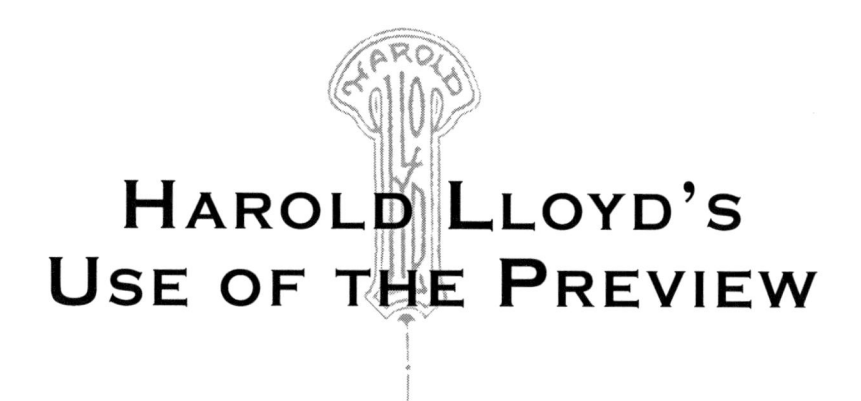

Follow the Crowd . . .
"To keep right in tune with what the audience liked or they didn't like."

In the May 23, 1926 edition of *The New York Times*, for an article entitled "The Public Is the Doctor," Harold Lloyd wrote of a facet of his filmmaking style that he had adopted over a decade earlier, during the Lonesome Luke one-reel days: the Preview. "The public is the best judge of what is funny . . . if they like what you have to offer they show their appreciation by spontaneous laughter. If they don't like it you can easily tell by the painful sighs . . . the public is eminently fair. These unprofessional spectators are the greatest help to a comedian who is trying to make something to please them."

A great number of the Lloyd films would have looked markedly different had Harold not utilized — trusted and valued — the preview, or a test of audience reaction to a film prior to its release. His adoption of this surprise screening as a gauge of popular opinion marked a turning point in his career, proving that he wanted the moviegoer satisfied, even if it meant changing sequences that he really liked. "Irving Thalberg, I believe, gave me credit for being one of the first if not the first to *really* use previews in the way that I did." [N]

"We did that with one-reelers. No one else was doing it at the time — in fact, when we'd do it, people in the theatre didn't know what we were doing, they didn't know what it was all about. The manager of the theatre would have to come out and explain to the public just what was going on — that it was something that had just been made, wasn't completed, and that they were using the audience as sort of guinea pigs to let us know whether we were on the right track. That we were going back and make a great deal of it over, which we did do — sometimes we'd come back and work for a month or longer after our first preview. Sometimes we'd have five, six, seven previews, if necessary, and keep improving all the time." [E]

"You see, I tried to tell the boys, 'Now, let's not take a century to make this picture because we know we're going to make a hell of a lot of it over. So let's make it as good as we can for the first time, then after the audience has seen it, we're coming back really to go to work and find out what's wrong with it.'" [J]

"And in that way we made the picture and then went back and took out the parts that we felt were not funny enough or that didn't have the right interest and either made them over or bridged them around another way, or embellished them . . . it was tremendously helpful to keep right in tune with what the audience liked or they didn't like." [N]

Harold made these changes even if it meant they superseded his own opinion . . . and his dependence on audience reaction was unprecedented ...

In an August 6, 1920 letter from Hal Roach to Frederick C. Quimby of Associated Exhibitors: "We were very disappointed with our preview on picture No. 8, *Get Out and Get Under*, and have made it over twice." The two-reel Lloyd pictures averaged between five and seven weeks to complete. *Get Out and Get Under*, however, was shot from the week of May 1-June 12, 1920, and then (after seven weeks at work on *Number, Please?*) re-shot key scenes during the weeks of August 7 and 14, 1920, totaling nine weeks in production.

The entire first reel of *I Do* (1921) was removed after previews went poorly. This was, originally, slated to be a three-reel film — the first reel centered on the elopement of Harold and Mildred, whose parents gave the young couple full blessings. The original release date planned was July 24, 1921; it would finally be issued on September 11. "At the first preview in three reels it disappointed so badly that we feared for a moment that it was a total loss.

Many of the Lloyd films, including *I Do* (1921) would have flowed dissimilarly, and would probably have been received differently, had HL not used and relied upon previews of his motion pictures.

> ## Fun Fact
>
> FROM *THE KID BROTHER* PRESS BOOK: "IF THERE'S ANYONE ON THE STAGE OR SCREEN WHO KNOWS WHAT THE PUBLIC WANTS, THAT MAN IN HAROLD LLOYD. HE HAS GIVEN HIS ADMIRERS MORE CONTINUOUS SUCCESSES THAN ANY OTHER SATELLITE OF MOTION PICTURES; YET, WHEN YOU COME RIGHT DOWN TO IT, HE LETS THE PUBLIC ITSELF DECIDE WHAT IT WANTS.
>
> "A PROMINENT NEW YORK DRAMATIC CRITIC RECENTLY COMPILED A LIST OF BROADWAY SHOWS WHICH HAD SEX AS THEIR MAIN THEME. HE ENUMERATED MORE THAN FORTY SUCCESSES, NEAR SUCCESSES, AND PLAIN 'FLOPS.' NEW YORK APPARENTLY WANTS THE SEX STUFF, YET THE GREATEST TRIBUTES EVER PAID MOTION PICTURES IN GOTHAM WERE GIVEN LLOYD'S *THE FRESHMAN* AND *FOR HEAVEN'S SAKE* WHICH SMASHED ALL RECORDS HELD BY THE THEATRES IN WHICH THEY WERE FEATURED.
>
> "LLOYD HAS ASSURED SUCCESSES ERE HIS PICTURES LEAVE THE STUDIO, FOR MORE THAN FIFTEEN THOUSAND CRITICS HAVE PLACED THEIR STAMP OF APPROVAL ON HIS PRODUCT BEFORE HE FINALLY OKAYS IT. THAT REPRESENTS THE PREVIEW AUDIENCES ON WHOM THE COMEDIAN TRIES OUT HIS WARES."

Further inquiry seemed to place the blame on the slowness of the first reel. Experimenting, we threw out the entire first reel, with such satisfactory results that I have always regarded *I Do* as one of our outstanding two-reel films." [I] As a result of the alterations to the picture (enhanced by some fun animated sequences, by Beverly Hills cartoon artist Elmer Young), the preparation (and consequently, the release dates) of other already completed Lloyd films was delayed: *Now or Never*, planned for issue on March 7, was released on May 5, 1921; *Among Those Present*, planned for May 9, was pushed to July 3, 1921.

Previews were not always tales of doom and gloom. The Lloyd company shot four reels' worth of footage for *A Sailor-Made Man* (1921), originally planned as a two-reel short. When previews went unexpectedly *well*, the short became Lloyd's first feature-length film.

As was the case with *I Do, Why Worry?* (1923) had its first reel significantly cut after it failed to harvest the desired level of levity. Stated Lloyd in his *Times* article, "If we had not previewed the picture, we would never have known that these first chapters would fizzle."

For Harold's first independent feature, *Girl Shy* (1924), a third fantasy sequence had been filmed for Harold Meadows' book, "The Secret of Making Love." The scene dealt with the romantic exploits of a rich sportscaster. Initial previews of this sequence were less than favorable, so it was discarded.

Lloyd scrapped a favorite gag in *Hot Water* (1924) after it failed to click with audiences. Let's see if you think it's funny: "I was carrying a group of bundles, and I was bringing home a turkey that I'd won in a raffle. I had taken my tie off and had tied it around the turkey's neck so I could lead it like a dog and carry my bundles at the same time. My shoe was untied so I set all of them down on one of these big mailboxes — you know, where you pile the mail packages on top — and as I sat down on the curb to tie my shoe, the postman came and picked up all my bundles with the mail, and I looked up just in time to see him starting to drive off with them. We always thought that was a very funny piece of business; it was a funny situation, but it never got a laugh. Oh, it got a titter, but not enough for the amount of footage we gave it. I never, to this day, have been able to figure out why that wasn't funny." [L]

Lloyd tried to shoot the Fall Frolic party sequence in *The Freshman* (1925) without Speedy losing his loosely basted pants (only his coat). However, audiences were disappointed in previews — they were led to expect to see something that didn't happen — so the scene was re-shot, Speedy lost his trousers, and Harold got his satisfied audience.

Also from Harold's college comedy: "In *The Freshman*, we have a scene where I invite some of my fellow students to have an ice cream cone or soda or something, and they accept. Now, I invite only five or six, but as we go out, on our way to the ice cream parlor, they invite a few more and a few more and we finally end up with about fifty students going along. Well, we thought *that* was a *very* funny sequence. Originally, we really made a whole sequence of it. We went into the candy-soda fountain and, oh boy, we had some comedy business in there, very good gags *we* thought. But we didn't get laughs out of it. Finally, we analyzed it — the audience felt too sorry for the kid. They resented these students taking advantage of him the way they did. So not until we cut it out did the thing pull together." [L]

For Heaven's Sake (1926), at six reels, was originally seven reels in length, but was cut by a reel after previews were disappointing. In the September 1926 issue of *Picture Play* magazine, Lloyd noted, "I protested against some scenes in *For Heaven's Sake* for being too far-fetched, and I was overruled. For instance . . . my gag men insisted it would be great to have me fall off the bus, catch hold of the rear bumper and go flipflopping behind it down the street at top speed. And they wanted the runaway bus to go ploughing into a building where a wedding was in progress, upsetting every thing and leaving the bride in the lap of the minister. Too much! Too much slapstick. Audiences won't stand for it. But they insisted both scenes were good. So we decided to make them. We previewed *For Heaven's Sake* before five different theatre audiences in and near Los Angeles before the film was released. Those two scenes lasted through just two previews, then they were cut out."

Previews for *The Kid Brother* (1927) allowed audiences to see one gag done two different ways. Option A surprised the audience, while option B let them in on the joke. Which one would work? "We finally left it a surprise. I think surprise has a *sharper* laugh to it." [L] We'll examine this gag a little later.

It is unknown whether the title of Lloyd's article for *The New York Times*, "The Public Is the Doctor," was coined by Harold or by someone at the *Times*. What is known is that, throughout his career, Harold came to depend on the preview as a necessary tool for filmmaking, a valuable element in a body of film output geared towards ultimate satisfaction of the audience, first and foremost. The preview, for Harold, can be likened to an injection that wards off illness, with the public the doctor that invented the serum — his audience consistently kept him on his toes, and kept his films better and funnier than, perhaps, even Harold could have imagined. As he wrote, "In my case, I am especially grateful for opinions and decisions that have been of great assistance in improving my comedies."

THE GLASS CHARACTER GOES MULTIPLE REEL

All Aboard . . .
"We had sown, plowed and fertilized, and now we reaped."

At the time that *Pay Your Dues* was produced, an intriguing series of telegrams and letters were sent between Hal Roach and Pathé:

A March 17, 1919 telegram from Roach to Paul Brunet, Pathé vice president and general manager: "I cannot make one reel a week alone and Lloyd is very tired of working every day including Sundays to keep up our release. Lloyd has expressed his willingness to sign for an additional two years at five hundred a week and a participation in the profits but we are interested only in a two reel proposition and one a month and I know the price we are offered for these comedies is more than Pathé would care to pay for."

A March 18, 1919 telegram from Brunet to Roach: "We decline to terminate contract and are willing to give you thirty three hundred dollars for comedy and study other proposition made from you by letter as we want you and Lloyd to be satisfied."

An April 4, 1919 telegram from Roach to Brunet: "Lloyd has expressed his willingness to sign for one more year providing he works in two reel pictures with a percentage of profits, which I have agreed to."

An April 5, 1919 letter from Roach and Lloyd, with Christine Rhodes as witness: "In consideration of your agreement to terminate the agreement under which the Rolin Film Company is producing for you one-reel comedies featuring Harold C. Lloyd, and of your agreement to make a new contract with this Company for the

The police are after HL in the final scene of *Bumping Into Broadway* (1919). This, the first Glass Character two-reeler, featured sumptuous sets and high production values.

production of two-reel comedies featuring Mr. Lloyd on terms more favorable to us, we, the Rolin Film Company and Harold C. Lloyd, jointly and severally agree that we will not enter into any agreement with any other firm, corporation, or individual for the production of motion picture comedies nor act, pose, or take any part in any motion picture play after the expiration of the agreement substituted for the present agreement above referred to without first giving you the opportunity to make a bid for our services for a period of one year following the date of the expiration of the agreement above referred to, and we further agree that if the bid for our services is as favorable in respect of money to be advanced or percentage of receipts to be paid as can be secured from any other source, we will accept the bid made by you." This letter was signed by Hal Roach and Harold C. Lloyd — a week later, the new contract was signed.

A lovely line art rendering for *Captain Kidd's Kids* (1919), the final film with Bebe Daniels as Lloyd's leading lady.

Virginia "Bebe" Daniels appeared in 144 Lloyd comedies from 1915-1919. She later went on to stardom with Paramount, and was voted Leading Vampire in a 1921 magazine poll.

The naming of his first multiple reel comedy was a serendipitous thing of beauty, particularly for Harold, in New York in November of 1919: "You may have never seen the Great White Way and know and care nothing of the theater, and still I need not tell you what it means to any actor to see his name in lights on Broadway for the first time. My heartbeat jingled the coins in my pocket, my legs wavered weakly and I stood staring, mouth open, until I woke to a fear that I might be attracting attention. So, closing my mouth, I strolled back and forth, but never took my eyes from that rainbow. The picture's title had been pure chance. *Bumping Into Broadway!*" [I]

The final Glass Character short, *Never Weaken* (1921), includes an elaborate suicide attempt which included inhalation of gas. You guessed it: it smelled repulsive.

The late Pacific Ocean Park set the scene for many wonderful sequences in *Number, Please?* (1920). Pickering Pier and the Blarney Racer coaster were used to great advantage by HL and cohorts in this marvelous two-reeler.

This was the first two-reel Glass Character short, under an April 12, 1919 contract with Pathé, calling for nine two-reelers in eighteen months. The contract allotted Harold half of the profits of the Rolin Film Company for the Lloyd comedies. For *Bumping Into Broadway*, Pathé forwarded Rolin $17,000. The film cost $17,274 to make. Gross rentals from theatres for the first three years were $150,356. Pathé deducted its take of 35%, plus its initial investment of $17,000. This left Rolin with a profit totaling $63,987, half of which was Harold's.

> **Produced by**
> *Hal E. Roach*
> ❖ **Pathé** ❖
> Distributors
>
> # HAROLD LLOYD *in the*
> ## Special Two Reel
> ## $100,000.00 Comedies
>
> The comedy is just as essential to the success of your program as the feature. It offers contrast; it gives relaxation; it brightens everybody up; *if it's the right kind.* Why devote much time and money to getting the right kind of a feature, and then take *anything* in a short length film, provided it's merely labeled "comedy?"
> Harold Lloyd Special Two Reel Comedies have a surpassing quality, based on four years' experience in the making of fine comedies by the best comedy producing organization in the business.
> They are the *best* that money can buy.
> One Two Reel Comedy Every Four Weeks, Beginning Nov. 2.

One of the bevy of print ads touting the series of Lloyd two-reelers that began with *Bumping Into Broadway* on November 2, 1919.

"During the life of this contract, less than a year and a half, the rental charged exhibitors in key cities for first runs rose from $300 on the first, *Bumping Into Broadway*, to $3000 on the final picture — *Number, Please?*

"Each was of the same length and approximately the same quality, and there was no remotely corresponding growth in manufacturing costs. The early Lonesome Lukes had cost from $1200 to $1500 to make and the one-reel glass pictures never more than $2000. The increased expense on the two-reelers was progressive, but moderate. It was not until we went into three-reel lengths and longer that the cost sheets began to mount dizzily, until now $1,000,000 is not prohibitive.

HL lighting his own smoke in *Among Those Present* (1921) — he didn't smoke in real life, but often did in his films. COURTESY BRUCE CALVERT.

"The jump in first-run rentals from $300 to $3000 in a brief time for two-reel pictures of much the same grade is explained solely by demand. We had sown, plowed and fertilized, and now we reaped. A letter issued from Pathé headquarters to all branch offices on September 24, 1919, just in advance of the release of *Bumping Into Broadway*, throws light on this:

"The letter calls attention to the special advertising campaign, including page space in *The Saturday Evening Post*, with which the New Million Dollar Two-Reel Lloyd Comedies are about to be launched and goes on to say:

"'Charlie Chaplin, Douglas Fairbanks, Mary Pickford and other big stars whose pictures to-day command big rentals, all had a turning point in their careers — a period in which their pictures jumped from small rentals to prices to which they legitimately are entitled. And the turning point in Harold Lloyd's career now has arrived. You know and we know that in the past the Harold Lloyd comedies were being sold at ridiculously low prices; so low that when on the first of March this year we started raising prices on one-reel Lloyds, inside of nine days all our branches combined showed an increase on collections for these subjects of 400 per cent without receiving one cancellation.'

"The letter also called attention to the fact that I had been averaging a comedy a week for five years and was therefore the 'most widely circulated comedian of all.' It closed with a notice that exhibitors thereafter would be required to book new Lloyd pictures on a separate contract calling for one every twenty-eight days." [I]

> **FUN FACT**
>
> THE FOURTH GLASS CHARACTER TWO-REELER, *HIS ROYAL SLYNESS*, FEATURED A NON-BILLED APPEARANCE BY HAROLD'S BIG BROTHER GAYLORD. THIS WAS HIS MOST SUBSTANTIAL PART IN ANY OF HAROLD'S COMEDIES, IN WHICH HE PLAYED A BOY-LOOK-ALIKE, THE PRINCE OF RAZZAMATAZZ. HIS NOT GETTING ANY ON-SCREEN CREDIT WAS PROBABLY INTENTIONAL, FOR MANY REVIEWERS NOTED THE EXQUISITE DOUBLE EXPOSURE SEQUENCES IN THIS FILM (VERY SIMILAR TO THE SAME NOTICES RECEIVED WHEN THE BROTHERS LAST PLAYED LOOKALIKES, IN *LUKE'S DOUBLE*, BACK IN 1916).

The September 1919 letter from Pathé was very right: this new contract did mark a true turning point in Lloyd's career. His one-reel days were now behind him; he'd now enjoy a longer period of time, and a larger budget, to produce films of double the length. The life of this contract — 18 months — saw the Lloyd films take a giant leap in terms of sophistication, quality and universal appeal. As all of Harold's films from this point, and beyond, are extant, it is highly recommended that they be viewed *chronologically*, in order of release. You will notice better production quality, finer stories, and increasingly superior acting by Lloyd and his cohorts, as he progressed as a filmmaker and story teller. This might have been a tremendously busy time for Harold, but "it wasn't work. When you're doing something, and you wish you were doing something else, then *that's* work. I had no desire to be doing anything else when I was working in pictures, so it really wasn't work. It may have been great effort, it may have taxed me mentally, but basically I was happy in what I was doing, so it wasn't work." [A]

HAROLD LLOYD'S BOMB ACCIDENT

Great While It Lasted . . .
"I resolved never to forget my good fortune."

There is no question about it; in the annals of life's turning points, for Harold Lloyd, August 24, 1919 ranks right up there with birth, marriage, and fatherhood. And that date, and its events, never left his memory, nor his lifestyle. That day changed his life, forever.

It all started, actually, in April 1919, when Lloyd signed his new contract with Pathé. An increase in advertising came along with the graduation from one- to two-reel films, and new photographs were ordered for the 26-year-old comic, currently in the midst of filming his fifth two-reel comedy, *Haunted Spooks*. New leading lady Mildred Davis, who took over in June 1919 after longtime feminine lead Bebe Daniels accepted a contract from Paramount, was not needed for this day's photograph session. An appointment was made for the afternoon of Sunday, August 24, 1919, at Witzel Photographer, located at 811 South Hill Street, off Eighth Street, in Los Angeles. Harold was accompanied by Frank Terry, an on- and off-screen member of the Lloyd troupe, best remembered (as an actor) for his appearance in *High and Dizzy*, in which he portrayed the man with the cane and top hat who met up with a drunken Harold in a hallway. Terry was also a gag man, and made numerous suggestions to Harold for props to bring to the photography studio — one such suggestion was a prop bomb, which Terry held up to his face, pantomiming using it as a cigarette lighter. Harold, always one to recognize a good idea, thought about the use of this bomb as a prop, and nodded agreement.

"Several of us were members of the Uplifters Club and five weeks before the studio had made two bombs for some stunt suggested by the news from Russia or the war at a club outing at Bear Lake. They were papier-mâché, rounded and painted black to represent the bombs anarchists always are to be seen on the verge of tossing in newspaper cartoons. The property man was not an explosive engineer and overdid the charge. When one shattered a heavy oak table at Bear Lake, the stunt was called off and the other bomb returned to the studio.

"All explosives were supposed to be kept under lock at the studio, and how this bomb got into a bin of property grenades, we never have learned. How this fuse came to be changed is more inexplicable. The two bombs made for the Bear Lake outing carried stock fuses. Property grenades are dummies carrying a special fast smoky fuse to heighten the comedy, and the one Terry brought along had such a fuse. He had no thought, of course, of finding a true bomb among the properties, and, had he, his suspicions would have been disarmed by the fuse. The weights of the true and the false varied and I believe that I would have detected the mistake had I gone for the properties myself, but I held the thing in my hand for the first time at the Witzel studio, the fuse already lighted, and my mind on the pose." [I]

The pose that never got shot was the first of the gag pictures scheduled to be snapped by the photographer. It called for Harold to light a cigarette from the wick of a bomb, characterizing his on-screen persona, devil-may-care, undaunted by life's obstacles — youthful and sassy — a youngster, laughing at adversity, perfectly embodying his films' character.

"Terry picked up the bomb, lighted it and handed it to me. I put a cigarette in my mouth, struck a sassy attitude and held the bomb in my right hand, the fuse to the cigarette. The smoke blew across my face so clouding the expression that the photographer, whose head was buried under his black cloth, delayed squeezing the bulb. As he continued to wait and fuse grew shorter and shorter, I raised the bomb nearer and nearer to my face until, the fuse all but gone, I dropped my hand and was saying that we must insert a new fuse, when the thing exploded." [I]

According to eyewitness Roy Seawright, Jr., "It was a big blast. I can tell you now that it affected his eyesight in his right eye and partially in his left eye, which he regained over a period of time. It shocked his ears — it shocked the ears of everybody.

"Then all bedlam broke loose. Everyone was running around. 'Call the hospital! Call the ambulance! Call the doctor!' and everything else. And now the pain was just settling in and he was still standing in his same marks where the bomb went off, and he grabbed his wrist. The thumb was gone. The first finger here was dangling, hanging right down in the front, swinging around. And he looked at it and you could see the look of terror which came over his face. His face was now registering the shock that we had already registered after the explosion."

A newspaper photograph of Frank Terry, gag man and Lloyd friend, who handed HL that fateful bomb.

The force of the blast tore a hole in the 16-foot-high ceiling of the studio. Frank Terry's upper denture cracked in half within his mouth. The photographer fainted. Most of the studio windows were shattered. Witzel's suffered significant damage, forcing the studio to close for some time. Harold Lloyd lost the thumb and the index finger of his right hand, and suffered painful injuries to his face and eyes. "Had I not lowered my hand at that instant I should have been killed instantly, my head probably blown off." [I]

Lloyd was rushed to the Methodist Hospital, 2826 South Hope Street, Los Angeles, which would be his home for the next 16 days, until September 9, 1919. The total hospital bill came to $235.85, of which $115 was for the room, $15 for the operating room, $15.50 for x-rays, $1 for laboratory fees, $3.05 for operating room supplies, $45.80 for dressings and drugs, and $40.50 for board for special nurses.

The general public first heard about Harold's tragic Sunday on Monday, August 25, 1919, in *The Los Angeles Times*' story entitled, "Reel Bomb Is A Real One." According to the article, "The force of the concussion blew out the glass roof of the studio, threw Terry to the floor and knocked the bystanders flat. All but a part of the index finger of Lloyd's right hand was torn away." Yes, the public *did* know about the loss of Harold's fingers — but, somehow, once he returned to the studio and resumed his career and his life, the maimed hand just didn't seem to matter much.

In early September 1919, Hal Roach sent a telegram to Paul Brunet of Pathé: "Harold Lloyd's condition greatly improved. He will lose a portion of finger and thumb of right hand. His face is in good condition. There will be only slight scars easily covered with makeup. His right eye, which we feared to be injured, is in good shape and will not be deformed in any way. This is far better than we expected."

Hal Roach received a telegram, dated September 16, 1919, from the Los Angeles office of Pathé: "Saw Lloyd today. He looks fine. His face not injured in any way. Eye doing nicely. Will not be affected. Worst feature loss of part of thumb and index finger which can be easily camouflaged. He expects to be able to work in a few weeks. Personally feel his future will not be affected in any way."

How *did* Harold go on as an actor? That can be summed up, simply, by adding courage to fortitude, then tossing into the equation a serendipitous cooperation between Hal Roach, Sam Goldwyn, and the principals of The Rubber Limb Company of New York. After Harold was released from the hospital, a rubber mold was taken of his *left* hand, then reversed to simulate the maimed right hand. From this mold, the portion that complemented the lost area of Harold's right hand was cut away. That rubber piece, with the remainder of Harold's hand, fit together perfectly — yes, like a glove. Roach and Goldwyn (who, previous to his film career, was Samuel Goldfish, glove salesman) then teamed to perfect the prosthesis. Sam devised a thin leather glove, skin-toned, and very tightly fitting, which fit over Harold's hand, with the prosthetic device inserted. The index finger and the middle finger of the glove were sewn together at the two knuckles — this provided movement for the rubber index finger: when the middle finger bent, the index finger followed alongside. The thumb remained immobile — the remaining fingers moved towards it. The leather glove was held on,

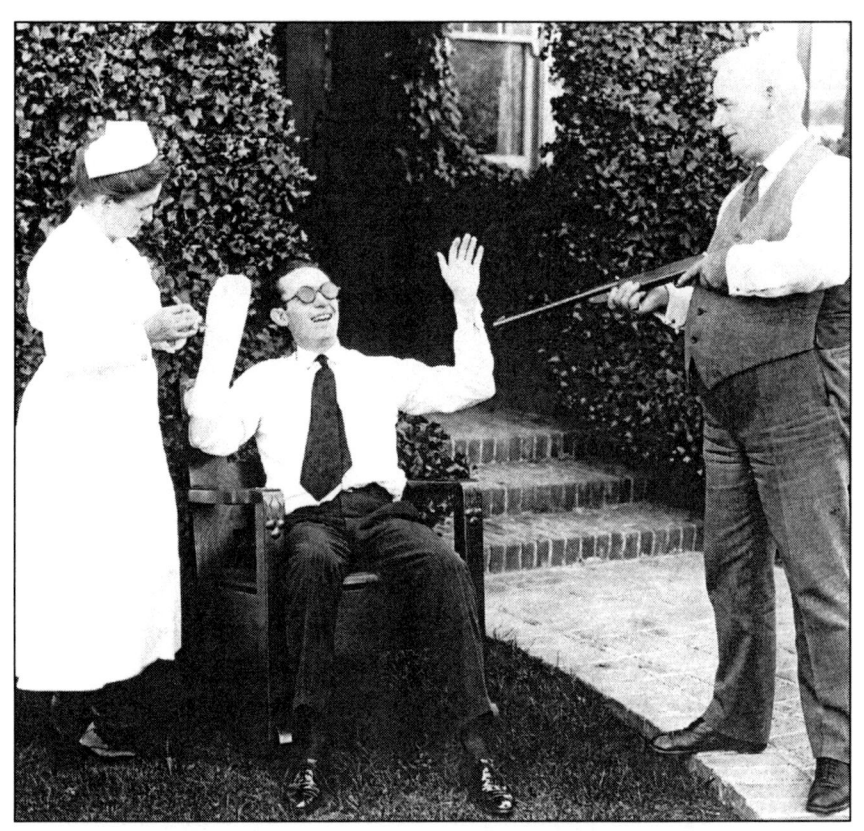

Following his release from the hospital, HL recuperated from his bomb accident at home, 369 S. Hoover Street. It is outside this home that we see a bandaged HL on the receiving end of fun with father Foxy. The nurse does not look amused.

tightly, by a rubber band garter system, which was fastened to Harold's upper arm. Just think about that, the next time you watch Lloyd dangle from the building clock in *Safety Last!* (1923).

Long time Lloyd fans know that, despite the fact that Harold never publicly discussed the loss of his fingers, he *did* mention his hand in print: "The accident accomplished two purposes. It speeded up a more realistic interpretation of my character. I discarded the flowing tie and any type of costume which differentiated me from the average man on the street.

"The accident also gave me plenty of time to think. And when I found that I had emerged practically unscathed except for my hand injury, I resolved never to forget my good fortune. I don't believe I ever have." [K]

However, in an October 1919 letter to Quebecois film pioneer Léo-Ernest Ouimet, who at that time was the Canadian distributor of Pathé films, Lloyd described the events and aftermath of August 24, 1919 in extraordinary fashion:

> "This accident occurred through the carelessness of someone connected with the property room, mixing real bombs up with other props and sham bombs, and Frank Terry innocently picked this bomb from among other props, to use in a still picture of me lighting my cigarette with a bomb. I had the bomb up before my face in a position to light the cigarette when, by chance, I noticed that the fuse had burned low and was not going to register well in picture, so lowering the bomb from my face to an angle of about 50 degrees, I told Terry he had better put a new fuse in the bomb, but just at that moment it exploded. (Had the bomb been before my face then — well, I wouldn't be writing you now.)
>
> "Mr. Terry and the cameraman were knocked over; I was thrown back, but never off my feet, and as soon as Terry struggled to his feet, he rushed to my side, and grabbing a newspaper, wrapped it around my hand to keep the air from striking it, and also, he says, to keep me from seeing it: but I had already discovered the damages, and knew that my thumb and finger were gone, and also that my face was badly cut or bombed, and as I supposed, powder marked, and my first words were 'my career is ended, Frank. I am done.' I had not yet considered my pains, as my thoughts were of my future. I was rushed to the hospital; I did not faint or give up, until placed under the dope on the operating table. The doctors discovered my right eye in very bad shape, and were in doubt for a few days of saving it; but at the end of 10 days, when the bandage was removed, I could see just a little, and it has been

gaining a little right along, and the eye specialists say it will come all right in a few months. My hand is healing very good, but I will have to return to the hospital for a short time soon, to have some more stitches taken in it, where the skin was not strong enough to hold.

"I have certainly had hosts of friends to sympathize, cheer me up, bring me flowers and good wishes, and God knows that their good thoughts and kind wishes have come from hearts of loyalty, and He has given me strength and courage to look on the right side, and feel that all is going to end well, and what seems all wrong, now must come out all right."

Harold Lloyd was a proud man, and a humble man. The last thing he wanted was for audiences to flock to his films out of pity, or curiosity, or sympathy. He worked too hard to achieve the fame he had — and he wanted to keep his fame through that same hard work, not through some tragic misfortune. Harold wanted to make his audiences laugh, and laugh again, which is why he never forgot his accident, never stopped trying to overcome its reminders, but why he also never forgot to be grateful for the second chance he did receive.

Richard Correll, son of Charles Correll of *Amos n' Andy* fame, was a longtime boyfriend of Lloyd's granddaughter Suzanne, and a prime personal archivist of the Lloyd films. "It's funny that a man who did so much physical business in so many films was injured posing for a still. I think the explosion was a turning point in his life, because what it really did was to make him gather up all the gumption he had to say, 'Look, I'm going to carry on. Sure, I've been in an explosion. I'm a comedian. I need my hands. But I'm not going to let this stop me.' It was a point where he sat back and said, 'Okay. I'm going to work even harder, and I need to take more time.' I think that the explosion actually helped him to become more critical of his own work and a better filmmaker altogether."

Further Impacts of Harold's Accident

In the midst of perusing Harold's filmography, astute Lloyd fans will notice that *Heap Big Chief* debuted in theatres on the day of Harold's bomb accident, Sunday, August 24, 1919. Lloyd and company would complete ten more films after *Heap Big Chief*, before the accident suspended production for four and a half months.

Bumping Into Broadway (11/2/1919) was all aglow on the marquee of the Strand Theatre on Broadway, when Harold was in New York, in November 1919, during his convalescence following the accident. The sight of his name in lights was a major boost to his morale, no doubt helping him recover more rapidly: within a month and a half, Harold would be back at work.

During his time in New York, Harold and Pathé ironed out a new contract — as Hal Roach had predicted, Pathé was very willing to bet on Harold's full recovery from his injuries. "The old and interrupted contract was scrapped and a new one written for a term of three years. It called for the completion of *Haunted Spooks* and the four remaining two-reelers of the original program, and for six further two-reel pictures, Pathé to do all financing of production, as in the past. Their return for this and for distribution ranged from 65 per cent of the gross earnings of the Lonesome Luke pictures, gradually revised downward to 37 1/2 per cent on the final contract, made in 1922. The great increase in gross earnings meanwhile much more than made up the difference, of course." [1]

Production on *Haunted Spooks* (3/31/1920) was interrupted, from August 23, 1919 to January 5, 1920. Immediately upon receiving word of Harold's mishap, Roach graduated costar Harry "Snub" Pollard to his own line of comedies. The first, *Start Something*, began shooting the week of August 30, and was released on October 26, 1919 (remembering that there were enough Lloyd films completed to ensure uninterrupted releases through February 1920 — by that time, Harold was well back at work — this also ensured no startling change in the actors' payrolls). Gaylord Lloyd, while brother Harold recuperated, appeared in 21 Snub Pollard comedies, most of which completed production by the end of 1919. Mildred Davis, in that time, appeared in 12 of the Pollard

Fun Fact

During the first days after Harold's accident, while he was hospitalized and afterwards during his convalescence at home, he received scores of telegraphs, notes, flowers, and cards. In an August 26, 1919 telegraph, Pathé executive Paul Brunet wrote, "Please accept my sincere sympathy on account of your most unfortunate accident. But, knowing you to be so courageous, I have every confidence for a speedy recovery for you and it will not be long before you will be feeling like your old self again."

Jack Warner wrote the following note: "To a real Pal, Hoping the boys see you real soon, and trusting you have a speedy recovery." From Mabel Normand: "Dreadfully sorry to hear of your grave misfortune, and hope it will not be long ere we see you on the screen again." Flowers arrived at the hospital on August 26, with a card that read, "A 'Bunch' from The 'Rolin Bunch.'" Other cards and telegrams were sent by Roscoe Arbuckle, the Uplifters Club, Hal Roach, Mildred Davis, Pathé Exchange, Vera Reynolds, Marie Mosquini, Bebe Daniels, Peggy Cartwright, Bobbie West, amongst many more.

"Showers of kindness had fallen daily on my head all the while I was in the hospital from friends and others who know me only as a shadow on the screen. In a heap of mail one day there was an unsigned card posted at Worcester, Massachusetts. It was just a stock greeting card, reading:

I've had some awful illnesses,
And accidents that stretched me flat,
But anyway I'm still alive,
And lots of people can't say that.

"I don't know about the meter, and the sentiment may lack something of being profound, but I was alive, and finding compensations in that statistically unusual state." [1]

comedies; by the end of her tenure with Snub (upon Harold's return to the studio), her weekly salary had been raised to $125.

Haunted Spooks is a fascinating film to watch, particularly when it is known that there was a four-month gap in the shooting schedule. There is no cut and dry point where filming resumed after the accident — many scenes in the first reel contain footage shot both before and after the accident (a prominent for-instance is the faction in which Harold and his rival for the girl's hand drew lots — via X's on paper — to see which suitor would approach the father first; a few parts of it were shot after Harold returned to the studio). However, the delightful sequence of newlywed Harold and Mildred in a car — complete with chicken coop — was what the company was shooting on Saturday, August 23, 1919: so that car ride can be watched with sure knowledge that it was begun in August 1919 and ended in January 1920. Interestingly — when viewers *look for* any variation between Lloyd's right hand, pre- and post-accident, there is no problem differentiating the actual hand from the prosthesis — but such diversions should never take away from enjoying the films. Harold wouldn't hear of it . . .

Lloyd's bomb accident often precipitated the need for a double for close-up shots which called for two hands to do some close-up action. In the October 18, 1970 issue of London's *The Sunday Bulletin*, Harold disclosed a little-known facet of filming close-ups of a single hand: ". . . I sometimes wore a glove, other times we shot scenes using my left hand and a mirror." In the scene in *Never Weaken* (10/22/1921) in which Harold writes his suicide note, one close up shows a *right* hand scripting, while in the next cut to full shot Harold is holding his pencil in his *left* hand. This mis-shot was apparently not detected in the editing process.

Harold Lloyd's salary, in addition to his films, were affected by his accident — in reality, his weekly pay fluctuated a great deal, rising as his star rose, and consistently allowing him a standard of living that he probably never imagined was possible, back in his Nebraska youth. Witness the progression of his salary changes, with dates and weekly amounts (the dates represent the week that the salary raise took effect):

February 1, 1915: $5. It was the inequity between this, Harold's weekly salary, and the $10 weekly pay given to co-star Roy Stewart that led Lloyd to leave Hal Roach's camp, joining Keystone.

June 19, 1915: $50. "More money than there was in the world," was Harold's reaction to this weekly salary, which pried Lloyd away from Keystone after Roach got a contract offer from Pathé.

August 5, 1916: $100.

February 3, 1917: $125.

February 10, 1917: $175.

March 10, 1917: $150.

February 9, 1918: $200.

February 16, 1918: $300. Lloyd quit the studio in early March 1918; it was not a financial matter, as Harold had already gotten the raise he wanted earlier in February. This disruption was primarily due to production disputes between he, Roach, and director Alf Goulding. It became necessary for an outside party to mediate, and Harold went to New York to meet with Pathé general manager Paul Brunet. Lloyd came back from the East feeling appreciated by upper brass, and fully recovered from the petty squabbles. Lloyd arrived in New York on March 9; while absent from the Rolin studio, his paycheck was slashed to $50 per week. When he returned to work, the week of March 30, his upgraded $300 weekly salary resumed.

April 5, 1919: $400.

August 30, 1919: $100. This dip was due to his absence from the studio post-accident. He received a $100/week salary from August 30-October 4, and then received $333.33 on October 11.

October 18, 1919: $500.

January 10, 1920: $750.

January 8, 1921: $1000. Lloyd's formal weekly salary would remain at this level for the balance of his career, though his income was substantially higher from this point on, owing to generous profit sharing clauses in his contracts.

"While I was laid up Mildred and Pollard had carried on at the studio, making one-reel comedies. Back on the job, we resumed *Haunted Spooks* where we had left off and made it, probably, our funniest picture to date. We had been so far ahead of schedule that we never lost a release date, our only difficulty the fact that women's clothes were changing so rapidly just after the war that there was a perceptible gap in skirt lengths in nine months' time." [I]

During his recuperation in November 1919, Harold took a trip to New York. Here, at the New York offices of Pathé, Charles Pathé (SEATED) **irons out a new Lloyd Comedies contract. Looking on are Hal Roach, HL, and Paul Brunet.**

Most of this statement is true, save for a memory lapse of Harold's, as he was penning his 1928 autobiography. In *An American Comedy*, Harold more than doubled his actual recuperation period: he cited, numerous times, that he was away from the studio for nine months, but it was actually a little over four. It must have *seemed* longer.

"The last vestige of the old comedy dress vanished from my character with *Haunted Spooks*, and my clothes thereafter were normal street wear, except when the role called for costume — that is, whatever I wore from then on was chosen to fit the character, not to draw laughs on its own. In the first four two-reelers I had worn a flowing Windsor tie, cloth-top button shoes, a checked suit, and at times my hats leaned a little toward the comic. I had been wearing the checked suit when the bomb exploded. Little remained of it, but had not a button been missing I still should not have cared to see it again. Thereby the accident speeded up the evolution of the character to a completely straight role." [1]

Not only did the events of August 24, 1919, change his on-screen character for the better — becoming more of *us* than any other comedy creator — but the accident changed Harold himself, for the better. He was markedly different after the bomb blast and recuperation period — and not just because he changed from a flowing tie to a four-in-hand style. He smiled more; he relied less and less on knockabout and slapstick gags, utilizing more realistic and relatable business in his comedies; he honestly gave the impression of being grateful to have survived. He went on, through two-reelers, into three-reelers, and then into features, and with each film he issued, his stories became stronger, his character truer, his comedy funnier, and his filmmaking technique more solid. Another person might have been defeated by a handicap which robbed the hand of two fingers. Another, weaker person might have been done in by such a malady. However, in summing up who we're dealing with here, friend Frances Metzger might have said it best: "We knew that wouldn't be the end of his career. Just to have your fingers blown off? No. Not Harold."

In the lives of each of us, there stand apart a few moments, events and circumstances that become, in looking upon them, true turning points in our lives. These become the major guideposts in the course our lives take: we can look back upon them, and identify them as the defining moment(s) that affected our every subsequent move. Harold Lloyd had many such turning points — hence the need for the book you are holding — many though they are, I feel that *the* single most important turning point, the date that most changed his life, was August 24, 1919. For many reasons, I feel that this day's events *most* changed Harold's life and career — and definitely made each richer and more memorable.

Harold Lloyd's Entry into Features

The Big Idea . . .
"It was a natural changeover . . ."

It was accidental; it was *not* planned — Harold Lloyd entered the feature picture arena chiefly by virtue of circumstances surrounding his new contract with his distributor.

"Only one of the six additional two-reel pictures specified in the revised Pathé contract stopped at that length. That was the third, *I Do*, which was made in three reels, but cut to two for exhibition. The first, second and fourth of the six additional pictures ran three reels, the fifth to four reels and the sixth to five, since when we never have made a picture under five reels. Each was begun with two reels in mind, but, the footage running long and the action and comedy justifying the extra footage, we threw in a reel or more to boot. Pathé was under no contractual obligation to pay us anything additional for this heaping measure. They did so voluntarily." [I]

The six pictures Harold referred to were *Now or Never, Among Those Present, I Do, Never Weaken, A Sailor-Made Man* and *Grandma's Boy*. The latter two are Lloyd's first two features, but neither was started as such — his first premeditated feature film was *Dr. Jack*, released on December 19, 1922.

"My whole situation was sort of an evolution. We made one-reelers, and we made a great many of them, and we went from one-reelers into the two-reelers, and from two-reelers we went into the feature pictures. And going into the feature pictures, I think, was very natural, because the first feature picture we made wasn't actually a feature picture, it was only four reels — it was called *A Sailor-Made*

Man. We got along, and we liked the footage that we had in it, and when we came to editing and cutting it down, we just hated to cut the rest of it out; so we said that it was too good to delete, and so we left it that way, and it became a four-reeler, and was really more or less our first feature." [E]

"So it was a natural changeover — it wasn't one of those things 'Now we'll do a longer type of picture.'" [L]

The production of these films is amazing when it is noted that, "In the early days, we didn't have a script. We just more or less got an idea of what the picture was going to be and we worked out, from week to week, a sort of schedule. Then we would ad-lib it, and it was completely spontaneous. All titles were always put in after the picture was completed. We had very fine title writer, his name was Beanie Walker — he was a former newspaper man, the sporting editor, of all things, for the *Examiner* in Los Angeles. He was an excellent writer for those types of titles, and always got his share of laughs." [C]

Harley M. "Beanie" Walker was a columnist for the *Los Angeles Examiner* prior to joining Rolin as a title writer in late 1917. He created the titles for virtually every Lloyd film from *Lonesome Luke Loses Patients* through *Why Worry?* (1923). COURTESY SAM GILL.

Not only were these films longer in length, but "they were much better in every way. A one-reel film runs only ten minutes; even in two reels there is little room both for establishing character and being funny; and confronted with that choice, it is character that must be sacrificed. Hence one- and two-reel comedies can only be a succession of gags loosely strung on the outline of a story. If the gags are good the picture is good; poor gags, poor picture.

"In five reels or more we can be both funny and sincere. When I say sincere, I use it with comedy reservations. Picture comedies cannot be true to life and be funny, for though life can be funny as all out-of-doors, the comic incidents are separated by long intervals of dull routine, with moments of drama and tragedy. Nature usually is a punk continuity writer. A good picture should crowd more comedy into five to eight reels than happens to most of us in a lifetime.

"If it cannot hold a mirror up to life, however, a film comedy can keep within shouting distance of verity. 'Is it plausible while you are looking at it?' is the only test it needs pass. It will be only if the characters are plausible. The action may be outlandish, but the characters — most particularly the central character — must not be. Every one in the audience should feel that he knows him, has known him, or might easily know him." [I]

A Swedish poster for *A Sailor-Made Man* (1921) — directly translated, it reads "Harold on the ocean blue."

This idea of believability is at the very heart of what makes Lloyd's Glass Character so enduring, important, and funny as generations pass. His resistance to the cinematic norms of the day — his gradual shedding of storylines or characterization that played upon quirk or unusualness — render the Lloyd films less archaic, antique, and old-fashioned than those of some contemporaries. They just don't have that time-worn look or feel — and that's because his character's normalcy is enduring. He continues to look, for all intents and purposes, like he could live next door to any of us.

When he graduated to two-reel film length, and particularly after his accident, Harold's films began to stress more believability and

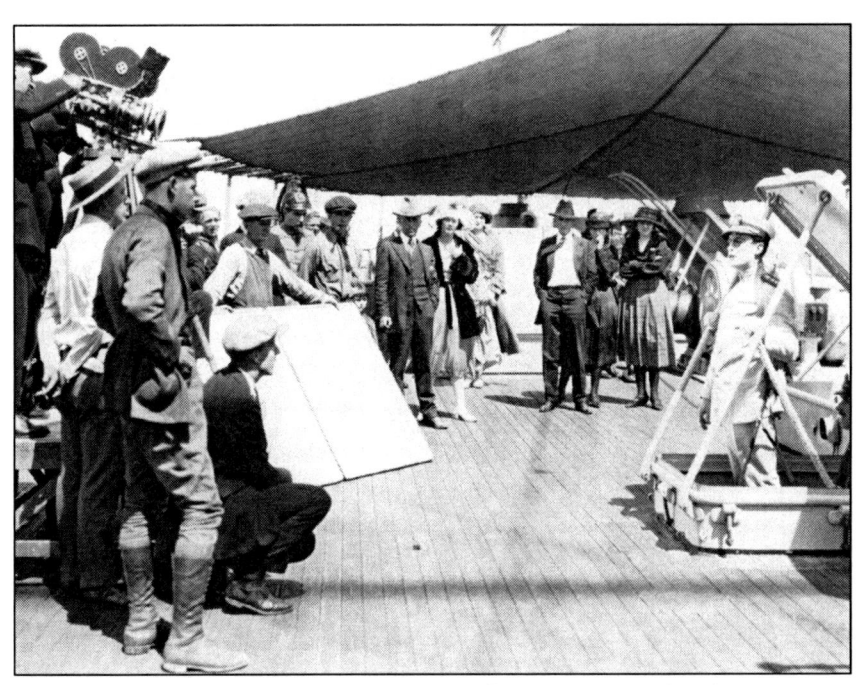

Shooting *A Sailor-Made Man* (1921) aboard the U.S.S. Frederick. Director Fred Newmeyer looks on (in straw hat, at left) as HL, in a dream sequence, runs the ship. Notice the light diffuser and the bounty of onlookers out of camera range.

normalcy, and to depend less and less on knockabout business, isolated gags, and the comedy involving farce and horseplay known as slapstick. "I think that the word Slapstick is misused in so many pictures made in the early 1920s or what we call the golden era. Take a picture like one of Charlie's, *The Gold Rush*, or take mine, *The Freshman*. Now those pictures are character comedies — they're as far away from slapstick comedies as you can get, not that they haven't got slapstick in them, but they've got many ingredients of comedy, they've got broad comedy, and light comedy, a small amount of farce comedy, and dramatic comedy, they're a whole blend of comedy, and to just dub them slapstick is completely erroneous." [C]

Lloyd's understanding of how to successfully make his brand of comedy was a gradual learning cycle; as he noted, an evolution. Of course, his use of the preview — allowing his audiences to unknowingly help him make his pictures better — helped, a lot. As well, the atmospheric conditions in cinema, at that time, were

"Freckles and His Friends" was a prominent newspaper comic strip from 1915-1971. In this March 19, 1923, installment, "Lloyd Has His Joke," the boys visit HL on the set of *Why Worry?* (1923). © NEWSPAPER ENTERPRISE ASSOCIATION

ripe for creativity: there was a bounty of competition. "There was sort of a friendly rivalry between the comedians of that day. I guess that's one of the reasons they called it The Golden Age of Comedy, because we did have so many comedians at that time, and there was sort of a rivalry where one would make a good picture and maybe have a lot of business in it that scored with the audience, so the other comics wanted to beat that, so they put their shoulder to the wheel. But it was all very friendly." [C]

Harold, however, was the first to admit that he did not achieve his level of success alone — he was far from a solo player in the film game, particularly by the time his films reached feature length. He employed a group of gentlemen, who he called his Gag Men, who assisted him in the formulation of stories and ideas, from which Harold would pick and choose the best for his character. These were the men credited in the Lloyd films for direction, story and/or screenplay — Sam Taylor, Fred Newmeyer, Ted Wilde, Jay A. Howe, Lex Neal, Jean Havez, Thomas J. Crizer, Tim Whelan, Thomas J. Grey, John Grey, Clyde Bruckman, Howard Green, Howard Emmett Rogers.

"I sit with them as frequently as possible. They may have agreed upon a story or have five more or less hostile plots, and I may like all or none, or parts of this and that. The result usually is a compromise so scrambled that no one and every one can claim the authorship." [I]

"These men, I would sometimes work with them en masse, with the whole group of them and I would sit with them and they would begin to throw ideas at me. And I'd begin to pick and choose ideas

> ## Fun Fact
>
> FROM THE DECEMBER 10, 1921 ISSUE OF *THE MOVING PICTURE WORLD* MAGAZINE: "ANY WHO DOUBT THE STANDING OF HAROLD LLOYD ARE REFERRED TO THE CONTEST STAGED BY *MOTION PICTURE* MAGAZINE, WITH ITS CIRCULATION OF 350,000 FANS, IN WHICH LLOYD HAS MADE A RUNAWAY RACE FOR THE HONORS OF 'LEADING COMEDIAN.'
>
> "IN AN ANNOUNCEMENT OF THE RESULT IN ITS DECEMBER ISSUE, *MOTION PICTURE* MAGAZINE CREDITS LLOYD WITH 4,650 VOTES, WHILE CHAPLIN, WHO FINISHED SECOND, RECEIVED 3,060. LLOYD ALSO WAS SELECTED FOR A PLACE ON THE 'IDEAL CAST,' WHICH INCLUDES GRIFFITH AS DIRECTOR, NORMA TALMADGE AS LEADING WOMAN, WALLIE REID AS LEADING MAN, JACKIE COOGAN AS THE CHILD AND BEBE DANIELS AS THE LEADING VAMPIRE.
>
> "INCIDENTALLY, PATHÉ CALLS ATTENTION TO THE FACT THAT BEBE DANIELS IS HAROLD LLOYD'S LEADING WOMAN IN ALL THE ONE-REEL LLOYD COMEDIES WHICH THE GOLD ROOSTER ORGANIZATION IS NOW RE-ISSUING UNDER A ONE-A-WEEK RELEASE PLAN. IT IS EXPECTED THAT WITHIN A WEEK THERE WILL BE 7,500 THEATRES, OR NEARLY 50 PER CENT. OF THE COUNTRY'S TOTAL, PLAYING THE LLOYD RE-ISSUES."

that I liked here and there. I would take an idea, here, and I'd say, this is good, it needs developing, it needs to fit this situation. So maybe I'd split them up into pairs, or threes, or maybe singly, and they'd go on their own and work on it. And then they'd throw them at me again and I would pick out the wheat out of all the chaff, and put it together, and do the assembling — that I always did myself — I knew what I really needed for my character; I knew my character and I knew what my character would be able to use best. Now, I had one gag man — he would give you the most terrible ideas, but under those different terrible ideas there was a kernel of something that was excellent. You had to be able to pick it out. Then I'd pick it out and I'd give it to two other boys to develop. Now, it wasn't their idea at all, it was this other man's. But, he was really one of my most valuable men. He probably gave me more original ideas — not in the form he gave them to you — but that's the point of saying that you must be able to pick the wheat out of the chaff. They were original boys, they were idea men — you know, I made directors out of about half of them. You see, I never put my name on the picture as directing it, but some of them I actually directed practically in their entirety, and I just had gag boys working with me, but in order to help them I put their names on the pictures. It was advantageous — you put the boys' names on the picture, they put that much more effort behind the picture. And they went out and became fine directors." [E] In case you're wondering who the gag man with the terrible ideas was: it was Frank Terry, the gag man who accompanied Harold to the studio on the day of his bomb accident. He worked in various capacities for Lloyd, dating back to *Spring Fever* (1919): he was an actor, an assistant director, and, in his gag exploits, was given sole credit for the stories of *An Eastern Westerner* (1920) and *High and Dizzy* (1920). And, regarding the direction of his films: as was noted earlier, Harold did take credit as director for two of his films, *Over the Fence* (1917) and *Just Neighbors* (1919).

By the time that Lloyd began making feature pictures, he had assembled a great and growing crew around him, had learned a lifetime of lessons, and was continuing to be a student of comedy. He was growing into a tremendous understanding of filmmaking, both from technical and creative standpoints, and seemed quite aware of this growth. "*A Sailor-Made Man* and *Grandma's Boy* were markers on the most important boundary line in our later history. Two such longer and better pictures, coming together, gave us a mighty thrust forward that carried us out of the middle ground into the foreground of picture business. They demonstrated, too, that the public wanted what we know as feature-length comedies." [I]

Harold Lloyd Releases Grandma's Boy

Grandma's Boy . . .
"It had a strength to it that we just couldn't keep in two reels"

By the end of his life, Harold regularly acknowledged four favorites amongst his films: *The Freshman, The Kid Brother, Safety Last!,* and *Grandma's Boy.*

"Story, in *Grandma's Boy,* is paramount, it comes first, because it had a faith theme in it, and it wasn't typical — that story was working for us, all the time. Funny thing is that I carried that story with me for several years. I tried to get it into a one-reeler, and finally we started this as a two-reeler, but it had so much to it, that we couldn't keep it as a two-reeler. It kept growing and growing, and finally grew to the five-reel stage. I got letters from all over, from people who said that it helped them, in that particular capacity." [A]

Once *A Sailor-Made Man* — which was begun as a two-reeler but grew to four reels — was in the can, completed, Lloyd and his team began work on a film that had two working titles; first, "The White Feather," then "He Who Hesitates." We might agree that the latter is the more fitting of the two.

"Now, for *Grandma's Boy,* the following-up picture, we intended to go back again and make another two-reeler, just because we had left that one long, and didn't mean that this was going to be our standard procedure.

"So, in *Grandma's Boy,* it started with an idea I had had for a long time, a very good idea, too, in my estimation, one of the best we ever had. And it was a faith idea. An idea of a boy who was a coward, and he was given a little talisman by his grandmother who he implicitly believed — she had never lied to him — and he was told that, with this talisman, that anything that he attempted he could accomplish, that he couldn't fail; he would overcome all obstacles. And, of course, having complete faith in his grandmother, he went out and acted accordingly — of course, he got into a tremendous amount of difficulties. But with the determination and the belief that he had to win out in the end, he just kept going, and through determination he overcame all of his obstacles. And then, of course, in the finish, when she had found out that he had righted all his troubles, and had changed his personality around, then she showed him that it really wasn't a talisman at all, it was just the handle to her umbrella, and that it was purely his own self, his own belief, which is mind over matter. Of course, he started to back slide, but then when she convinced him that he had accomplished these things and that it was himself — then, from that time on, he went on and, well, we assume that he did the same things he did with the idol. But it was a very fine, we thought, idea, and when we started it, it was for a two-reeler, but it had a strength to it that we just couldn't keep in two reels. And it kept going and going and finally we said, 'so let's just play it out,' and it developed into a five-reeler, which was really our first true feature picture, and was quite successful for us; gave us a different call at the box office from a monetary standpoint, and from that time on, we went into feature pictures. So, the next one that was followed up was one we called *Dr. Jack*, and that actually was a feature picture that we had intended as such." [E]

The film grew to the length that it did, admittedly, because after initial previews, the original vision of *Grandma's Boy* — more drama than comedy — was disappointing to Lloyd audiences, because it lacked the usual injections of laughs and gag situations. Lloyd had tried to put a real dramatic intent in the picture, but the result was not as funny as moviegoers expected from Lloyd. So, after seeing the writing on the wall, as it were, Roach and Lloyd, along with gagmen Sam Taylor, Jean Havez and T.J. Crizer, went back to work on adding more comedy sequences. This improved the film, along with increasing its length.

Thanks to Sonny's grandmother, who shined his shoes with goose grease, the kittens in Mildred's house are satiated. Mildred will fill *his* belly, too — unfortunately, with the moth balls he rushed from his suit to the candy box. From *Grandma's Boy* (1922).

The film's comic nuances — the finishing additions to the final release — are excellent, and blend well with the dramatic and sympathetic moments in the picture. Witness the Civil War sequence, in which the officers were enjoying their beverages, the strength of which was characterized by the superimposition of a kicking mule in the punchbowl; the vision of Harold after being thrown in a well and walking home, "Mostly uphill, and no shade" — his "Never-Shrink Brand" suit *didn't* quite live up to its shrivel-proof expectations; the exceptional comic timing of the townsmen attempting to capture the malevolent hobo The Rolling Stone (beautifully portrayed by Dick Sutherland, who had a similarly menacing role as the Maharajah of Khaipura Bhandanna in *A Sailor-Made Man*), and the frightened goose peeking around the corner after Harold emerged as the successful conqueror of The Rolling Stone. The comedy beautifully counteracted the intensity of the dramatic tones in the film, adding needed relief to rather dramatic and often heavy content.

The sequence in which Sonny was told of his grandfather's conversion from coward to hero was pivotal to the success of *Grandma's Boy* (1922). Here, HL dons square-rimmed glasses with lamb chop sideburns, and will soon be a granddaddy of a military hero. COURTESY PAUL E. GIERUCKI.

Throughout the making of *Grandma's Boy*, Lloyd was keenly aware of the potential influence this kind of film could have on his audiences — the faith idea actually *did* emerge as an inspiration to audiences, in a way that no other of his films had to that point. As such, he was extremely careful to insert gags and business that viewers could fully relate to. His character, Sonny, had to represent the people watching, and had to be as viable as possible.

"The boy went to the party and his grandmother had shined his shoes with goose grease. And when he was courting the girl, a little kitten came along and liked the goose grease and started licking it. Well, that's very embarrassing and could happen today to anybody. He got rid of it and it brought back all its little brothers and sisters, about a half a dozen or more of them, and they all started going on it. The same thing with the suit that had moth balls in it, and he inadvertently put the moth balls into a candy box and then was fed them back and he had to eat his moth balls. Now, that *could*

> **FUN FACT**
>
> The following rhymed review of *Grandma's Boy* appeared in *The New York American* on September 8, 1922. Rose Pelswick was the poet/reviewer (she actually was the movie critic for the *American*):
>
> All those subtle spots are heeded
>   Which comedians agree —
> When they are interviewed — are needed
>   For a comedy to be
>
> A success; a situation with an
>   April shower mood,
> As it were, a correlation where both smiles and sighs intrude,
>   Shows a chap who was presented
> With ambition badly dented
>   And a timid disposition that resented being rude.
>
> So his grandmother decided
>   To reform him, and she gave
> Him a charm, which she confided
>   Would unquestionably save
> Him from harm; and so he tackled all the trouble in the place;
>   Caught a bandit who was captured in a syncopated race;
> Fought his enemies, succeeding
>   In his love affairs, and speeding
> Through amusing complications at a palpitating pace.

happen to anybody. Now, that was one thing that my character did that was a little different from the others. I'd say in about 98% of the time, I never did anything that couldn't actually be done — it might be a little improbable, it might be stretched — but it *could* happen." [C]

Harold also recognized *Grandma's Boy* as the most sentimental film he had made to date. "*There* is a picture that I did that was closer to a sort of method with pathos that Charlie used to do an awful lot. A lot of people said that my character didn't work that way, but he did very much — that picture could easily have been a drama as well as a comedy — he was right on that borderline of being a coward. You could have made a dramatic coward just as easily. He was a coward from birth, and his grandmother gave him this symbol that had made his grandfather brave. He believed his little grandmother, and he went out and completely conquered everything — he got into many difficulties, got beat up and had tremendous hard times in doing it, but finally won out in the finish, and then found out that it was just a handle to an umbrella, and that it was all within himself. It was a lovely faith scene. But that whole thing was done with purely a dramatic basis and pathos that ran throughout the whole picture." [C]

In one of the only instances of comment on his contemporary's films, Charlie Chaplin noted of Lloyd's *Grandma's Boy*, in a May 23,1922 quote to journalist Rob Wagner, that it was "One of the best constructed screenplays I have ever seen . . . The boy has a fine understanding of light and shape and that picture has given me a real artistic thrill and stimulated me to go ahead."

At the time of this film's release, September 3, 1922, *Grandma's Boy* took its place as a highly influential film, helping to pioneer the then-new idea of comedies that could be feature length, combining both character development and gags, *and* keep audiences engaged all the while. However, what truly makes this film a landmark turning point in his career, was that it firmly broke ground on the adaptability of Lloyd's Glass Character in serving up comedy to any kind of audience. From this point on, he would never replicate the same kind of Glass Character in two consecutive films. "Whereas my character was always the boy with the glasses, and whereas he was always fighting odds, fighting the big fellows, still his attitude of thinking was entire different from one character role to another — not that we didn't occasionally repeat the same type. Sometimes he was a brash character, sort of a go-getter like we have in *Safety Last!*; another time, like in *Grandma's Boy*, he was a bashful, shy type of character. Sometimes he was rich, sometimes he was poor, sometimes he was a sophisticate, sometimes he was a dreamer, and each quality would motivate a lot of gags we'd do. Take the sophisticated character, for example. Do you remember the one I did in South America? Yes, *Why Worry?* — now, that was a sophisticated type of character; he was sort of a hypochondriac, and your gags for that differed entirely – so did his thinking and his type of action — from the character in *Grandma's Boy*. So, in that way, my character was never just one straight-line character." [L]

THE HAROLD LLOYD THRILL COMEDIES

Look Out Below . . .
"Just a small portion of what we did."

"Out of all the pictures I made, only five of them, as I recall, were thrill pictures. But the funny thing is, no matter where you go, they seem to remember those pictures. They must have had a tremendous impact on people's minds. Some of the ones we made were *Safety Last!*, that was a feature, *Feet First*, in which we use the scaffolding, but before that we made *High and Dizzy*, we made *Look Out Below*, and we made *Never Weaken*. Those were the five pictures we made — I wasn't a human fly in any of them. The only one that came closest was *Safety Last!* — and of course, there, I was substituting for my pal who was a human fly." [C]

John & Mary Q. Public know Harold Lloyd, chiefly, as a thrill-seeker, a human fly, because of the predominance of the picture of Lloyd, hanging from the hands of a clock in *Safety Last!*. Harold knew it: yet, he couldn't escape it. "People generally know me as a thrill comedian; but, that was just a small portion of what we did." [F]

He was right: of his 200-plus film appearances from 1913-47, only *five* (roughly 2 1/2%) can be considered thrill comedies. There were tense moments in many of his pictures, but a mere handful has, at their core, a central thrill element. These *were* exceptionally popular comedies, filled with tense laughs and downright fright.

Precious little is known as to exactly *why* Harold Lloyd strove to make the stunt comedy genre so much his own. It was dangerous; it was unnerving; it was hard work — harder than normal; it scared

The piled mattresses below HL – here in a candid still from the set of *Feet First* (1930) — vividly show no railings; had Harold not, if needed, fallen flat, the final bounce would have been a doozey.

the movie-going public. Why risk your own *life* to make an audience laugh, when a good scenario writer could get the job done?

Outside of the niceties of the films themselves, an understanding of the man, Harold Lloyd, is important in order to ascertain his work ethic for these pictures.

In the first place, the stunt work that Harold did do himself was tremendously hard on his body. It would have been hard on *any* man's body, but the envelope was definitely pushed when his disability is recalled. Lloyd, for the rest of his life after his 1919 accident, had occasional pain in his right hand — many of the tendons and muscles of the hand were blown off along with his thumb and index finger — and the use of it was challenging at best, particularly with a rubber prosthetic device underneath a leather sheath glove holding real and fake hand parts together. Harold was, by nature, a very athletic guy — but his accident left him with limits to his own active ability.

A rare shot of the set in *Feet First* (1930), which was built to look like the Orpheum Building, at 842 S. Broadway in Los Angeles. Sitting in the left window, feet dangling, is Lloyd double Harvey Parry. Barely visible, at extreme right, is HL looking up at Parry.

The whirlwind vertigo- and acrophobia-inspiring thrill sequence in *Never Weaken* (1921) has HL regretting his former death wish. Here, two famous stills are blended into one dynamite lobby card.
COURTESY PAUL E. GIERUCKI.

Secondly, Lloyd, the man, the filmmaker, the star, was not reckless by nature. He took extreme precautions in the execution of his thrill sequences, and he *did*, when necessary, use stunt doubles. For instance, in sequences utilizing horseback riding, he would bow to a more adept equestrian for long shots, and in the shooting of factions that his insurance company would flat out not let him do, he would reluctantly agree to a stunt double. However, Harold never *chose* to be doubled: each time, he had to be forced to.

All told, considering both his physical challenges and the advanced stunt work needed for his films, Lloyd worked harder than he, perhaps, needed to. Hanging in the balance, as it were, was much more than the laughs of the audience: his safety and well-being hung on each tense laugh. He did not have to go that cinematic route: he chose to.

Of all the strengths of the Lloyd film repertoire — and there were many — the most enduring and famed remains the Thrill

Photographer Gene Kornman with HL on the top of the mockup of the building roof in *Safety Last!* (1923). The two were great friends — Lloyd called Kornman "Genkie."

Picture. Lloyd's formula — a laugh, a scream, and a laugh — provided a most unique kind of comedy, in which the laughs were both humor-based and driven by fear. It is generally agreed that, as Harold noted above, five films encompass the thrill picture family, but prior to them all was *Ask Father*, in which Harold, hastily excused from the office of his girl's father, climbed the exterior of his building to get to the window in order to gain re-entry to the office. That was a thrill sequence which lasted all of ten seconds. However, the remaining five films — *Look Out Below, High and Dizzy, Never Weaken, Safety Last!,* and *Feet First* — all feature major sequences, most lasting over half the film's length, in which Harold put himself in harm's way, yet emerged unscathed. In each, the circumstances that brought about the danger increased the comic irony, which added to the nervous laughter.

"The recipe for thrill pictures is a laugh, a scream and a laugh. Combine screams of apprehension with stomach laughs of comedy and it is hard to fail.

"*Safety Last!* came of an old family. Its original progenitor was a one-reel glass character picture called *Look Out Below*. For it we built a frame of wooden girders, painted to likeness of steel, two and a half stories high, over the southern portal of the Hill Street tunnel. It was our first thrill picture depending upon height for its effects, and was original with us as far as I know. Neither it nor any of its descendents contained any doubling, double exposure or trick photography in the usual sense. The illusion lay in deceptive camera angles of drop and height.

"The second member of the family was a two-reeler called *High and Dizzy*, taken on the same scene, but presumably on the ledge of a completed ten-story hotel instead of bare girders, and having nothing in common with *Look Out Below* except the height theme.

"The third generation of the family was *Never Weaken*, a three-reel *de luxe* edition of *Look Out Below*. The thrills came of my efforts to commit suicide in the belief that Mildred had thrown me down. This time we built our framework of girders on the roof of the Ville de Paris department store. We used the interior of the same store for the department-store scenes in *Safety Last!*, the next thrill picture, working from closing time until two and three o'clock the next morning.

Safety Last! (1923) was the fourth of Lloyd's five thrill comedies, and remains his best-known work. This segment of the climb, on a set erected on the roof of 908 S. Broadway in Los Angeles, was shot on August 8 and 9, 1922.

"The success of the thrill idea in one, two and three lengths suggested trying it at full-program distance." [1] Thus begins the story of the granddaddy of Lloyd's thrill pictures — the film he remains best-known for — *Safety Last!* This film, unquestionably, is one of a handful of turning points in Harold's life that can still be considered, by cinema history, as a ground-breaker.

The 1920s were a special frame of time, unique beyond, perhaps, any other decade. Emerging victorious from World War I, witnessing endless new innovations, and experiencing more confidence than ever before, America *was* roaring with frivolity, excess, and thrill seekers. One such "typical" American was North Carolina native

Bill Strother, a professional steel worker and an occasional "Human Spider," who spent his leisure time scaring people. One summer day in 1922, Bill contracted to climb the twelve-story Brockman Building, located on the corner of Seventh Street and Grand Avenue in downtown Los Angeles. That day found Harold Lloyd in the area (it should be remembered that, when not wearing his magic horn-rimmed glasses, the star was virtually unrecognizable):

"First place, I was walking down Seventh Street in Los Angeles, and I noticed at one of the corners this tremendous crowd that was there. And in making inquiries someone told me that a man was going to scale the side of a building, this was about a ten-story building. And, being curious, I waited around, and the man came out and was introduced and said a few remarks, and then proceeded to start to climb up the side of the building. Well, by the time he had climbed up about two stories, and started on the third one, I began to feel so sorry for him, and I said, 'Oh, he can't *possibly* make it.' It was a very difficult building; he really climbed up just the windows — went from one window to the other — I still don't see how he did it. So, being, oh, I don't know, a little chicken I guess they call it, I walked on up a block, intending that I wasn't going to watch him kill himself. But, my curiosity got the better of me, so when I was about a block away, I went around the corner so that I was out of sight, but I could peek around the corner every so often to see where he'd gone. So I watched him scale this whole building by just occasionally peeking at him.

"He finally reached the top. Then he got up there, and he had a bicycle, and he rode the bicycle around the edge of the building. Then he got on the flagpole and he stood on his head. Well, it made such a terrific impression on me, and stirred my emotions up to such a degree, that I said, 'My, if it can *possibly* do that to an audience, if I can capture that on a screen, well, I think I've got something that's never been done before.' So, back I went, and up to the roof where they were, and made myself known, was introduced to the young man that did the scaling, and gave him a card, and told him to come out to the Hal Roach Studios — that we would like to talk with him, that we may have an idea that would be both beneficial to himself and to us." [E]

"It attracted a tremendous amount of people. What was the reason for it? They wanted to see this man perform an exceptional feat. And underlying it was that there was great danger in it. The man could easily be killed. In fact, many of them had been killed. There's something fascinating with people on that end of it. I felt, and I think that I'm normal to a degree anyway, that if I could get that terrific feeling within me, that I could hardly bear to look at it, but still I was so fascinated that I didn't want to leave, because I just wanted to know what the finish was, and what the outcome was with this climb. So it's just one of those things that you've just got to feel that, as you react emotionally to it, and that you're normal, that others will react to it the same way." [A]

You might be thinking, at this point, that Lloyd, Roach and associates went immediately to work hammering out the entire story around which Bill Strother might be utilized in the new picture, still untitled at this point. You'd be mistaken.

"We made the last part of the picture first — now, remember, I didn't know exactly what the beginning of the picture was going to be. I knew that we had to climb this building to get money for a certain reason — we hadn't worked out those reasons. Now, after we made that climb and we had made it, we knew we had a fine finish. Then we sat down with our gag men, and we figured how the boy was going to leave his home town, we knew he was going to do this for the girl, so we worked out all our reasons, and then the picture was built and brought up to the climb. And, I might say that this was one picture, that on our first preview, we were delighted with as far as having to go back and make a lot of it over." [E]

The climb — again, the first part of *Safety Last!* to be shot was the end of the film — is a thing of beauty to behold. A tense, exciting, scary and exhilarating sequence marrying humor to fright — however, the first thing Lloyd had to do was reconcile the use of Strother in the film. Think about it: how funny would it have been, really, to watch Bill Strother climb a building? It would have been thrilling, yes, but not all that humorous. The way Lloyd and his gag men inserted Harold into the climb was ingenious:

"The more you had good business that was really working for you, the more chance you had to get a good picture out of it. When I say something working for you — let me make an example out of

The beginning of the thrill sequence, when HL commences (*and* finishes) the publicity-stunt climb for his pal, who is in trouble with the law — this *Safety Last!* set was built and filmed at Hal Roach Studios.

the climb in *Safety Last!*. This pal of mine was to make a climb — the steeplejack — he had gotten into an altercation, a little difficulty, with one of the local policemen there. Even though his picture was printed, that he was going to do the climb, without the face showing, the policeman recognized the clothes. So, when the climb was to start, the policeman was there, because he had a grievance against this particular character, and was going to arrest him, which would naturally ruin our climb.

"So we saw the policeman standing there, and he said, 'I can't go out there until we get rid of the policeman.' So I made several efforts to get rid of the policeman without too much success, so finally he said, 'Look, here's what we'll do. You go out and pretend that *you* are the mystery man who's going to make the climb. You just climb up to the first floor, and then, for a moment you slip right into the window. I'll change, and put on your coat and hat, and I'll go the rest of the way.' Well, that was all right, except that

I was scared to death to even climb the first floor! I said, 'I'll break my neck!' So he finally talks me into it. So I go around, and I'm introduced, with all the fanfare, and I climb the first floor. But, while I'm climbing from the ground to the first floor, the cop happens to see him peeking around the corner, and takes after him. So he runs into the building and the policeman after him. So by the time I reach the first floor, he manages to just open the door long enough to see me there at the window and says, 'You've got to make just one more floor till I ditch this cop.' So, I looked at him in amazement — my God, I made it to the first floor, but the second floor, well, it's just unheard of! But, I go ahead, expecting to be killed at any moment. And, of course, that continues on during the whole climb — he doesn't ditch the cop, but every time we see this little interjection coming in, 'Go one more floor till I ditch the cop.' And, in the last scene, we saw the policeman chasing him over the roofs of the adjoining buildings, and a little title comes out, 'You'll have to continue until I ditch the cop.' Well, that's what I mean by something working for you. Because all the time, they felt that I was going to be relieved, or that I couldn't go any more than one more floor, and then that makes all the other business so much stronger, because you've got something that is anticipated, when will the fellow help him out? How much more can he do?

"Now, then, the same thing applies with a major story. The more interesting that you can make your character — I don't mean he has to be eccentric, but he has to be a personality that is not just the ordinary run — when he gets into difficulties, someone can envision that there's going to be fun here. He won't act like the normal person. Wait till he gets into that trouble — what is he going to do? Then, right away, there's anticipation of what's going to happen, with trouble, of course. In comedy, trouble is one of the great ingredients: there's so many variations. You take newspapers. What gets printed most in newspapers? I'd say 75%, maybe that's an understatement, honestly, most of it is trouble, grief, more disasters. I think that they do that because people, somehow, get a feeling, well, they're all right, someone else is in trouble, not that they're wishing it on them, but at least it might make them feel a little better, that someone else is having difficulties too. And, of course, in trouble, with a picture, if everything was happy, and you were going along, you wouldn't run into any particular difficulties. But, if you get yourself into situations where you're liable to be killed, or you're going to be sent to jail, or you're going to lose all your money, or you're going to get beat up, or any numerous things, right away, that's trouble, and you say, now, how is the man going out of it? So, it's the getting out of it, the surmounting it, the overcoming of obstacles, that gives you the opportunity to create comedy." [A]

Thus emerged the skeleton story of the professional who contracted to make a climb but who, for some reason, couldn't, and had to be replaced by Harold.

The Bolton Building was the fictional name given to the building in question (a wide-view sketch of the LA Investment Building, located at 1016 South Broadway off Tenth Street, served as the representation of the Bolton Building in the sequence in *Safety Last!*, although the actual edifice that Strother climbed for long shots was the International Bank Building, located at 116 Temple Street, corner of Spring Street). The bottom of the building, just as Harold was commencing his climb, was actually a set, constructed at the Hal Roach Studios.

True, some of these thrill pictures were shot inside an actual accommodation, but for all intents and purposes, for Lloyd, "the streets were our studio." [D]

The technical end of the filming of the building-climbing sequence is nothing short of brilliant, when it is remembered that this was 1922 — there were, as of yet, no such innovations as *process* or *chroma-keying* (the optical or electronic insertion of an image into a different background). Couple that with Lloyd's famous answer to skeptics who doubted the integrity of the shots — "We were up just as high as you saw: when we were four stories in the air we were four stories up; when we were at ten stories, we were just that high" [E] — and it would appear that he was being completely truthful. Well, he was — *sort of.*

"What we did do was to build platforms. And the platforms were built at least, probably, 20 feet below us, which as you know that's quite a distance, and they had no railings around them — we put as many mattresses on them as we could, and we made the platform as large as we could, but there was a limit to what you could do. So, consequently, when you got up there, it did look something like a

This lobby card for *Safety Last!* (1923) shows two portions of the thrill sequence. On the left half is Bill Strother, costumed as HL, climbing the International Bank Building on September 17, 1922. On the right is HL showing off on the in-studio building-at-street-level set.
COURTESY DAVID KALAT.

postage stamp when you looked at it from there on down. And it meant that if anything happened to you, you had to jump to this platform, and you had to fall flat, because if you bounced, that would be the end of the whole thing. One time, I was working up there, I believe around the clock, and I felt that there was a good chance that I might lose my balance, so I just let go and fell flat.

"It took quite a long time to make this sequence — I guess we were about a month and a half, two months on it — because we could only work a certain length of time in the daytime. You had to work from about 11:00 to around about 1, and then the shadows came in, and the shadows would have been very noticeable.

"The funny part is that when I first started, about the first two days, I would do nothing. Of course, I had done several before this, but in a different way. But the first two days, when you get up to the heights, it's that fear of heights, of even looking over that people have, you just feel like you want to jump. So, I was very careful, and

I did very little. But, as you were up there, and you got to doing things, then there's a situation took place that you become a little overconfident — because I would walk clear out beyond the platform, and the boys would say, 'There's no need of that, Lloyd,' and of course they would get scared then, because it was silly. But I had developed, by that time, a great deal of confidence, I felt I knew what I was doing, and I felt I could even jump to the platform from there, I thought. Whether I could have or not, I don't know." [E]

"I have no desire to break my neck and it would be very foolish of me from a business standpoint. All the staff, the company officers, the distributors and others have a like business interest in keeping me alive and whole. So the amount of risk I take in a thrill picture becomes a compromise between the necessity of taking some and the foolishness of taking too much." [I]

"The only time, in those days, that I used a stunt man was to do something that I actually couldn't do. If it were to do some rodeo work, or some acrobatic feat that I was unable to do, then we used a stunt man. That was the only time. I think there were only some scenes that the human fly did on a couple of them where we had absolutely no platform at all. But, with him, he wanted to it without any and I wouldn't let him. I put a very strong thin wire cable on, and we had him do that. That was one where I would have been afraid to have ever taken a chance, and that was on the real building; that wasn't on our building. See, we picked a certain building in Los Angeles, and when we built our sets, we built them to match that building, so that they were just the same, and we chose a building that had little crevices." [E]

Following the pattern of his previous thrill comedies, faux building exteriors were constructed for Lloyd to work upon; however, for this film, the ascending height (conducive with a continuous climb) had to be fully reflected. Thus, *four* separate buildings, each differing in height, were chosen to hold four different sets, each representing another section of the building. Long shots of Strother, outfitted as Lloyd's double, were shot on September 17, 1922, as he climbed the crevice-laden ten-story International Bank Building (which, years later, was demolished to make way for the Los Angeles City Hall; eagle-eyed TV viewers will know the City Hall as the rapidly tilt-shot building in the opening sequence of the 1950s series

Superman). Bill was secured to the building with a heavy piano wire. The chief cameraman on duty that day was Walter Lundin, assisted by Harry Gerstad, Ed Norris, and Fred Guiol: four cameraman, capturing different angles, making up one dynamite sequence.

Commencing on August 1 (*before* Bill shot his portion: after seeing the rushes, Strother knew better how to climb, in order to *look* as if he were Lloyd) and for the next three weeks, Harold did his work on the mockup building-portion sets. For each, the four cameramen (who, admittedly, were as brave as Lloyd) were perched upon the edges on neighboring buildings, shooting towards Harold. Careful attention was paid to angles — while it appears, in watching the film, that Harold is climbing a single building that is on the *left* side of the street, he was actually working on mock structures erected on buildings on the *right* side of the street. Each set was built on the roof top side nearest to the street: through precise angling and framing, the illusion of both height (provided by how high the building was) and placement (positioning of the camera lens) were expertly accomplished. It took a keen eye, and knowledge of the facts, to know that there was, indeed, an honest trick being played on the viewer. Yet, unlike present-day technology, packed with computer-generated ways to dazzle the audience, Lloyd and company did nothing but organize their surroundings, and shoot them creatively.

"The danger, while not as great as it might appear to the public, was nevertheless still very real." [I]

With the release of *Safety Last!*, on April Fool's Day, 1923, audiences recognized that they were witness to a cinematic milestone — ambulances were on call in many theatres, to treat those who became wobbly from the tense excitement. The laughter emanated both from nerves, and from the peppering of gags throughout the climb: pigeons descending upon Harold, whose hat is covered with peanuts dropped by a child watching him from an upper floor window; a mouse running up his leg as he was struggling up a ledge (the rodent-in-pants shimmy dance, which ended in a desperate hanging off the ledge — and the mouse falling out of the pants and onto an onlooker's toupee — was actually performed by a double, Robert A. "Red"

> ## Fun Fact
>
> Lloyd speaks, in the Winter 1958-1959 issue of *Sight and Sound* magazine, regarding *Safety Last!*: "We didn't have process shots in those, you know. Every shot was real. If I was hanging from the fifteenth floor, then I really was up there. All we did was build wooden platforms that jutted out beneath us. The camera shot down so that these weren't seen. But often the platforms were fifteen feet below me. I used to take three or four days to get acclimatized to the heights. We built that clock in *Safety Last!* on the actual building. No, people didn't look up at us. They didn't see us or thought we were builders. My wife was Mildred Davis then and starring with me in that film. She was petrified of heights. That last scene at the top of the building — 'Get this over fast,' she screamed.
>
> "I always did the improbable but never the impossible. I never hit the pavement and bounced up again into a room. I aimed for reality. I was the first comic to be a guy you could believe in. I had that gimmick of the glasses, but that was all I needed."

Golden, an assistant director for Lloyd); a sprawling net falling on Harold, who frees himself from it, only to have it fall onto a drunk (Earl Mohan) on the street — clearly, the Lloyd gag team strove to inject as many humorous obstacles as they could so, while not putting Harold in any unnecessary visible danger, his building climb could be seen more naturally as a faction of a comedy film.

Safety Last! was intensely praised, both in its day and since. Cinematic great Orson Welles wrote that "The construction of *Safety Last*, for instance — as a piece of comic architecture it's impeccable. [French playwright Georges] Feydeau never topped it for sheer construction. He was, almost entirely, his own gag man. Really a writer who acted, if you know what I mean."

This installment of "Freckles and His Friends" deals with *Safety Last!* (1923). The strip appeared in papers 11 days before the film debuted in theatres nationwide. © NEWSPAPER ENTERPRISE ASSOCIATION.

Lloyd's second talkie, *Feet First*, released on November 8, 1930, was shot in the same fashion as in *Safety Last!*, with similar shooting platforms and building facades. Sounds like a repeat formula for mirth-invoking success, right? Well, in this case, wrong. The film fails to capture the same glee as had its silent predecessor. The chief dilemma was the injection of *sound*. Harold's audible grunts, groans, and cries for help, made the climb seem somehow more real and, thus, more terrifying and less humorous. There were gags, to be sure: a paint can which just happened to fall onto Harold's head;

a hose which was lowered to Harold by the building janitor (Willie Best), only to be turned on, spraying the street below with water; a cigar butt dropped onto Harold, who shook it loose, only to have it fall into the straw hat of a man on the street. However, despite the sprinkled funny spots, the vividness of Harold's plight, *through sound*, made audiences feel sorry and desperate for his character, not root for him as had been the case in *Safety Last!*. If it is possible to compare two films, one silent and one sound, that share a single nervous-comedy element, inevitably the more *realistic* will be that with sound. And, in so doing, the nerves will suffer more negatively because of that realism.

Frankly, many of the audiences of 1930 were horrified by Lloyd's character's cries for help — it just wasn't all that funny — a theatre owner in Berlin solved the problem by turning off the sound track during the ascent. The audiences responded favorably.

Every Lloyd fan must never forget — and this is as good a place to be reminded of this as any — that the stunts that Harold *did* perform himself, and there were many, were accomplished (from 1920 on) with a major handicap. Two fingers were gone from his right hand; partial paralysis stayed with him for the balance of his life, and it was certainly not easy maneuvering a right hand with only three remaining fingers. That which Lloyd *did* accomplish on his own, in the arena of thrills, was immense, and becomes cataclysmic when his accident is added to the picture. Be that not forgotten.

Harold Lloyd Corporation Makes Harold His Own Boss...

Heap Big Chief...
"It was a one-man operation."

Anyone who works has dreams of being his or her own boss... calling the shots, steering the boat, ultimately guiding his or her own success or failure. Harold Lloyd was no exception, and with the creation of Harold Lloyd Corporation, he saw his dream realized.

From the earliest days of the careers of both Harold Lloyd and Hal Roach, the two had worked side by side, with and for one another. By the early 1920s, however, Lloyd was establishing himself as an important star, and Roach was broadening his own horizons with interests such as *Our Gang*, Laurel and Hardy, Will Rogers, Snub Pollard, and Charley Chase. Roach's preoccupations, combined with Lloyd's intense desire to exercise increased control over his films, precipitated Harold to break from the Roach camp after the completion of filming *Why Worry?* (1923).

"*Why Worry?* was the last picture to be made under the Roach banner. By contract I had the exclusive use of the big stage at Culver City and first call on everything, including Hal's time. He was trying to work four or five other units on the one remaining stage and we came to a point where his own best interests, he agreed, dictated turning me loose.

"It was the friendliest possible severance after nearly ten years of teamwork." [I]

This was a tremendous turning point in Harold's career: on April 24, 1922, Harold Lloyd Corporation was born, and would begin

The standard envelope used by Harold Lloyd Corporation, mostly for sending out autographed photos requested by fans worldwide. Another variation of the company stationary had a picture of a smiling HL on the left side of the envelope.

operations the next year. The Corporation's offices were initially located at 1040 Las Palmas Avenue in Hollywood. Harold predictably assumed the Presidency of Harold Lloyd Corporation. Assisting him were his father, James Darsie "Foxy" Lloyd as Vice President and Treasurer, his mother's brother, William Royal Fraser as Secretary and General Manager, and John L. Murphy as Production Manager. Harold took on these men to assume managerial and financial duties "for which I had neither taste nor training, and which was demanding more and more time that I preferred to give to the picture and to plain enjoying myself." [1]

The Moving Picture World trade journal broke the news of the Lloyd/Roach breakup in its July 7, 1923 edition, and released other studio changes. "Lloyd's entire staff has been released by Mr. Roach and will immediately go over to the comedian. Sam Taylor and Fred Newmeyer will go with Lloyd as directors; Tim Whelan and Ted Wilde as 'gag' men; Robert A. Golden, assistant director; Walter Lundin, staff cameraman; Gaylord Lloyd, Harold's brother; Roy

One of the lobby cards issued for *Hot Water* (1924): this card features but one of the marvelous titles written by Thomas J. Grey.

Brooks, Charles Stevenson and Wallie Howe, actors; Gene Kornman, still photographer. Jobyna Ralston, who has taken Mildred Davis' place as Lloyd's leading lady, will continue with the comedian. Joe Reddy will handle the publicity."

Though Harold delegated some responsibilities, "I was the full boss of my pictures — I financed them and I produced them, and hired my own directors and cast, and had my own studio, so it was a one-man operation. There were very few people who did that at that time; Douglas Fairbanks, Sr., did it, and Mary Pickford did it and Chaplin did it. I don't know whether there were any more at that time who did that; I think we were the four who were in that category." [E]

Harold Lloyd Corporation produced each of Harold's feature films from *Girl Shy* on. The company also guided other units . . .

In 1927, Harold Lloyd Corporation founded a division called "Hollywood Productions," releasing through Paramount, for the express purpose of producing Edward Everett Horton comedies. Eight films were produced, many of which are extant.

In the early 1940s, Lloyd produced two films for RKO-Radio Pictures. *My Favorite Spy* (1942) costarred Kay Kyser, Robert Armstrong and Jane Wyman. *A Girl, a Guy and a Gob* (1941) costarred George Murphy, Edmond O'Brien and a talented brunette (later a redhead) for whom Harold was a true inspiration. Their affection was mutual: "My personal opinion is that I think that Lucille Ball is the best comedienne that we've had, at least in my lifetime. I think so. Take Marie Dressler and Mabel Normand and Mae West — they're all excellent and all splendid and I wouldn't take a thing away from any of them, but I still think Lucille has got more to give from a comic standpoint — she is a real comedienne. I don't say that Lucille can't go wrong, the same as we all can, everybody can have their moments where they've up the wrong street, you see — there's no one wearing wings — but I don't know of anyone who comes closer to the contemporaries that I worked with, as far as being a real comedienne, than Lucille Ball. Lucille was always after me, for quite a long time after, to make a sequel of it. She was just great in it. She wouldn't let me off the set. I was the producer, I wasn't directing that particular picture — I was supposed to be working with writers and many other things, but they kept me on the set every time Lucille was on it. For instance, she had to drop a purse off of a balcony down onto Edmond O'Brien's head. She'd say, 'Harold, come here, how would you drop this purse?' So I had to figure it out and do it for her — 'Oh, that's right,' — but she could do it immediately. All through the picture, I would do the scene for them, and time it and space it, and then they were just magnificent, they could just catch it immediately." [C]

Lloyd, who was years between his own 1938 and 1947 starring vehicles, added his own touch to the film, in his own unique fashion. The script featured directions like "The growing sequence," and "The handkerchief gag." No stranger to comedy on paper, even Ball was bewildered, asking her producer, "What's it all about?" She would find out, as three words on paper would, inevitably, become 500 very funny feet of film footage. Lucy was properly apologetic to her veteran producer, later noting, "Watching him every day on the set was an inspiration. His quiet, reassuring knowledge of his

HL with Lucille Ball and Desi Arnaz on the set of *A Girl, a Guy and a Gob* (1941): the affection between actress and producer was mutual and deep.

art and how to get the job done was something that stuck with me. His authority and understanding, coupled with his great vitality, is what made him one of the greatest comedians of our time. His incomparable timing, his awareness of material, his enchanting quality of being able to develop what I call a 'sense of play,' and his ability to execute them all with a complete credibility, are all the things that made Harold Lloyd a giant among giants."

Another important consequence of Harold Lloyd Corporation, aside from the production end of things, was the growing influence of Harold, himself, in the industry. Even at the outset of his role as producer, Lloyd had pull. "I was responsible for bringing Harry Langdon into pictures. I saw Langdon in Vaudeville on the Orpheum circuit in a skit that he was doing called 'Johnny's New Car.' I came back and told Hal Roach that he was a natural for the screen, and I suggested that Hal talk to him and sign him up. He came out and he was most willing, but they differed a little on a matter or two of about $100 a week difference. I don't know if it was [Sol] Lesser or not, but Lesser gave him what he wanted and he went off, and I always told Hal, 'You were very foolish, Hal, he was easily worth that and much more to start with.' They wanted me to handle Langdon after I had gone away from Roach, and I considered it for a while, because Harry needed handling. His own judgment on what he should do wasn't as good. He went from Lesser, I believe, to Sennett, and they were working him entirely wrong there — they were working him like they had Ford Sterling and they were working him like they did Chaplin to start with. Chaplin's first character was a heavy, villainous type, and he was very funny with it, but he never reached the heights he did with the Little Tramp when he changed. So Harry came to me and said, 'What's wrong? I don't seem to be capturing what I was doing in Vaudeville.' I said, 'Harry, they're working you too fast. Let them work to you and work much slower.' Now, here's where his judgment was bad: so, they did, but then he worked much too slow — he went from one peak down to another without hitting a medium. Same thing when Harry went out for himself, on the choice of some of his material and some of the things he did. He was one of our really great comedians, but the pictures he made didn't really prove that. He needed guidance. He was a lovely character and should have been infinitely better — if he'd have used his material better and used more judgment." [C]

With the commencement of operation of Harold Lloyd Corporation, Harold's films truly became *his*. From *Girl Shy* through *The Milky Way* (1936), Lloyd was solely responsible, technically, artistically, creatively and critically for the product that bore his name.

THE FILM THAT STARTED IT ALL ... *GIRL SHY*

It was not accidental that Harold Lloyd chose to release his first independent feature on April 20, 1924, his 31st birthday. This was a special film for him — always would be — although it is not known if he ever cited *Girl Shy* amongst his favorite of his films (the four he always noted were *Grandma's Boy, Safety Last!, The*

Foxy Lloyd showing his famous son some of the fan mail received in the office. Note the stacks of envelopes on the desk, the variety of already-autographed photographs strewn about, as well as the portrait of Jobyna Ralston on the wall behind HL.

Freshman and *The Kid Brother*). However, it was an important film in his evolution, for in it, he raised the bar in the film arena, both for himself and for the industry as a whole.

The great chase sequence, arguably the heart of *Girl Shy*, was filmed first, before any other scenes in the film were shot. One of the greatest factions of the chase, in which the horse wagon "runs over" the audience, was later borrowed by a friend of Harold: director Fred Niblo was in the process of shooting his epic *Ben-Hur* (1925), when he saw *Girl Shy*. So struck was he by this "under the street" camera technique, that he employed it for the great chariot race sequence. Actually, to execute *Girl Shy*'s brief yet magnificent shot, cameraman Walter Lundin mounted a camera within a manhole on Grand Avenue in downtown Los Angeles, providing the remarkable illusion (Lundin was a master of sight gag execution, a really excellent camera artist). Harold, always one to recognize an opportunity, left

Jobyna Ralston was leading lady opposite HL in six of his most important features from 1923-1927, and is revered and beloved by Lloyd fans, many who consider her his finest female foil.

the studio during the filming of *The Freshman*, on May 24, 1924, to watch the Ben Hur chariot race being shot.

Girl Shy was Lloyd's first independent feature, for which he both produced and starred. As such, the veritable second half of the film — the race to rescue his girl (Jobyna Ralston) from a doomed marriage to a known bigamist (Carlton Griffin) — was a crowning achievement, utilizing a bevy of vehicles to help him get to his

Some fundraising at the Corporation? Key members of the team flank a kneeling HL: standing, from left, Warren Doane, Charles Stevenson, Charley Kelvin, Red Golden, Tom Crizer, and Sam Taylor.

destination faster. Of course, had he caught the train in the first place, there would have been no need for a frenzied race. But, he missed the choo-choo, and made desperate use of any contrivance he encountered — a couple of cars, a motorcycle, a trolley car, a fire truck, a sand wagon and a horse car among them. For sheer excitement, and variety of conveyances, this multi-reel finish cannot be topped.

"In this picture, he was a boy that stuttered. That made it very difficult, and it gave him quite a lot of difficulty in trying to get to the place he had an hour to get to. And, of course, it's one of those charge to the rescues. But what we did in those days, when riding on streetcars running wild, and driving a team of horses right down a main street, and missing automobiles — we actually did that, you see, there was no process in those days. I did about 90% of my own stunts; occasionally, I'd find something I just couldn't do, and then you'd have to get someone else. But I did practically all my own stuff." [C]

In the chase sequence, we witness a rare event: a scene in which Lloyd was injured. Harold's character was to ride the back of a fire engine by grabbing a hold of the truck's hose as the big red machine traveled at 35 miles an hour. Harold received six stitches to the forehead in the accident, explained here, from the *Girl Shy* press book: "A fractious fire nozzle got away from Lloyd, striking him with trip hammer force across the forehead and knocking him off the fire engine. For a minute, the other members of the Lloyd company who witnessed the accident thought he had suffered a fractured skull, but it was soon apparent that, while painful, the injury would not prove really serious. Lloyd received immediate treatment at the home of a nearby physician." The article closed by saying, "... the danger of the situation is said to be quite palpable upon the screen." This is very correct.

> **FUN FACT**
>
> JAMES DARSIE LLOYD, HAROLD'S FATHER, HELD THE TITLES OF VICE PRESIDENT AND TREASURER FOR HAROLD LLOYD CORPORATION. HOWEVER, HIS DUTIES ON THOSE ENDS WERE MINIMAL — HIS CHIEF RESPONSIBILITY WAS HANDLING HIS SON'S FAN MAIL. FOXY WOULD OFTEN AUTOGRAPH THE THOUSANDS OF REQUESTED PHOTOS OF HAROLD. THIS POSES A QUANDARY FOR CURRENT-DAY MEMORABILIA COLLECTORS AND AUTOGRAPH SEEKERS; THUS, IT IS VERY IMPORTANT TO BE ABLE TO TELL THE DIFFERENCE, AUTOGRAPH-WISE, BETWEEN A FOXY AND A HAROLD.

A side-by-side comparison of the most widely known autographs of the name Harold Lloyd. On left, as Foxy signed photos of his son, and on right, the authentic HL autograph. He frequently accented his name with a whimsical sketch of his magic horn-rims, and had a distinctive capital L.

The ending of *Girl Shy*, in which Harold arrives at the Buckingham estate just in time to stop the wedding of Mary Buckingham (Ralston) to Ronald DeVore (Griffin), inspired the similar ending of *The Graduate* (1967). Director Mike Nichols, as had Niblo years earlier, invited Harold to watch the filming, which he gladly did.

The climactic ending of *Girl Shy* (1924) — which saw Harold Meadows succeed in stopping the marriage of the girl he loved — inspired the similar ending of *The Graduate* (1967).

For all the kudos and awe that the chase to the rescue inspires, *Girl Shy* also offers a genuine piece of Americana to today's audiences. In the hustle and bustle of contemporary travel, full of freeways and gridlock, this film's sequence in which Harold Meadows and Mary Buckingham share a ride (as well as a box of Cracker Jack *and* a dog biscuit) upon a train is a reminder of a gentler, easier time. Train travel allowed time for conversation — heck, these two fell in love, for all intents and purposes, during that ride — and was a relaxing way to go. Those who drive cars to and from work on a daily basis will, doubtless, watch that train ride scene and wax most nostalgic for those good old days.

One other thing that is so lovely about Harold's inaugural independent production is its showcasing of Lloyd's talents as an actor, comedic *and* dramatic. One sequence in particular stands out: Harold has just found out that his book, "The Secret of Making Love," which he wrote with the most honest of intentions, is going to be retitled "The Boob's Diary" and marketed as a comedy book. He is heartbroken, particularly as he had determined that, once his book was a success, he would propose marriage to his beloved Mary. Thinking himself an utter failure, he realizes that it would be better to send her out of his life than to keep her hanging onto false hopes. They meet in a park, and he purposely lies to her, telling her he was only kidding her to get new material for his book — she is heart-broken, and so is Harold, as he fights through tears, forcing sarcastic laughter, to make himself look all the more loathsome to her. To top it all off, he then leaves Mary standing by a tree, and walks off with another girl — and as the ultimate indignity, he buys her a box of Cracker Jack (he had famously bought one for Mary on their train ride, and she had kept that beloved box in her purse since). In this scene, as in perhaps no other, you see both the power of Harold Lloyd as an actor, and the glorious ability of Jobyna Ralston to bring out the best in her leading man, through her own prowess as an actress. This is a powerful, and pivotal, moment in the film, and expertly showcases Lloyd's undervalued mastery of the peppering of comedy with dramatic moments.

Girl Shy offers so much for so many different kinds of audiences. The shy audience member will find hope in Harold's conquering of his timidity, in order to save the girl he loves. The stutterer will see

A frame capture of the chase sequence of *Girl Shy* (1924), in which the camera was mounted in a manhole cover, soon to be run over by the horse wagon: this exciting ocular choice motivated director Fred Niblo to add a similar shot to his epic *Ben-Hur* (1925).

that this malady need not squash ambitions. The aspiring author will witness the struggle for ideas, the pride in a finished product, the agony of rejection, and the potential success of a project. Those attuned to fantasy will revel in timid stutterer Harold Meadows' book, "The Secret of Making Love," and his internal visualizations of the conquerings of "My Vampire" and "My Flapper." In this one film alone, we might see more Glass Characters than ever before — there is a great deal of role-playing throughout the picture's seven reels. This film is a golden example of Lloyd's ability, through his Glass Character, to stretch himself into an infinite number of storylines, in the process reaching all kinds of people, and inspiring them all the while. And, because he went independent, he had supreme control over every direction his character took. The establishment of Harold Lloyd Corporation not only made Harold a much richer man, it made him a much finer filmmaker.

Marriage and Fatherhood

Let's Go . . .
"To me, he was the best."

Life imitating art definitely rang true for Bebe Daniels and Harold Lloyd. The two, partners on screen in a successful series of comedies, saw their professional pairing turn into a romantic bond that was forced to sever in the early summer of 1919. They were an exclusive couple — and Bebe was not yet out of her teens — but the strength of their affection could not withstand the power of Bebe's desire to be a great actress on her own terms.

There was intensity in Bebe's manner, with her wide, attractive eyes and expressive face, which was present on and off the screen. Harold and Bebe, however, did have basic incongruities — prime among them was Bebe's strong will and fully developed career plans. This strength of ideal was rare, and not altogether popular, for women to exhibit in the pre-1920s. Eventually, she caught the eye of director Cecil B. DeMille, who offered Bebe a contract with Famous Players-Lasky; hesitant at first, she waited for Harold to stop her from accepting, but he didn't — perhaps because he respected her ambition, but more likely because, at this point in his young life, he didn't feel ready for marriage.

So, after a four-year pairing, on and off the silver screen, Harold Lloyd and Bebe Daniels parted ways. Their affection never waned — they kept in contact for the rest of their lives (and their lives ended eight days apart, in March 1971). Yet, both moved on. Professionally *and* personally.

The 1919 breakup of Bebe Daniels and Harold Lloyd was a sad one for both. Harold felt unready for the marriage that Bebe desired; she then changed gears and moved on with *her* career, leaving Lloyd and Rolin for greener pastures at Paramount.

Enter the woman who was Harold Lloyd's next female lead in a mere fifteen films (eleven shorts and four features), yet later took on a more prominent role as his leading lady in life. Mildred Davis, known to friends and family as "Mid," remains the one woman, save for Elizabeth Lloyd, closest to Harold for the longest period of time.

Mildred Hillary Davis was born on February 22, 1901, in Philadelphia, Pennsylvania. Mid's long blonde curls and large expressive eyes were of her time: she very closely resembled a young, and mightily popular, Mary Pickford. She was an average schoolgirl, part of her education having been received at Stadium High School in Tacoma, Washington. However, she had big dreams — of Hollywood fame over books and studying. Thus, when on an extended vacation in Los Angeles, she immediately sought out the casting directors, and auditioned. She won a minor role in Metro's vehicle for star Viola Dana, *The Weaver of Dreams* (1918). However, her winning of the role of Betty Thompson in Bryant Washburn's comedy *All Wrong* was, in retrospect, a bigger break than she would imagine. The film was released on June 1, 1919, through Pathé.

Two who saw the film in previews: Hal Roach and Harold Lloyd.

Mildred's reviews were good — characteristic conclusions were that the young heroine was "pretty and vivacious," and that she "leaves nothing to be desired." Kind sentiments, indeed — but the really important words were found within this trio of wires from May 1919:

A May 19, 1919 telegram from Hal Roach to Paul Brunet, head of Pathé: "Bebe Daniels has signed contract with the Lasky Company to be featured by Cecil B. DeMille in big productions. Impossible to keep her with us. Have you any suggestions to advise for leading lady with Lloyd?"

Hal seemed to answer his own question in a May 22 1919 telegram, again from Roach to Brunet: "I am trying to get Mildred Davis who played lead in Bryant Washburn picture All Wrong to play leads with Lloyd. Kindly ask the opinion of people there regarding this girl."

A May 22 1919 telegram response, from Brunet to Roach: "Mildred Davis very satisfactory. We suggest that you get her."

Sounds like a done deal? Think again. By the time that Roach and Lloyd decided to pursue Davis for the Lloyd series, 18-year-old Mid had grown weary of Hollywood, and returned to school in Tacoma. The men finally located her, and requested that she return to Los Angeles to test with Lloyd. "Before appearing at the studio she bought a new wardrobe — one intended to express maturity. It included a large hat ornamented with a large and wavy plume, and Mildred adjusted her deportment to the grave dignity of the plumage.

"Our first meeting was mutually disappointing. She knew little of Harold Lloyd, and, in make-up and character clothes in which we met, I fell something short of her ideal leading man. For my part, I exclaimed to myself, 'Can this be the girl in the Washburn picture, or have those roguish little pixies, the telegraph boys, put a changeling in our nest?' The very qualities that had charmed us Mildred had effaced so painstakingly that it was some time before Hal and I realized that it was only her clothes that were wrong."

[I] Mildred Davis eventually signed her contract on June 2, 1919, for $100 weekly, and commenced her tenure with the Hal Roach Studios.

Mildred Davis appeared in 15 films opposite her future husband, and was his leading lady at the time of his steadiest and steepest growth as a comic innovator.

Her popularity was swift and sure — she was never compared, per se, to Bebe Daniels, and immediately became a hit with Lloyd fans, at a time when his status amongst cinema's mirth makers was on the rise. Perhaps more than any of Harold's leading ladies, Mid was with him at the time of his steadiest and steepest growth, and as a positive consequence, her value rose alongside his (as did her weekly salary, which began at $100, and was raised by $25 every six months).

On March 7, 1922, Harold Lloyd sent a telegram to Pathé's publicity director: "No foundation to reports of my engagement to Mildred Davis. —Lloyd."

Less than a year later, on February 10, 1923, Harold Lloyd and Mildred Davis were married.

The union of leading lady and leading man is nothing new — in fact, nowadays, it is actually commonplace (at least in a casual manner; divorces are brisk after many such on-set romances). So, the fact that Harold and Mid stepped out on occasion was hardly unusual. They began to seriously date during the filming of *A Sailor-Made Man*, between August and October 1921; they went dancing, saw shows, frequented amusement parks and beaches, and really enjoyed each others' company. Lloyd stated that the whole idea of marriage evolved from the pending expiration of Mid's contract, which would occur after shooting for *Safety Last!* was wrapped. As the leading lady for, arguably, the most popular comedian of the decade, Mid was quite visible in very widely distributed comedies. The possibilities were strong that she would begin receiving lucrative offers, which would afford her wider scopes for her acting range — in other words, she most likely would receive more money, and a greater variety of roles, than the Lloyd camp could offer. However, "it needed the prospect of losing her to bring home to me the fact, apparent for months to every one else from the increasing ardor of my devotion, that I loved her. Mildred paid me the handsome compliment of giving up a future in dramatic pictures by saying yes, and we were married in the midst of *Why Worry?*" [I]

"After being with me for about four years, she had an opportunity to play leads in the pictures, so I thought the way to keep her my leading lady for the rest of my life was to do what I did." [C]

Hal Roach stated, according to a few interview sources, that on the night before his marriage to Mildred, Harold offered him money to think of an honorable way to back out. If Hal Roach's account is correct, one has to wonder why Harold would make such a request. Some clues found in Harold Lloyd's Last Will and Testament point to a monumental rationale for marriage: Mildred's pregnancy.

Harold's Last Will and Testament is a formal, legal document, signed on March 2, 1971, six days before Harold died. Two errors were made in the typing of the 29-page Will. Each error was crossed out, corrected, and initialed by Harold and his witnesses (Linda Hayward Hoppe, Joseph G. Gorman, Jr., and Thomas Waterman). Therefore, any information left pristine, or uncorrected, is considered legally binding and assumed to be correct.

Daughter Gloria's birth date was listed twice within the document. On two separate pages in Harold's will, on Page 1, paragraph 2, and Page 11, paragraph 3, Harold's firstborn child is listed as "Gloria Mildred Lloyd Guasti, born May 21, 1923." If this is correct, then it becomes crystal clear that Mildred Davis was pregnant at the time of her marriage to Harold Lloyd.

However, the family has (and continues to) recognize May 21, 1924 as Gloria's birth date. This is coincident with comments made by family friend Diana Doyle, whose grandmother was a longtime friend of Mildred Davis. According to Doyle, her grandmother and Davis were in The Hospital of the Good Samaritan during the same period, giving birth to girls — and Doyle stated that her grandmother was born in May of 1924.

So, the mystery lingers. On one hand, the family and close friends are certain that Gloria was born in 1924. On the other hand, Harold's Last Will and Testament states that Gloria was born in 1923. Consultation with Gloria's birth certificate was little help, as all that is available is a supplemental report, sates 1/11/1925 — on it, her birth date is May 21, 1924 — however, the absence of the orignal certificate, as well as the legal bindings of the Will, keep the mystery most alive. For posterity, it is important to at least acknowledge the ambiguity.

Mildred Davis and Harold Lloyd were married at St. John's Episcopal Church, 512 West Adams Boulevard, Los Angeles, in a ceremony performed by Rector George Davidson. The official witnesses were Mildred's mother, Caroline Davis, Harold's brother and best man, Gaylord Lloyd, and Mildred's maid of honor, friend Jane Thompson. In a funny coincidence, at the time of her marriage, Mid lived in Los Angeles, at 5443 *Harold Way*. After a honeymoon in San Diego, the Lloyds settled, at first, at 369 S. Hoover Street, along with Foxy, Gaylord, and his son, and then, in 1924, at 502 S. Irving Boulevard, which was their home until 1929, when they settled in Greenacres.

It was not the easiest of unions. The Lloyds' personalities, on the surface, were drastically different. Though the film fan magazines portrayed the marriage as singularly strong amongst the Tinseltown community, it was, in fact, more normal (by Hollywood terms) than the public could have imagined. Harold was much more active

Newborn Mildred Gloria Lloyd with her mother and father, taken in the spring of 1923, around the time HL was finishing the filming of *Why Worry?*.

and lively than Mid, who was more quiet and reserved. Perhaps due to this, and coupled with his being out of the house much more often than she, Harold soon partook of a number of extramarital affairs — most notably with 1923-27 co-star Jobyna Ralston, as well as with subsequent leading ladies, models and starlets, throughout his life. However, breakup of the family was never an option: having come from a broken home, filled with inconsistency

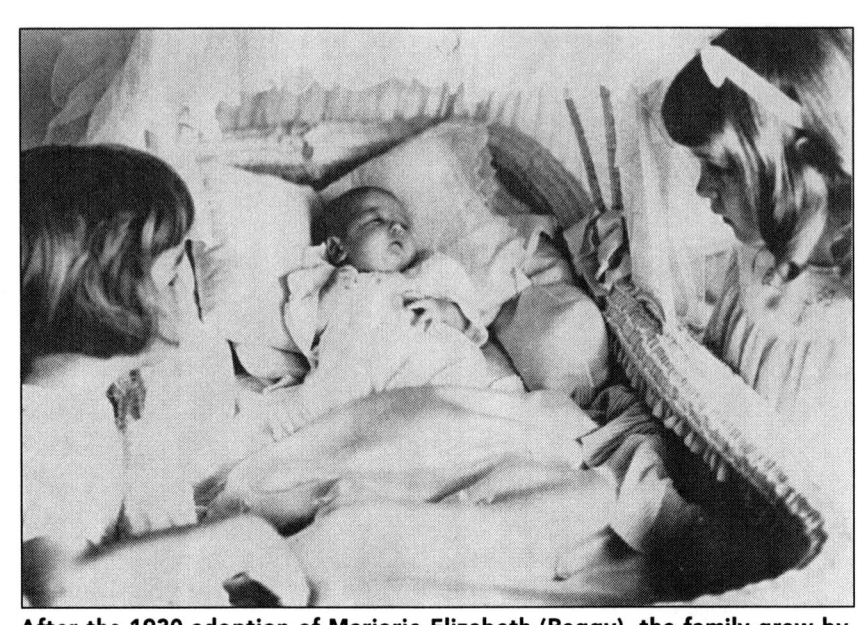

After the 1930 adoption of Marjorie Elizabeth (Peggy), the family grew by one with the 1931 birth of Harold Lloyd, Jr. Here, sisters Peggy (LEFT) and Gloria gaze upon their new baby brother. COURTESY DAVID KALAT.

and instability, Harold was determined not to put his family through the same turmoil — their marriage remained intact, for over 46 years.

Harold and Mildred adopted daughter Marjorie Elizabeth, nicknamed Peggy, on September 2, 1930, after years of trying to have another baby, and numerous miscarriages. Peggy, born Gloria Gabrielle Freeman on April 15, 1925, became the playmate and life mate that Gloria yearned for. "We got along fine. I was just hungry for somebody to love, and to be loved back." [G] However, the family was not complete just yet. As if scripted in a Hollywood think tank, right around the time the three-month trial period for Peggy's adoption began, Mildred became pregnant. Forty-one days after Peggy's adoption became legal, Harold Clayton Lloyd, Jr., was born, on January 25, 1931.

As parents — to Gloria, Peggy, and Harold, Jr. — Harold and Mid were generous to the point of overindulgent. The entire family had the best of everything. Gloria Lloyd, his first-born child, still has very fond memories of her father, even almost four decades after his death. "My dad was not a dictator, but he was a very caring father, and we had to do certain things in a certain way. He would say to us, 'Now girls, there are a couple of things you must do in life. First of all, you must get a good education. Then, you should go and get yourself a little job. Then, there are a couple of other little things — you have to learn words. There is a book called *Thirty Days to a More Powerful Vocabulary* — Funk and Wagnalls — I want you to learn five new words a day. You come in, in the evening, after we have dinner, and tell me what you learned. Another thing you should learn is your times tables. I'll go over it all with you' — and he did. He was there to help us.

"He was not detached. If anything, you detached yourself from him! Oh, we had some arguments about things, but that's all right, it's good — it's family — everyone gets like that. It was normal. I was opinionated, he was opinionated, but our opinions would have to come to an end, so we would make an agreement. And we did: I didn't give in! No, I'd never give in." [G]

Considering the great wealth of the Lloyd family, the children were, at the very least, *introduced* to the value of a buck. Mildred's parents lived down the street from Greenacres and, at 13, Gloria and her friends had a lemonade stand on Benedict Canyon Drive at Angelo Drive. "Grandmother provided the lemons. We girls were dressed in little sundresses with ruffles, looking like little waitresses. We charged a dime a glass. We were making a little money. Well, my mother came to us. 'Now, you girls cannot just keep all this

> **FUN FACT**
>
> MILDRED DAVIS WAS QUOTED IN THE APRIL 7, 1923 ISSUE OF *MOVIE WEEKLY* MAGAZINE, IN AN ARTICLE ENTITLED "WHY HAROLD LLOYD MARRIED MILDRED DAVIS": "THERE WAS ALWAYS SOMETHING NICE ABOUT HIM, SOMETHING CLEVER AND DISTINGUISHED FROM OTHER BOYS, EVEN IN HIS COMEDY MAKE-UP. I USED TO WISH I KNEW HIM . . . AND JUST IMAGINE THAT HE SHOULD HAVE SOUGHT ME OUT AS HIS LEADING LADY, AND NOW I'M HIS WIFE! . . . OH, I DON'T REMEMBER WHEN HAROLD FIRST PROPOSED. HE DID IT TWO OR THREE TIMES. BUT I THINK THE FIRST TIME WAS ONE MOONLIGHT NIGHT AT THE BEACH. I WAS AFRAID IT WAS JUST THE MOON THAT WAS THE MATTER WITH HIM, SO I DIDN'T SAY YES, THAT TIME."

A really beautiful couple — Mr. and Mrs. Harold Lloyd.

money that you say you're making' — maybe it was five dollars. 'You have to give it to the Church.'" [G]

Through the 1920s and 1930s, Harold was quite busy with either acting or producing. Mildred was, essentially, a housewife — she kept close to home, busying herself with friends, gardening, and crafts, yet fighting loneliness and a growing dependency on alcohol. The 1940s home life at Greenacres became one of increasing seclusion and solitude for Mid. With Harold always immersed in either a hobby or various work-related activities, she did not share her husband's propensity for the limelight, and found shelter at home.

Her sporadic, isolated alcoholism cast a melancholy over the house, particularly owing to Harold's teetotaling and non-smoking lifestyle. Heated arguments were common between Harold and Mildred, though the tenderness they felt for each other never waned. The pressures of an often-absent husband and father were omnipresent, but the Lloyds chose to make the best of it, rather than disturb the family unit. Harold and Mid, together, had a sweetness and a love between them that was evident; often, when Harold was away, he would send cards and telegrams to his wife; their love was more comfortable than passionate, more surface than deep, yet their devotion was strong enough to keep them together, needing each other in life and home until Mid's death on August 18, 1969. That, when all is said and done, *is* far superior to today's average Hollywood marital union.

What kind of *father* was Harold Lloyd? "To me, he was the best. And he was so understanding. He was a great humanitarian, too, to people, and I think that rubbed off on family. You could go to him with any question — it was such a comforting feeling. We understood each other very well; we really did. I miss him a lot — he had so many good ideals about living with people, and how to treat them — and he was so cheerful — he was a very cheerful man in the morning." [G]

One memory, however, is most clear and enduring for Harold's eldest child, and it gives us a glimpse of an indulgent father who tried his level best to appear just the opposite: "My 21st birthday. We went shopping, and I wanted a watch, which had little rubies and diamonds on it. We went to Weinstein's, a downtown Los Angeles store at that time. He went in there, and I saw a watch, with a flip-up face. And it was beautiful — it had little rubies and little diamonds, and it was very unusual for that time. And, I imagined it wasn't cheap. I didn't push him for that, but I liked it. Well, he was pretty rough on us about overspending money. He said, 'Well, we'll think about it, and we'll see.' He didn't give me any clue either way. I said, 'Oh, Dad, I really like that watch.' He said, 'Well, it's pretty expensive.' You know, to him, money was something you worked hard for.

"We looked at other watches that day, and I didn't know what I was going to get. So, I opened up my present on my birthday, and

The Greenacres *L'Orangery* was the site of many a family card game — here, Harold does not seem to be headed towards victory against wife Mildred.

there it was! It was in a beautiful box — I still have it — and it was engraved, 'To My Darling, Gloria, I Love You So Much, Your Daddy.'" [G] That diamond and ruby watch is still one of Gloria's most prized possessions, and a most cherished memory.

Unquestionably, the marriage of Harold Lloyd to Mildred Davis, and subsequent fatherhood, was a significant turning point in his life, for it set a clear course for his life from then on. True, it was far from a perfect union, but *is* there a perfect one? Theirs was a marriage and life filled with excess, in many respects, and his parenting style followed suit. But, while one might think of a grand film star as too preoccupied with toys, sniffles and holidays, Harold proved the cynics wrong — he was a strict father, Victorian in many respects, but one with a sight on fun. He was a busy man, but made time for his family, when at home. When you see an enthusiastic Lloyd on screen, know that this was how he was at home — loud, almost-childlike in frivolity, and most lively. I do think that fatherhood was good for him, for, unlike his own father, he *was* able to provide a stable environment for his family, and that was quite satisfactory to Harold.

HAROLD LLOYD RELEASES THE FRESHMAN

The Freshman . . .
"We just couldn't engender that enthusiasm."

"*The Freshman* was a long overdue ship. When I first began to grope about for something better than Lonesome Luke, I had a dim outline in my mind of a college-boy character, but discarded it as too limited in scope. A college picture, even a college series, would be well worth trying, I was convinced, but I did not care to go on being a freshman for life, and that would be the risk. When the glass character finally evolved, I thought of him as of an age and type that could be fitted easily into a college story and intended to make one in one reel, then in two reels. One thing and another sidetracked it; meanwhile, the number of students in colleges and the public interest in college football grew tremendously, and when we did make it at last in seven reels we made it most opportunely." [I]

The Lloyd formula of filmmaking was a great success to this point — he would film the climax of the picture first, and then shoot the prefacing rest of the story (to Harold, a good clincher, a magnificent ending, was primary, and would often times suggest the story line that led to the end). This had been the case with most of the Lloyd features to date. Lloyd began *The Freshman* with this plan in mind: shoot the big game sequence first, and then, assured of a great ending, capture the rest of the film. Build the entire story from its culmination.

"That was your clothes rack, but the clothes were the pieces of business — that's what either made the picture good or just made

Harold Lamb next to his model for collegiate popularity, in the opening of *The Freshman* (1925). The poster was for a fictitious film made by a made-up company – but it incorporated Lloyd's own nickname, Speedy.

it just another routine picture. So then we had to sit in and devise these gags. Now, we didn't just get them all at once, because we would work out a sequence, or a series of sequences, and then we would shoot those, then we would suspend action and come back and work some more. Because we kept changing our story as we went along, and we found out that it worked better to go along a certain story direction, or idea line, why, we would change it. So that would naturally change other things that we did. So our whole story was very, very pliable. In fact, deviating from this particular one, we made many of them where we did the finish first. We did the finish on *Safety Last!* first. We photographed that first. We had an idea of how we were going to do the first part of it, but we weren't sure. But, we did the climb to start with. Of course, we had finished the climb, and we were so gratified with it, because it looked like it had what we were trying for, and then we had tremendous enthusiasm to go back and get the beginning and the middle for it. And we worked up to the climb. Now, we tried that in another picture, called *The Freshman*, which had a football game for the finish. Well, we worked about two days on the football game, and there we just couldn't engender that enthusiasm or that feeling that we should have had in the football game, so we gave it up and went back and, with *The Freshman*, we went back and started from the beginning. In *The Freshman*, practically all we started with was a little one-line scene — that was that the Boy had a great desire to go to college and be the most popular man in school. And we felt that he would get off on the wrong foot, and his father stated, as he left, that they would either break his heart or his neck. And, they almost did both. But, that was the whole thing. The whole thing was that the boy wanted to be the most popular boy in the school, and the difficulties that ensued from that." [A]

This was a complete departure from Lloyd's norm, and marks a turning point in his filmmaking career. He had a formula, a procedure that was extremely successful — however, in starting *The Freshman* as he had every preceding feature, he almost instantly felt that he didn't know his character well enough — did not understand *why* it was so important for Harold "Speedy" Lamb to win the game, and did not have the all-important spirit of the character in him — and feared that the film might suffer as a result. So, Harold shot *The Freshman* in total sequence, from start to finish, and in so doing, thoroughly personified Speedy — this translated into increased motivation for the climactic end of the picture. Here, he changed his *modus operandi* for the good of the character and, in so doing, probably made the picture a better one.

For the "new end," the company traveled to northern California's Berkeley Bowl on November 22, 1924, and shot an actual game between Stanford and the University of California-Berkeley, complete with zealous pom-pom-waving crowds. Lloyd's crew worked before the game and during halftime, with the enthusiastically filled stadium as the backdrop: ". . . we felt very much at home and we had a nice audience of about 90,000 to witness half a dozen of the scenes and we had to work pretty doggone fast there." [L] The final close-up shots, sans crowds in the background, were later shot at an empty Rose Bowl in Pasadena.

The Freshman was one of Harold's four favorites of his films, and with good reason. It got a lot accomplished, particularly from the point of view of its main character, Speedy (which, coincidentally, was Harold's own nickname): "That had an idea was all — the idea was simply that the Boy had an obsession, to go to college and be the most popular boy there, because his idol in that same college had been the year before. The only thing was that he went with the wrong impression of how to go about it. His idea of what to do to be popular was wrong, so it got him into trouble, and that was your whole story." [C]

One main avenue for popularity, in Speedy's mind, was success in football. Owing to the fact that Chet Trask, Speedy's idol, had been both most popular man on campus *and* captain of the football team the year before, Speedy — gridiron neophyte extraordinaire — decided to take on the sport that he barely knew how to play. In the faction involving Speedy doubling for the dilapidated tackling dummy, it was *actually* Lloyd. Dozens of strong men, some professional players and some film extras, lined up to deck him. "When the professional football players tackled me, I didn't feel it because they seemed to know how to tackle without hurting a person. However, when the amateurs hit me, it was really painful. After that scene, I felt sore for a week." [E]

Each of us who starts a new school, a new job, or a new relationship, wants to be liked. But, Speedy took this to the extreme: "In his desire to be the most popular boy, he threw a party. His suit wasn't ready, it was just basted. So he had no choice, he had to wear the suit basted, and the tailor went along in case he'd have trouble — and he did. So the whole party — and that's something we did then that they don't do very often at all — we took one theme and built upon that one theme of his going to a party in a basted suit and all the things that happened to him at the party he was hosting with his clothes coming apart. And it ran for a long

On board a train headed for Tate College, Harold "Speedy" Lamb first encounters Peggy, "the kind of girl your mother must have been," in *The Freshman* (1925). COURTESY BRUCE CALVERT.

sequence — I think it's one of the funniest sequences we ever did." [C] Of course, as we read earlier in our discussion of Harold's use of previews, they *tried* to shoot the Fall Frolic party sequence with Speedy losing only his coat, not his pants, but the result was less than satisfactory. "We had to redress the set, call back the cast . . . and unravel the trousers." [A]

At the beginning of *The Freshman*, we first learn of Harold's desire to be popular at college. The character of Harold Lamb stares longingly at a poster for the fictitious film, "The College Hero," on his door. On the poster, Lester Laurel, the star of the film and Harold's hero, poses by his mantra quote, "I'm just a regular fellow — Step right up and call me Speedy!" Harold adopts the nickname of Speedy from there on. He also decides to use Lester's line, accompanied by the jig Laurel did in the movie, and deliver them each and every time he meets someone new at Tate College.

> **FUN FACT**
>
> According to the text of the infringement trial brought by H.C. Witwer against Harold Lloyd Corporation over *The Freshman*, ". . . over 100,000 feet of film were taken in connection with the play, only 7,000 feet of which was actually used . . . Physical preparation for making the picture started on August 11, 1924, and until October 13, 1924, the day that actual photographing commenced . . . The photographing or 'shooting' of the picture was completed on March 27, 1925."

From that point on, *The Freshman* succeeds in personifying the comedy of embarrassment like, perhaps, no film has ever. Speedy, systematically, is subjected to pranks, humiliation, degradation, and eventually to poverty, at the hands of both fellow students and faculty. Each time he is thrown to the ground (figuratively *and* literally), he picks himself up, dusts himself off, starts all over again, and is thrown down anew. It is hard not to cringe when you see all the things that happen to Speedy in his quest for the golden ring of popularity — and this might be the only contemporary negative that can be said of Harold's college comedy.

In this film, as in conceivably no other, Lloyd may have paid the highest price for his characters' reflection of his audiences. Harold Lloyd, as opposed to most of his contemporaries, is a veritable chronicle of the Roaring Twenties — filled with ambition and overall positivism, a really regular fellow in look and demeanor, lacking the eccentricities and quirks of other characters. Yet, think about the sequence in which his Fall Frolic suit was not yet completed, but was just cursorily sewn together. In this day and age, a fellow could have easily said, "Oh, well, my suit isn't ready; I'll wear jeans and a tee-shirt, and I'll get by." And, he probably would. But, not in the 1920s — decorum, correctness and style were law. Lloyd's character forged ahead, and wore the delicate duds — and, as a result, was subjected to the highest form of mortification: his suit's disintegration before the entire student body. In 1925, men in the audience fully understood

Joseph Harrington (right) portrayed an alcohol-addicted tailor who only had time to lightly baste Speedy's suit in *The Freshman* (1925). The undoing of the stitches caused some of the most jovial laughs — and a prime sting in the comedy of embarrassment — that this film offers.

Speedy's *need* to wear the suit, even though it was just basted; today, the mere thought of it makes one squirm. Sequences like this, and the other Speedy knock-downs, are closer to outright satire of social conventions than Lloyd had ever tried; however, the film is not satirical. Lloyd's character conforms to his environment, convincing us — by persevering — that the misery he is undergoing is worth all the trouble. Yet, there is a fine line — in subjecting your character to too much ridicule — between inspiring your audience to root for your character, or pity him.

Ultimately, those of us who were born after 1925 are very fortunate that we can see this film at all. Read on, and learn why we are lucky that this film survived a landmark legal ruling . . .

Harold and his uncle, business manager William R. Fraser, had a pre-filming luncheon at the Armstrong Café on Hollywood Boulevard with producer and friend H.C. Witwer, and had mentioned the premise for their college picture. Witwer outlined

The sumptuous Fall Frolic sequence in *The Freshman* (1925) was filmed on a set, but was treated like an actual party – many of HL's friends and family attended, and thus can be seen frolicking on the dance floor.

for them the coincidental plot of his *Popular Magazine* article, "The Emancipation of Rodney." Witwer had sold the story to the magazine on August 27, 1915, and the tale appeared in the November 20, 1915 issue. While alike in many respects, the crux of the 1915 story was a magic formula that the college athlete had perfected that guaranteed victory. When Lloyd and Fraser relayed that story line to their gag crew, it was agreed that the idea would not make good film, and their *The Freshman* continued on as planned. After the fact, it was thought a good idea to invite Witwer to the studio to alleviate any possible controversy, and allay any thought that the Lloyd team had used any of Witwer's story in their new film. It was believed that meeting would smooth over any potential ill-will; that is, until the money started rolling in. The casual naïveté with which Lloyd and Fraser dealt with the issue proved to be very costly: on April 11, 1929, Witwer sued Harold Lloyd Corporation for infringement. H.C. Witwer died on August 9, 1929, but his widow, Sadie, pressed on. On July 9, 1930, judgment was in favor of Witwer, and a bulk of the profits of *The Freshman* was handed over to the widow. However, an appeal followed, and a reversal was

Harold "Speedy" Lamb is about to lose most of his college fund, in this sequence from *The Freshman* (1925). The filmed scene that followed — in the ice cream parlor — was later scrapped after previews, due to a lack of laughs over Speedy's dire predicament.

rendered by the Ninth Circuit Court of Appeals on April 10, 1933.

Interestingly, H.C. Witwer tried much earlier to sue Lloyd. On December 26, 1925, Witwer brought some kind of action in the Los Angeles County Superior Court, but the action was dismissed: when Witwer sold "The Emancipation of Rodney" for $75 to *Popular Magazine* on August 27, 1915, he sold the story *and* all rights in it. Years later, on February 13, 1929, the sole legal ownership of the story was handed over, by written agreement, back to Witwer. Two months later, with Witwer now free to pursue a ton of potential money, Lloyd's ordeal began.

In the trial phase, most of those involved in the production of *The Freshman* were called to testify. It was important for Lloyd Corporation personnel to stress the ad-lib nature of the building of the Lloyd pictures. During co-director Fred Newmeyer's testimony, it was revealed that, on all Lloyd's films, the titles were made up

The final moments of the big football game, and the resultant celebration, in *The Freshman* (1925) were filmed at the Rose Bowl in Pasadena, California — no spectators witnessed these pivotal gridiron shots; the stadium was empty. COURTESY PAUL E. GIERUCKI.

after the picture was completed (including explanatory matter and dialogue). He also stated that, right after *Safety Last!* wrapped, the initial idea for a college comedy crystallized. Plans were even made for the camera crew to get some stock footage of a football game; then, according to Newmeyer, ". . . They had a chance to get this great big giant, and the stock stuff was put away," and *Why Worry?* was born. However, most intriguing was the following testimony of Newmeyer regarding the Lloyd company's method of preparation of the story: ". . . Shooting it 'from the cuff,' was typical of all of Lloyd's stories up to that time. No schedule. Harold surrounded himself from the beginning of *Grandma's Boy* with the best available gag men. He never believed in a scenario; in fact, if he did have a scenario, he would never follow it." According to Newmeyer, Lloyd once asked him, "'Do you think I would gain anything by shooting from a scenario?' I said, 'No, you would just waste your time and throw it away,' because he won't follow one of those things; if he did go out there, he would change it on you; he couldn't do it, it is impossible."

It was revealed, later in the 1933 appeal phase paperwork, that in the initial 1930 infringement finding, Harold Lloyd Corporation was prohibited from further distribution or exhibition of the picture, and that all prints of *The Freshman* were ordered destroyed. In addition, the Corporation was to pay to Mrs. H.C. Witwer all profits directly or indirectly received from the film from April 11, 1926 on (three years prior to the commencement of the initial suit). The appeal that followed was in Lloyd's favor, returning all money to Lloyd, and saving *The Freshman* from perpetual destruction.

Thus, we can consider ourselves very lucky to have had the chance to meet Harold "Speedy" Lamb, at all.

When *The Freshman* was re-issued in 1960, it was shown with a prologue by Harold Lloyd. Dissolving from a close-up on a pair of horn-rimmed glasses, Harold appeared on screen to share the following introduction: "Hello! I remember a few years ago . . . taking a pair of glasses and creating what we called the 'Glass Character.' Now, among the many pictures that we produced with this character, there are some that seem to have a spirit that ignores the time barrier. I believe that the picture that we are going to show now is one of these. Of course, it was made long before many of you were born. Before pictures began to talk. It was in an era that we affectionately called The Roaring Twenties. It was the time of the Model-T and the Flapper and the Charleston. Prohibition of alcoholic beverages was the law of the land. And, of course, kidding around, it was the national pastime. There have been lots of changes since then . . . but there is one thing that hasn't changed. That's the spirit of youth! Its hopes, its humor, and its unfailing courage! And it's to that spirit that we dedicate this picture!"

HAROLD'S RISE WITH THE SHRINERS

The Rajah . . .
"That has been one of the great pleasures I have had."

It might be hard to believe that joining a club can change a person's life. Yet, it can happen, and when we fully understand Harold Lloyd's 46 years in the Ancient Arabic Order of the Nobles of the Mystic Shrine, or the Shriners, we can see that joining this organization, as he and his father did in 1925, so greatly enhanced Harold that it must be classified as one of the supreme turning points in his life.

> *"Shrinedom has given me a greater appreciation of what it means to be an American. In the Shrine, I have found myself surrounded by men full of the joy of living, men of hope and optimism and understanding."*
> —Harold Lloyd, June 1950

In his second year as a Shriner, Harold joined the Al Malaikah Temple, with headquarters near the campus of the University of Southern California — non-members will know this home, the Shrine Auditorium, as the site of such events as the Academy Awards, the Grammy Awards, and the American Ballet Theater. Harold became a life member of the Al Malaikah Temple on October 25, 1926; within 13 years, he was the head, or Potentate, of his Temple.

"By going to the Shrine, I have met so many wonderful people; really, you meet a cross-section of what really represents America.

Prior to an outdoor luncheon at the yet-to-be-completed Greenacres, HL poses with his friend and social secretary, Roy Brooks. This photo was taken on August 22, 1928.

You see how wonderful a country this is. Because going to these different cities, and through the Shrine, meeting them on a different ground from what you would ordinarily do, with a certain intimacy, you really find out the qualities of what this country is made up of." [A]

In the 1940s, Harold, owing to his status as an internationally renowned celebrity, began to rise within the national organization — without question, this was a supreme benefit for the Shriners, which had seen its membership numbers decrease through the Depression years. Harold's visibility and instant recognition factor was a huge boost for the group. On July 21, 1949, 56-year-old Harold was elected Imperial Potentate of the Shriners, the highest

HL in 1949. The five stars underneath the Shrine emblem on HL's fez signify his stature as the national head, or Imperial Potentate.

national office; he retired on June 22, 1950.

"The Imperial Potentate is head of all Shrinedom. He is elected for one year. He makes visitations to practically every principal city in the United States, in Canada, in the Hawaiian Islands and in Mexico. Of course, he has to preside over meetings, and do many things along that line. But you give practically your full year to the Shrine, which is one of the greatest organizations in the world. And it is a marvelous work — and I'll be furthering that during the year, and very happy to be doing it." [B]

It was around 1942 that Lloyd spearheaded plans for a charity that captured him for the rest of his life: the Shriners' Hospitals for Children. His own 1919 bomb accident rendered him especially concerned with the burn unit, which he helped add to the Shriners' care system in the mid-1960s. "They are responsible for one of the world's finest philanthropies: they have these marvelous hospitals, all over North America, that do nothing but cure little crippled children. And that's without regard to race, creed or color. No discriminating at all. And it's 100% charitable — the Shrine does not seek aid outside; it's all done by the Shrine. And the Nobility — which the Shrine is called — that's one of the things they look with great pride upon doing." [B]

By July 1963, Harold was elected Chairman of the Hospital Board of Trustees. He accepted the post while in France, and spent the rest of his life working tirelessly on behalf of this charity as Chairman of the Board. So much so that granddaughter Suzanne, who was raised by Harold, knew her grandfather professionally as a hospital administrator, only to find out later that he was a legendary film star.

> **FUN FACT**
>
> During his one-year term, Los Angeles hosted the 1950 Shrine Convention, and held a million-dollar electrical pageant in the Los Angeles Coliseum. At the convention, Lloyd discussed his belief in the organization:
>
> "I am a Shriner," he said, "because I believe in the ideals on which the Shrine was founded . . . We believe in the brotherhood of man, and in the dignity of the individual. We believe it is the function of government to preserve the rights and freedoms of the individual. We oppose an ideology that seeks to degrade human beings. We oppose any philosophy that declares the police state to be the highest human social achievement, and which would invade the sacred sanctuary of a man's conscience where only God may enter as judge."

The Al Malaikah temple of the Ancient Arabic Order of the Nobles of the Mystic Shrine was headed by Imperial Officer Harold Lloyd in 1940.

Being a member of the Shriners, truly, was one of the most rewarding aspects of Harold Lloyd's life. He greatly appreciated the opportunities the organization gave him — the chance to belong to something worthwhile, and the prospect of participation in the charities that the group supported. Joining the Shrine was one of the happiest and most meaningful turning points of his life.

"That has been one of the great pleasures I have had. It's a magnificent organization; I think a third of our Presidents have been Shriners. I was the national head of it. I think their philanthropy is one of the greatest that is done any place at any time. It's a great altruism." [C]

Harold Lloyd Releases The Kid Brother

The Kid Brother . . .
"I'm the little puny fellow."

The New York Herald Tribune, in its January 25, 1927 issue, stated, "All of Lloyd's other pictures have been perfect and so is *The Kid Brother.*"

The January 29, 1927 issue of *The Moving Picture World* wrote, "Technically this is the best piece of work Lloyd has done. It should prove one of his great successes with any audience."

The Boston Herald, in its February 1, 1927 review, raved: "Where, oh, where does Mr. Lloyd find all his gags, rare, snortingly funny gags that trip upon each other's heels they come so fast and are so spicingly amusing."

Consistently, across the nation, praise was heaped upon Lloyd and company for this, his indubitable masterpiece, his most technically and artistically beautiful film, and your author's personal favorite.

Lloyd called *The Kid Brother* "an idea we had been holding since the Roach lot." [I] In it, "I have a father and two older brothers who are behemoths, and I'm the little puny fellow, the boy that thinks and, in the end, outwits the ones that just use their muscles." [J] A film that *The Kid Brother* greatly resembles in plot and character is the dramatic *Tol'able David* (1921), starring Richard Barthelmess, directed by Henry King. Both films center around mountain folk, a young sibling longing for acceptance, and a nostalgic slice of Americana. (For Barthelmess, as young David, this was a breakthrough role; one that is still, perhaps, his most

Following the medicine show fire, and as rain poured down outside, Harold Hickory's brothers Leo (Leo Willis, left) and Olin (Olin Francis, right) endure a outdoor soaking as their kid brother serves hot coffee and bread to Mary Powers (Jobyna Ralston). From *The Kid Brother* (1927).

memorable. *Tol'able David* was noticed, and admired, by Lloyd: he cast one of its three outlaws, Ralph Yearsley, in the role of the town bully, Hank Hooper.) The two films differ, however, in that *The Kid Brother* managed to tell a rural story of the same poignancy, action, and victory as did *Tol'able David*, but with a delightfully humorous twist.

The Kid Brother marked Jobyna Ralston's final appearance as Harold's leading lady, Lloyd's last characterization of an innocent country boy, and his last film set in a rural environment. Some of Lloyd's finest films, which featured a rural setting, were set as far from the big city as possible. Donkeys, horses, bad guys, trees, wooden ramshackles, and the ten-gallon hat predominated in such Western comedies as *Two-Gun Gussie* (1918), *The City Slicker* (1918), *An Ozark Romance* (1918), *Billy Blazes, Esq.* (1919), and *An Eastern Westerner* (1920). Lloyd took a gentler rural approach, particular to the central character, in the classic features *Grandma's Boy* (1922) and *The Kid Brother*.

The central premise of this film — the young dreamer craving to prove himself — is similar to many other Lloyd films, before and

Shooting *The Kid Brother* (1927) at Catalina Island in 1926. Seated at farthest left is the film's assistant director, HL's brother, Gaylord Lloyd.

after. But it is *how* Lloyd accomplished this eight-reel wonder that makes *The Kid Brother* a cinematic turning point, beautiful, witty and amazing.

One of the most poignant moments in this film, which is resplendent with warm beauty, occurred after the medicine show burned to the ground, rendering Mary Powers (Ralston) homeless. As she watched the final remnants of the show melt away, she sat upon a wicker box, in which Harold Hickory hid from his father (for inadvertently causing the chain of events that led to the fire). When she got him out of the box, she let down her guard and emotionally collapsed in Harold's arms. She cried — her tears fell, one by one, onto Harold's hand. Slowly, at first, and then in massive doses, the drops soaked his hand — he continued to snuggle closely as his hand became drenched. He looked at her, utterly amazed at how many tears she could cry: then he realized that it had begun to rain, and that her sorrow had not inspired that particular downpour. This was one of those lovely, quiet moments that this film is so famed for: and it is doubtful whether anyone can watch it with a totally dry eye.

The goodbye scene between Harold, Mary, and that wonderful tree, was accomplished in extraordinary fashion. Leading up to the scene, Mary had been frightened by the medicine show strong man, Sandoni (Constantine Romanoff), and encountered Harold in her attempts to flee her assailant. Harold scares off Sandoni with a stick that, unbeknownst to Harold, held a snake. Harold is both surprised and inwardly proud to have frightened the heavy; when he realizes that what actually scared Sandoni was the snake, Harold is dejected, and throws the reptile-ridden stick away. Mary, upon first glance of the slithering snake, jumps into Harold's arms: it is love at first sight. Harold gently returns Mary to the ground and, after some conversation, they say their goodbyes. The scene could have satisfactorily ended there, but in true Lloyd fashion, the topper must be topped; more magic was up the sleeve. Mary walks off and Harold watches as she disappears over the crest of the mountain. He runs to a tree, and begins to climb to keep his lady love in view.

I've often thought that, *if a man ever did that for me, I'd faint.* Yes, Harold Lloyd *was* an effective romantic comedy leading man.

Watch the sequence, and think about this: the ascent would have lost much of its effectiveness had it been captured simply via camera tilt. Maintaining the camera at an even level with Lloyd — rising as he rose, and preserving contact with his emotions and motivations — made the entire faction all the more effective and touching. Cinematographer Walter Lundin's employment of a camera-upon-elevator effect, used so elegantly in *The Kid Brother*, was actually first executed by D.W. Griffith's crew in *Intolerance* (1916) — however, Lundin conceived the use of this technique purely because of its benefit to the sequence, and as an aid to the story and the character. After *The Kid Brother* was released in January 1927, its technical ingenuity was copied by others — in very similar fashion to the inspiring camera work in *Girl Shy* — two films that utilized the upwardly moving camera technique were Frank Borzage's *Seventh Heaven* (1927) and Buster Keaton's *The Cameraman* (1928).

To make all of this look as good as it did, Lundin utilized the relatively new technology of panchromatic film, which rendered colors (even in a black and white film) more vividly represented by shades of gray, making everything look clearer and richer. It is very important to recognize cinematography when celebrating good film — without Walter Lundin, Lloyd would not have, as a general rule, looked as good.

And, without good directing, the best of films will no doubt flop. However, the number of directors who helmed *The Kid Brother* is staggering, one of a kind for a Lloyd film. Lewis Milestone (who would later direct the 1930 classic *All Quiet on the Western Front*) was the original director on the picture, back when it was still known by its working title, "The Mountain Boy." Milestone, though, could not stay with the Lloyd project, due to contractual problems with Warner Bros.: he asked that his name not appear in the credits of the final product, since he did not participate in the post-production work or in the editing room. Ted Wilde assumed the directorial duties, until he came down with pneumonia in November 1926. J.A. Howe, a Lloyd gag man, and Lex Neal (co-director of childhood pal Buster Keaton's 1925 film *Go West*) took over. Both Wilde and Howe are given on-screen credit for direction; Wilde, however, is given sole credit as director in the film's copyright paperwork.

Without a good cast, no film can thrive. And we're not just talking *human* cast here: little did Lloyd and co-star Constantine Romanoff know, but Harold and Sandoni were to be outclassed by a simian cohort in one of the film's most exciting sequences on an abandoned ship. Harold, after being knocked out by Hank Hooper and left for dead aboard a row boat, comes to and boards the massive ship The Black Ghost — his zeal to mount builds after realizing that bad guys Sandoni and Flash (Eddie Boland) have stashed the town's stolen dam fund money aboard the vessel. (Their pet monkey [Chicago] threw down a piece of paper from the ship to Harold — a Medicine Show Announcement — which tipped Harold off and proved that the thieves, along with Hickoryville's dam fund, were most likely aboard ship.) Harold quietly climbs aboard, just in time to witness Sandoni killing Flash (who had tried to split the loot a tad unevenly, in his own favor). Harold hides in a locker, but the monkey finds him. Sandoni is in a nearby room — suddenly, he hears footsteps up on the deck. He rapidly follows the sound — you can almost hear it yourself. In the meantime, Harold retrieves the stolen money. What the audience knows, but Sandoni

HL with his talented simian cohort Chicago aboard "The Black Ghost" in *The Kid Brother* (1927). This monkey headed one of the finest directed and executed scenes ever presented in a Lloyd film.

doesn't, is that Harold placed his own shoes on the monkey, who then gingerly climbed the stairs up to the top deck, producing the footsteps, and thus distracting the villain. The moments surrounding Sandoni's following of the pitters and the patters were brilliantly timed, spaced and directed: every time Sandoni attempted to surprise the stepper, the monkey had just gone out of sight. It goes to show you one benefit directors had before sound technology: with the monkey's movements as the lead, the director could yell

Harold Hickory retrieving Hickoryville's "dam fund" in *The Kid Brother* (1927). Sandoni (Constantine Romanoff) has his hands up, but does not yet know that the gun barrel-like object in the window is just a well-positioned copper pipe.

out and *perfectly* time Romanoff's moves, resulting in split-second timing of each hilarious moment. Finally, thinking he is about to nab Harold, Sandoni positions himself around a corner, arms outstretched — only to look down and find the monkey wearing shoes and scurrying by him. Truly, this is one sequence that defies explanation — it has to be seen to be fully appreciated — this was one of the best directed and executed factions Lloyd and his crew ever conceptualized.

Fun Fact

Exploitation and advertising for the films was in high gear, and rare form, during the time Lloyd's *The Kid Brother* was released in early 1927. Paramount, the distributor of the picture, made some suggestions for, as they would say, "Putting It Over Right." This was another way of saying, Getting People Into the Theatres. Some of their ideas:

"A contest in which persons of all ages can participate is the following suggested 'Word Contest." Through the medium of your newspaper, or special circular, announce a KID BROTHER WORD CONTEST, informing the public that the theatre will award ten passes to those ten persons who can submit the longest and neatest list of words that they can form out of the letters in the title, 'THE KID BROTHER,' using each letter but once in a word. Arrange the above contest, so that its conclusion comes on the day preceding the opening of the picture."

A suggestion for a lobby exhibit: "Place a satchel of money on display, with sign — "THIS SATCHEL CONTAINS ONLY A PORTION OF THE MONEY FOUND BY 'THE KID BROTHER.' See how he finds it — INSIDE. Decorate with stage money, etc."

One suggestion for an exploitation stunt was called "THE KID BROTHER Identification Contest," in which newspaper photographers ran around snapping pictures of male youngsters for publication in the paper. "Another angle on 'The Kid Brother' contest would be to obtain photos of prominent citizens when they were youngsters. With each set of photos published in the newspaper give a complete list of the names in the contest, the readers to fit the names of the group to the photos. A suitable caption might be: FAMOUS KID BROTHERS IN CENTERVILLE. DO YOU KNOW THEM?"

Two film trailers were produced for *The Kid Brother*. One was the Service Trailer, containing typical shots from the film, 90 feet in length (approximately one minute of air time, with film cranked at 24 frames per second). The De Luxe Trailer was 200 feet long (a bit over two minutes at 24 fps), had "marvelous art titles," and "carefully selected scenes showing the drama and thrills of the film."

Constantine Romanoff appeared in five Lloyd features from 1926-1938. He turned to acting after being blackballed from his first career, as a professional wrestler.

In that portion of the film, Lloyd and his team decided to let the audience know that it was the monkey, wearing Harold's shoes, that Sandoni was hearing. Therein lies one of the most crucial tests in comedy — whether to let the audience in on the joke, or surprise them. In *The Kid Brother*, Lloyd exercised both sides of that coin, with equally fine results. As ever, the generation of maximum laughs was always the goal. Every once in a while, however, a scene — and how to screen it — would stump Harold. One such sequence in *The Kid Brother*, involving the mutual pursuits of Harold and Sandoni, proved a puzzlement . . .

"This big fellow — we were having a fight — he was trying to kill me and nearing that objective." [L] "This one piece of business was a bracket, an iron bracket that was fastened to the side of the ship. One part was fastened to the ship and then there was a prong that came out. Well, he grabbed me and in my getting away from him I went up against the ship and this iron bracket fit right into my hair on top of my head — you couldn't see it. So, he had one of these iron belaying pins, and he came over and grabbed me by the chest, and with his other hand he had this iron pin, and of course he wanted to crush my skull so he hit me over the head with it. Well, of course, he didn't hit my head, he hit this iron pin that was into my hair, and of course he didn't know it. And he gives me this terrific blow, and all I do is blink my eyes. And he can't imagine what's happened. So he hits again. And again I don't do anything — it should have killed me. Of course, I get away then, and as I get away and run, the audience sees why I wasn't hurt — that he was hitting a big iron. Now, one thing was to see me thrown into that position and let the audience know that the iron was up there, and that he didn't know what it was, but they did, and the other one was to surprise both the audience and the assailant. We previewed that both ways, and in this particular one they both got laughs. But we thought the surprise had a little the best." [E] "The surprise is feasible here for two reasons: The action is fast and the blows are funny in themselves. Thus the audience is alert and already laughing when overtaken by the unexpected denouement." [I] "But sometimes that doesn't work. Sometimes one is three times the laughs that the other one is — and you never can tell whether it's the surprise or the way of letting

The brute Sandoni (Constantine Romanoff) holds the iron belaying pin that he *thought* would crush Harold's skull in *The Kid Brother* (1927). The execution of that scene provided one of the heartiest surprises in any Lloyd film.

the audience know what's happening. So it's all different things in making a picture that you can never set iron-clad rules on." [E]

The scenes taken in and around the water, involving Harold and Sandoni, are downright exciting, tense and at times scary. Not only was the action thrilling, but the difference in stature between Harold Lloyd and Constantine Romanoff provided quite the contrast. Lloyd, five feet ten inches in height and weighing around 170 pounds, looked rather hopeless next to the towering Romanoff, a former professional wrestler whose tall, trim frame held massive and burly muscles, covered by a broad-shouldered and brutish appearance. Romanoff had a reputation as a domineering opponent who, in the words of Howard Angus of the *Los Angeles Times*, "uses [his legs] like most wrestlers their hands." Lloyd might have been intimidated by his screen opponent's wrestling acumen, but he told his co-star not to hold back in their celluloid fisticuffs: as a result, their fight is effective and very physical.

Harold eventually conquers the churlish brute — not because of a punch or a kick, but because Sandoni can't swim, and Harold succeeds in getting him into the water in the hull of the ship. This, in and of itself, was thrilling — that Harold could have possibly conquered Sandoni — and proved downright inspiring to audiences. As Harold noted, "I'm the little puny fellow, the boy that thinks and, in the end, outwits the ones that just use their muscles." It was a great lesson, in a great film — Lloyd's true technical, artistic and sentimental masterpiece.

And, of course, knowing that, at the end of Harold Lloyd's life, the film he traveled with and exhibited more than any other was *The Kid Brother* — well, that secures this well-loved picture as a true and enduring turning point for its star, as well as a perennial treat for its lucky viewers.

BUILDING GREENACRES

Bliss . . .
"This is our home."

"Traveling for pleasure has been denied me, but money is a means to most ends eventually and, once my wages passed the margin of ordinary living expenses, money became an ambition. Not only money for its own sake, which I do not pretend to despise, but money as a measure of achievement . . .

"About the time my salary jumped from $150 to $300 a week I set up that good old destination of $100,000 as a goal. One hundred thousand dollars used to be another way of saying independence . . .

"Success had been a long time on the road, but, when it did arrive, it came with such a cumulative rush that the $100,000 nest egg was laid before the nest was warm . . .

"An income of considerably more than $50,000 a year to-day requires no vast labor to manage nor ingenuity to get rid of . . .

"The first true luxury I ever allowed myself was a swimming pool at the Hoover Street home in my single days . . . There is no swimming pool or other luxury about our present home; there will be, however, in our new place in Benedict Canyon, Beverly Hills.

"We have been conservative in everything so far except this new home, and we have tried, though with little success, to be conservative in this. I have the good judgment of my business manager, Mr. Fraser, to thank for owning the property — sixteen acres of the old Benedict ranch, including the home site." [I]

Groundbreaking day in 1926. HL joins wife Mildred and daughter Gloria, along with key family members and architectural staff, to watch the acres become a little greener. Harold took a break from filming *The Kid Brother* to witness this momentous event.

In 1923, William R. Fraser, Harold's maternal uncle, suggested that Harold purchase ten acres of an old ranch owned by Colonel Edson A. Benedict. Both Mary Pickford and Joe Schenck had desired the property, but Benedict wouldn't sell: eventually, when he changed his mind, Lloyd won the site, valued at $60,000. Later, he added six acres to the lot, having purchased the property of the late Thomas Ince, who had built in the canyon just above the original ten acres. The Benedict home was remodeled, and Harold's mother, Elizabeth, lived in it for two years.

The Harold Lloyd family became a trio with the birth of daughter Gloria — then living in a lovely white home on Irving Boulevard in Hancock Park, southeast of Hollywood — and the crystallization of Greenacres slowly formed. What resulted was a sixteen-acre triumph of the wonders of technology and imagination, a thing of magnificence, a veritable fairy tale, with Harold himself as the scenarist.

The architectural firm of Webber, Staunton, and Spaulding, A.I.A., comprised of Field Staunton, Jr., and Sumner Maurice Spaulding, offices at 627 South Carondelet Street in Los Angeles,

A sketched rendering of the layout of Greenacres. Ten of the acres to the right of the house, including the pool, lagoon, golf course and canoe course, were subdivided after the estate was auctioned — now, private homes grace that area, comprising what is now known as Greenacres Drive.

was chosen to design the Lloyd home on the Benedict Canyon property, with A.E. Hanson hired as the landscape architect. "After a year of consultation, planning and revising, we scrapped the first draft entirely. We wanted no formality. Our architect designed an Italian Renaissance house, formal and growing progressively more so." [I]

However, the first order of building business was the completion of Gloria's playhouse, a miniature thatched roof cottage with every "amenity": a working kitchen and bathroom, with running water, lowered ceilings (Gloria was only four at the time) and playrooms. "The only mistake they made was the bathroom. They didn't have a potty in there — we had to go down to the tennis court — it just had a little sink. The bedroom was fine, but the kitchen, as we grew, got a little small. We would have movies screened — Felix the Cat, Mickey Mouse — we were always doing something creative." [G]

The main house on the estate was indeed a mansion — 32,000 square feet, with 44 rooms — its size was just short of an acre itself.

Finishing this structure first was a wise choice, allowing Mother and Father the piece of mind of knowing Daughter had a safe place to play amidst the hustle and bustle of construction.

Daughter Gloria surely appreciated this venue during what was a turbulent time in the life of a young girl. "When I left there, and went back to the Irving Boulevard house, I was so lonely. The little house — I thought it was so beautiful, but I lost my friends when we moved. It was kind of scary for me. I used to sit with a little pink tutu, and a little crown, and my dolls, and I would sit at little tables, and my dolls and I would entertain each other — I was very lonely." [G]

While Lloyd was in New York during mid-1927 (filming *Speedy*), the architects were hard at work. In a letter to Harold, dated September 29, 1927, Spaulding reported, "The house itself is well started and the pavilion at the pool is being framed. Although the hill still looks as if some great calamity had struck it, it is encouraging to see the house grow."

The initial vision for the landscaping was a definite reflection of Harold's roots, natural, beautiful, and self-sustaining. A large driveway wound through the grounds (resembling a large upside-down question mark), leading to the walled forecourt of the house, boasting a large stone fountain. This fountain was inspired by one in

The first edifice completed at Greenacres was Gloria's playhouse – a miniature thatched roof cottage befitting a cinematic princess. There she safely played while construction bustled around her.

Viterbo, Italy, the small town made famous by the Villa Lante. The reinforced concrete walls of the house, inspired by the Villa d'Este in Rome, were stuccoed a warm grayish-tan, with trim in stone. The forecourt, with the fountain as its centerpiece, gave ample space for several cars' parking. The simple area was always bordered by many flower pots of various sizes and colors, as was the fountain and gardens and terraces. The bell tower atop the home was a gift from King Alphonso of Spain, and Mildred commissioned the statue of Peter Pan in the central court. Happily, this masterpiece of a home still stands, and will endure, having been named to the National Register of Historic Places on February 9, 1984.

Greenacres boasted seven separate gardens, with each garden section interconnected by extensive arbors, lawns and cutting beds; twelve major fountains (daughter Gloria was married by the fountain on the great lawn in 1950); a one hundred foot waterfall with a canoe lake and a mill pond below; a 250,000 gallon Olympic sized (85' long by 40' wide) green and white tiled swimming pool (one of the largest in Beverly Hills, which cost over $400 a month to

The hand-carved circular oak staircase balustrade, seen as one entered Greenacres, was an award winner.

heat; according to daughter Gloria, Harold could swim the length of the pool totally underwater). All water was supplied by a 50,000 gallon reservoir of spring water located under the house. In that pool, such aquatic legends as Johnny Weissmuller and Buster Crabbe gave the Lloyd children swimming lessons, which Harold photographed through windows for capturing underwater scenes. The pool was adjoined by a Pavilion area, which was used for lavish nighttime summer parties and film screenings, with its own

One of twelve fountains on the estate, this one has the distinction of boasting Harold's monogram, along with the year they moved in (1929) designed in stones around the base.

bandstand and bar facilities. Completely surrounded by terra cotta ceramic tile, the Pavilion boasted a lovely ornamental iron fence, and housed numerous varieties of fragrant and extensive plants and flowers. Two men were responsible for maintaining the swimming pool and tennis court, there were sixteen full-time gardeners, and there were two chauffeurs. The estate held the nine-hole "Safety Last" golf course, named after Harold's thrill comedy.

To describe the home — its elegance, its beauty, its magnificence — is a study in superlatives. The property was just under 16 total

The dining room at Greenacres: the city line ran through this room, meaning that half of it was in Los Angeles, and half in Beverly Hills.

acres, 12 of which were within Beverly Hills and 4 within the City of Los Angeles (the boundary line ran through the dining room: it is said that Mildred best enjoyed dining in Beverly Hills, sending Harold to Los Angeles — the *other* end of the table — to dine). The mansion — 32,000 square feet, forty-four rooms — was just short of an acre wide itself. In the main house, there were two cooks, two butlers, two governesses, three maids, and three personal secretaries, all presided over by the chief housekeeper.

"We had a basement, the first floor, the second floor — the second floor was a mole hole, and it was just one room, for one of the servants — and that's all. We had an elevator to get to the second floor — they wanted to build another floor — and Dad said, 'Listen here, I'm not running a hotel! I don't want any more levels!'

"We didn't have thousands of bedrooms. It was spaced out — we had a lot of acreage. We had upstairs rooms, and most of them had porches — these were regular rooms. The blue room, the green room. My mother's little boudoir — they were all connecting rooms." [G]

A majestic hall in Greenacres, complete with one of a kind antiques, hand-sewn tapestries, priceless art, and exquisite tile flooring.

Entry into the home with its towering 16-foot ceiling and its magnificent circular hand-carved oak staircase balustrade, designed in wrought iron, gives a sincere feeling of grandeur (it was given the Honor Award by the Southern California Chapter of the American Institute of Architects in 1930). A handsome paneled elevator gives additional access to the upper level. The 50-foot long sunken living room accents this feeling of elegance, with coffered ceiling of gold leaf, intricate paneling, and a stone fireplace. Behind a wall of carved wood columns is a complete 35mm projection booth. At the other end of the living room is a 40-rank Aeolian theater pipe organ. A magnificent fireplace, one of fourteen in the house, dominates the formal dining room. Harold's library, which was built with a hidden dumb-waiter (ever the thoughtful teetotaler, Lloyd was mindful of Prohibition with this feature), still boasts the elaborately carved heavy wood desk that he used. "He put a lot of money away. He had that feeling — if you make your money, save it. In his desk, he would put money away — after he died, we found thousands of dollars in coins, in desks, in walls." [G]

"The sun room — the *Orangery* — was painted by an Italian man, Mr. Durante. It was a beautiful room." [G] The 20' by 40' Sun Room was the site of Lloyd's famed Christmas tree which stood, year-round, from 1965 until 1975. "Let's get this established. First place, to do what I do, you've got to be a nut. Of course, most comedians are nuts. We've been doing this for about 15 years. Most of the ornaments are imports, a lot of them were made for us. It's really two trees in one. We cut limbs off other trees and put them in here, and they're all bambooed and strung up. And, last year's tree, we put it up in December and took down the following December. Generally, we only leave them up for only a couple of months afterwards. We intend to take this down, but somehow, it just seems to be staying up." [D] The name of the room, *L'Orangery*, was inspired by the hand-painted ceiling of indigenous plants, flowers, leaves, and a couple of parrots. The completion of the painting has a humorous tinge: after several years of painstaking work, the artist finally received an ultimatum from Harold. Either finish in three weeks, or be fired. This explains why the tiny leaves expand to nearly ten times their size in one part of the room.

One foyer in the mansion was to the front of the entrance hall, and led past the men's coat room to the library. The remaining two foyers were on either side of the fireplace in the entrance hall. One foyer led to an elevator, the main dining room and the kitchen wing, while the other opened to the formal breakfast room, which was highlighted by an imported French marble fireplace and a hand-painted scene on the domed ceiling. The Music Room boasted portraits of Mildred over the white piano, Peggy over the fireplace mantle, and Gloria over the settee. There were fireplaces in both Harold and Mildred's twin dressing rooms and in their sitting room.

The second story master bedroom suite, the size of a small house, has two of the home's 13 bathrooms (actually, each of the home's six bedroom suites has its own bathroom). The children's nurseries were adorned with hand-painted murals by illustrator Eulalie M. Banks. All of the oversized and well proportioned main rooms were highlighted with oak-paneled inlaid walls, hand-painted ceilings, hand-sewn Oriental rugs and huge tapestries over tile or parquet wood floors. All Persian rugs, either used on floors or as wall hangings, were hand-woven to Harold's strict specifications.

A curving stairway led down from the entrance hall to a spacious circular vestibule. The lower level of the house gives visitors a good look at the 14" thick walls of the architectural masterpiece. A long underground passage leads to a hidden downstairs game room and cocktail bar — this hallway is lined with Lloyd's Rogues' Gallery, graced by personally autographed photos of luminaries, started by wife Mildred as a 1937 Christmas present to her husband. Currently, 139 photographs hang in the halls of Greenacres; there are 254 portraits in the total inventory of the Rogues' Gallery. Almost all of the portraits are personally inscribed to Harold Lloyd. One of the more whimsical examples of personalization came on the photograph of Cecil B. DeMille, who wrote, "May the public never find my spectacles as funny as they find yours."

If any flaw could be found in the plan of the mansion, it was the location of the ladies' powder room, off the first landing of the main stairway. Imagine the nuisance for well-dressed women to have to climb up a flight of stairs to make themselves more alluring!

"Growing up in that house was fun — Mother loved parties. She loved costume parties, birthday parties, Valentine's Day, St. Patrick's Day, Christmas. We were a true family — it might have been like a circus at times, but it was mostly centered around children and very personal friends. Part movie people, part socialites, always good friends." [G]

The family moved into Greenacres in August 1929, and it would be the Lloyd home until the estate was sold at auction in July 1975.

Harold's library – to this day, that desk, boasting intricately hand-carved wood, sits as a reminder of the magnificent sense of style of the home's brainchild.

Granddaughter Suzanne moved into Greenacres as a young child. "It was my home. There was a great security in it. There was always a lot of love in the house, and laughter. I had a wonderful time. I had secret places that were my own private places, where I could go to read, or think — in the summer, it had this cool smell, with cool breezes. The house had a personality and a life to it — it was a lovely feeling — there was warmth and laughter, but there was also structure, strength, and integrity; there was a form to it that was really a statement. The main thing is that it was used as a home, not necessarily as a showcase." [H]

On January 29, 1956, *The Sunday Spectacular*, a 90-minute color television program, chronicled life "Inside Beverly Hills," and focused much of its attention on the Harold Lloyd Estate. As host Art Linkletter entered the property, he spoke: "This is Harold Lloyd's driveway — his private Route 66. If we don't meet with mishap we should reach the house before nightfall . . . We paused at the main swimming pool and bathhouse to go up for the rest of

The 50-foot sunken living room, complete with grand piano, parquet oak flooring, and delicate window treatments.

the journey . . . It is now the next day and no sign of the Lloyd home — we know it's on the grounds as we hear voices from a far-off Hi-Fi . . . We are passing through the Cypress Gardens and the lily pond . . . to the Poplar Gardens . . . one of the most beautiful scenes in all Beverly . . . So beautiful that when I get home I'm going to kick my eucalyptus tree right in its euc."

This Xanadu was, indeed, grand in Depression-era California. And its realization marked a sincere turning point in Lloyd's life. With an estate that cost over two million dollars to realize, it was evident that the instability of his childhood was far behind Harold. Long gone — but never forgotten — were the days of living in a cardboard box atop a building roof, with only a nickel left to his name. His home — admittedly grander than most of us could ever dream of inhabiting — was truly a symbol for Lloyd. It embodied his success, both as a professional and as a man, and represented permanence. For Harold, to be able to build and sustain such a grand estate was a tremendous point of pride. Though he honestly defined Greenacres as "home," it also signified his place in the film world — the estate was, indeed, his grand home that laughter built.

Harold's dream, laid out in his Last Will and Testament, called for the estate to be used as a film industry museum after his death. On April 20, 1973, on what would have been Lloyd's 80th birthday, the doors of Greenacres were opened to the public (the first tour was given to the Shriners of the Al Malaikah Temple, to which Harold belonged). Private bus tours were booked through May 1973. In June, public tours were conducted daily from 10am to 5pm through the Gray Line Bus Company, which departed from the Wilshire entrance of the Beverly Hilton Hotel. Beginning on September 1, a double-decker bus, imported from London, shuttled visitors to and from the estate. These expeditions were a day-tripper must until mid-1974, when the tours ceased, due, in part, to neighbors complaining about the noise and traffic. The next year saw estate upkeep costs mount, and the strain of finances became too high an obstacle to overcome, even for the Lloyd tradition. With taxes alone in six figures (just before the estate was auctioned in July 1975, $500,000 in back taxes and mortgage costs loomed), and the home became too costly to maintain.

On July 27, 1975, Greenacres was auctioned to the highest bidder. Iranian Nasrollah Afshani, a retired importer of industrial supplies, bid $1.6 million for the estate that Lloyd spent over $2 million to build in the late 1920s. The property was then subdivided into ten one-acre lots (lining what was the Lloyd driveway, and what is now Greenacres Drive, off of Benedict Canyon Drive), at the crest of which is a six-acre plot preserved intact, including the Lloyd mansion, Gloria's playhouse, the great lawn, the tennis courts, the lovely Rose Gardens, and the exquisite and welcoming entry courtyard. Nasrollah Afshani never actually lived in the home, but such is not the case of Greenacres' later owners: recording executive Bernard Solomon (purchased from Afshani in 1979 for $3 million) and entrepreneurs Ted Fields (purchased in 1986 for $6.5 million) and Ron Burkle (purchased in 1993 for $20 million).

Many theatrical films, and television programs, have used Greenacres as a location backdrop, prime among them the 1958 UA drama *Kings Go Forth*, the 1973 MGM feature *Westworld*, a 1975 episode of ABC TV's *Baretta*, a 1976 ABC made-for-TV movie *Death at Love House,* starring family friend Robert Wagner,

The glorious hand-painted ceiling and upper walls in L'Orangery *— the sun room — featured elaborate vines, indigenous plants, sparrows, cherubs, pheasants, flowers, parrots, grapes, and an elegant framework at its core.*

and the 1992 Warner Bros. film *The Bodyguard*. The home, in the years since Ron Burkle purchased it, has also garnered quite a reputation as the site of some of the most exquisite political fundraising party venues, with only the most glittering guest lists. "Ron Burkle owns Greenacres, and he loves that place, and Harold is very lucky that his place is now owned by a man who loves it, preserves it, takes care of it — and you couldn't ask for anything more. What Harold did for film preservation, Ron Burkle has done for Greenacres preservation." [H]

In the September 1932 issue of *Photoplay* magazine, Harold told author Gladys Hall, "This is our *home*. I'm going to be comfortable in it. I'm going to wear what I please when I please. When I come home from the studio at night, or from golf or wherever I happen to be, I'm tired. I want to relax. I want to be myself. And I can't relax in a museum. It's *got* to be a home. And a heck of a home it would be if I had to 'live up' to my surroundings. I'll make my surroundings fit *me*. It's swell to live in the midst of beauty, but you don't have to be a stuffed shirt about it."

Perhaps Greenacres was not all that far from Harold's vision for it — he *knew* that he wanted to build something singular, unique and memorable — but there is no questioning its enduring importance, both to Beverly Hills and to the film community. Decades after his death, Greenacres is still referred to as "The Harold Lloyd Estate." To this day, as well, its grandeur is sure, its structural integrity admired, and its essence lasting. Today, as in his day, Greenacres remains one of Harold Lloyd's crowning achievements.

"It was his home — he was very proud of it. Every part of it." [H]

> **FUN FACT**
>
> THE 1973-74 PUBLIC TOURS OF GREENACRES — YOUR AUTHOR MISSED OUT ON THEM, AS SHE WAS THEN YEARS AWAY FROM EVEN KNOWING LLOYD'S NAME — WERE VERY COMPREHENSIVE, ALLOWING VISITORS TO GET A VIEW OF THE WHOLE OF HAROLD'S ESTATE. AMONG THE PLACES OF INTEREST INCLUDED IN THE TOUR WERE THE HANDBALL COURT, THE SWIMMING POOL, THE GREENHOUSE, THE LILY POND AND GAZEBO, THE CASCADE REFLECTING POOL, THE MAIN COURTYARD, THE MAIN HOUSE, THE FORMAL GARDENS, GLORIA'S PLAYHOUSE AND "GROUNDS," AND THE TENNIS COURT.
>
> AFTER THE TOUR, ONE COULD VISIT THE TOUR RECEPTION AREA, OFFICES AND GIFT SHOP WHERE, AMONG THE SOUVENIRS THAT COULD BE PURCHASED WERE A SERIES OF TEN SLIDES OF ESTATE SIGHTS, A TEE SHIRT, BUTTONS, BUMPER STICKERS, CHARMS, AND POSTCARDS.

Harold Lloyd Releases Speedy

Speedy...
"It was an ambitious undertaking."

"Speedy" was Harold Lloyd's own personal nickname, pinned to him by his father when son was but a teen. Yet, that is not what makes Lloyd's 1928 comedy so important.

Speedy was the final silent in the film career of Harold Lloyd. That too, in and of itself, is not why this film stands apart.

The great baseball legend George Herman "Babe" Ruth has a cameo appearance in *Speedy* — a very rare, if not singular, instance in which Lloyd shared screen time, in one of his own films, with one as famous as himself. However, that isn't the big deal either.

Your author was born in New York, and *Speedy* offers generous and important views of, arguably, the largest big city in the land in the Summer of 1927. Alas, in my view, that *still* is not what makes this a crucial picture in Lloyd's cinematic arsenal.

It is the very fact that he *did* shoot the film in New York... that he had the confidence as a filmmaker, and the courage of his convictions, to travel across the country to shoot location scenes, when it would have been easy enough to build a series of sets, have some remote film of New York shot for him and sent back home, and produce the whole shebang in California... *that* is what makes *Speedy* a turning point film in Harold Lloyd's career.

The name of the film, *Speedy*, as was noted earlier, grew from Harold's own nickname. "When the character of the current picture began to take shape, it was seen that the name fitted him like a glove. Moreover, Speedy is brief and suggestive; therefore an intrinsically good title." [I]

The driving might not have been easy for Harold Swift in *Speedy* (1928), but the riding sure was light on the pocketbook: The Only One Cab fare was 15¢ for the first quarter mile, and 5¢ for each additional quarter mile.

Lloyd intended, after *The Freshman*, to change gears (as was his mode) and make a big city picture. The original idea, dealing with the underworld, grew in scope, as the team searched for a bounty of gag potential. The premise gradually morphed into the eventual franchise plot — "But it called for a set that would cost $80,000 and for a trip to New York. The season was unfavorable for working in New York, so we filed the story away and adapted the underworld faction into *For Heaven's Sake*." [1]

News of Lloyd's pending location shoot first broke in the May 28, 1927 issue of *The Moving Picture World* trade journal: "Harold Lloyd has determined upon the story for his next production, a story possessing a New York background that will take him to the Eastern metropolis for at least four weeks during the height of the baseball and the Coney Island season . . . Both the Yankee stadium and the world's greatest amusement center have important settings in the new Lloyd story, for Paramount release."

Then, in mid-June, Harold caught a mighty cold, which almost turned into pneumonia — this delayed the company for a few weeks, but owing to his prime physical condition, Lloyd recovered swiftly. *Moving Picture World* reported on July 30 that "Production on the newest Harold Lloyd picture is so far advanced insofar as the sequences filmed in Hollywood are concerned that the comedian and his staff will reach New York several weeks ahead of schedule. Originally, Lloyd planned to start filming in Manhattan around the end of August or early in September, but progress has been so rapid that he will probably get to New York early in August."

Harold, accompanied by wife Mildred, her mother, Caroline Davis, and their daughter Gloria, along with a crew of approximately 50 actors and technicians, arrived in New York's Pennsylvania Station at 10:40am on Thursday, August 18, 1927, aboard the Broadway Limited train. While in New York, Harold made his professional headquarters at the old Paramount studio in Astoria, Queens; he, along with his family, maintained personal headquarters in an apartment on upper Fifth Avenue.

The production crew, headed by ace cameraman Walter Lundin, utilized equipment from the Astoria facility, as well as essentials brought with them aboard the train. This was an extremely ambitious location shoot — and would prove to be a very important two-month trip, both because of the final product, and because of how it all happened.

Speedy offers many valuable glimpses of 1927 New York — it is, in many ways, an historic film, a treasured slice of nostalgia for those of us for whom New York is home — and the City was thrown open to Lloyd and associates, who made exceptionally good use of the beauty and grandeur of Manhattan and environs. Locations included Central Park, Washington Square, Sheridan Square, Pennsylvania Station, New York Harbor, Times Square, Fifth Avenue, the El (elevated subway), Battery Park, the South Ferry (the Manhattan side), the (then-new, now-old) Yankee Stadium, the Queensboro Bridge, the Plaza Hotel, and Tilyou's Steeplechase and Luna Park at Coney Island. The NY Police department gave Lloyd and company complete freedom to use the City however they chose, controlling the crowds and blocking off streets as necessary. This was not the first film to use New York as

HL poses with members of the New York City Police Department, a dedicated bunch that saw to it that the Lloyd Corporation got *Speedy* filmed with relative ease.

a location, and certainly wasn't the last, but the courtesies granted Lloyd for this shoot without doubt were unprecedented and spectacular.

Harold's final silent film, whether intentional or not, endures as a supreme love song to the Big Apple, and remains a grand visual tour of one of the most famous amusement parks in the world: Coney Island. Lloyd and his female lead, Ann Christy, rode many of the more popular rides, and helped audiences (of yesteryear and today) to better appreciate Tilyou's Steeplechase and Luna Park, and all the wonderful features of this New York landmark. What fun they had, riding the airplanes, maneuvering their way through the fun house, and eating all the food the vendors had to offer. Of course, a Coney Island highlight (of so very many) occurred as Harold and Ann were walking down the boardwalk. He was blissfully unaware that a live crab (with very active claws) had fallen into his pocket — courtesy of a visit to a vendor who just happened to be selling not-yet-dead crustaceans (go figure). As the couple paraded through the crowded boardwalk, on that sunny Sunday afternoon, the crab's claw captured a piece of lingerie out of the bag of a beach bather. Once she realized that she had been "robbed," she confronted Harold, grabbing her stolen wares, and informing him that it was men like him "that make women afraid to wear underwear." Now that smarts.

"We began work on *Speedy* in mid-summer. At Christmas, the picture three-fourths or more finished, we first turned our minds to devising an opening sequence, and not until a month later did we consider how to end the story.

"All of the baseball and Subway, virtually all of the taxi and Coney Island, and much of the horse-car faction were made in New York and the picture completed in the studio and on location on the Coast." [I]

The crew was in the Big Apple from mid-August through mid-October 1927 — what was planned to be a simple four-week shoot took twelve weeks to complete, due to the large crowds that inundated the locations. Interestingly, Buster Keaton's location trip to New York in Spring 1928 for *The Cameraman* was significantly cut short, because of a lack of crowd control. Somehow, the Lloyd camp succeeded in capturing what other companies tried and failed to film in New York — and *Speedy* fans have the NYPD to thank for this triumph.

"However many the extras or elaborate the pains you take, it is impossible to manufacture a crowd or a traffic scene as convincing as the real thing. The best effects usually are had by mixing the genuine and the synthetic. The difficulty about tying actual crowd and street scenes up with a picture is that the public should not be aware of the camera. If they are, they stop, stare and grow self-conscious. The enlisting of a crowd without its knowledge is called 'stealing a shot.' We stole several shots at Coney Island for *Speedy* with much success and attempted to steal another in Times Square.

"The police department gave its sanction, an actor in regulation police uniform took up station at Forty-third Street and Seventh Avenue and the two cameras were concealed in a laundry wagon which was to be parked at the curb. When we were ready, another car was found parked in the selected spot. We appealed to the actual traffic policeman on the corner. He ordered the car away, but its

With the imposing Queensboro Bridge as a backdrop, and with the well-behaved citizenry of New York in attendance, HL and crew film a faction of *Speedy* (1928). Lloyd can be seen leaning off his classy taxi.

four occupants drew back their coats, disclosing police badges. They were city detectives on watch for a thief who, they knew, would stroll up Broadway sooner or later that day. The scene was postponed; then, as we were about to begin a second time, a bundle-laden woman shopper approached our movie policeman for information and refused to be shooed away. The efforts to get rid of her tipped off the crowd and made any further attempt impossible that day, so the bit was put aside to be taken in Los Angeles." [I] The thief-watch occurrence, which really happened, inspired a similar sequence, which was shot in downtown Los Angeles for *Speedy*. The shot they were actually going for that day appeared at the start of the film, when *Speedy* was attempting to deliver flowers to his boss' wife . . .

"In Los Angeles, in December, we set up a dummy Subway kiosk on a corner in a neighborhood business center, assembled a crowd

FUN FACT

A novelization of the picture, aptly entitled *Speedy*, was written by Russell Holman, who had written a similar book for *The Freshman* in 1925. Both books were published by Grosset & Dunlap, which released a bevy of such film novelizations.

In his 1928 offering, Holman fictionalizes the story nearly exactly to the film. Comprised of 16 chapters, and 274 pages, Holman (as he did in his 1925 novel) combined the film scenario with filler material. As a result, a lot more happens in the 274 pages than does in the eight reels of the film.

The book was dedicated to Harold Lloyd — "King of Comedy, who has made life brighter for millions all over the world." From his home in Sound Beach, CT, on February 11, 1928 (almost two months prior to the release of the film), Holman wrote his acknowledgment page:

"The real author of *Speedy* is Harold Lloyd. The famous comedy star, assisted by his very efficient staff — Ted Wilde, John Grey, Howard Emmett Rogers and Lex Neal — originated the characters and plot and developed them in their every detail for the screen. This book was written from the picture after its completion, although the undersigned author did have the pleasure and benefit of discussing its theme with Mr. Lloyd personally. As far as possible the incidents in *Speedy* are used here exactly as they appear in the photoplay.

"The undersigned is deeply grateful to Mr. Lloyd, his staff and the Harold Lloyd Corporation for permission to novelize the picture and for their splendid cooperation without which this book would have been impossible.

"That this novel has caught, even in small measure, the buoyant spirit and gay entertainment qualities which *Speedy* displays on the screen, is the hope of
Russell Colman."

of extras and a fleet of automobiles with fake New York license plates and made the postponed bit which called only for Speedy to stop, tie a shoe string on the running board of a parked car, go on, and, finding the traffic signal against him, reach out, seize the traffic cop's whistle, blow a blast and proceed through the parting waves. But no amount of dressing will make a suburban intersection in California look like Times Square." [I]

Director Ted Wilde was nominated for an Academy Award for "Best Comedy Direction" (1928 was the only year this category existed). He lost to Lewis Milestone, who was the original director of *The Kid Brother*. Wilde also had another *Speedy* distinction: he was able to get baseball's most famous player, Babe Ruth, to appear in a cameo role (Wilde had directed Ruth in his 1927 feature, *Babe Comes Home*). This was a unique and singular achievement for Lloyd who, at this point, was amongst the most admired and successful film stars in the world — he hardly needed a celebrity co-star to help one of his films. The employment of Ruth was not just to exploit baseball's greatest hitter: it was a tremendously imaginative idea, given that Speedy Swift was such a big Yankee fan (spending most of his time as a soda jerk on the phone, finding out the latest scores, and cleverly sharing them with the kitchen help). Ruth and Lloyd were something of a mutual admiration society, and their collaboration for factions of *Speedy* only adds to the historic and popular importance of this picture. (As a side note, Babe later gave Harold the bat with which he hit his record sixtieth home run that season.)

Lloyd, along with key members of his staff, visited the then-four-year-old Yankee Stadium on August 27, 1927, planning for sequences to be shot when the Yankees returned home from a grueling 18-game road trip on August 29. They did get those shots, during the August 31 game against the Boston Red Sox (won by the Yankees, 10-3; in the game, Ruth hit the 43rd of his 60 season home runs — and that round-tripper can be seen in *Speedy*). Also shot was a dizzying ride through city streets, as taxi driver Speedy is commissioned to take Babe Ruth to the Stadium. The star-struck driver, gazing back at his idol at frequent intervals, ignores the road and the traffic around them, making for a hair-raising fare. Actually, the taxi was mounted on a truck, driven through the

Manhattan streets with the help of an under-cranked camera; the street route was closed by the police, and all cars and pedestrians were Lloyd Corporation hires. These shots were alternated with lightweight camera shots of general avenue travel, cranked at even slower speeds so that, when projected at normal and sped-up speeds, the end result dazzled the senses. Even Ruth, upon arriving at the Stadium, notes to Speedy, "If I ever want to commit suicide, I'll call you."

Lloyd certainly did his homework in garnering atmosphere, in the human form, for his New York shoot. On one occasion, according to the *Speedy* press book, Harold and Ted Wilde, disguised in beards, visited a rescue mission in the Bowery section of the City, and succeeded in obtaining a slew of extras, most of which appeared in "the fight between old men and rough roustabouts. Needless to say, Lloyd and his directors were enthusiastic when their new found friends swung into action. Plenty of first aid material was used after the scenes were taken."

The chase sequence which ends the film, as Speedy races through New York City to save his girlfriend's grandfather's trolley franchise from doom, was not with its perils. At one point, the horsecar crashed head-on into a girder that held up the Washington Bridge. Harold was *not* the driver in these establishing long shots (he would use a double to accomplish something Harold felt he could not do well — one of these, which he would freely admit, was rodeo work, and this included any work with horses). The driver was thrown from the trolley; the horses were shaken but not hurt — and the whole accidental crash had been captured on film! The crew got together and actually rewrote for that bit *right on the spot*, a most serendipitous accident, making for a wonderfully tense moment in the chase.

Perhaps the only downside to *Speedy* was another consequence of the New York trip: once the film was in the editing phase in Los Angeles, it was found that no *medium closeups* had been shot of Speedy on the trolley during the final chase sequence — only close-ups of Lloyd, and long shots of the double, had been filmed — and it would be too expensive to return to New York to capture just a couple of shots, however needed they were. So, Lloyd decided to utilize a new technology, the "Williams Process," to fill in the gap.

HL and costar Ann Christy on the Human Roulette Wheel, one of the most popular rides in the Pavilion of Fun at Coney Island.

Process was another term for a traveling matte, or back projection: film footage would be projected onto a translucent screen from a rear projector to provide what appears to be a moving background for actors being filmed on a set. Generic shots of travel along a street (it could have been *any* city avenue, and in this case, streets in downtown Los Angeles doubled for New York) were shot at slower speed, and then were projected at normal rate, giving the impression of racing. Later, Harold was shot in the studio, at the helm of a horsecar, with reins in hand, and a mock trolley just behind him, appearing to be scurrying at breakneck speed along the streets. In theory, the objective was met — however, owing to the infancy of the technology, the process shots lack reality; truly, when watching *Speedy*, the viewer knows *exactly* which sequences utilize process. It breaks up the effectiveness of the film's climax, but can be forgiven, when the pioneering nature of the situation is pondered.

There were other desired shots — lengthy and detailed — that the trip to New York just couldn't provide. To solve the problem,

Lloyd's company constructed an exact replica of the Sheridan Square district in Manhattan on Lloyd's 40-acre Westwood location ranch. The set, which cost $80,000 to erect, was correct in every detail, and required several months of carpentry work to complete. The crew utilized nearly 500,000 feet of lumber in the construction of the street and buildings; 6000 pounds of white lead, 400 pounds of oil, 3000 pounds of paint, one mile of fencing to secure the location (comprised of over 1500 slabs of brick facing), nearly 30,000 feet of lime brick facing, 20,000 square feet of plaster board, and an equal amount of composition board backings. Asphalting that amounted to several city blocks. Street car tracks, totally over a half mile in length, were built, as were mock fire escapes for the faux buildings, and plate glass for store windows. This was said to be one of the largest orders for building materials ever ordered by a motion picture company.

It was noted, in the September 24, 1927 issue of *The Moving Picture World*, that "before Lloyd leaves New York on his return trip to California, he will have played to nearly 2,000,000. Sounds extravagant, but during the next four weeks, Lloyd will be working on his new picture in the most congested centers of Manhattan and Brooklyn, providing a free show for Fifth avenue, the financial center, baseball fans and residents of various other districts in New York from the Battery to the Bronx River. Lloyd has already been seen working around New York by at least 300,000 persons, and he is really just warming up to the task which brought him across the country. The comedian will have to complete his work before cold weather sets in, for his story is virtually laid in the summer time, and derbies and topcoats are hardly significant of warm weather. John L. Murphy, Lloyd's production manager, feels that with the wonderful co-operation the unit is receiving here, the company should be ready to hit the long trail back home not later than the middle of October." Home they did go — *Speedy* was released on April 7, 1928, and its reception cemented his domination of financial and critical film matters.

It can be argued that, with his New York location shoot in the can, Harold Lloyd perfected a blueprint for the successful accomplishment of the challenging and grueling task of cross-country on-location filming. He didn't have to go across the

A long shot of the Old New York set, built at Lloyd's Westwood Location Ranch. It was designed to mirror the Sheridan Square neighborhood on the lower west side of Manhattan. This set was utilized for both *Speedy* (1928) and *The Cat's-Paw* (1934). COURTESY EUGENE L. HILCHEY, CENTURY ARCHIVES.

country in a 12-week trek for genuine and ultimately historic footage — he could have simply hired a freelance cameraman to provide b-roll of the sights and locations that made New York famous; he could have built elaborate sets at home to mimic *the real thing*, and could have easily shot on Los Angeles streets as substitutes for New York avenues — and by cutting such corners, he could possibly have been just as successful in producing a fine motion picture.

However, at this juncture in his career, Lloyd was at the height of his powers — a confident and sure filmmaker who spared no expense in order to make his films excellent (and, remember, he was producing his own films at this point, bankrolling his productions, and put his own personal fortune behind this film and its elaborate New York shoot). Lloyd, possibly as no other independent producer could, commandeered the entire fleet of the largest police department in the country to allow unfettered access to the streets, the neighborhoods, and the landmarks of New York City and environs. It was a supreme achievement for Lloyd, then just 35 years old — and it made for a dynamite cinematic result.

Perhaps the *Speedy* press book said it best: "The bespectacled comedian is a firm believer in authentic atmosphere and locale in all his pictures, which brought him to transport his entire company from Hollywood to New York, just for the sake of obtaining authentic scenes which his script called for. It was an ambitious undertaking, but with the completion of the comedy, it was very well shown that his time and efforts spent in New York were worth while."

With *Speedy* completed, so closed Harold Lloyd's "Golden Age" of silent film comedy. This would be his final silent feature — even though he planned his next film, *Welcome Danger*, as a silent, he later embellished it with sound. The period of 1922-1928 (encompassing *Grandma's Boy* through *Speedy*) represented Lloyd's best work, in which he both reflected and inspired the spirit of the Roaring Twenties. Now, it was on to further pioneering: sound on film.

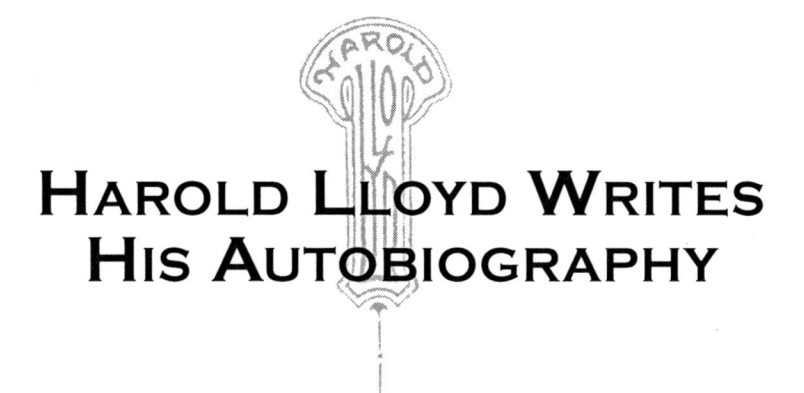

Harold Lloyd Writes His Autobiography

Take a Chance . . .
"I have no desire to be or knack for being comic in my off hours."

"Birth was one of the least interesting things that ever happened to me; but there must be an opening shot in a war, tears at a wedding, a raccoon coat on a sophomore and a birth in a biography, experts tell me." [1]
—*The first line of* An American Comedy.

Before the days of unauthorized biographies, the stars themselves (often with the assistance of a ghost writer) wrote their life stories, confident in the sales potential of such a book, provided their films remained popular. Lloyd, the world's top screen comedian, who had been credited with writing scores of stories in the press and fan magazines, took the plunge (aided by writer Wesley Winans Stout) with the September 12, 1928 publication of *An American Comedy*, Acted by Harold Lloyd, Directed by W.W. Stout, and published by Longmans, Green & Co.

The titling of the book was very shrewd and quite appropriate. In life and in art, there was no more American a comedy actor than Harold Lloyd . . . hailing from the country's heartland, battling poverty and uncertainty, learning his craft not from genetic roots but from hard work and perseverance . . . evolving before audiences' eyes . . . changing his character from film to film and reaching more of an audience base in the process — yes, *An American Comedy* was a perfect moniker for Lloyd's life story. And the penning of his autobiography marked a turning point in Harold's life — how could it not? I mean, *really*, how many of us — driven by worldwide popularity and curiosity about our very existence and motivations — will ever need to publish a book about our lives?!?

After a second paragraph chronicling his birth and providing some background for his life's beginnings, he wrote, "In this third paragraph I stop to serve fair warning — or unfair, as you prefer — that I am not a funny man off the screen. In pictures I am as funny as I know how to be, like the job and have no secret sorrows that I am not John Gilbert or Adolphe Menjou; but I have no desire to be or knack for being comic in my off hours. Such comedy as there will be here — and there should be plenty of it — will lie in the humor of events, not in any conscious effort of the author to be cute." [1]

Inside the 204 pages of *An American Comedy* are a marvelous compilation of both film stills and candid family shots, accompanying a whimsical text, which boasts a true command of the language (on either Lloyd's or Stout's, or a combination of the duo's, part). The autobiography chronicles Harold's youth, adolescence, his evolution from stage to film, and delineates most of this films, with the most detailed discussion of his then-current production of *Speedy*. Reviews were wholly positive: the *New York Herald-Tribune* praised how the book "tells his story with a young man's zest."

However, it seems such a shame that Harold chose to undertake such a book — his life story — at the relatively young age of 35, particularly considering he still had upwards of 42 years left on this earth. There was so much left to say, so many stories remaining to share, and so many facts to clear up for posterity. (On the latter, I can say, personally, that had he written his autobiography years later, it would have made *my* job infinitely easier, and would have made my own brand of Lloyd archaeology more fun and less frantic!) Yet, we can be grateful for the tales he did tell — valuable glimpses into filmmaking in its infancy, and wonderful firsthand chronicles of his rise to superstardom.

In the final chapter of the book, "Recipe for a Laugh," Lloyd is at his most contemplative, sharing, perhaps, to this point his only full acknowledgment of his stardom and his importance to contemporary cinema:

The front cover of the first edition of *An American Comedy*, the autobiography that HL wrote in 1928, at the tender age of 35. It includes stills from *Safety Last!*, *Grandma's Boy*, *Why Worry?*, and *The Freshman*, as well as a portrait from *Speedy*, which he was filming at the time of publication.

> **FUN FACT**
>
> **MORE FROM THE CHAPTER "RECIPE FOR A LAUGH":**
> "ANY PICTURE STAR IS UNDER CERTAIN OBLIGATIONS TO WHAT SOMETIMES IS KNOWS AS 'MY PUBLIC.' ANY PICTURE STAR SOUNDS A BIT OR MORE SILLY WHEN HE TALKS ABOUT 'MY PUBLIC,' BUT NEVER THINK HIM OR HER HYPOCRITICAL. THAT PUBLIC IS EXACTLY AS IMPORTANT AS SHE OR HE PRETENDS, WHICH IS AS IMPORTANT AS A PARACHUTE TO A BALLOON JUMPER. TO BE A SUCCESSFUL STAR IN PICTURES, WHERE AUDIENCE AND ACTOR NEVER MEET AND AUDIENCES ARE WORLD-WIDE, DEMANDS EVEN MORE TRAFFICKING IN THE ACTOR'S PERSONALITY THAN THE STAGE HAS SET A PRECEDENT FOR. THE WHOLE PURPOSE OF PUBLICITY IS TO CREATE A PUBLIC INTEREST IN THE ACTOR, TO MAKE A PUBLIC CHARACTER OF HIM. HAVING DELIBERATELY SOUGHT THAT INTEREST, THE ACTOR CANNOT SAY: 'YOU MUST EXCUSE ME; I AM ON PUBLIC VIEW ONLY FROM THREE UNTIL FIVE ON ALTERNATE WEDNESDAYS. THE REST OF MY TIME I AM A PRIVATE CITIZEN AND I MUST ASK YOU TO RESPECT MY PRIVACY.' THAT IS, HE CANNOT SAY THIS IF HE GOES ABROAD IN PUBLIC PATHS AND IF HE HOPES TO KEEP HIS PUBLIC.
> "IT IS NO OVERPOWERING MODESTY THAT PREVENTS ME FROM SHOWING MYSELF *SANS* MAKE-UP AND OUT OF CHARACTER ANY MORE THAN I CAN HELP, SO MUCH AS THE FACT THAT I DO NOT GIVE A GOOD SHOW. I NEVER HAVE GOT OVER BEING SELF-CONSCIOUS AND CONSTRAINED ON PARADE WHEN OUT OF MAKE-UP, AND I DO NOT LOOK AS I AM SUPPOSED TO LOOK." [1]

"Sooner or later I shall be asked, 'And to what do you attribute your success, Mr. Lloyd?' and I shall not blush and dimple and reply coyly that it is not for me to say. Nor shall I pretend to think that it was largely luck, for I do not think so, except in so far as all of life is a set of circumstances. The only ultimate answer would be 'I attribute my success to being born,' but the ingredients may be guessed at. The accident of growing up with a new theatrical form, enthusiasm, hard work and business sense have had much to do with it, but principally I have been an unusually successful picture comedian, I think, because I have an unusually large comedy vocabulary.

"Vocabulary is not the right word, but I do not know a better. By it I mean the tools of my trade, the store of knowledge of comedy effects, what they are and how to obtain them, accumulated by long experience and observation, and sharpened by a natural instinct for the theater. The theater caught me young and no experience in it — cellar stage, amateur, stock company, stage hand, picture extra or one-reel slapstick — was wasted. Specialization plus aptitude plus work seems, therefore, after much figuring, to be the formula, which is no discovery. That answer was in the back of the book all along.

"We have kept our pictures clean and will continue to do so. The easiest of laughs is the off-color gag. If it is well done and not too vulgar, adult audiences may enjoy it hugely yet not care to have their children see it, and we aim a picture at the whole family. Children are the easiest of audiences, business men the most difficult, and it is our particular pride that we draw both extremes as well as the middle.

"How long I continue to make pictures will depend on how long I hold my popularity and avoid monotony in my stories. One, even two pictures, are no criterion, but if ever three fail consecutively the handwriting on the wall will need no translating. I can only hope that when the time comes I shall not try to fool either the public or myself, but will bow my way out as gracefully as I can manage and turn to directing, producing or developing a younger actor. I will not have the excuse others have had, if I do not. There are men and women in Hollywood who were so overwhelmed with sudden riches that they spent as they made. When their popularity waned they had no choice but to go on, good or bad.

"If I keep my character genuine, however, and vary the theme sufficiently, I should continue in the comedy field indefinitely. The character is youth now. As my youth passes, either the character must grow older with me or I must switch to a new character." [I]

The Saturday Evening Post serialized portions of Lloyd's autobiography in their 1928 issues of March 24 and 31, and April 7, 14, 21, and 28. *An American Comedy* was later republished, in its entirety, shortly after the death of Harold Lloyd, by

Dover Publications. The 1971 reprint included 37 photographs, a new index, an introductory comment by Richard Griffith of the Museum of Modern Art Film Library, and an appendix comprised of an excellent 1969 interview between Lloyd and Hubert I. Cohen, entitled "The Serious Business of Being Funny."

All of it is valuable . . . it is good, fun, honest reading, not boastful (as it could have been), but rather reflective, I do think, of Lloyd's natural humility. Of course, he was justifiably proud of his accomplishments — having to write his autobiography at 35 is not a norm — but, through his words in *An American Comedy*, Harold seems not only genuinely happy to have achieved his level of proficiency and stardom, but fully aware that he *earned* it, through hard work and ability. And, ultimately, how sweet it must have been for him to share that message with the world.

The Sunrise of Sound, and Welcome Danger

Hear 'Em Rave . . .
"I decided we had missed the boat."

"That was quite a sad era for the silent screen actors and actresses; so many of them never seemed to bridge the gap between silent and sound." [E]

Following the production of *Speedy*, Harold Lloyd began his next silent film, tentatively titled "The Butterfly Catcher." Its theme — the underworld of Chinatown — was one that Lloyd and crew had stored up for years; the underworld had been explored in his 1926 comedy *For Heaven's Sake*, but the then-newsworthy issue of Chinatown corruption, married to the gangland storyline, seemed both timely *and* gag-laden.

"We had made that picture in its entirety in silent; in fact, it was probably one of the longest pictures in its primary stage that we had ever made. In other words, I think we previewed in about 16 reels, that's about 16,000 feet. And the funny part is, it went beautifully, in that tremendous length, but we knew it was ridiculous; we wanted to get it down to somewhere around about 10,000 — so we had to cut it down by around 6000 feet. Well, to cut 6000 feet out of a picture is an ordeal. So we had to do it by stages. So we cut out around a reel and a half, and we took it back to another preview, and it went terribly; oh, gracious, we were just — I was almost on the point of walking out on them; I think I really did walk out. So then we went back and cut another reel out of it. I think we had something like ten previews on this picture, and we kept cutting it down and it kept getting worse and worse. Till, finally, we got it down to between nine and ten reels, and then she started to perk again. We were fairly happy with it, after a long ordeal of having the first preview excellent and the rest of them very poor." [E]

At this point, the novelty of talking pictures was taking hold on the moviegoer's imagination. One evening, Harold was passing the Million Dollar Theatre on Broadway in Los Angeles, when he heard waves of laughter. He purchased a ticket, to find out what was making the audience laugh so: inside, a short subject was being screened, which simply showcased everyday objects, and the sounds they made. Bacon frying; ice tinkling in a glass; a crank on an old Model-T Ford; a man striking an anvil: these ordinary sounds, accompanying what the audience was seeing on the screen, produced *laughter*.

Seemingly instantly, Harold decided that his latest silent must become his inaugural talkie. "I decided we had missed the boat, and to the consternation of my crew and my associates, I said we're going to make it over — which cost us over $400,000 to make it over. The picture was the most expensive I ever made, at over $900,000; of your own money, that's quite a bit, you know. But, it paid off in a very large degree, so the gamble was well worth it." [C] This gamble commenced with reworking the story, replacing some crew and cast members (including swapping original female lead Mary McAllister with Barbara Kent), scrapping most of what had been shot, and starting all over again.

The tradition of humor inherent in Lloyd's Glass Character was largely optic, gag-related, and the story being told was contingent on the craftsmanship and physical stamina of Harold himself. Now, with the dawn of talking pictures, a new angle, and a new challenge, was being forced upon scores of silent stars, Lloyd included.

"My bridge over from silents to talking was most natural, because I had made this picture as a silent picture, and when I turned it into a talking picture, I kept about half of it and dubbed it, and the other half we made over. But, we had the same action, and the same procedure, pattern, and it was just a natural changeover. Sound gave me just a different facet to work with." [C]

"In those days, no one knew very much about dubbing. In fact, in our dubbing room, when we tried to dub the one half that had

Botanist Harold Bledsoe contemplating relieving his nerves with alcohol in this still from *Welcome Danger* (1929). Notice the exceptional lighting technique, which captures the mood of the tense scene perfectly

been shot silent, it was like an insane asylum — we had about seven or eight different people who were all making different effects. One man was walking up and down stairs, and another was rattling and another was hammering on this, and another one was coughing." [E]

"In one situation they wanted to get some ice in a glass to sound natural. And after going through one effect after another, someone came out with a glass of ice water and clinked the ice in the glass and someone said, 'My God, that's it!'" [N]

"It was very difficult, and of course we never had as good a sound in that picture as we could have, because we had done that. But one thing that it did accomplish was that we had the pace of a silent picture in a sound picture. It had a silent picture pace to it, and still it was a talking picture. And consequently, it took on a little different quality, and was very fortunate for us, because we didn't just flop over like a pancake and go from silent into sound, we really did a blend through there. And *Welcome Danger* had a very lovely pace into it; unfortunately the sound wasn't as good as it should have been, and it wasn't one of our best pictures, although it was a very humorous type of picture." [E]

The normal mode of production greatly changed with the new sound genre. One particular sequence from the beginning of the picture, involving Lloyd (as Harold Bledsoe) and leading lady Barbara Kent (as Billie Lee) proved a revelation to the star. "I remember we went out to do a scene with a girl and myself sitting on a bench, in a place called Griffith Park — it was just the two of us — and I think in the company was something, on one of these talking pictures, I think the crew amounted to somewhere around 40 or 50 people. Now in silent days, before that, I had taken a scene almost identical, with a girl and myself, doing a love scene on a bench, and I think there were four people. I directed the picture, and we had a property man and the camera man, the girl and myself. Now we couldn't do that today, even if we wanted to. Those things are passed and gone now. The sound end of it brought many, many changes of all different kinds." [E]

Silent and sound scenes were mixed in the final release of *Welcome Danger*. The silent portions are dubbed in spots, some appearing out of synch with lip movements. The look of the film is reflective of the silent, nonverbal influence — Harold looks much more comfortable in those scenes that had been shot for the silent version — yet the simplistic approach to the integration of sound effects and dialogue mars the final product significantly.

Other things changed for Harold, as he contributed to what truly was the pioneering of sound on film. "It required our more or less having definitely a story. It was much more necessary when you put dialogue into it; before we could say whatever came to our mind, and it was the pantomime and the action that was paramount. The audience couldn't read your lips. But when dialogue came into it, it meant that you really had to sit down and really work out some normal everyday dialogue — that demanded more of a story, and a little different type of procedure. I think that if we had had more competent dialogue writers at that time, we could have made that phase of it infinitely better." [A]

Paramount Pictures put HL front, center, and huge on the cover of its *New Show World* magazine, touting its coming film releases for 1929-1930.

 The emphasis on physical comedy, so much a hallmark in the silent era, quickly became the exception rather than the norm as sound films caught on. "It was easier to sit down and talk, and to make up verbal quips, to get dialogue, instead of visual action and ocular business, gags, as we used to call them. The spoken word

Shooting *Welcome Danger* (1929). Leading lady Barbara Kent is seen at lower right, along with Walter Lundin at camera, Malcolm St. Clair (silent version director) behind him, Wallace Howe (behind light diffuser), Jimmy Anderson (standing), head electrician Anderson "Bard" Bardwell (kneeling), and Lloyd double Jake Jacobs (holding the slate).

seemed to be much simpler to get their laughs from, and much cheaper. They could make a picture for much less, because visual comedy is expensive. It takes timing. It takes spacing. It takes rehearsal to bring it off correctly. And, as time went on, comedians seemed to lose the art, or the knack you might call it, of doing pantomime. It just became a different school of thought." [E]

Lloyd understood that the earliest of talkie films had virtually taken the *motion* out of pictures, leaning too far towards the ear, and too far from the eye.

"There were very few comedians who seemed to weather the sound situation, because it was a different technique, to a certain degree. It didn't have to be, but it developed that way. Of course, in the early days, it was quite hectic — you see, some studios had talking picture equipment, and some didn't. Right at that very time, because there were certain difficulties in handling the sound

> ## Fun Fact
>
> From the Associated Press, February 24, 1930, dateline Shanghai: "Initial showing of Harold Lloyd's first talking motion picture, *Welcome Danger*, by the International Settlement Foreign Theater last night resulted in a demonstration by 350 Chinese students in the audience. The students handled the theater manager roughly, demanded their money back and one of them hurled a giant firecracker into the center of the theater, causing a near-stampede.
>
> "A portion of the film depicting asserted underworld life in San Francisco's Chinatown, in which Chinese opium smugglers were portrayed, caused the displeasure of the students, who declare the picture is 'unfriendly and derogatory to the Chinese people.'
>
> "Police dispersed the demonstrators, who had asked and obtained a refund of their admissions, and arrested the ringleader, who is said to be a scenario writer for a Chinese motion-picture company.
>
> "As a result, possibly, of the publicity, large audiences today witnessed the film, which was shown in two foreign settlement theaters guarded by police."
>
> A day later, on February 25, the AP reported that *Welcome Danger* was being withdrawn from showings in local theatres in China by Paramount Corporation.

and the sound equipment, they seemed to go to dialogue. I'm not talking particularly about comedy, but they seemed to take on a stage type of production. You were held down, in cranking a camera, to 24, because that seemed to be a speed that is necessary for the voice, to capture the voice naturally. When we worked in silent pictures, we could say anything we wanted, you could say anything, even stupid if you want, and people didn't know what you were saying — even in a love scene, you could have said something idiotic if you wanted, if it didn't take you out of the mood. But, when dialogue came on, you had to have real writers do it, not that they always did. And in so many different ways, by having the spoken word, and having little comedy witticisms that meant as much as the visual type of comedy, it was almost after a certain length of time, they stopped using the visual type of business, they went to the verbal, and the ocular seemed to just kind of pass on out. And today, it's an amazing thing how little visual type of action is used compared to the spoken word. Most of the directors and the actors — they know nothing about how we did it in the silent days; it's kind of a lost procedure. So many of them think that if you're not talking, there's something's wrong. It's not right." [E]

"You *don't* have to talk every moment that the film is running. We don't do that in real life; that just because you're doing some business you must have dialogue to accompany it — it isn't necessary. For a long period, people thought they had to talk all the time." [A]

Harold's first talkie cost $979,828 to realize, yet grossed nearly three million dollars — much of that *curiosity cash* — most of the silent stars' talkie debuts followed suit: what *do* they sound like?!? "I'm a comic — I could have had any kind of voice I wanted. It didn't make any difference — even though I didn't use my voice correctly to start with, it didn't really seem to matter much, because they accepted the comic for what he was. That's one advantage that a comic has, to a degree." [E]

While audiences had been mesmerized by various films that featured loud sneezes and sizzling fried eggs, the thrust of *Welcome Danger* did not provide hilarity . . . curiosity, yes, but not hilarity. However, one marvelous touch to the sound version — perhaps as a sarcastic shot at the new genre — had Lloyd and Noah Young performing a scene in total darkness, with only sound to carry them.

The recurring sounds chosen for aural enhancement were chiefly those of crushing skulls and squeaking secret panel doors. The awkwardness of the acoustic experience was heightened by the sappiness of the dialogue (for example, when Bledsoe was on board the train, arriving in the town of Newberry, he cracked, "Newberry? Well, I've heard of raspberry and strawberry, but this is a new berry on me." Mercy . . .). Then there was the almost-unbelievable ungraciousness of Harold's character. Harold Bledsoe is downright unlikable as the picture begins, primarily due to his incessant verbal putdowns of Billie Lee. Consequently, as the early scenes

WHEN HAROLD LLOYD MADE HIS FIRST SOUND PICTURE, "WELCOME DANGER,"
HE WENT INTO THE QUIET COUNTRY TO SHOOT A PEACEFUL RURAL SCENE

From *Motion Picture Classic* magazine, March 1930: a whimsical (and all-too-realistic) look at the rigors of early sound filming, sketched by artist (and later production designer) Harold Michelson.

progress, you find yourself, instead of rooting for his character, hoping that Billie will either sock him or leave him in the meadow.

For that reason, perhaps more than any other, I feel it might have been a wiser choice to keep *Welcome Danger* as a silent feature, Lloyd's twelfth. Harold Lloyd's Glass Character, as he would aptly agree, needed the association and support of his audiences — story lines and situations were always designed towards inspiring moviegoers to *want* him to succeed. With the conversion of the film from silent to sound — a major career turning point for Lloyd — and with the incorporation of incredibly uncouth dialogue for Bledsoe, audiences, for the first time, were introduced to a Lloyd character that was rude, obnoxious, and actually a negative distraction within the opening sequences of the production. No where in the film is this clearer than in the scene introducing Billie, the girl whose face Harold Bledsoe had fallen in love with at a photo machine, but whose sloppy appearance (when her car breaks down) leads him to think her a boy. He proceeds to lodge every imaginable demeaning statement toward Billie, and only because she is not fixing her car rapidly or efficiently enough, and Harold needs a quick ride back to town. Billie really didn't do anything to deserve such a tongue-lashing: this shows a random sort of violence, in this case of the verbal kind, the likes of which had not been seen in a Lloyd film since the Lonesome Luke days. How she even considered forgiving him is truly beyond anyone who experiences the first fifteen minutes of *Welcome Danger*.

The silent version of *Welcome Danger* was not scrapped, but rather was issued to theatres that could not yet screen sound films. While the differences between the two might be looked upon as minor, the silent version just seems *funnier*. It is better paced and snappier — without the bounty of sound effects and that hard-to-swallow dialogue as distractions, the action flows easier, and its star looks obviously more at ease in the sequences shot for the silent adaptation.

For someone who had played nice young men for years, it must have been an interesting — possibly even refreshing — experiment for Lloyd to portray a character with repellent tendencies. However, it wasn't successful then, and does not work today. The introduction and development of Lloyd's Bledsoe persona, then as before so vital

GOES EAST TO HELP SEE EVERYTHING IS O. K.

JOHN L. MURPHY

You have heard people say "What a Pal" in speaking of the friendship existing between folks these days. Well John L. Murphy has been working with Harold Lloyd as his production manager ever since the famous comedian was with Hal Roach and when he decided to come on his own as a star and producer, why John L. stuck with Harold, and all through his years of working on his own, Mr. Murphy has seen to his welfare in every business way as far as production is concerned.

Harold Lloyd is heading East to attend the world's premiere of his first talkie, "Welcome Danger," for Paramount, so it is only natural that John L. Murphy should go East to check up the projection of the picture when it opens at the Rialto and look after the business of his "Pal" and co-worker who will be in the Metropolis and make a personal appearance at the opening. Lloyd leaves for the East accompanied by Joseph Reddy, his personal press representative, on Saturday.

From the *Hollywood Filmograph*, October 5, 1929 – a tale, surrounding *Welcome Danger*, that typifies the lifelong friendship between HL and his production manager, John L. Murphy.

to the success of his pictures, merely stands to this day as a rare instance of incorrect judgment on the star's part. Why he let that happen remains a prime mystery.

Owing to the initial disgust Harold Bledsoe inspires at the commencement of this film, it makes fans — including me — a tad uncomfortable with the prospect of disliking one of Lloyd's characters. However, it is the dialogue that makes him so initially despicable, and this feeling of angst is not as prevalent in the silent counterpart. Your author *guarantees* that if you ever have the opportunity to see both the silent and sound versions of *Welcome Danger*, you *will* prefer the silent. It makes for a much less uncomfortable viewing experience.

Mind you, the *original*, complete silent version is not known to survive to this day, but fragments do — the original picture negative was missing the first reel, but the dupe picture negative was used to fill in that missing reel and other segments. These fragments comprise a mock "restored silent version" that has screened in some archive theatres. Actually, on August 13, 2008, UCLA's film archive screened both versions of *Welcome Danger* — the silent and the sound — on the same evening. The response to the "new" silent has been overwhelming — mirroring the curiosity and enthusiasm of 1929 audiences. According to UCLA film archive preservationist Jere Guldin, "After we screened it, I believe it played for five days at the Film Forum [in New York]. They sold out the shows every day."

Lloyd's pioneering contribution to the development and facility of sound in film is unquestioned, and should never be downplayed. He bravely forged into talkies at a time when his powers in the silent cinema arena were virtually unrivaled, and it took a lot of guts to take this leap — but the final product stands out as less than ideal, in my humble opinion.

The final release's reviews were mixed, from "It is hilarious, but never as appealing as *Speedy*" to "Should Harold Lloyd have stuck to pantomime in the first place?" Without question, Harold Lloyd, though he felt he *had* to forge into the sound game, was not ready for it. *Welcome Danger* shows that clearly. Lloyd's judgment had served him beautifully through eleven silent feature films. But with premature tackling of delicate new technology, a poor script and even poorer character development, it let him down on his first talkie.

Harold Lloyd Releases The Cat's-Paw

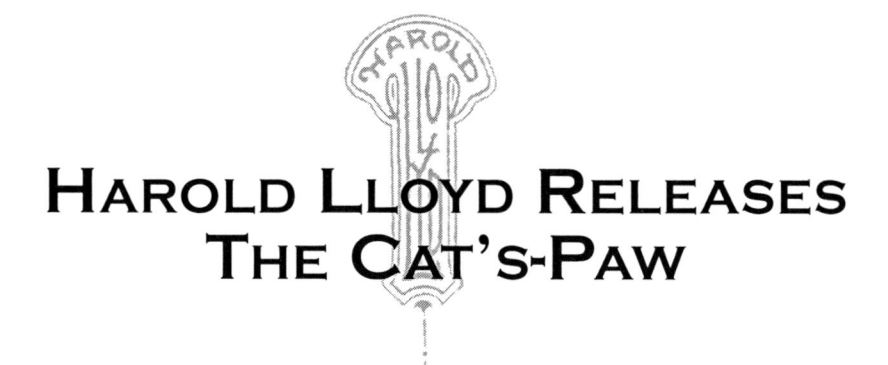

The Cat's-Paw . . .
"There were two ways we could do it."

As Harold Lloyd's sound film career progressed — he produced *Feet First* in 1930 and *Movie Crazy* in 1932 — he found that the condition of the nation was affecting him in more ways than one. The Great Depression had hit — and had changed his, and every movie maker's, mode of operation. He discussed this with writer Gladys Hall in the article "Looking at the World Through Horn-Rimmed Specs," in *Motion Picture* magazine, in September 1933.

"I've got to dig deeper for my stories. Laughter is not enough any more. Horn-rimmed specs are not enough. A pretty girl is not enough . . . There will have to be deeper thought back of the gags and something to think about in the story.

"People have been through too much, have had too many vital problems and too much stern grief to be satisfied with something merely funny, superficially funny. People who have known financial disaster and hunger and unemployment will feel they have been given soda pop when they needed bread, if I give them only laughter. Not that I disparage laughter. Very far from it. Because, among the many things the so-called depression has taught me is the vital need of laughter . . . I really feel now that I am not a mere entertainer, but a man with a mission in the world — the *serious* mission of being *funny*, of invoking laughter where no laughter was before."

It is clear that, at the time that he began seeking ideas for a new picture, Harold sensed that his beloved Glass Character was reaching its natural end. The dawn of both the sound era and the Great Depression can both be seen as direct reasons for the beginning of the end of the good times for Lloyd filmmaking. Despite the fact that Harold's voice suited his screen personality well (as Lloyd would say, "I'm a comic; I can sound any way I like"), the Glass Character was the problem. Harold's "up-'n'-at-'em" persona did not synch with the bleak Depression era, yet Lloyd faithfully stuck by the screen presence which had successfully seen him through the past seventeen years. Lloyd did not suddenly become unfunny; the audience simply lost its identification with the Glass Character.

As a result, Lloyd and crew had to do something that had been done for no Harold Lloyd film since the earliest Lonesome Luke days: they went outside of their team for their next story. This marks a turning point, professionally, for Lloyd, in that it hinted at his realization that he and his character needed help. Perhaps the team's idea well went dry; maybe they simply found a story they felt couldn't miss — whatever the reason, it marked a complete departure from their norm.

"We did make a change on a picture called *The Cat's-Paw*. It was a story we bought that ran in *The Saturday Evening Post*; Clarence Budington Kelland was the author." [E] The story had appeared in the *Post* from August 26-September 30, 1933; when Harold read it, he decided to buy the rights to it for $25,000.

This trend of film adaptation of the written word was quite popular in the early 1930s, and Harold had hoped to continue the vogue.

"We bought this story; we liked the idea, and there were two ways we could do it. We could do it the way we had always made all of our pictures, with business and gags, along the same line, or do the picture the way Kelland had written it in his *Post* story; in other words, do it straight, and let dialogue more or less take the prominent place in the picture, and let the business kind of drop into wherever it belonged. Now, we didn't know which way to go. We knew we had been successful the other way, and we thought this was a departure, and we would be able to get more out of the Kelland story by following the lines as Kelland had written it. So

A climactic scene in *The Cat's-Paw* (1934), in which Ezekiel Cobb (HL), finally stands up to the corrupt Ed Morgan (Alan Dinehart), as Morgan's sidekick Strozzie (Nat Pendleton) looks on.

we put two pieces of paper into a hat, written one way or the other way, the old way or the new way. And we drew out the new way. And we abided by it." [E] This coin flip of sorts — quite reminiscent of the way Harold and his family got to California in the first place — definitely was a maturing turning point in Lloyd's career. The *word* was triumphant, essentially overriding the *gag* and, with it, nearly two decades of established filmmaking practice.

"As I look back, I think if I had my way to do over again, I would have done it the old way, and we'd have still captured and gotten more out of it. By doing it the new way, we didn't collect the amount of laughs we had in some of the previous ones, but the story end of it was better, because if we had put so much business in, and gone in another way, we'd have had to make the story secondary, and in this, the story was the major. See, in most of our pictures previous to that, story was very secondary — it was action that counted." [E]

Uniformly, nearly exclusively across the board, *The Cat's-Paw* is cited both as Lloyd's most unorthodox film and *not* his best sound picture. While the former might be true, I must humbly disagree with most of the world's critics and scholars:

I feel that *The Cat's-Paw* is Lloyd's premier talkie.

Now, I might be a committee of one on this, but please hear me out — and then judge for yourself, by watching the film (which can be found on the DVD box set *The Harold Lloyd Comedy Collection* on Volume One, Disc 2, Side A).

I contend that *The Cat's-Paw* is the best sound film that Harold Lloyd ever made — but it does not, in my estimation, contain what I construe to be the best *sound scene* he ever appeared in. That distinction goes to his screen test sequence in *Movie Crazy*. If I have to show *one* scene from a sound film of his, it is that one. In it, he was funny, believable, honest, and he perfectly executed the physical and verbal demands of the faction. A close second to the screen test, also from *Movie Crazy*, is the dance sequence in which Harold unwittingly created havoc by accidentally donning a magician's coat.

However, that being said, I think that *The Cat's-Paw*, as a package, is the finest of his talkies. Perhaps it is because he had a professional writer's words as his script, or maybe because he was perfect for the role, or conceivably because he was growing as a talking actor, but I feel that, as Ezekiel Cobb, missionary from China, Harold Lloyd showed the depth of his abilities as an actor. He handled the part beautifully.

Witness the scene, taken in his boarding house bedroom, in which he found out that he not only was elected Mayor, but also that he was the patsy — the Cat's-Paw as it were — for the incumbent political machine. Witness the moment in which Mayor Cobb decides to veto the bill containing the machine head's chief graft, and the strength of his work opposite costars George Barbier and J. Farrell Macdonald (Harold's co-director on *Over the Fence* 17 years before). Witness the climactic point in the film, when he tricks every known gangster in town into confessing their crimes or risk being "beheaded," and realizes that he has cleaned up both the town and his reputation. Each of these sequences stand alone as some of the best acting Lloyd had ever done.

Possibly more than any other Lloyd film to date, *The Cat's-Paw* contains drama — allowing Harold to exercise his skills as a dramatic actor which had been honed in his early stage career. In its August 21, 1934 critique, *Variety* noted that "*The Cat's-Paw* is a big departure for Harold Lloyd in that it is the most adult comedy yet

Fuzzy Knight stutters his way through a confession of sorts — prompting Mayor Ezekiel Cobb (HL) to hand him a pad and pencil — in the ironic ending of *The Cat's-Paw* (1934).

attempted by him." This is very true. And, had he not had such a depth of background in *non*-comedic acting, he might not have been able to pull it off as well as he did. However, he fully utilized his *comedy* skills of timing and spacing to excellent advantage in his dialogue delivery, while also personifying the calm and unrattled exterior that is so indicative of the missionary lifestyle. *The Cat's-Paw* was the most complex and realistic script he had handled to date — fully believable, and peppered with proverbial language, which was actually quite appropriate for Harold's vocal characteristics, which were capable of affectation.

The character of Ezekiel Cobb based most of his moral decisions on the teachings of Ling Po, a fictitious Chinese philosopher whose writings were studied by Cobb from young boyhood. In the film, Ezekiel shared much of the wisdom of the sage in explaining his decisions and his actions.

"*The blind man, lest he stumble in darkness, welcomes the guiding footsteps, even of an ass.*"

— Ling Po

Newly elected, and recently awakened Mayor Ezekiel Cobb (HL) addresses the citizenry of Stockport in *The Cat's-Paw* (1934). This scene utilized the Old New York set, originally built for *Speedy* (1928) at Lloyd's Westwood Location Ranch.

Compare the story in *The Cat's-Paw* to some of his other sound films. And weigh its script against any of his other talkies. In terms of sophistication, story unity, and flow, his 1934 offering stands up extremely well. And, Lloyd had more of a hand in the actual story than might be realized: according to the August 27, 1934 issue of *Time* magazine, Lloyd bought Kelland's story *The Cat's-Paw* on the strength of its first chapter in *The Saturday Evening Post* — subsequent chapters were enhanced by Lloyd's own suggestions to Kelland for the character of Ezekiel, undoubtedly with an eye towards a film adaptation.

And the transfer of short story to film was brimming with the Lloyd touch. The romance factor — one that Harold often talked about as a strength of his Glass Character — was better developed and more believable in *The Cat's-Paw* than in any other Lloyd talkie, in my view. Lloyd's chief female lead in this film, Una Merkel, was not thrown at the audience as an obvious choice to become Mrs. Cobb by the end of the film — theirs was a relationship, a friendship, which grew as the story progressed. It was very realistic, much more so than most of the previous Lloyd talkie pairings, as

> ## FUN FACT
>
> Long before late-night television made it fashionable to laugh at politics and its practitioners, Lloyd used his films to poke fun at the legal system. Though it is a lost film, one can only imagine the courtroom frolics in *Lonesome Luke, Lawyer* (1917). Corrupt politicking in a rough neighborhood set the scene in *Count the Votes* (1919). The Kingdom of Thermosa was given the razz in *His Royal Slyness* (1920), with those in charge depicted as drunken bumblers. In *The Cat's-Paw* (1934), corruption and embezzling from within the political machine was showcased, with the faction's candidate with the least chance of winning the mayoral race — Lloyd's character — emerging victorious after fisticuffs with the incumbent delighted the constituency.
>
> Of all of these examples of Lloyd political films, for ultimate satisfaction, you cannot beat *The Cat's-Paw*. Mayor Ezekiel Cobb (Lloyd) was framed in a phony scandal and professionally ruined by his enemies. However, being from China, he grew up with the teachings of great philosophers telling great tales of great men: one in particular dealt with a Chinese leader, Fu Wong, who experienced a predicament similar to that of Cobb. Wong solved the problem by beheading every known criminal, ridding the city of crime. Needless to say, Cobb didn't commit mass murder — but, he made the town's bad guys *think* he would, and got them all to confess to their wrong doings in lieu of losing their heads. This exonerated Cobb, and ridded the town of corruption. Actually, this is one politically charged film that most politicians should *not* see — it might give them ideas.

well as those to come. Perhaps the only other credible romantic pairing, post-*The Kid Brother*, was that of Barbara and Harold in *Feet First* — again, the pairing of the two by film's end was not exploited through unrealistic means, yet made sense, because they were each underdogs as the story progressed. On the other hand,

Stockport Mayor Ezekiel Cobb (HL) informs Jake Mayo (George Barbier, left) and Police Chief Pat Shigley (J. Farrell Macdonald, leaning) of his plans to rid the town of corruption, in *The Cat's-Paw* (1934). Macdonald had directed HL at Universal in 1914, and also directed the first Glass Character short, *Over the Fence*, in 1917.

look at *Welcome Danger* — now, really, what woman in her right mind would even *consider* taking on Harold Bledsoe if he talked to her the way he spoke to Billie at the film's outset? Ponder *Movie Crazy* — realistically, are we to believe that Harold didn't know that Mary Sears (Constance Cummings) was also the Spanish señorita? And that, with the probable bevy of male movie stars at her avail at the studio, she could actually fall in love with a guy she called "Trouble"? (Now, don't get me wrong — I adore *Movie Crazy*, which is generally considered Lloyd's best talkie — but I feel that the development of the romantic angle, and the dialogue that Lloyd and Cummings were given for their scenes together, just didn't work.) Similarly, look at the eventual marriage in *The Sin of Harold Diddlebock* — now, how *could* the youngest of the Otis girls (Frances Ramsden) really be drawn to, and eventually marry, a middle-aged man who wears a tattered and moth-eaten jacket to work, and then parades around town in a checkered suit that rivals any of the 1960-era's loudest curtain patterns? Really!?!

No — for my money, the film's-end marriage of Petunia "Pet" Pratt and Ezekiel Cobb represented the most natural romantic progression ever presented in a Lloyd talkie. She, wise-cracking and street-smart, took a slow-but-sure liking to the innocent Ezekiel. Her gradual understanding of him opened him up in a way that, potentially, saved the character from doom. She helped the Chinese missionary to broaden his social horizons, to embrace his new political post, and to realize his capacity to achieve good, both for himself and his new town of Stockport. Along the lines of most of Jobyna Ralston's silent-era characters, opposite Lloyd, Una Merkel portrayed the finest of Lloyd's talking female foils, and brought out the best in Lloyd's character.

Ezekiel Cobb was a persona that did, truly, follow the basics of Lloyd's Glass Character — in this case, a meek and mild-mannered young man who used his wit, resourcefulness and inner goodness to get himself out of a pinch, a number of times. This was a believable character, too, in that little guys (or those perceived to be as such) are pushed around frequently — in the spirit of the best of the Lloyd characters, we are rooting for his success, however unlikely it appears at the outset. The story provides plenty of opportunity, throughout the film, for the audience to rally behind Ezekiel, as he genuinely pursues, and honestly wins, the Mayoral race in corruption-ridden Stockport, and then ultimately destroys the town's machine politics and rids the municipality of scandal and crime. It's a great story — filled with ups, downs, surprises, and excitement — it might not be the funniest of his films, but it surely is the best scripted and the best performed of Lloyd's sound offerings.

I believe the reason that most critics and scholars, and even some fans, dismiss *The Cat's-Paw* as a misstep in Lloyd's filmography is due to its emphasis on story, and not on gags. It is not like other Lloyd films. It doesn't feature gag business that builds, one on top of another, as most of his pictures had to that date. It might not have been built in the normal Lloyd fashion — heck, even *he* called its production "the new way" — but I think its departure from the usual *is* its major strength. Its uniqueness showcased Harold's versatility, and his ability to handle, and wonderfully execute, words and actions that didn't come directly from his own gag team. It also

The first victim is about to be handed his head in *The Cat's-Paw* (1934). Holding the bowl, at left, is frequent Lloyd costar Constantine Romanoff.

showed what a fine actor he was — it might not prove him a master comedian, but it is a tremendous example of *really* good acting.

And why *does* a Harold Lloyd film have to be a total gag fest, anyhow? Since when does taking a chance on something different qualify you as a "dog" (the opinion, on this film, of esteemed Lloyd author Richard Schickel)? Why, I think that Harold must have thoroughly enjoyed escaping from the boundaries of gag comedy and graduating, if you will, to something a bit more legitimate and straight. It was a stretch — a gamble — but, what worthwhile variation from the status quo isn't? From a financial point of view, the film — shot between January 30 and April 23, 1934, it cost $617,000 to produce, yet only grossed $693,000 domestic dollars — was a clear loss for both Lloyd and distributor Fox. Yet, for my money, in terms of his acting and his character's story line, *The Cat's-Paw* is a definite winner.

Now, go watch the film, and see if you don't agree with me . . .

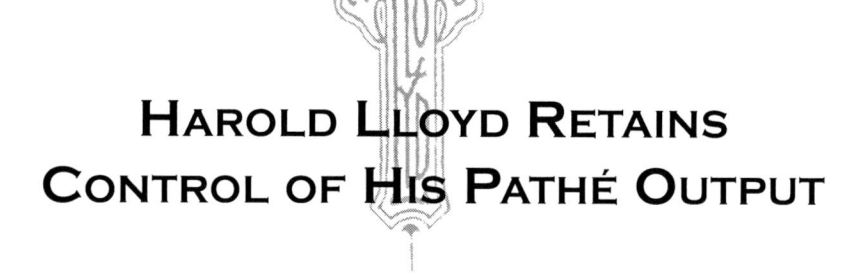

Harold Lloyd Retains Control of His Pathé Output

Fireman, Save My Child . . .
"My character had an individuality."

"Some of the fondest memories in my entire career date back to my association with Roach. There was a close bond between us. I doubt that any two people could understand each other better. As time passes my feeling of indebtedness to Hal Roach grows." [K] Indeed, those early days were fun, for both men, and the films they made together, while perhaps not all masterpieces, were deeply important to Lloyd.

On January 17, 1938, a series of explosions, following a fire in the boiler room of Pathé Exchange's East Bound Brook, New Jersey plant, seriously damaged its two-story warehouse, and destroyed a large quantity of the films that were stored there. Among them were many of the early movies that Roach and Lloyd collaborated on.

Consequently, in July of 1938, Harold purchased the negatives of the surviving 114 of his early films from Pathé. *Variety* called this a purchase made for "sentimental and business reasons" — and while Lloyd the businessman might have liked the idea of gaining sole ownership of his films (so he could, for instance, safely and ethically recycle a successful gag from a past picture), there is no question that Harold wished to take care of his cinematic legacy himself. This marks a definite turning point in his career . . . it couldn't help but, because he now owned the output of his own evolution.

Amongst the films now in his possession were what survived of his Lonesome Luke output, and of the Glass Character one-reel, multiple-reel and feature-length films. With a few exceptions,

Harold now owned the only existing print of many of his films — it bears noting that, at this time, theatrical motion pictures were not viewed as relics of an era, bearing historic significance; most film stock was recycled, or merely filmed over, and was largely not kept for posterity by any film company. Thus, the very fact that Pathé had his earliest works at all must have been awfully attractive to Harold, who was an historic-minded man. Lloyd stored his prized possessions in a newly constructed film vault, connected to the service buildings on his Greenacres estate. A little over five years later, something went terribly wrong.

On August 5, 1943, a nitrate explosion and fire ripped through the film vault, destroying most of the films Lloyd took possession of in 1938. Harold tried, diligently, to save as many of the cans of film as he could, running in and out of the vault, frantically tossing unhurt reels to safety. However, the damage was immense, and not just to the films.

Harold collapsed in the doorway of the vault; he was revived by his wife Mildred. Seven firefighters and one Greenacres employee were overcome by smoke inhalation, and were taken to a nearby hospital. The damage to the actual structure and surrounding property was estimated (by Harold) at $2 million.

After the 1943 fire, Harold built two concrete vaults in the cutting fields near the Victory Garden at Greenacres, for the surviving films, and made duplicate negatives from the best surviving prints of the films whose original negatives had perished. There they sat . . . alive, but hardly kicking.

Then, in 1966, Harold met his granddaughter's boyfriend, Richard Correll, who was awestruck and gleeful to meet this cinematic giant. Correll, then a film student and now a major Hollywood director, was saddened to see the collection of film cans in disarray within the vault. He and friend Dave Nowell volunteered to put the films back in order for him — separating negatives from positives, nitrates from safeties. Harold was so delighted that he offered to pay the young men for their services.

"Then we started to screen the pictures, and he would attend," noted Correll to film historian Kevin Brownlow. "The whole time he was involved in the process, because initially he didn't know if he should trust us, then after he did trust us, he just let us have everything — the keys to all the vaults — he'd say, 'You take care of it.' I was real lucky."

"We're going through the throes right now of trying to keep a lot of one-reelers from being lost. Richard Correll and David Nowell are doing a very good job handling nitrates for me. More than half of all the pictures made — more than *half* — have been lost through nitrate negatives because they're very expensive. Nitrate, as you all know, is a very dangerous form of film and very tricky. It turns into jelly and for no reason at all just explodes. It gets to a certain point, activates, and away it goes! And they're such nasty fires because of the fumes and everything. I lost an awful lot of films. They were stored in New Jersey, in a place called Bound Brook. Everybody stored them there. They had a tremendous fire and everything — Lonesome Lukes, etc. — were all lost. And I had a nitrate fire at the house. Fortunately, I didn't have the ones that I treasure the most. They were in another place. So that's where a great many films have been lost, and a lot of them have been lost because no one knew who could preserve them. They didn't think it was valuable. If we had known that they were going to have a certain value afterwards, we'd have saved a lot more. The picture was made, we were happy with it at the time, and we went on to make something else. That was that." [J]

> **FUN FACT**
>
> THE TRUE VICTIM OF THE EVENTS OF BOTH JANUARY 17, 1938 AND AUGUST 5, 1943 WAS FILM HISTORY, FOR A LARGE PERCENTAGE OF THE EARLY FILMS OF HAROLD LLOYD PERISHED IN THOSE BLAZES. OF THE 81 SINGLE-REEL GLASS CHARACTER FILMS PRODUCED, 18 ARE NOT KNOWN TO SURVIVE, AND MOST OF THEM POSSIBLY DIED ON ONE OF THOSE DAYS. A WHOPPING 53 OF THE TOTAL 67 LONESOME LUKE FILMS ARE NOT KNOWN TO SURVIVE — ONLY 14 EXAMPLES OF THE CHARACTER OF LONESOME LUKE ARE KNOWN TO BE EXTANT. GRANTED, THESE LUKE FILMS WERE ALMOST CERTAINLY NO MASTERPIECES, BUT THEY WERE STEPPING STONES IN THE CONTINUING EVOLUTION OF LLOYD'S GREATNESS — AND THEY'LL NEVER BE SEEN — IT'S STILL A SHAME.

HL surveys the damage done by a nitrate explosion and fire at Greenacres — and holds a destroyed reel of one of his films that will never been seen again.

Richard Simonton, a friend of Correll and Nowell, was in on the fun — the film work and the screenings — and also graduated to a career in film preservation. "Rich and Dave, mentioned above, were the best thing to happen to the film collection. With youthful enthusiasm, they aired out hundreds of reels of nitrate film that had been sealed in cellophane bags (which had only concentrated the deteriorating fumes) and began a preservation program for titles that had not previously received attention. They printed all the one-reelers they could, though some were already too far gone. Harold optimistically ordered those reels of film buried against the time when future technology might find a way to reverse the decomposition. (After his death, they dug them up and had a bonfire.) The good news is that many one-reelers were saved in the nick of time." [M]

The films that were lost, and the films that survive to this day, *all* have importance: "I was glad to find a character that I could say was truly my own, that was different from all the other comic characters on the stage and screen. My character had an individuality." [K]

"Watching one of his films with him was great," continued Correll. "He was like a director. If you sat and looked off to the side instead of at the screen, you would see him react much like the character was reacting; you would see him take his hand when something was about to happen and then hit with it, you know. He was like a director watching someone he was directing — a lot of directors are like that. They do the expressions as they're watching the subject."

Simonton still looks back on those days with warm and important memories. "We had never seen *Girl Shy*, Lloyd's 1924 feature, so half a dozen of us sat down one day in 1970 to watch a silent screening of it. Without music or the laughter of a larger audience, the film received a far less enthusiastic response than expected, so Harold (having cringed all the way through it) said, 'Put the print back in the vault. I don't ever want it shown again.' It's too bad we had watched it that way, because proper presentation makes a world of difference. After Harold died, I showed *Girl Shy* in a theater with live accompaniment by Gaylord Carter and people were helpless with laughter—as they have been ever since." [M]

Richard Correll had, and still does have, a thorough understanding of the man and his methods. He, like Harold, was a tremendous study. "He also always referred to the character on the screen as 'he' or 'the boy' or 'that fellow' — he never said 'I did this.' It was always the other guy. As a matter of fact, in real life, he was much like the character on the screen. People used to say to me, 'What's Harold Lloyd really like?' I always thought he was a lot like the character in his films, because even at an older age, he was very youthful, pretty high speed most of the time, had a great sense of humor and was always up to something — always up to a joke, or up to pulling a trick on somebody.

"I think my association with Harold Lloyd was one of the luckiest things that ever happened to me. I think, having been brought up around people like Harold, and having access to all those films, and all of the time he spent with me, it has really helped my career a lot. I've always been very, very grateful to him. As far as I'm concerned, he is still one of my best friends."

All of this happened, primarily, because Harold Lloyd decided to buy back his films from his original distributor. And, in so doing, he showed the true depth of his friendship for his pictures.

A Curious Human Being Turns Interested Hobbyist

Bees In His Bonnet . . .
"You don't have any boring moments by doing that . . ."

Harold Lloyd completed work on *Professor Beware* in May of 1938. He then took a break from the filmmaking game.

"I didn't really quit. I was more or less forced into doing one picture that I finished and didn't like. I had a picture before that, it was a veterinarian picture, and there was a king in it, a very democratic type of king, and I more or less was the veterinarian, brought the kitchen to him; in other words, ordinary things in life. And he felt that he liked my philosophy and he wanted to abdicate — he did finally abdicate in the story. This was right around the time that David Windsor was King of England, and he was thinking of abdicating. So the foreign department called me in and said, 'Harold, I don't think you ought to do the picture you're figuring on, that veterinarian picture, because we don't think you'll be able to release it in England. It won't be a good market for it because they're a little upset.' So I went ahead and made this other picture, and I was never really happy with it, it was a picture called *Professor Beware*. It had lots of good things in it, but I didn't think it was up to the others. So I said to the boys, 'I'm not going to shoot another picture until I get a story that I actually like.' Six months went by, I didn't find it, another year, two years — and finally I was having lots of fun, with hobbies, avocations, traveling; I was having fun." [D]

"His interest and joy of doing things in life — he was like a kid in a candy shop — he got into painting, microscopes, magic. It was all a challenge — his whole life was a challenge — to be as good as he possibly could. And he wanted to be a winner. He had that push that you have to have, in order to get somewhere in life. He pursued everything, to the very end." [G]

"My broad interests came after, more or less, I had achieved a certain amount of success in the theatre. Then the more that I began to accumulate what you might call avocations, or hobbies, the more interested that I became. I found that just something to do as a hobby wasn't enough. It had to be something that, more or less, captured you *completely*. That inspired you to probe all of the different facets of it. It had to give you an anticipation of arriving at a solution of how to do this, or where to go to get that, and ways of working this out, and how could you do this that would be a little better than maybe it had been done. It's that quest for it — that urge to keep going — that I think that makes a hobby a tremendously interesting activity in life. In fact, I think that it completely enriches your life. Not only in that you get up in the morning with wanting to pursue it, and learn more about it, but it allows you also to contact and meet so many personalities, people that you would never have met or known anything about, if you had stayed in just your own vocation." [A]

"You don't look for a hobby. You have to have something that's fun to do. You have to have something you like to pursue — that obsesses you, that you want to get up in the morning and do something about it, learn more about it, get something that has to do with it — then life is very interesting. You don't have any boring moments by doing that; there's not enough hours in the day. You must let it take over." [D]

"I have no idea what he'd do with the technology today and with computers — I'd be scared to death — he wouldn't sleep! The house would be wired up with every computer, every disk, every satellite dish, every form of information he could get his hands on! Because, he had encyclopedias, he had *National Geographics* that he saved, and he was a ferocious reader." [H]

SOME OF HAROLD'S FAVORITE HOBBIES . . .

"Painting, microscopes, showing dogs, judging, photography, color, music, stereo music, magic — oh, they go on and on." [D]

Let's examine these, and more of Harold's favorite leisure pursuits — and understand why they meant so much to him, and why their exploration marked individual turning points in his life . . .

THE STUDY OF COLOR — BY THE STAR OF BLACK & WHITE FILMS.

Harold Lloyd was once described as a primitive abstractionist, making a prime study of color theory, studying physical and chemical properties of color, and collecting and cataloguing samples of every hue of paint manufactured in the U.S. and abroad (Lloyd invented a color supply panel for artists, fitted with 72 tubes that squeezed out matched, harmonious shades). His painting grew out of his fascination with color. What began as working out color harmonies on swatches of canvas, grew into creating actual paintings. However, Harold was always clear on the purpose of this hobby.

Harold's interest in painting grew out of his research and appreciation of color. One has to wonder, though, how often he dabbled while in a suit and tie.

"We live in a world of color," Harold noted in "It's Tremendous," in the January 19, 1953 issue of *Time* magazine. "If you like the color forms, that's what pleases me. Then it's a success." He continued, "I don't give a damn about drawing . . . I start painting 90% of the time without any idea . . . Eventually it suggests something."

Painting — Suggested by Color.

Harold was a quite talented artist, investigating painting chiefly, at first, due to his preoccupation and fascination with color research. He eventually graduated from creating color harmonies to building images. His paintings were known as "Imaginettes" and "Fantascapes." They do conjure fantasy, and activate the imagination, just because of their non-descriptive character. You don't know quite what you're looking at, resulting in every spectator seeing something unique.

"From color, I finally got into the realm of painting, mainly because I like to work with color. So I paint landscapes, still lifes, and so forth. Finally, it was because of color that I started to paint some non-objectives. They were very imaginative ones — so finally, one of the men who was head of one of the art galleries, he was intrigued with them and gave me a one-man show which lasted for about a month. Of course, I was very puffed up and thrilled about that — I think anything you do that is different from your own

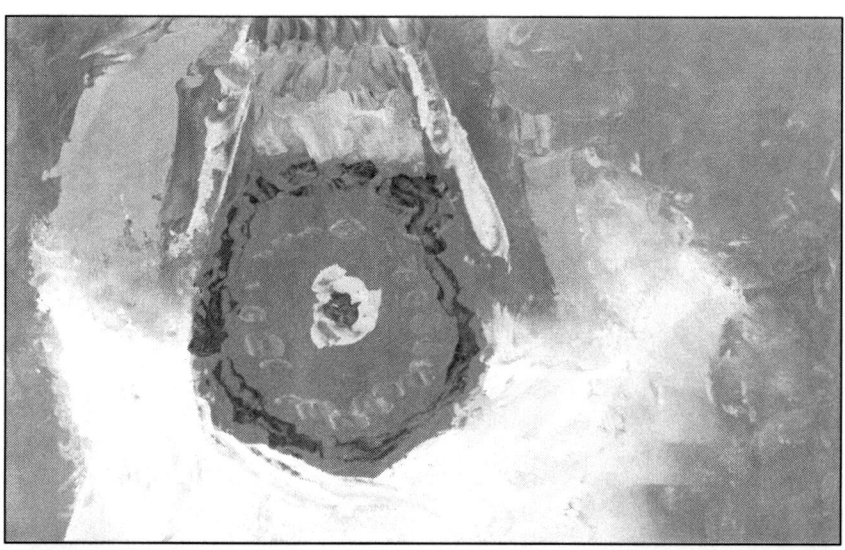

Three examples of HL's "Imaginettes." All created in vivid colors, one can look at them and *imagine* what he endeavored to communicate . . . but you're never quite sure . . . exactly as HL wanted.

occupation, the one that you actually earn your living on, that you get after you've achieved a certain amount of success, I guess you feel you've had it to a certain degree, then when you accomplish something in another field, you get a tremendous thrill out of it." [A]

In the January 19, 1953 edition of *Time*, Lloyd was profiled in the midst of his first exhibition, held from January 16-February 14

Harold played a lot of marbles as a child – here, he examines one of his collection, a whimsical branch of his research of color. The box is perched upon some of his books on color and painting.

at the Frank Perl Gallery in Beverly Hills. His works were called "bright as rainbows, and just as vague . . . objects occasionally turn up in his work." This might be an intentional theme, as Lloyd never named his paintings. He explained: "They're all non-objective, completely abstract, pure color harmonies. Maybe they strike you as ships burning at sea, or old temples with hordes attacking them, but the moment you get up close there's nothing you can point to and say this is that or that or that. If I gave them titles, you might object that they didn't look like what I called them. With no titles, you start with an open mind."

HL attends to an angle detail at the exhibition of his paintings in 1953. Each painting (here, the larger "Fantascapes" are on display) was untitled and "non-objective, completely abstract."

"There was a theme between the color in photography and the making of color paints to the edge, in finding new colors, and then having them patented. He really liked painting. This he did with the family — he did it with Mid, he did it with Harold, Jr., he did it with Glo — Dad didn't go to art classes, but Glo and Mid did. That was something that the family kind of did together — that was a hobby that brought the family together." [H]

Stereo Photography — Harold Snapped It Up.

In the June 1924 issue of *Photoplay* magazine, an author asked stars about "Their Pet Aversions," the chief peeves in their lives. Douglas Fairbanks told of his hatred for castor oil; Mary Pickford cited the color cerise; Marie Prevost noted how monkeys gave her the willies. Harold Lloyd, in an ironic choice, stated that his pet aversion was a still camera. "I hate a still camera . . . A camera in my house is — to me — like an unfriendly eye at a keyhole."

The "Chaos Room" at Greenacres — filled from floor to ceiling and wall to wall with photographic equipment for, arguably, his favorite hobby.

However adamant he might have sounded then, Harold *did* change his tune, particularly once he was introduced to the world of Stereo Photography, which allowed for 3-D images, in 1947.

According to the April 1954 issue of *Photography* magazine, "I met Jerry Holcher, a Sunset Strip camera shop owner, and Russ Dyer of the David White Company — those two conniving so-and-so's who baited me with a stereo slide and hooked me into a world of 3-dimensional photography that's been my padded cell ever since."

The thing about stereo that differentiated it from all his other hobbies is that it *lasted*. Whilst Harold tired of most of his other hobbies, stereo stuck, for life. And, in the life span of this hobby, Harold took upwards of 300,000 stereo images — one example, viewable in *The Stereo Realist Manual*, for which Lloyd wrote the foreword in 1954, saw Harold climb to the top of San Francisco's Golden Gate Bridge, just to get "the" shot. He also, famously, took thousands of 3-D images of topless models (vivid portraits, to say the least). He was a dedicated, enthusiastic, and fun-loving practitioner of the art and science of stereo photography.

Again from April 1954: "When I start shooting, I concentrate to a point where I'm liable to do anything to get a picture. I've stopped my car dead in the middle of Miami traffic to grab pelican shots while my fellow motorists blasted at me with their horns. At Grand Canyon, I crawled out on a rock overhanging the canyon to get a picture (a week before, someone was killed

A 1949 advertisement for the Stereo Realist camera, featuring one of its most famous customers — Harold Lloyd. At the bottom, the Realist is called "The camera that sees the same as you."

A wonderful shot of HL at his Stereo Realist camera — obviously enjoying himself. Note the hc/L monogram on his shirt's left pocket.

trying the same crazy stunt, but I didn't know it then). I've leaned out of the 85th floor of the Empire State Building, shot down from the top of the Eiffel Tower in Paris, and once, in New Orleans, when people on my balcony vantage point blocked my view of the main float in the Mardi Gras, I climbed out on a rickety electric sign to get my shot. I've done many foolhardy things which I don't advise anyone to emulate, but when my stereo and I are on the prowl, I'm in a fool's paradise."

Lake Tahoe sets a most spectacular backdrop for a beautiful image of photographer Harold, 1955. He often went to great lengths, and to fabulous venues, to capture his exquisite photographs.

The "chaos room" of Greenacres was where he stored and tinkered with his equipment. It resembled the rummage department of a second-hand camera store in war time — open shelves and all available floor space were crammed with Stereo Realist and Rolleiflex cameras, electronic flash equipment, stereo slide viewers, lighting paraphernalia, 3-D projectors, and slide-mounting gear and supplies. His photographer friend, John Meredith, estimated that Harold spent nearly a half million dollars taking pictures.

"He had a freedom to be creative, to be innovative, to travel, to have the freedom to be out of the house, and go anywhere he wanted — it was a tool to get him into places." [H]

Harold's granddaughter Suzanne has published two books on her granddad's favorite hobby. In *3-D Hollywood*, published in 1992, she shared images of Harold's friends — a veritable stereo time capsule of Tinseltown, captured by Lloyd himself. More recently, in 2004 she released *Harold Lloyd's Hollywood Nudes in 3-D!*, an examination of the racier side of Harold's pet avocation.

HI-FI STEREO — TO THINK HE WAS ONCE SILENT.

In the mid-1950s, Harold became very interested in hi-fidelity stereo — however, this was not a hobby that he immediately mastered. His first attempts were, well, less than aurally ideal.

Lloyd purchased marvelous speakers for his first system, housed in the living room. However, he did not take the speakers out of their boxes, opting instead to cut twelve-inch holes in the enclosures. His Bell amplifier, seated upon a folding card table, was cheap and, frankly, not up to snuff: as a result, his initial sound system was severely lacking in quality. He would learn great lessons from a young friend, Henry Joncas, thirty years Harold's junior, and would eventually have a refined and perfected system in his beautiful wood-paneled living room.

"My dad literally lived in the living room, and I spent a lot of time with him there — with his music. He did these things to the Nth degree. In his eyes, it was a project, a production — he loved it — I used to sit with him, holding his hand while he changed the records." [G]

When all was said and done, Henry helped Harold accrue an audio set-up to be most proud of, consisting of (for the time) state-of-the-art equipment: McIntosh amplifiers, a Marantz preamp, Rabco tone arms, two D & R turntables (so he could switch back and forth), huge custom subwoofers (designed by Gordon Mercer), and a pair of Isophase Electrostatic speakers (the original equipment, however, did not get thrown out: the old Bell amplifier and everything *but* the speakers in the cardboard boxes remained in their original place until he died. He just added more card tables each time new equipment was purchased).

Lloyd's record collection was immense, as was the volume he set for his enjoyment. At times, the level of his music would rock the living room, creating a slight but steady rain of the gold leaf from the ceiling. He once claimed that his favorite composer was Beethoven, though his tastes were entirely eclectic.

"He loved music — all kinds of music — from show tunes, to jazz, to classical — I guess classical was his favorite. He had something like 25,000 albums, and he had reel-to-reel tapes of live recordings and performances." [H]

"We used to argue over what to listen to," noted Joncas. "He listened to the classical and opera which I loved, but occasionally wanted to listen to some more popular singers and music. Finally, when I arrived one night, Harold said, 'I have the perfect idea for how we will pick the music.' Harold proudly brought out a simple little kitchen timer that rings a bell after the preset time. He said, 'Now what we are going to do is this. You pick a selection and we set the timer for 10 minutes. Then at the end of ten minutes, if I don't like it, it will be my turn to pick. If I do like it, we keep on listening to it, but we just take turns . . . O.K.?' And so it went."

MICROSCOPY — A HIGH-POWERED HOBBY.

Such a strange hobby, especially considering the fact that Harold would staunchly refuse to actually kill anything in order to study it under a microscope. He would only handle live things, leaving it to others to do dissections, which Harold would study afterwards.

Harold's microscopy hobby dated back to a trip he took to Germany in the early 1930s. He visited the Carl Zeiss plant (where world-famous lenses were made, and still are today), and decided to purchase the highest of the high-powered microscopes for Jack Davis, Mildred's brother who was then studying medicine at the University of California. Only thing was, once Harold got the "new toy" home, he grew so fascinated by it that he kept it.

Once Harold's press agent, Joseph Patrick Reddy, found out about this new hobby, he sent out the story about Harold's microscope to the press, and soon Harold was receiving things to look at, including live bugs, from perfect strangers. He and brother-in-law Jack set up a mock laboratory in the Greenacres cellar, and made a particular study of one species, the Black Widow spider. The

Microscopy was a comparatively short-lived hobby for HL — it only lasted around five years — but in that time, he and his scopes helped combat a Black Widow spider plague.

December 1937 issue of *Motion Picture* magazine featured an article by Dan Camp on "The Black Widow's Love Life (Not a Movie Star) — Discovered by Harold Lloyd." In it, we learn of Harold's "dissection" of each detail of the Black Widow's courtship, and the mating, followed by her eating her husband. Harold, according to the article, would watch and study the Black Widow's habits as no other species, and would not allow anyone, except himself and Jack Davis, inside the laboratory.

Harold was credited with a major discovery, in the midst of all this gawking. He and Jack found that a certain wasp from Texas is deadly to Black Widow spiders — this in the midst of a Black Widow plague, and as a curb was being sought — and conducted experiments to prove it. They tested two varieties of wasps with the spider: the first one met a quick end, but the second was quicker than she and, with speed and accuracy, stung the Black Widow to death. Harold received many commendatory letters for his discoveries.

"Microscopes. Oh, that obsessed me for about five years, I guess. I bought these microscopes, and I probed into the other world, and it is the most *fascinating* world. I put out about four microscopes at a party that we had one time — no one wanted to have conversation! They were all so interested — one of the things that had the most interest was an unwashed strawberry. I'm telling you — that was on the stage for an hour. It was one of the most interesting articles that anyone could imagine." [A]

Our Mr. Lloyd was a man of great intelligence, in case you didn't know that already. From the "I Bet You Didn't Know This" department, by Harold from the aforementioned article: "You can tell the real Black Widow . . . by a reddish mark on the bigger part of her body. It's shaped like an hour-glass, this mark, and definitely identifies *Latrodectus Mactans*, which is the Black Widow's scientific name. Aside from that, her body is glossy, her legs are long . . . and she's about an inch long, from leg-tip to leg-tip."

MAGIC AND MENTAL TELEPATHY — "CLAYTON THE GREAT."

Harold's general love of magic, actually, dated back to his childhood. His favorite trick was hypnotism — he enjoyed watching it, and did get the chance to play a famous prank on a young friend, Paul Herrin. Harold decided to teach Paul how to hypnotize him, with ironic consequences. "He was shown the mesmeric stare, the passes of the hands and, finally, the finger snapping that brought the subject out of his trance. He was an apt pupil and I a splendid subject, a trance resulting immediately. For half an hour he had me cavorting around the yard supposedly at his will, and how he enjoyed it! I was older and bigger, yet he was my master. When he no longer could think of anything more to order me to do he snapped his fingers to end

The three cohorts in "The Mental Marvels in Crystal Gazing Supreme" — from left, John "Swami" Summer (HL Corporation secretary), Harold "Clayton the Great" Lloyd, and Roy "Yogi" Brooks (HL's social secretary).

the entertainment, but the subject failed to snap out of it. He snapped his fingers again, he experimented with other fingers, waved his hands, commanded, coaxed, pleaded, pretended to go home and leave me, to return again to more finger snapping. My uncle John came home to luncheon to find all the snap gone out of Master Herrin's fingers and the boy nearly hysterical, but Uncle John had the family liking for horseplay and insisted that he was powerless. I was one to squeeze the last drop out of any joke, but when the boy broke into sobs his subject began to rub his eyes and manifest other signs of returning consciousness." [I]

Harold's appreciation for magic and tricks did sneak into his films — like the fly-in-his-hand trick to divert officer Charles Stevenson's attention in *Never Weaken*, and the hiding within a coat in both *Bumping Into Broadway* and *Safety Last!* — but never was magic more prevalent than in the dinner dance sequence in *Movie Crazy*. In it, Harold showed a deep understanding and a high grasp for the props that the professionals used to such great advantage — his choice of gags in this bit were outstanding.

The mental telepathy branch of Harold's magic hobby was more an extension of his love of performance than a fascination with the mystics — it involved mind-reading and memorization. One research source mentioned that Lloyd got the idea from reading about Tibetan monks, but in reality it grew out of some simple word games that Harold and Wally Westmore, among others, used to play at Paramount during the filming of *The Milky Way*. Harold, at first, didn't do too well at these word quizzes, and the loser always had to buy lunch — to solve the problem, he hired three secretaries to record every three-, four- and five-letter word in the dictionary, which Harold would then memorize. He did whatever he had to do to succeed. From that time on, he never lost a game, nor a lunch.

Speaking of lunch — one day in 1937, Harold hosted a luncheon at "A Bit of Sweden," on Lexington Avenue; this was one of his favorite New York City restaurants. This occasion was built around his new act, comprised of "Clayton the Great" (Lloyd), with "Swami Summer" (Harold Lloyd Corporation secretary John Summer), and "Yogi Brooks" (social secretary Roy Brooks). The show was called "The Mental Marvels in Crystal Gazing Supreme." The ad read on: "The Super Mentalists of the Age; Stupendous? Colossal? Astounding? Mediocre! Readings for What We Can Get, Ten Cents or Down; Come to Us with Your Troubles; We See All! Know practically nothing."

Surrounded by the restaurant smorgasbord, Harold set to work reciting the numbers off of dollar bills, backwards and forwards, and could identify any object, present or elsewhere, of which a guest was thinking. Their act went something like this: Someone passed Harold a dollar bill; Roy Brooks covered his face with his hands and proceeded to read the serial number on the bill. Harold, apparently, gave no signals nor did he say anything. Roy also read names written on papers held by Harold. The key: if a name of an object were whispered to Harold, he would concentrate on it and then, a few minutes later, one of his assistants in the next room would call out what it was.

The secret to the act was an elaborate mnemonic code that Harold developed. This code allowed Lloyd to transmit verbally to Summer and Brooks the identity of nearly every object, unbeknownst to the audience. This code was later preserved in several bound manuscripts — intact to this day — but there remain no directions which allow for deciphering it. The secret to the magic died with Harold.

Magic was a fun hobby for Harold; one that bonded him with other celebrities who had similar interests. Orson Welles noted that "I got to know Lloyd through magic — we were both members of the same magical fraternity. What a lovely man!" One famous story has it that Harold and Orson needed a sub trunk (one of those boxes that has an escape door in the back, making it look like the entrant has disappeared) for a gig they were hosting at the Players' Club on Gramercy Park South in lower Manhattan. They called upon Al Flosso, then owner of Martinka's Magic Emporium on Sixth Avenue in the Chelsea district in New York City. Lloyd and Welles were loaned a top-of-the-line Jack Gwynne original design trunk. The store was on the second floor: visualize, if you will, Harold Lloyd and Orson Welles lugging the large trunk down the stairs of this elevator-less building themselves, and then back up again! Anything, for the right gag!

CANINE BREEDING — HAROLD GOES TO THE DOGS.

Harold's interest in canines began in the mid-1920s — and as was indicative of his nature, he took this interest quite seriously, and did it up in a big way. *Big*, as in the size of the dogs.

At one point, the Lloyds had upwards of 70 Great Danes in his kennels (at his Westwood location ranch), and boasted a $500 a month food bill for the high-appetite pooches. His personal favorite was Great Pal Prince Ludwig. Prince would frolic with Harold and family at the beach, and was often photographed *on* his daddy. The family's home movies feature a sequence of Prince, along with Mildred and Harold, on a porch swing. These animals' weight averaged 150-200 pounds and, when standing on hind legs, the Danes met or exceeded Harold's height, of 5' 10". In the 1920s and 1930s, dog-wise, the bigger they were, the harder Harold fell for them.

HL frolics with his favorite Great Dane, Great Pal Prince Ludwig, circa 1927. Prince remained a vital member of the Lloyd family until his death in 1931.

As his collection of dogs grew, Lloyd began showing them in canine competitions throughout California. He not only judged the contestants, but earned a staggering number of "Best in Show" blue ribbons for his own dogs.

In late May 1930, Lloyd was saddened by the poisoning death of one of his Great Danes, along with three other dogs, at a Los Angeles Kennel Club show at the Ambassador Hotel. The dog, Champion Illo von der Rhon, was imported by Lloyd from Germany in 1927, and was valued at $2500 — he was found dead fifteen minutes after being returned to the kennels from the show by L.J. McGuire, who oversaw Lloyd's kennels. An immediate autopsy was performed, and traces of strychnine were found in the dog's stomach.

Harold's favorite Great Dane, Great Pal Prince Ludwig, died on December 19, 1931, of dropsy (an accumulation of excess water in body), in Harold's bedroom at Greenacres. He was 9 years old, and weighed 180 pounds; Prince had been a perennial Best in Show winner when in competition, but had retired in 1928.

Where, in his thirties, Harold bred the largest possible dogs, in his sixties and seventies, Lloyd preferred smaller canines. He often traveled with small poodles Pepi and Pierre, and visitors to Greenacres were met by cocker spaniel Nicki. He was a true animal lover, but Harold always held the highest fascination and affection for dogs.

Handball — powering Harold's left hand.

After Lloyd's 1919 bomb accident, he found himself suddenly without half of his dominant right hand. In order to function — not just in the acting of his films, but for such everyday activities as writing, eating and driving — he had to strengthen his left hand. To accomplish this, Harold turned to handball, one of his earliest sport hobbies.

"Handball keeps me thin during the making of a picture, golf from getting too fat between pictures . . . Handball is practicable because it may be played in the studio any idle hour.

"One day Roach jeered me onto the court by offering to spot me twenty points. Twenty-one is game.

"'You mean that I have to make only one point to win?' I demanded.

"'Right,' said Roach, and won 21 to 0. I not only made no point, but rarely came within six inches of the ball." [I]

Humble roots, indeed: the sport, with the pinpoint accuracy needed to hit the ball, assisted Harold when he needed to strengthen his left hand's mobility and, particularly, make it his new dominant hand. It succeeded.

When Lloyd was headquartered at his Hollywood Metropolitan Studios, production manager Jack Murphy built a three-wall, open-air court. "The smack of the hard rubber ball on the wooden walls may be heard most any time of day at the Metropolitan studio, but, whether we find time to play during working hours or not, a set of handball concludes most every working day." [I]

GOLF — PAR FOR THE COURSE.

One of the grandest features of the Greenacres estate was the golf course that Harold built in the front yard. He called the nine-hole arena the "Safety Last" course.

Par for the course was 30. Every hole had a water hazard, for the canoe path ran through the entire links. Many professional golfers, for that reason, considered Harold's the trickiest course in the area.

In 1927, as construction on his estate was bustling around, Harold held a tournament at the "Safety Last" course, entertaining some of the foremost golfers in the country, among them Tommy Armour, George Van Elm, Bobby Cruikshank, and Eddie Loos, who established a course record of 28. For his efforts, Loos was presented with a gold golf ball — Lloyd kept another such ball in his deposit vault, for the golfer who could best that record.

Jack Warner, one of the famed Warner Bros., also had a nine-hole course at his neighboring estate. Sometimes he and Harold would erect a temporary walkway over the fence, so that their guests would be able to play a normal eighteen holes.

HL and daughter Gloria tackle the final hole on the "Safety Last" course at Greenacres. Their canine companion looks rather disinterested.

Bowling — Lloyd goes on strike.

One of Harold's very favorite hobbies which he, miraculously, was able to continue with a hand disability, was bowling.

In March 1927, Harold entered the American Bowling Congress, yet was enjoying the sport long before then. At that time, as well, a Los Angeles-based bowling team took the name of "The Harold Lloyds," and Harold often played with his team, participating in a tournament with them on April 5, 1927. The team members were captain O.M. Gregg, J.B. MacKenzie (more on him later), Walt Ashfield, Joe McCord, and Harry Hopping.

Years later, after Greenacres was completed, a handball court was his favorite hobby spot on the estate for about the first ten years or so. Then, he wanted to build a bowling alley on the grounds. The lady of the house, Mildred, emphatically refused to let her husband do it, citing the excessive noise from the collision of ball and pins.

So, as any good millionaire would do, Harold Lloyd decided to build his *own* bowling alley, off the estate, and commissioned architect W. Douglas Lee to design a state of the art building on two lots in Santa Monica. Built in the famed Streamline Moderne style of architectural detailing, the Llo-Da-Mar bowling alley was erected at a cost of $29,000, opened in 1940 (the name is an amalgamation of owners' names, Harold **LLO**yd, Ned **DA**y, and Hank **MAR**ino), located at 507 Wilshire Boulevard in Santa Monica. The manager of the alley was one of the members of "The Harold Lloyds," J.B. MacKenzie. The building still stands today, boasting a large rectangular field of glass brick in the center of the central bay. The bay is offset towards the west, and is asymmetrical in form (very indicative of streamline design). The two-story building branched out into two extensions, both boasting a lengthy band of windows with unique protruding outer sills and hoods. The large one-story bowling alley also included a mezzanine area of offices, as well as a coffee shop and a cocktail lounge. The building was named to a prestigious list of Historic Properties by the Santa Monica Conservancy, on February 10, 2003, both for its architectural genius and for its historical significance.

How could Harold Lloyd bowl, one might ask, with only three fingers on his right hand? The customary bowling ball varies in weight, but normally has three holes, for the thumb, index, and

A rare shot of HL bowling — allowing you to see the full extent of the damage done to his hand in 1919. Thanks to a specially designed ball, he was able to continue participating in a sport that he greatly enjoyed.

middle fingers to brace the ball, which rests on the palm just prior to release. Harold was a natural *rightie*, but lacked the thumb and index finger. So, a special ball was designed for him, with a slot, approximately two and one half inches long and seven-eighths of an inch high, into which Harold would insert his middle, ring, and pinky fingers, resting the ball on his right palm before launching it at the ten pins. How did he do with such a revolutionary ball? He bowled three perfect (300) games in his lifetime.

Finally, Harold's Hollywood Hobby Horse — a Mutinous Mount.

Harold's Hollywood Hobby Horse — the wooden equine that got HL into the toy business for a spell.

Harold inspired the design of a toy in the late 1920s which was a party favorite at Greenacres. Friends at gatherings would try to play with it, and fall right off. It was Harold Lloyd's Hobby Horse.

Lloyd family friend Clyde Payne designed the hobby horse, which woodworker Fred Silch carved, and Harold financed the undertaking. However, Silch accidentally put a pivotal bolt in the wrong place, resulting in what was called a "mutinous mount." The toy horse, according to a March 4, 1940 article in *Life* magazine, "is next of kin to the Dodge 'Em and the Pogo Stick, and first cousin to the yo-yo." The most talented riders, at celebrity parties, were reportedly Jack Benny and Judy Garland. Among the worst: Harold himself.

Harold copyrighted the toy in 1929. Each of these recalcitrant equines was uniformly around thirty one inches high, twenty inches long, and thirteen inches wide, and was painted various colors with a red mouth, brown nostrils, blue eyes, rubber ears and a rope tail. The toy was a product of the Hollywood Hobby Horse Company, Inc. (Harold was President), located in the Beaux Arts Building, Los Angeles.

> ## Fun Fact
>
> Harold *did* let some marvelous hobbies into his life – his avocations were a tremendous source of joy for him, mentally challenging him, and keeping him active. Now, there are those who criticize Lloyd's bevy of pastimes — calling them rich man's toys or cures for the boredom of life — but the reality is that his life was better, and more interesting, because of his hobbies. Actually, Harold's staggering number of dedicated hobbies was less a product of his wealth and free time, than a result of his curious and enthusiastic nature. His tendencies, both on and off the screen, were to shrug the perennial shoulder at obstacles, laugh at challenges, and look a goal head-on — this explains his investigation of so many avocations, his pursuit of them, his conquering of them, and his essential discarding of them, moving on to the next. The joy of hobbies for Harold was to master something he didn't know before. Perhaps this way of thinking arose from his not having finished high school, and never having attended college — he absorbed as much information as he could, all his life. Lloyd was a very smart man.

Harold Lloyd Releases His Final Film

The Sin of Harold Diddlebock...
"I entered it with great enthusiasm."

Through the 1930s, Harold Lloyd made, essentially, one film every two years. With his final two features during that decade, *The Milky Way* (1936) and *Professor Beware* (1938), he saw his box office numbers dropping significantly, and an increasing lack of association between the public and his Glass Character. Perhaps it was due to his age . . . maybe filmmaking was growing less fun . . . possibly he wasn't getting good enough stories . . . whatever the reason, as he foresaw in his 1928 autobiography, he decided to bow out of active filmmaking when the handwriting on the wall needed no translating. Lloyd decided to slack off — for a while, at least.

With active filmmaking behind him, he turned to other activities — alongside his bounty of hobbies, he produced two moderately received films for RKO, and hosted a weekly radio program, *The Harold Lloyd Comedy Theatre*, for NBC and Old Gold Cigarettes. Here, Harold's main responsibility as host was providing narration and verbalizing visual plot elements — an ironic twist for a former silent film star.

"For an actor not to be active in his profession, it's like a golfer who hasn't played golf for a year or so. You get pretty rusty . . . A lot of people wondered why I had, more or less, stopped making pictures. It wasn't that you just decided to quit, you just kind of tapered off." [K]

Harold maintained a close friendship and a mutual admiration with Preston Sturges, the writer/director for whom billionaire

HL in *the* world's loudest suit, and wearing a ten-plus gallon hat, in *The Sin of Harold Diddlebock* (1947), embodying the post-war years' version of The Wardrobe Misfunction.

Howard Hughes had created California Pictures. It was, actually, Sturges who got Lloyd the radio show gig. However, and more crucially here, Sturges was not only a friend of Lloyd's, but a big fan, particularly of his 1925 college comedy, *The Freshman*. Preston encouraged Harold to come out of "retirement" to do one more picture with an intriguing twist: the investigation of what might have happened to Harold Lamb after he won the big football game for Tate College at *The Freshman*'s end. A satire all the way, the new picture was entitled *The Sin of Harold Diddlebock* — why the character's last name was changed from Lamb to Diddlebock is anybody's guess. It just might have sounded funnier.

The fact that Harold came out of retirement for this picture marked a turning point in his career, for a reason yet unknown to him: *The Sin of Harold Diddlebock* would become his final film. And, for all the excitement with which it began, it emerged as a quite disappointing close to his career.

"I came out of retirement because I thought we could make one of the best pictures I'd ever made. And I entered it with great enthusiasm." [E]

The film began shooting in September 1945. The picture commences with a clip of the climax of *The Freshman*, then quickly inter-cuts 1925 Harold with 1945 Harold — amazingly, twenty years had done little to his appearance — Lloyd could still pull off the college-aged character.

"I thought they used that to very good advantage. They took the football game which was the finish of our picture, *The Freshman*, and started off the picture with me as the young man who had won the football game, had scored, and got a job because of what he had accomplished there. Of course, 20 years elapse, and then you went into a character with me as a man around 40, but it was very good at sliding me in that way. Using *The Freshman*, we used the football game to finish the picture with — we'd built up to the character, you knew what he was trying to do, what the football game meant to him, and of course, the football game scored beautifully for us in that picture. But, then, starting it off without knowing who the character would be, how's it going to go? But, it didn't seem to make any difference — it had the same type of humor in it, and they laughed practically the same.

"They wanted to blend into *The Freshman*, from the old football game, into the present picture. And they tried, they had to make about four or five scenes, and they tried to get doubles, and each time they brought one in I said, 'Oh, no, that doesn't look like me, it won't work.' So finally, Wally Westmore, who was head of makeup

The thrill element in *The Sin of Harold Diddlebock* (1947) packed little of the punch of his earlier nail-biters, chiefly because the sequence began at the highest height. Jimmy Conlin hangs onto HL's leg, which is attached, via chain, to Jackie the Lion.

at Paramount, said, 'Harold, I think with a little makeup you can do it.' I said, 'Oh, Wally, you're kidding me.' 'No, really, we'll pull it up here, and put a little false teeth up there.' And, it was amazing — and I don't want to say it to be egotistical — but the funny thing is with very little makeup and the way they did it, they

Producer/writer/director Preston Sturges with HL in a posed still, ostensibly designed to create anticipation of a new Lloyd thrill sequence in *The Sin of Harold Diddlebock* (1947).

put it on me, and I walked onto the stage, we were doing some testing, and Sturges was sitting there, and he turned around and he looked at me in dumb amazement. And he said, 'Harold, I just don't believe it!' He followed me around for ten minutes; every place I'd go he'd be standing there looking at me and say, 'I can't believe it!' We took some of the stills, and we cut off the edges so you couldn't see the advertisements and we mixed them all together. The acid test was that I tried them out on Mid. And, she couldn't tell which were the new ones and which ones were the old ones." [B]

> **FUN FACT**
>
> FROM PRESTON STURGES' NOTEBOOK: "HAROLD LLOYD STORY: UNSUCCESSFUL WORM. DRINK AND MANY DIFFICULTIES. DIFFICULTIES FORCE RESOURCEFULNESS. RESOURCEFULNESS BRINGS SUCCESS. SUCCESS BRINGS CONFIDENCE."

A calendar montage shows the passage of 22 years in Harold's life, from June 1923 to June 1945. *The Freshman*, though released in 1925, set the opening scene in *Diddlebock*.

"We had a lovely idea. It was an idea you could say in one sentence, which is so good for any play. Well, it was just a young man who had all the enthusiasm and the ideas, and he was offered this opportunity when he finished college. And when he finished college, the man had forgotten that he had offered him this opportunity, so he was given a position of a bookkeeper. He thought he was going to get to be an idea man, which would gradually lead to him onto being one of the general managers or a vice-president, and finally the president — he had great ideas. And, of course, he ended up, 30 years later, as the senior bookkeeper. And it was a bottleneck, and he was let go, given a little extra money which they had held out. Having done that, he went out, without knowing what to do, he got talked into taking his first drink, and got roaring drunk, and a whole day went by without him knowing what happened." [C]

"And during that day he did more things — he bought a defunct circus, he got married, he played the races, and he made a tremendous amount of money. When he woke up the following day, he inherited all this trouble." [E]

The entire premise for the film was perfectly summarized by Harold; as he explains it, it does sound like a very inspiring and interesting picture. "A young man who had ambitions was given a position. This position kept him, for many years, where he stopped thinking. When he was fired, he got himself into trouble. When he got into trouble, he had to think again. When he thought again, he got back again what he had in his youth. He was a very nice character. He had just been subdued." [C]

"It was just this one day — there was a lovely motive in it — he had fallen in love with about seven different sisters. That was a nice scene. I can say this: that the first third of the picture, I thoroughly liked. If I were to make it over — I haven't seen it for many years — but I don't think I would want to change it much, the first third. It was from the time we got into a barber shop that we really went downhill, as far as I was concerned." [C]

"The theme of the story — the fight against the smugness which comes from security — is a very fine theme. But the way it turned out didn't please me." [K]

"I think Preston fell in love with a certain portion of it — he had way too much dialogue in it, in my opinion. Now, the first third of the picture, I liked very much. In that section of the picture, Sturges and I worked completely hand in hand. Anything that I had to do, he'd say, 'Harold, how do you figure you'd like to play that?' So I said, 'I'll think it over and bring it to you in the morning.' I'd come in the morning with a version of how I thought it should go and he'd say, 'That's it.' We had no trouble. We just seemed to be in complete harmony.

"Preston took about three or four months to write the first third of it. The last two-thirds he wrote in a week, more or less. And in that last section he had preconceived ideas of how the character should go. And there we didn't see eye to eye at all.

"I didn't agree with how he wanted me to play the character, and I had a section in my contract that if I didn't like it that I could play it the way I wanted. But I also had to do it the way he wanted. That meant in the projection room we had to argue it out, and we didn't fare any better in the projection room than we had on the set.

"Sturges got completely in love with this circus idea. He should have built the other ideas. There were so many things that could

A film that began very enthusiastically for HL evolved into a trial of his patience and fortitude — the 1950 reissue of *The Sin of Harold Diddlebock* was renamed *Mad Wednesday*, and reduced Harold Lloyd's name on all advertising so it was barely noticeable.

have come in there. He didn't want gags to come into it. He wanted his dialogue. It called for business; it just cried for it. He said, 'Harold, this business is too good for my dialogue.' I said, 'Preston, that's terrible!' 'Well, it'll kill the dialogue.' I said, 'Then, *let* it kill the dialogue! What are we after? We're after entertainment, laughs.' 'Harold, I just can't do it.' So I stopped looking for business. And that was the difficulty we had." [E]

Rather heated projection room arguments between Sturges and Lloyd began when takes were being chosen based on how leading lady Frances Ramsden looked in them, rather than their strength, according to Jean Nugent (the first choice for the role of Miss Otis in the film, but who later lost the part to Ramsden). A perennial tug of war developed between Sturges and Lloyd, she told historian Kevin Brownlow. "This started a kind of nasty feeling between the two of them. And I think Harold felt he wasn't getting a fair deal. And he proved that he was right many times when we were viewing the dailies. Sturges would say, 'And now we have Mr. Lloyd's preferences — we will show his prints.' And Harold would say, 'You *see*, Preston?' They were like little rotten kids. But many times Harold was right, and a lot of times Sturges was right. But it became a conflict, and I think this is what Harold began to show in the picture. He wasn't his happy, happy self as the picture went on."

Harold had further problems with his screen alter ego. "Preston wanted this character to be a schizophrenic, which I felt was an irritating character, that the audience wouldn't like him. And they must like you; they must feel sorry for you, they must work with you, and, of course, laugh at your idiosyncrasies and your mistakes. With this schizophrenic, you couldn't do that with him, the way he was.

"While I'm saying this, I don't want you to get the idea that I don't think he's a very astute and talented man. He's a tremendous power in the theatre. He just got imbued with this idea, in my estimation, and that spoiled the picture. Plus, Howard Hughes, who put all the money up and had a right to do what he wanted, he had other ideas and he did them, and in my estimation — probably not in Howard's — he didn't help the picture either." [E]

After Hughes pulled the plug on the original 1947 version, he cut it from 89 to 76 minutes, added a talking horse ending, and

The year before HL began work on *The Sin of Harold Diddlebock*, he was hosting a 1944-45 NBC radio show, *The Harold Lloyd Comedy Theatre*. By this time, his glasses had corrective lenses for reading.

re-released it as *Mad Wednesday* in 1950. "He changed the title and added the talking horse thing, much to my consternation." [C]

"So, consequently, even though some people may like the picture, I was terribly disappointed because I know it could have been a magnificent picture, probably one of the best that I'd ever made, and it wasn't, in my opinion." [E]

"I never particularly liked that picture; I thought it had missed very badly. I didn't make it. I wouldn't have made it that way. I thought it could have easily been one of the best pictures I ever made. But, it wasn't, by a long ways. Don't get me wrong — I think it had some excellent moments in it, and I think my work in it was as good as anything I'd ever done." [C]

The Sin of Harold Diddlebock does contain two examples of excellent handling of dialogue by Lloyd. Upon being fired, he explains his fate to Miss Otis; later, a dejected Harold gets drunk and spews his own special brand of wisdom. In these two sequences, Harold displays a tremendous ability to convey verbal emotion, further showing his many *histrionic* gifts that were admired in the review of Harold's first major stage appearance, forty years earlier.

Evidently, in addition to his admiration of Lloyd's *The Freshman*, Sturges also revered *Safety Last!*, for he incorporated a height thrill into *The Sin of Harold Diddlebock*. Amazingly, at 53, Harold could still handle the athleticism of the scene, but Sturges filmed the sequence against a process (trick) background, and commenced the thrill at the highest height. Harold realized that viewers knew the difference — *he had some experience in this area* — he understood the contrast between the current sequence and a similar height element from his silent thrill picture. "If you were nine stories in the air, you were actually that high, the people were underneath you at the time. We were actually up there because we didn't have the benefit of process in those days, or trick photography. Now, in *Diddlebock*, or *Mad Wednesday*, we had a lion scene up high — that was done with process; that was a process scene, but it didn't have nearly the impact that the earlier ones did." [C]

"He'd have you put to a height, and then if you wanted to go any higher, you couldn't; you were already there. You don't leave any space to reach a climax." [E]

The whole experience left Harold with an unexpectedly bad taste in his mouth, cinematically speaking. This project, which he had entered with such hope and enthusiasm, had ended so badly, particularly after *Mad Wednesday* was released by RKO three years after Diddlebock, and the 1950 advertisements not only did not give Lloyd star billing, they reduced the font size of this name so as to make it barely visible amongst his costars' billings. Angered by the whole situation, Harold vented his spleen by suing Hughes, California Pictures, and RKO, for damages to his image "as an outstanding motion picture star and personality," and for $750,000. The defendants' final counter offer of $30,000 was later accepted.

It is often said, particularly of athletes, that it is far preferable to go out on top of your game, rather than limping. In the case of cinematic superstar Harold Lloyd, to have such a disappointing and frustrating overall experience as he did in his final film appearance seemed a quite unfair way for it all to end. Thankfully, for him and for his fans, he was not quite done yet . . . it would take more than a decade, but Lloyd's name *would*, again, be on movie palace marquees. For this, we can be glad, for he *did*, ultimately, bow out of the movie game feeling like a champion.

> "The sin of Harold Diddlebock was that he had stopped using the brain that God had given him and the moral is: trouble is the grindstone that sharpens our wits."
>
> —*The film's end card*

Granddaughter Suzanne Enters Harold's Life

Luke Wins Ye Ladye Faire . . .
"It's really an incredible gift."

"I know the response his films get — I've never, in my life, seen people leave a theatre not liking what they saw. It was like you'd found your new best friend, and you hooked up with him, and he was a friend for life." [H]

If ever a granddaughter could be as close to a man as his own child, then Suzanne was that to Harold. If ever a grandfather could be his grandchild's hero, then Harold remains that to Suzanne.

Suzanne Gloria Lloyd Guasti was born on July 28, 1952, to Gloria and William Guasti. With parents who separated during her infancy, and a mother abroad throughout her childhood, Sue was essentially raised by Harold and Mildred Lloyd as their own child. She grew up in Greenacres. She called Mildred "Mimi." She always did, and still does, refer to Harold as "Daddy." Harold used to point to Suzanne and say, "There's my prize."

"He was very loving, very caring. He had a mission with me — I think I was the second shot — he got me through his daughter. He cared about spending time with me — he wanted to know what made me tick, what made me think, what made me feel, and he was truly involved. He had a boyishness about him, that he enjoyed doing things that children enjoyed — like going to the circus, going to the movies — he liked showing me things that he enjoyed.

HL inspects his legendary Christmas tree, housed in the Greenacres Orangery. Christmas was a big deal in the Lloyd house, particularly after Suzanne came to live there full time.

"He tried to make me more cultural. We played a game at the table, with an atlas — we'd pick a town or a country, and we'd have to have a discussion. It was a mental exercise — he wanted me to be connected." [H]

Life was filled with fun and luxury, peppered with a definite Victorian sense of discipline, and an omnipresent feeling that, in Harold's eye, Sue was being groomed for something special. For years, she dated Richard Correll, son of Charles Correll of Amos 'n' Andy fame, and his interest in film fostered Sue's curiosity alongside. She and her friends — most children of stars and industrialists — would play football on the spacious lawns of Greenacres, and Harold, desirous yet unable to participate, would provide refreshments and a hearty cheer from the sidelines.

One particularly whimsical ongoing memory of her childhood was the annual Christmas celebration at Greenacres. Not many children could boast of their family tree resplendent with over 5000 ornaments, with more in the basement. One Christmas shopping spree, at Saks, saw Harold starting to purchase a few ornaments and then, unable to resist, buying the entire display tree and taking it home on the spot. The twelve-foot beauty went to Greenacres, leaving a huge empty area in Saks.

"He's like a renaissance man before it was hip to be a renaissance man. He did his own thing, while being a very imaginative, creative genius." [H]

Not only did Harold lavish love and affection on Sue — providing a stability that she is perennially grateful for — but he also began grooming her, from a very young age, for her future role in his legacy.

"He did it pretty cleverly. He would pose questions, 'Well, if you were in this situation, how would you do this? What do you think of this? Would you do this or would you do that?'" [H] Harold took Sue on a business trip when she was just fifteen — that was the beginning of her life's true education, under Harold's tutelage.

One day in 1967, grandmother Mimi took Sue to the porch outside the dining room. "She said to me, 'I want to tell you where we were this afternoon. Daddy and I have given you a very special gift.' She said, 'You'll know what it is. I can't really explain it, but Daddy and I have given you something very, very important, and you're going to have to always take care of it. It's really an incredible gift.' And, she said, 'You'll understand, and it's really wonderful.' What she was trying to say was that

Seven-year-old Suzanne and HL, in the Poplar Garden at Greenacres, 1959.

'We trust you, and we really believe in you.' And, that was how I was written into the will, really young, at the age of 15." [H]

Sue, perhaps for the first time, realized the depth of her role in family affairs when Mildred Lloyd died in 1969. Harold gave Sue Mid's wedding ring, and put Sue in charge of her final arrangements. Such a daunting task for a 17-year-old girl. Then, a year and a half later, Harold succumbed to cancer, and Sue's role in the Lloyd world grew monumentally. She and four others were named in Harold's Last Will and Testament as the Trustees of the Harold Lloyd Foundation, now known as the Harold Lloyd Estate and Film Trust. In this expanded role, 19-year-old Sue learned more lessons than a Phi Beta Kappa scholar could possibly absorb. And, in so doing, she showed the depth of her devotion to Daddy.

Her courage would be tested during those dark days in July 1975, when Harold's beloved Greenacres had to be auctioned to the highest bidder. Unable to raise the significant funds needed to save the estate, after numerous attempts, an Iranian developer won himself a $1.6 million prize. "I think this is one of the largest crimes that has happened to the film industry — to let this house go," Suzanne noted, cognizant of Harold's wish that Greenacres would be made into a museum, open to the public, a Hollywood landmark to the golden era of silent cinema.

The years that have followed have seen Sue tirelessly defend her grandfather's legend, even when the battle seemed endless — as in *Grandma's Boy*, "Mostly uphill, and no shade." In her capacity as the sole remaining Trustee, Sue has donated significant funds to the American Film Institute, established scholarships in Harold's name to the University of Southern California and Pepperdine University, has dedicated the Harold Lloyd Motion Picture Scoring Sound Stage at U.S.C., and has traveled worldwide with Harold's films, presenting them to live audiences, just the format that Lloyd preferred. In 2005, Sue oversaw the production of a mammoth 7-disc DVD set, *The Harold Lloyd Comedy Collection*, which *The New York Times* declared the box set of the year. It has already been established that, in his lifetime, Lloyd shunned any small-screen viewings of his films. However, Suzanne feels he would have approved of cable and DVD as venues for screenings: "I think he would have loved it, because it was a controlled element, in which he could show his product the way he wanted." [H]

Today, Sue single-handedly runs both the Harold Lloyd Estate and Film Trust and Harold Lloyd Entertainment, overseeing the release of the Harold Lloyd Comedies, through theatre and television/DVD screenings, as well as publishing books, promoting his photography work, and marketing use of his image and likeness. "We're almost in our infancy of what can happen with, especially, a lot of his intellectual property — from remakes, to advertising and licensing, to merchandising, to games, to his influence on pop culture. It can grow — it is just a small little plant right now that needs to be fed and nurtured, to grow, and take root again, the way he was.

Fun Fact

Suzanne Lloyd is exactly what her grandfather wanted and needed: a businesswoman who knows her product, and believes in it. She currently oversees both the Harold Lloyd Trust and Harold Lloyd Entertainment.

"I had to have a company to be able to release the films, and put them out, to do screenings, and it could be a Trust asset which all of it is owned by the Trust, but it had to be a working company where I could get employees and some help, and work it so it was an arm of the Trust. So, I thought that, by having a corporation, I could publish books, I could do photography work, do remakes, do licensing of him as an individual for a commercial entity for any kind of product — but I could decide on how to use his image in the most tasteful way — and not to just hand him over to somebody who didn't really know his thinking or his philosophy, or really what he was about. This was really a vehicle to put myself into running it.

"I'm just now getting to a point, a plateau, where I'm going to see the work I've put into restoration, and for preparation to send him out. I know how his films do with audiences — and thanks to Sony, his films are being seen again in theatres — the reaction has been amazing. I hope that the DVD package is fulfilling — because I've put a lot of time, and work, and energy into it. As to how for it can go, I think there's a long way to go, and there's so much more to be done. And, it's been done with people who really cared, like you [Annette], Rich Correll, Richard Simonton – people who have come through and seen the potential. There have also been other people who have come in and pilfered and not cared, and just looked for their own enjoyment. Unfortunately, my grandfather's business sense of who he trusted his estate to was very short-judged." [H]

Sue definitely inherited her grandfather's sense of fun. Here, in 1996, the family and some friends take in the sights at the M-G-M Studios at Walt Disney World. Back row, from left, Paul Wing, Hugh Ragan, Jamie O'Neil, and yours truly, Annette D'Agostino Lloyd. Middle row, from left, Linda Trugman, son Christopher Hayes, Suzanne Lloyd, and daughter Jacqueline Hayes. Oh, in the front? You might recognize them: Goofy, Minnie, Mickey, Pluto, Donald and Daisy.

"If I had not been the person, straight off, to take the bull by the horns in this whole thing, and start Harold Lloyd, Inc., or carry on with the Trust, or do anything, this would not be in existence. Nobody would do it in my family. There was nobody in my family to do it — I have no brothers or sisters; I have a mother who was not put into a position of power by her father, to have any say about his films — he did not put any of his children in this kind of authority. It was always me, and it was only me. And I fought for him, for a long time.

"The most frustrating thing was to convince people to believe in Harold and what he could do. That was the hardest thing in the whole process — I never minded doing it — but he is a product I believe in so highly. I knew that I wasn't scared, because what I was selling, I believed in. But, I know the response his films get — I've never, in my life, seen people leave a theatre not liking what they saw. It was like you'd found your new best friend, and you hooked up with him, and he was a friend for life." [H]

Harold took on the responsibility of raising his granddaughter Suzanne when he was close to 60 years of age. This, for most men, is normally a time in which retirement looms, and parenting duties melt into guiding friendships. However, in conscientiously assuming her upbringing, Lloyd unwittingly reached a succinct turning point in his life. True, he had given himself a renewed and unsullied chance at fatherhood, but he also purposely and carefully molded his granddaughter into the kind of businesswoman he needed, a fierce believer in his life's work. He chose her for this vocation — and she has run with it from day one.

"It's a lot of responsibility, and I've had some major fights. Sometimes I just sit and I think, 'What would he think, what would he do?' I have responsibilities — I've got a family to raise; I'm a single mother with two children to raise. But, I'm really happy. When I go into a theatre, and you see those really great responses — kids jumping around saying, 'He's great, he's great,' and they don't even know who he is: *how great is that?* I'm really proud of him — I love him to death as a Dad or a Grandfather — but also the person who was the career person, the star. The work that he did, and the joy that he keeps on giving to these people and children, who don't even know who he is, and the joy that he's bringing back to people who did know him. That's just a remarkable thing: what a great gift to know that you've been dead for years, and you're *still* making people laugh and be happy, and in some places you haven't been on a screen in 80 years — and your magic goes up there, and your art, and your character which you developed and discovered, from your own personality, is still entertaining people of all ages today. I think that's just an *amazing* thing." [H]

Harold Lloyd, her grandfather, has become her career, and she savors the role that was given to her. "People need to know who he is. I need to carry the torch for him." [H]

HAROLD LLOYD IS RECOGNIZED WITH AWARDS

Count the Votes . . .
"This is a very cherished moment."

"They do forget you. I know in my case that I've been off so long that I know that I've lost practically a full generation. I think kids from 24 on down, they might have heard of me through their older brothers or mothers and fathers. I had a funny little incident coming out of the Sherry Netherlands — a group of youngsters came chasing after me, this was about a year ago, and wanted my autograph, and I said, 'Now, wait a minute, kids, you don't really want my autograph; you don't even know who I am.' They said, 'Oh, yes we do, Mr. Lloyd.' I said, 'Now, you haven't possibly seen me in a picture.' They said, 'Yes, we have.' I said, 'Now, where?' 'Well, over there at the Museum.'

"Every so often I have someone come up to me — and I know they're as old as I am, and sometimes I think that they're a little older — and they look at you and with the greatest of sincerity say, 'Yes, sir, we certainly like you. I saw you when I was a little girl.'" [B]

Whoosh! Even in his day, Harold realized that fame was fleeting, and that a star's adulation lasted only as long as his most recent release. As such, it must have been both a joy and a relief to be granted a number of very special honors and awards in his lifetime. Each marked very happy turning points in both his professional and personal life — each denoted recognition; each signified appreciation; each singled him out as one of the greats. However, one, in retrospect, did significant damage to his enduring legend, far beyond even his realization. Read on.

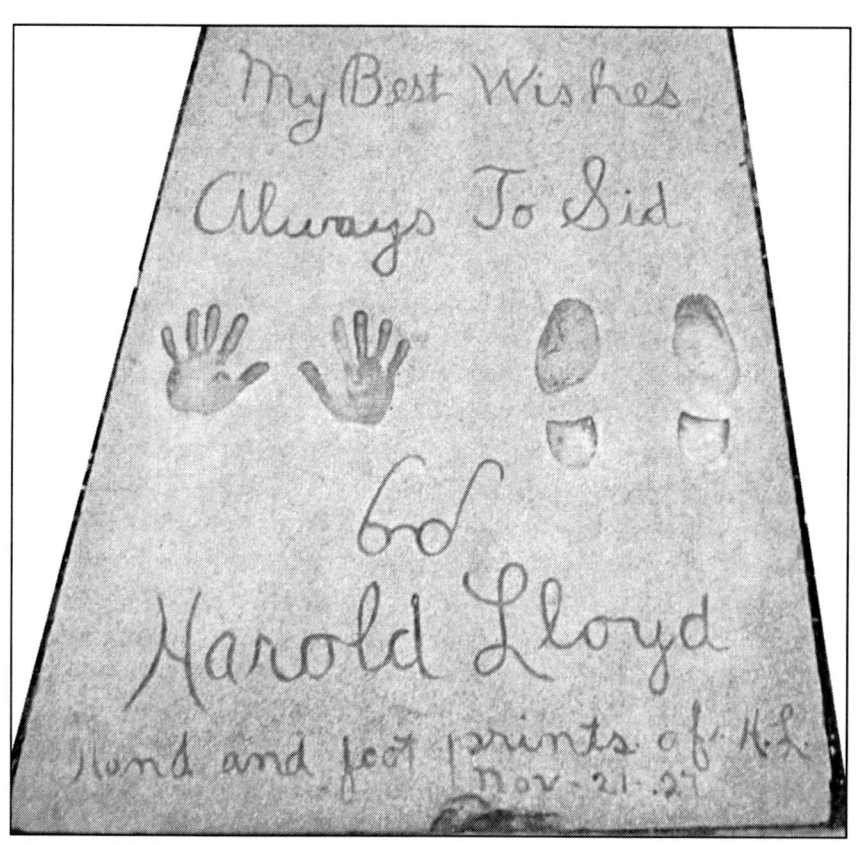

The Harold Lloyd block in the forecourt of Grauman's Chinese Theatre, on famed Hollywood Boulevard.

GRAUMAN'S CHINESE THEATRE — CEMENTING HAROLD'S STARDOM.

The world-famous Chinese Theatre, located on the 6900 block of Hollywood Boulevard, was the final picture palace constructed by "Hollywood's Master Showman," Sid Grauman (1879-1950).

Groundbreaking for the property, which was the site of the home of actor Francis X. Bushman in 1915, was marked by a ceremony at 7pm on January 5, 1926. Construction took just over one year, and cost approximately $2,000,000. Opening night, May 18, 1927, saw 2,258 spectators (its then-capacity) experiencing the Los Angeles premiere of Cecil B. DeMille's epic (almost three hours long) *King of Kings*.

The forecourt of the Chinese Theatre remains, to this day, a lasting memorial to Hollywood luminaries, and the enduring tradition of placing hand and foot (primarily, though not exclusively) prints in wet cement began on April 30, 1927. That much is known. *How* the idea was hatched is widely speculated (at least nine published versions are known to exist), yet is not important. What is important is that it continues, and probably always will (though real estate is now at a premium!).

After Mary Pickford and Douglas Fairbanks (ceremony #1, April 30, 1927), Norma Talmadge (ceremony #2, May 18, 1927), and Norma Shearer (ceremony #3, August 1, 1927) came Harold Lloyd, who was granted the fourth ceremony, on Monday, November 21, 1927. Harold's square (which is not really square, but an uneven brand of quadrilateral) was inscribed "My Best Wishes Always To Sid." Under the inscription was, to the left, his hand prints and, to the right, his foot prints. Under them is a whimsical, and singularly unique, cement rendering of Harold's famous glasses. Directly underneath is his autograph (neat, yet not at all indicative of his normal signature), followed by the verification that the above are actually the "Hand and foot prints of H.L."

The poignant element to this ceremony, one which visitors can see — but may only notice upon mention — is the effect of Lloyd's bomb accident on the hand print impression. Of course, Harold wore his prosthetic device underneath a glove for the ceremony. However, it is evident, upon looking at the *right* hand print, that the thumb and index finger could not be pressed as heavily or deeply as the other (real) fingers. Yet another souvenir of that fateful August day eight years earlier, preserved for posterity in cement.

HOLLYWOOD WALK OF FAME — LLOYD HAS TWO STARS.

It runs, east to west, from Gower Street to Sycamore Avenue along Hollywood Boulevard, and is intersected by Vine Street, running north to south from Yucca Street down to Sunset Boulevard. It is the Hollywood Walk of Fame, and it is, indeed, a star-studded walk.

The first ceremony took place in 1961, showcasing square coral terrazzo stars outlined in bronze, with celebrity names, inset in three-foot square black terrazzo blocks. Underneath the name is an encircled symbol of the industry for which the honor is bestowed: a camera for film, an antenna-laden set for television, a microphone for radio, an LP disk for the recording industry, and comedy/drama masks for live theatre (the final category, added in 1984).

Harold Lloyd was the recipient of *two* camera-emblazoned stars, one for his acting in film, and one for his producing talents. One star is found at 1501 Vine Street, at the intersection with Sunset Boulevard, at the northwestern corner. The other is located at 6840 Hollywood Boulevard, directly in front of the Hollywood Masonic Temple: it was dedicated on June 5, 1969. That day, coincidentally, was Harold Lloyd Day in Los Angeles County, so bestowed by the County Board of Supervisors.

GEORGE EASTMAN HOUSE — HONORING HAROLD.

Long revered as one of the premier film history libraries and preservation houses in the world, the George Eastman House, located in Rochester, New York, presented three distinct honors to Harold Lloyd during his lifetime.

On November 19, 1955, the First Annual George Eastman Festival of Film Artists presented gold plaques to ten outstanding stars of the silent screen. The Medal of Honor was inscribed, "For Distinguished Contribution to the Art of Motion Pictures, 1915-1925." The honored stars were chosen by a poll of over 300 Hollywood actors, actresses, producers, and directors. This decade of stars was Mary Pickford, Charles Chaplin, Buster Keaton, Ronald Colman, Gloria Swanson, Lillian Gish, Mae Marsh, Richard Barthelmess, Norma Talmadge, and Harold Lloyd.

Two years later, on Saturday, October 26, 1957, the Second Annual Festival of Film Artists was held at the Eastman Theatre at George Eastman House in Rochester. This Medal of Honor was awarded to those who contributed to the industry from 1926-1930. Rouben Mamoulian was the Master of Ceremonies, the recipients were Clara Bow, Joan Crawford, Greta Garbo, Janet Gaynor, Norma Shearer, Maurice Chevalier, Gary Cooper, Fredric March, Ramon Novarro, William Powell, Gish, Pickford, Swanson, Barthelmess, Chaplin, and Lloyd.

On October 24, 1965, Lloyd was honored at the Dryden Theatre Film Society Festival. Eastman House Vice-Director James Card hosted a tribute and presentation to Harold, who was gifted with a rare 28mm print of *Luke's Double* (1916), as well as an antique 28mm projector.

THIS IS YOUR LIFE — HAROLD LLOYD, AND OTHERS.
This classic roast of a series, which aired on NBC from 1952-1961, was hosted by the late Ralph Edwards. Its premise, honoring a singular person with testimonials from family and friends, gets to the very heart of what really matters in life: making every day count, and acknowledging those you love each of those days. After having been a guest on *This Is Your Life* episodes honoring Mack Sennett (March 10, 1954) and Bebe Daniels (September 29, 1954), it was Harold's turn to be the roasted.

This Is Your Life: Harold Lloyd aired on December 14, 1955; a half-hour long program presented live in glorious black and white over the airwaves of the National Broadcasting Company.

Harold was at dinner at the legendary Brown Derby, with friend Jim Coulter, when he was surprised (to put it mildly) by Edwards and his accompanying camera crew. It should be remembered that this program was aired live, as it happened. Harold was almost upstaged by neighboring diner, Groucho Marx, who was at the adjacent table with his family, and was in particularly good humor that evening. Actually, once Lloyd and Edwards arrived at the El Capitan Theatre, you could hear the host boast, ". . . *Without Groucho Marx!*"

By the time of this program, Harold's parents and brother had all passed away. Guests included Paul Herron, a childhood friend, who reminisced about Harold's prankishness as a youth; Hal Roach, who looked back at their early days as extras on the lot at Universal; Mildred Davis Lloyd, who recalled her first meeting with Harold; their children, Gloria, Peggy, and Harold, Jr.; Jackie the Lion, Lloyd's "co-star" in *The Sin of Harold Diddlebock* eight years earlier (the only caged guest); makeup genius Wally Westmore, who recalled word games they used to play to pass the time at Paramount, and former Shriners' Hospital patient Patty Lee Britton, who acknowledged Lloyd's visit to her while a resident at the Hospital.

Harold was, obviously, every nervous about this surprise, for he mistakenly placed his *left* hand in his pocket during the opening segment of the program, and gestured openly with his right; the viewer, as a result, has a very clear view of his maimed right hand. Though shaky at first, Harold calmed down, and seemed to enjoy himself immensely. He smiled throughout the program, and was very animated in his commentary about his childhood and his entry into film. "Ralph, I never thought you could do it," Lloyd commented to Edwards on being chosen a *Life* honoree.

THE AMERICAN FILM INSTITUTE — NAMING A SEMINAR SERIES AFTER HAROLD.

The American Film Institute was founded in 1967 as a national arts organization designed to train filmmakers and preserve America's film heritage. Two years later, on September 23, 1969, the AFI held its first Master Seminar, a series of discussions with participants who represent a cross-section of cinema's talents. The series is now known as the Harold Lloyd Master Seminars, after its initial guest, and continues to attract luminaries from around the world.

Harold was delighted to have been chosen as the inaugural subject of this seminar program. Coming a month after his wife's death, the timing of this colloquium could not have been better for Harold's morale, and for his feeling of permanence within the film community. "May I just say that . . . I feel highly honored being in on the initial shove-off . . . It's a pleasure to have been your guest tonight. I'm happy to say that I have the honor of being one of the original men of the Academy of Motion Picture Arts and Sciences, and I don't believe it was as big as this when we started, to tell the truth. I'm sure that everyone here, every guest you have, is rooting that it's going to go tremendous places." [J]

THE 25TH ACADEMY AWARDS — HAROLD AND OSCAR FINALLY JOIN HANDS, BUT AT A HIGH COST.

On January 11, 1927, the Academy of Motion Picture Arts and Sciences was born. Thirty-six people who represented a cross-section of the film world met that evening to discuss the formation of an organization which would serve the motion picture industry. Of this group of thirty-six, two were lawyers — their client? Louis B. Mayer, head of Metro-Goldwyn-Mayer. The two legal men, Edwin Loeb and George W. Cohen, became "special members," seeing to the legalities of drawing up a Constitution and By-Laws. Mayer, on that night, was elected Chairman of the Committee on Plan and

Honorary Academy Award recipient Harold Lloyd, March 19, 1953.

Scope. The remaining thirty-three persons present signed to become "founding members" of this Academy.

Five Academy "branches" were initially established (as of 2008, the tree had grown to 15 branches) — the initial quintet of discipline representations was Actors, Directors, Writers, Technicians, and Producers. The Actors Branch was comprised of Richard Barthelmess, Jack Holt, Conrad Nagel, Milton Sills, Douglas Fairbanks, Mary Pickford and Harold Lloyd.

Each year, the Academy recognized excellence in the industry, and the most sought-after prize in the film galaxy was its Academy Award, later nicknamed Oscar. The first Academy Award ceremony was held at Hollywood's Roosevelt Hotel on Thursday, May 16, 1929. Sadly, most of Harold's finest work had pre-dated possible awards. Imagine how crammed his mantle could have been, had such films as *Grandma's Boy, Safety Last!, Girl Shy, The Freshman* and *The Kid Brother* been eligible for Best Picture honors.

However, one of the Actors Branch's founders was not forgotten by the organization he had helped establish. Twenty-five years after its inception, "Oscar" had a date with Harold Lloyd.

Thursday, March 19, 1953: the 25th annual Academy Awards presentation, which had the historical distinction of being the first *televised* Oscar ceremony. *Variety* estimated that over 91,000,000 people either watched or listened to the entertainment world's party of the year, which was telecast live from bi-coastal locales. The Hollywood portion originated at the Pantages Theatre, hosted by Bob Hope, while the New York portion was held at the NBC International Theatre, hosted by Conrad Nagel (a founding member of the Actors Branch himself). This was 1953, but the Academy was awarding honors for outstanding achievements in films released in the year 1952.

In Hollywood, Bob Hope mused about the current vogue of 3-D pictures, all the rage, popularly-speaking, in theatres nationwide. "It's hard to say what effect 3-Dimensional pictures will have on the world," Hope began. "The next generation of children may be born with square eyeballs." In a later reference to 3-D's impact on Oscar, Hope joked, "This is the last year the statuette will be presented in this form. Next year, it will be wearing glasses."

Academy President Charles Brackett, late in the over-90-minute telecast, had the distinction of presenting the Honorary Academy Awards, voted by the Board of Governors. This year, six honorees were lauded for their various contributions to the industry: George Alfred Mitchell, Joseph M. Schenck, Merian C. Cooper, Bob Hope, *Forbidden Games*, as Best Foreign Language Film of 1952, and a very special honoree, whose introduction, by Brackett, went as follows:

"On most arrangements of the Greek masks, the mask of comedy is placed a little higher than the mask of tragedy. And, why not, you ask, after seeing what a laugh will do toward lifting the human spirit. The next award goes to a high practitioner of comedy. A man who, in a dazzling series of movies, permanently dislocated the funny bone of America. But, he was more than a comedian; he was, and is, that most difficult of all things to be: a good citizen. On its Silver Jubilee, the Academy is pleased to announce the voting of an Honorary Award to its beloved Freshman: Harold Lloyd."

Prior silent film greats who had received the Honorary Academy Award included Charles Chaplin (1927/28), David Wark Griffith (1935), Mack Sennett (1937), and Douglas Fairbanks, Sr. (1939). Joseph M. Schenck shared 1952 honors with Lloyd; Buster Keaton would be lauded in 1959, Lillian Gish in 1970, Chaplin again in 1971, Mary Pickford in 1975, and Hal Roach in 1983.

Lloyd, who had not previously received an Academy Award, (despite his final silent, *Speedy*, being nominated for a "Best Comedy Direction" Oscar in 1927/28), received his prize with the following short statement:

"Thank you. I am most grateful, and highly honored, to the Academy, for this award. This is a very cherished moment. You know, when you get one of your own, they kind of seem different. As Bob said, next year, they'll have glasses. I guess I'm just a year too soon. Thank you very much."

A cherished moment, on the surface, it indeed was. However, in retrospect, *Harold might have been better off without this award*. I'll explain this unconventional turning point . . .

Harold Lloyd was given the 1952 Honorary Academy Award, inscribed to a "Master Comedian and Good Citizen." The dedication was very carefully worded, and while it was honest and, on the surface, complimentary, two of the words on the plaque would later have detrimental overtones, and would prove significantly damaging to the recipient and his reputation.

It is true, and undeniable, that Harold *was* a master comedian, and owing to his monumental charitable work, particularly on behalf of the Shriners' Hospitals for Children, was a good citizen. However, the choice of the two words "good citizen" can be interpreted as not solely directed towards Lloyd, but rather squarely at . . . Charles Chaplin.

From the earliest of his films, Chaplin and his Little Tramp persona presented pictures that championed the underdog — much as Lloyd did with his Glass Character — but Chaplin (perhaps because he was not born in America, but more probably because of the preponderance of poverty in his films) was much more attractive to liberals and leftists and intellectuals than Lloyd. Commencing in the early 1920s, the Federal Bureau of Investigation kept tabs on Chaplin and his activities, and failed (though they tried) to find evidence that he supported the Communist Party. By the 1930s, Chaplin's films were increasingly more political in scope and message. Chaplin gave a speech in 1942 in support of America's then-ally The Soviet Union — this caused a great deal of controversy, especially within the McCarthy era, when everyone and their mother was running scared of being branded a Communist on the basis of his/her associations. Soon, organizations and clubs were campaigning against Chaplin, and theatres showing his films were picketed. Conditions rose to a fever pitch, poisoning Chaplin's name to a level where many in Hollywood were afraid to be associated with him or his filmmaking world. Finally, on September 17, 1952, Chaplin and his family ventured to London to attend to world premiere of his film *Limelight*. While on board the *Queen Elizabeth*, Chaplin was informed that the re-entry permit he would need to return to the United States (Chaplin never renounced his British citizenship) had been rescinded. He decided not to return to America, making a new home in Vevey, Switzerland. Chaplin only returned to the US once, in April 1972, to receive his second Honorary Academy Award.

The awarding of an Honorary Oscar to Harold Lloyd was long overdue — beyond his prominence as a founding member of the Academy, he had a body of work that should have been honored years before. That being said, recognizing him as a master comedian would have made perfect sense at *any* time.

However, the timing of the Academy's recognition of Lloyd as a "Master Comedian *and Good Citizen*" in 1952 seemed kind of strange — true, he did serve as a Delegate from California at the Republican National Convention in 1952, and had helped found the Shriners' Hospitals back in the early 1940s — but he did nothing out of the ordinary to warrant such a "good citizen" laud that year.

> ## Fun Fact
>
> This might not have been a formal award, but it was a delight for Harold, nonetheless: his caricature at the Hollywood Brown Derby, located at 1628 Vine Street, was a joyful presence at, truly, one of his favorite dining spots. These caricatures began in 1933, when Bob Cobb, owner of the Brown Derby, was approached by a young man from Poland, Eddie Vitch. He offered to do some sketches of his famous patrons in exchange for a meal. The result so delighted Cobb that he hired Vitch on the spot, and a tradition was born. Harold Lloyd was a vivid and memorable part of the Hollywood Wall of Fame, indeed.
>
> And, serendipitously, Harold and childhood pal (and fellow stereo photography enthusiast) Jim Coulter were dining at that very restaurant on the evening of Wednesday, December 14, 1955 – the night Lloyd was honored on *This Is Your Life*.

Why *did* Harold get *that* award, worded *that* way, *that* year?

Simply put, it was more of a slap in the face to Charlie Chaplin than a reward to Harold Lloyd.

And, the aftermath was terribly damaging to Lloyd — a backlash that can be felt to this day. Whether the Academy realized what their wording of that award would eventually do to Lloyd, one can only surmise. But, the reality is that Harold Lloyd's reputation, critically and popularly, suffered, and badly, as a result of being deemed a "good citizen" that year. And he's still paying for it.

Critics and intellectuals, who all adored Chaplin, began looking at Lloyd differently — assaulting the attack on Chaplin, through Lloyd's award, by sacking Harold altogether. It didn't help that, at this juncture, film criticism began to evolve into an erudite and scholarly pool of murky confusion for those lacking Ph.D.'s in cinema. The Lloyd films, non-"Auteur," non-intellectual, ultra-American and diverse in character scope, began being viewed as outside the realm of film criticism, and unworthy of serious examination. Lloyd's movies, with their emphasis on conquering obstacles and endeavoring to move upwards, did not resonate with a new arena in film critique that tended to celebrate the cinema of the left, of the liberal, of the perennially downtrodden, and leaned away from America and towards Europe in terms of cinematic importance. Lloyd's Glass Character, which essentially changed in personality with each release, was not viewed as a relevant regular character with an ongoing message. Essays and studies of the Lloyd films were practically non-existent, compared with the bounty of assessments of the works of his contemporaries. Soon, Lloyd was an outsider in the arena of serious film criticism, replete with its historical and political overtones and its psychological musings.

The kids of the 1950s, who not only read this stuff, but also grew up without Lloyd films on television, evolved into the authors and critics, historians and scholars we all know today — and they started elevating the Charlie Chaplin and Buster Keaton they knew and understood, while dismissing the Harold Lloyd they hardly knew. Harold's standing really began to suffer. And, owing to the fact that *he* didn't create the problem, *he didn't deserve it*. It was mean and unfair.

Hopefully, as new generations — now armed with the knowledge of the more accessible Lloyd films — grow to become the burgeoning image movers and history chroniclers, the critique of film and filmmakers will advance into what it should have been all along: an assessment of each individual's talent, and the worth of each standalone motion picture, not an endless study in comparison and contrast. I've often noted that the comparison of the "Big Three" in silent film comedy, Chaplin, Keaton and Lloyd, can be likened to a link between any given "big three" in fruit — say, apples, oranges and bananas. Just as those three are generally known as fruits, Charles, Buster and Harold are all generally known as silent film comics. However, just as the cited fruits all have different colors, textures, tastes and nutritional values, each of the gentlemen cited have markedly different styles, characters, motivations, strengths, weaknesses, and talents. Comparing the three fruits, as well as the three geniuses of the silent film comedy, is merely an exercise — a *fruitless* one, if you'll pardon the pun — in trying to push a personal preference on others. If you like one better than another, fine, but comparing them has no practical purpose. There's no room for that in serious film study. And, it has been universally practiced for generations. *And*, most crucially here — it has been rampant since Harold Lloyd received that award in 1953. He might have been better off without it.

THE CRAFTING OF
TWO FILM COMPILATIONS

Harold Lloyd's World of Comedy . . .
"It isn't just a reintroduction. It is a rebirth."

"I think Charlie was really one of the great figures; but speaking of him as such, sometimes, one gets so strong about Charlie that they make him the only one, and I can sit down and name ten that are just magnificent in my estimation, equally as good in their way as he was in his. So, I think it's wrong to pick any one person as being the only one." [E]

Indeed, by the late 1950s and early 1960s, Harold started to think that the time was right for a re-introduction to the baby boomer generation. *How* to do it? That was the basic dilemma.

Many of his pictures, including *The Freshman* and *Movie Crazy*, had been re-issued by Harold throughout the 1940s and 1950s, in theatres worldwide. "Their reception had been excellent. Those had been about the only occasions on which I have dusted off my old films and given them a public airing since they were originally released." [K] However, he was hesitant to literally re-issue all of his films: they were made during a different time — the audiences who would be seeing the films, teenagers, and even some adults, were not even born when Lloyd's films first came out, and the frame of reference in the movies might be lost on most viewers. Harold knew that, to them, his name was not as widely known as some of his contemporaries. He was fearful that his beloved pictures would be slighted by a generation for whom they were not made in the first place.

Throughout the early television era, Lloyd had repeatedly shunned attempts to air his films, which he totally controlled; he didn't want his films edited for time restraints or broken up for commercials, but wanted them seen in a complete, uninterrupted form. Despite the fact that Harold had produced compilation films specifically for the Shriners (*Down Memory Lane* in 1949 and *Harold Lloyd's Laugh Parade* in 1951), he seemed to completely dismiss the idea of screening isolated moments from his films to the general public via edited-together clips.

That being said, it was a curious compromise when, in 1955, Harold announced his intent to produce a compilation film for general release — a collection of moments from his pictures, featuring such elements as surprise, action, thrills, situations, satire, chases, and sound. He began with a working title, "Harold Lloyd's Festival of Comedy," and went to work on what he hoped would be a renaissance picture. It would take close to seven years to complete.

"I got the really basic idea for doing this because my son, who is now around about 24, naturally wasn't born when I made practically all these comedies. But he has run the biggest majority of them; yes, he's seen them all. And he's gotten, you might say, such a kick out of them — he said, 'Why don't you pass these onto the generation I belong to? I think that you're keeping them all bottled up.' So, it was really because of that that we started. It may meet with a lot of response; it may not. Of course, that's what we did with every picture we presented. Really, you never knew — and of course, you see, I produced all my own pictures. I hired all my own personnel, and I worked with them; when we completed the picture, I got in with the distributors, and I was with Pathé, then I was with Paramount, then I was with 20th Century Fox. What we did was we merely released through these companies. I financed my pictures entirely. I didn't go through the banks to finance them; I financed them myself. What I'm getting at is — when you put several hundred thousand dollars into a picture, and you haven't previewed it, you don't know whether it's going to be, in the terms of the theatre, a turkey or not." [A]

On March 5, 1962, Harold received the copyright on his first compilation for public release, which he finally called

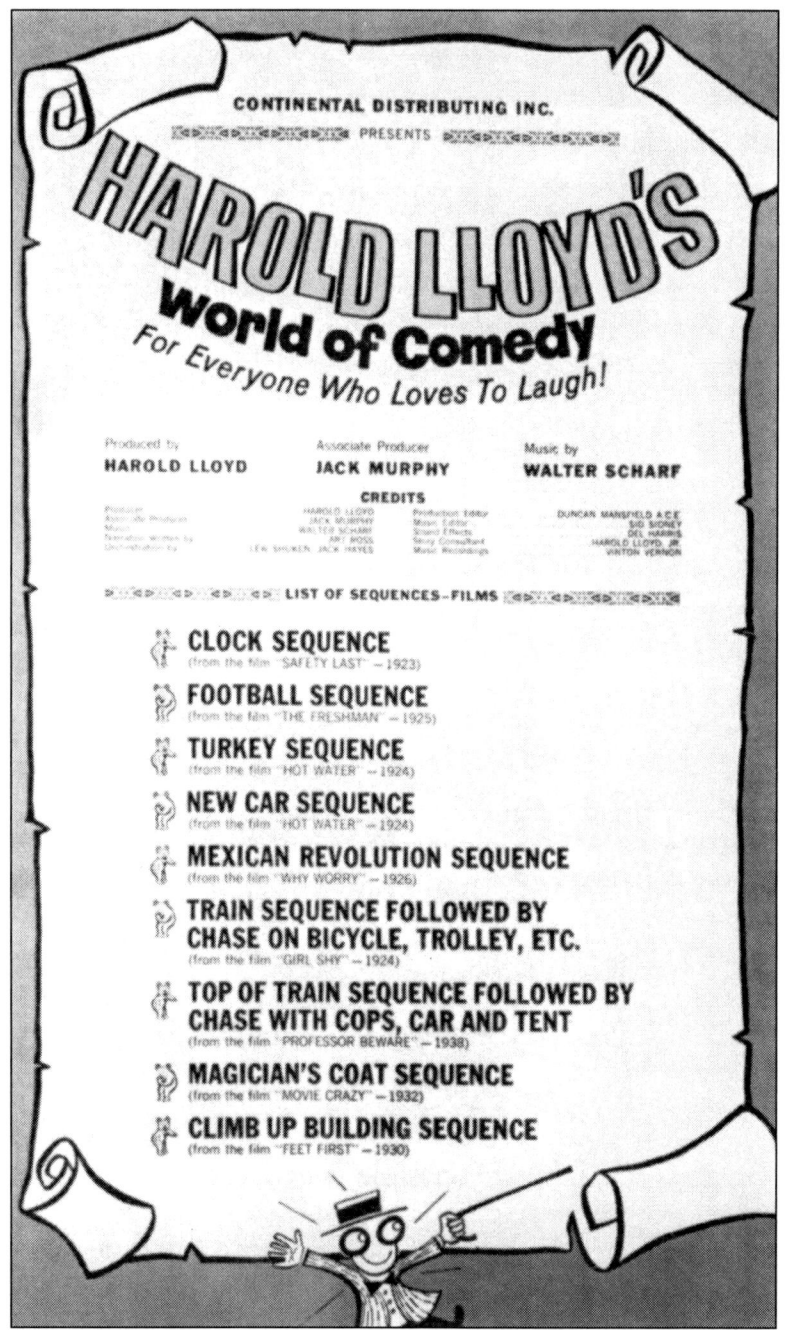

A poster for *Harold Lloyd's World of Comedy* (1962): eagle-eyed viewers must have noticed the error on the sheet, as it cited the release year for *Why Worry?* as 1926, instead of 1923.

Harold Lloyd's World of Comedy. Always a true believer in gauging public opinion, Lloyd organized a preview of his latest film in Bakersfield, California, before an audience comprised, chiefly, of teens. Harold crafted a questionnaire of sorts for those in attendance. One question comprised the poll: "Mr. Harold Lloyd is interested in learning your opinion of the Picture shown tonight. Did you like this Picture or not? Why?" The responses were uniformly excellent:

"Yes! Very Much! It is great to have an opportunity to laugh at sheer nonsense. There is so much that is sordid and depressing, that this kind of movie is refreshing indeed."

"Yes. It kept me in stitches from beginning to end. Should be great. Would like to see more."

"I loved it. There are far too few things to laugh about in this tangled mess of a world today. Thank you, Mr. Lloyd, for a wonderful evening with my husband and our 4 children."

"Being a teenager, I liked the film because I have never had a chance to view such entertainment. It is entirely original and very refreshing."

Then, in releases for critics and reporters, the reviews for the compilation glowed with such adjectives as rich, glorious, great, thrilling, hilarious, lively, funny, the side-splittingest thing seen in years. Needless to say, Harold was delighted.

"I found that when I put the first film together and had it shown to certain preview audiences, it appealed to the youth exactly as it had when it was first made, many years before." [K]

"It's amazing how children respond to Harold. They have no idea who this guy is but they just seem to love him. I think it proves that these films are simply entertaining and that makes a connection with people of all ages." [H]

"I always regarded myself as a character on the screen, which I was. Basically, I wore glasses, but my character changed with a different picture. One time he might be very brash, another time an introvert, another time a hypochondriac type of person, but it was according to the picture we did, and that lent a little different type of comedy. That's one reason I think that, my having been off the screen for so long and coming back, the type of picture we're doing, *World of Comedy*, will be a good introductory one, because it will show a certain gamut of the type of comedy that we did." [F]

> **FUN FACT**
>
> IN 1966, HAROLD VISITED THE SCHOOL FOR VISUAL ARTS ON EAST 23RD STREET IN MANHATTAN, TO TALK TO THE STUDENTS ABOUT HIS FILMS. HE FOCUSED HIS DISCUSSION ON HIS FINAL COMPILATION, *HAROLD LLOYD'S FUNNY SIDE OF LIFE*, RELEASED IN NOVEMBER 1966. IN HIS OPENING STATEMENT TO THE SEVERAL HUNDRED STUDENTS OF COLLEGE AGES, LLOYD NOTED, "I MADE *THE FRESHMAN* IN 1925. I ASSUME MOST OF YOU SAW IT AT THAT TIME."

Then came Cannes, the yearly festival in France. *World of Comedy* was not entered in any competition, but was shown off-hours. The response of the jammed audience, international in flavor, was overwhelming, ranging from hearty laughter to prolonged applause to standing ovations. "It was all the more amazing to me that this international audience enjoyed the picture, in view of the fact that there was a language barrier. But, I shouldn't have been surprised — because humor has always passed over language barriers. It is the one universal language." [K]

On May 13, 1962, Cannes recognized Lloyd's enduring popularity by awarding him with a plaque, engraved "To the Grand Prince of Cinema," and presented by Robert Favre Lebret, the festival director. He might not have been entered in any actual competition at the Cannes Film Festival in 1962, but Harold Lloyd certainly won many new fans amongst, arguably, the most sophisticated audience in Europe, during that wondrous show.

"I was sitting up in the balcony, where they generally put the people who are in the pictures. The ovation amazed me. And then they called on me to make a speech. Now, I've never been particularly fond of speech-making, and I haven't changed with the years. But the enthusiasm and warmth of the evening moved me deeply." [K]

In the summer of 1963, Harold produced a second compilation, which he called *Harold Lloyd's Funny Side of Life* — however, this one was built by Lloyd for the retrospective of his works at New York City's Museum of Modern Art. As opposed to the 1962 film, only moments from his silents were utilized (but also incorporated a soundless sequence from his 1932 talkie *Movie Crazy*), with an abbreviated, but virtually complete version of *The Freshman*. Theatrically released in 1966, and mainly in Europe, it was not as successful as its predecessor, and was pulled out of international theatres by Lloyd.

One positive aspect of these two compilations was the continued reawakening of interest in Lloyd, though misconceptions still survived about his work. People saw Harold chiefly as a thrill comedian, whose screen persona was brash and sassy — exposure to his work allowed for an awareness of the wide range of vivid characterizations that Lloyd brought to the screen. It still does, to this day.

And, for Lloyd, the overall production and reception, particularly of *Harold Lloyd's World of Comedy*, was a very happy turning point in his life. "It isn't just a reintroduction. It is a rebirth." [K]

Harold Lloyd Succumbs to Cancer

For Heaven's Sake . . .
"He Just Said, 'I Can't Suffer.'"

Harold Lloyd lost his bride, Mildred Davis, on August 18, 1969: her death affected her husband greatly, giving Harold, perhaps for the first time, a glimpse of his own immortality.

"Harold was not the same after Mimi died." [H]

In the late spring of 1970, Harold began to lose weight, and was tiring rather easily. Originally thought to be ill with a kidney ailment, doctors diagnosed carcinoma (cancer) of the prostate. He had surgery on July 15, and made frequent outpatient visits to St. John's Hospital in Santa Monica.

Harold Lloyd's final public appearance was at the Cinema City exhibition, marking the first 75 years of cinema, at the Round House, Chalk Farm, London, on September 22, 1970. The event stayed open until October 17, 1970, and was co-sponsored by the National Film Archive and *The Sunday Times*.

Lloyd opened the exhibition, despite the fact that he was still recovering from his cancer surgery. He chose, of all his films to show at the event, *The Kid Brother*, which in his later years was a particular favorite of his. Some 43 years after its initial release, the house rocked with laughter and praise. "Critics and the public were entranced by the refreshing originality and ingenuity of its comedy," the papers raved. Later, Harold traveled to Yorkshire to open the Regional Film Theatre for the British Film Institute. He, again, presented *The Kid Brother*. While in town, Harold paid a visit to Bebe Daniels who, with husband Ben Lyon, had been living in

To help celebrate the first 75 years of cinema, an ill Harold journeyed to London to help with the party. While in the United Kingdom, he regularly screened *The Kid Brother* (1927).

England since the late 1930s. In a touching point of sentimentality, Harold was still wearing cufflinks that Bebe had given him over fifty years before. It was evident that the feelings the two once shared had not totally disappeared: their affection was quite strong.

In October 1970, after returning home, he received a visit from Dr. John H. ("Jackie") Davis, Mildred's brother. Dr. Davis had not seen his brother-in-law for some time, and he was startled by

> ## Fun Fact
>
> ON FEBRUARY 9, 1971, AT 6:01AM PACIFIC STANDARD TIME, THE SYLMAR EARTHQUAKE ROCKED SOUTHERN CALIFORNIA, MAGNITUDE 6.6, ABLE TO BE FELT INTO WESTERN ARIZONA AND SOUTHERN NEVADA. THE QUAKE CAUSED OVER $500 MILLION IN PROPERTY DAMAGE, AND KILLED 65 PEOPLE. THE TREMORS ALSO AFFECTED BEVERLY HILLS, AND HAROLD LLOYD.
>
> DESPITE HIS GRAVE ILLNESS, HAROLD FELT THE EARTH SHAKING ON THE MORNING OF FEBRUARY 9. HE SHRUGGED OFF THE PROTESTS OF FAMILY AND DOCTORS, AND DECIDED TO SURVEY HIS HOME, TO SEE HOW IT WEATHERED THE QUAKE. "HE CAME DOWN THE HALL AFTER THE EARTHQUAKE — HE WAS OUT OF BED FOR THAT — AND HE SAID, 'GO DOWN TO CHECK THE CHRISTMAS TREE AND THE OSCAR AND YOUR GRANDMOTHER'S TEA SET.'" [H] HE PROCEEDED TO ROAM THE HALLS OF HIS XANADU, HEARTENED BY HOW IT STOOD, VIRTUALLY UNSCATHED. ONE CAN ONLY IMAGINE WHAT HAROLD WAS FEELING AS HE WALKED THROUGH THE ABODE THAT HE BUILT AS A SHRINE TO HIS MAGNIFICENT CAREER. DID HE SENSE THAT THIS COULD BE HIS FINAL VISIT WITH HIS BELOVED HOME? THE AGONY, COUPLED WITH HIS PERSONAL PRIDE IN HIS PROPERTY, MADE FOR, NO DOUBT, A BITTERSWEET TIME THAT HE HAD, ALONE WITH HIS GREENACRES ON THAT CHILLY FEBRUARY MORNING.

Harold's thinner appearance, so much so that Jack immediately ordered a new bevy of tests on Lloyd. The worst fears were realized: the cancer had spread to Harold's legs and chest, and was moving at a violent speed. The prognosis was bleak, considering Harold's age (77), and the acceleration of the disease. Cobalt treatments were undertaken, but to no avail: Harold's death was imminent.

"I was completely shattered at the prospect of losing him. It was when Jack Davis said to him, 'You're dying, you'd better get your affairs settled,' he just felt like someone ripped the plug. If no one had said anything to him for a few months, he might have lived longer. He just said, 'I can't suffer.'" [H]

Exactly *when* Harold Lloyd developed his prostate cancer is undeterminable, save for his death certificate, which states that he was under doctor's care for the cause of death from June 6, 1970 through to March 8, 1971, the day Harold died.

Close friend Richard Correll recalled the final obstacle Harold had to fight: "When he was determined terminally ill with cancer, he was very unwilling to accept that. He said, 'I have to fight it; there must be another way around it.' Almost, again, like the screen character, he wanted to see if he could outsmart his way out of it.

"When it was determined that he couldn't, the doctors said, 'Look, Harold, you've got to get your affairs in order; you're not going to live; you're only going to live for perhaps another half a year.' And he gave up. When he knew there was no chance and that the fight was over, he just gave up. And he went to bed, and died in about 3? weeks.

"Once he gave up, he gave up. He didn't want to linger. I never knew him as someone who was sick or feeble or slow or senile or unable to get around. When he was faced with the prospect of being something like that, he just talked himself into not getting into that position.

"And, that's how he died: in bed, at home, which is probably the way he always wanted to go."

Harold Clayton Lloyd died at 3:45pm, on Monday, March 8, 1971. He was 77 years old, 43 days shy of his 78th birthday. He passed away at home, 1225 Benedict Canyon Drive, Beverly Hills, California, in his second floor bedroom.

On Thursday, March 11, 1971, services for Harold Lloyd were held at the Scottish Rite Temple, 4357 Wilshire Boulevard, Los Angeles. Over 1000 persons attended, as Lloyd was eulogized by George M. Saunders, of the Shriners Hospital for Crippled Children. "Millions of words have been written about his talent," Saunders said. "The key to it was his wholesomeness, on screen and off." Among those present were entertainers Charles "Buddy" Rogers, Jack L. Warner, Morey Amsterdam, Red Skelton, and Milton Berle, who called Lloyd "a teacher for all the comics who followed him." The pall bearers were all Shriners.

Private entombment followed at The Great Mausoleum in Forest Lawn Memorial Park, Glendale, California.

One of the last public pictures taken of Harold Lloyd, in the fall of 1970, in London.
COURTESY DAVID KALAT.

Just eight days after Lloyd's death, on March 16, Bebe Daniels, 70, succumbed to a cerebral hemorrhage in London, survived by her husband, Ben Lyon, and two children. As could be expected, Bebe had been devastated by Harold's death.

In 1926, Albert Einstein wrote that "Our death is not an end if we can live on in our children and the younger generation. For they are us; our bodies are only wilted leaves on the tree of life."

True, death is always a turning point in *all* of our lives — as it was for Harold Lloyd – but he has definitely lived on in his ancestors, and will continue to thrive as new generations meet and experience the film work he left behind. His death was *not* the final turning point. More was, and is yet, to come, keeping alive, perhaps, *the* finest of his qualities:

"I think it's his humanity — he was a refreshing person to be around. He was not depressed — if he was, he kept it to himself. You could count on him; his wholesomeness of living; he really cared; he was a gentle man, a wonderful man. When you see his sweetness on the screen — that's the kind of man he was." [G]

HAROLD LLOYD LIVES ON

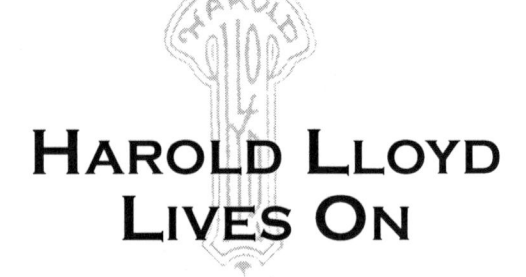

Next Aisle Over . . .
"Hooray for Harold Lloyd"

"While I think I'm quite well known with the nostalgia group, I'm known very, very little, if at all, with a great many." [J]

Harold Lloyd's legacy lives on — chiefly, and most sweetly, through his fans, who continue to remember him and his films, and who, plain and simple, want him to hang in.

I find it very interesting to hear how people were introduced to this undiscovered country. How did *you* get to know Harold Lloyd? What was the first vehicle that catapulted him into your world? Chances are that one of two responses is likely. You either met him through the marvelous DVD set, *The Harold Lloyd Comedy Collection*, which came out in 2005, or on a syndicated 1970s TV series called *Harold Lloyd's World of Comedy*.

THE TIME-LIFE SERIES — A FIRST GLIMPSE OF HAROLD LLOYD.
Harold Lloyd's World of Comedy was a half-hour long program (mostly; some episodes were an hour in length) that contained clips of the Lloyd films, edited and packaged for commercial television. Kind of strange, isn't it, that most of us met this silent screen legend on that newfangled gadget affectionately nicknamed "the small screen". . . and via clips at that?

This program was initially aired in 1977, sadly before most of us had video cassette recorders. TimeLife Films compiled twenty-six (26) episodes from the wealth of Lloyd silent and sound films at their disposal, following the company's acquisition of the worldwide rights to the films of Harold Lloyd in 1973. A marvelous opportunity, this was, to introduce to new generations the man who was the most popular comedian of the 1920s, the star who was, sadly and chiefly at his hand, virtually unknown to the public-at-large, and the films that made millions laugh themselves right out of their seats. The series met its challenge, didn't it?

"*Hooray for Harold Lloyd . . . Harold Lloyd . . . Laugh a while, dig that style . . . A Pair of Glasses and a Smile.*"

Yet, *Harold Lloyd's World of Comedy* was less than ideal. Hardly the way Harold would have wanted us to be introduced to him. With a banjo strumming, Henry Corden's narration veritably inspiring the invention of the mute button ("Poor Harold . . . It's doom for the groom if he enters that room!"), and cruel edit points (for almost a decade, I thought that *Hot Water* was a two-reel short, because it had been reduced by three of its five reels for this series) — these shows would have been loathsome to Lloyd. Yet, *we* recall it with such warmth, and such great memories. Why?

Simple: it allowed us to glimpse the genius. The show gave me, a Kennedy-era baby (whose parents, of the FDR years, had never even heard of him), the opportunity to see what excited my McKinley-era grandparents, two generations earlier. Within a split second from my first viewing, I saw a guy, rather good looking at that, with glasses, brown hair, and a dynamite smile. Within the next minute, I was laughing, enjoying what I was seeing (would that I could recall the first film I saw that evening!). I didn't think much about the fact that what I was seeing was not only in black and white, but it was silent. There was music, honkytonky and jazzy at the same time, but I didn't hear it. All I did was watch. And, in so doing, my life changed.

It was the series that introduced me not only to the man, but to an overall appreciation of silent film. That series pushed me to want to learn more about him, to buy books on him — to write three or four of them myself — and to endeavor to, somehow, help bring him back to a public that so sorely lacks an attachment to film's roots. *Harold Lloyd's World of Comedy* was not a perfect series. But, it certainly did its job, and well.

Harold Lloyd: The Third Genius — Two Masterful Hours on Harold.

This groundbreaking and lovingly built documentary, done for the *American Masters* series on PBS, first aired in the United States on November 15, 1989, written, produced, and directed by Kevin Brownlow and the late David Gill. An eager audience of Lloyd fans learned more about Harold in these two hours than any prior book had accomplished. With the full cooperation of the Lloyd family, Brownlow and Gill had unfettered access to the Lloyd family/career archives — and the result was nothing short of gloriously fascinating.

"He had become," noted Brownlow of Lloyd, "a name people automatically added to Chaplin's and Keaton's without really knowing why. It was our duty to provide the reason."

This 120-minute program did a great deal to seal Lloyd's place among the supreme triumvirate of silent film comics, along with Chaplin and Keaton; some of us might think Lloyd is higher than "third" amongst the geniuses, but such radical thinking is not for a book. *The Third Genius* was nominated for an Emmy for Outstanding Television Documentary for 1989. In the eyes of Lloyd's fans worldwide, this program remains a clear winner.

The Harold Lloyd Centennial — 1993 Was Quite a Year.

From April 22-25, 1993, the state of Nebraska celebrated the centennial of the birth of Harold Lloyd, who was born in Burchard on April 20, 1893. It was during that trip that I first met Suzanne Lloyd and Rich Correll — and they've been cherished friends ever since.

A major highlight of the weekend was the Saturday, April 24, showing of *Safety Last!*, at the Stuart Theater in state capital Lincoln. The massive crowd was treated to the musical accompaniment of legendary organist Gaylord Carter, whose career was launched by Lloyd in the 1920's. For me, this showing marked the first time I had ever seen Lloyd on the "big screen," and the thrill of it was immense. It had often been written that "Lloyd films cry for an audience," and that night I finally understood what that meant. The contagious laughter that rippled through the audience as Harold battled obstacle after obstacle on the Bolton Building was

Your author's favorite portrait of Harold Lloyd, taken in 1922.

positively inspiring! As a purely television viewer previously, I never realized how the presence of an audience can heighten the laugh quotient, and how your own appreciation of a film can be increased, as it mushrooms off of your fellow viewers. I never thought I could enjoy a Lloyd film more — I learned quickly, and well, that night, that with fellow fans laughing beside you, spending time in the cinema with Harold is positively magical. It was also during this evening, as never before, that I learned the true power of conventions and gatherings with people of like interests to your own — much like you catch a cold when around a sick person, you can catch the most wondrous of infections — those of enthusiasm and fandom — at such events.

Directly after that gala weekend came "Harold Lloyd 100," a centennial retrospective held from April 30-June 3 at the New York City repertory house Film Forum. Still working on my first book (*Harold Lloyd: A Bio-Bibliography*, published in early 1994) during that time, I went to every card. I saw over a dozen shorts and nineteen silent and sound features — all (except for *Safety Last!*), for the first time on the big screen, and some for the first time ever. What a tremendous opportunity that was for fans to absorb a concentrated dose of these wonderful films.

During 1993, newspapers and magazines carried articles about Harold; movie houses, colleges and film museums the world over screened his pictures — he was getting attention, the likes of which he had not received since the Time-Life series went off the air in 1981. It was a great year.

The Silent Screen Stars Stamps — They Cost 29 Cents Then.

On April 27, 1994, the United States Postal Service released a new set of 29¢ stamps: "Stars of the Silent Screen." While there were a number of very worthy stars who could have been so honored, only ten were chosen to be so immortalized. The ten on the final issue — Rudolph Valentino, Clara Bow, Charlie Chaplin, Lon Chaney, John Gilbert, ZaSu Pitts, the Keystone Cops, Theda Bara, Buster Keaton, and Harold Lloyd — were *not*, however, the first ten of choice.

As far back as 1981, it was hoped that, somehow, the design of

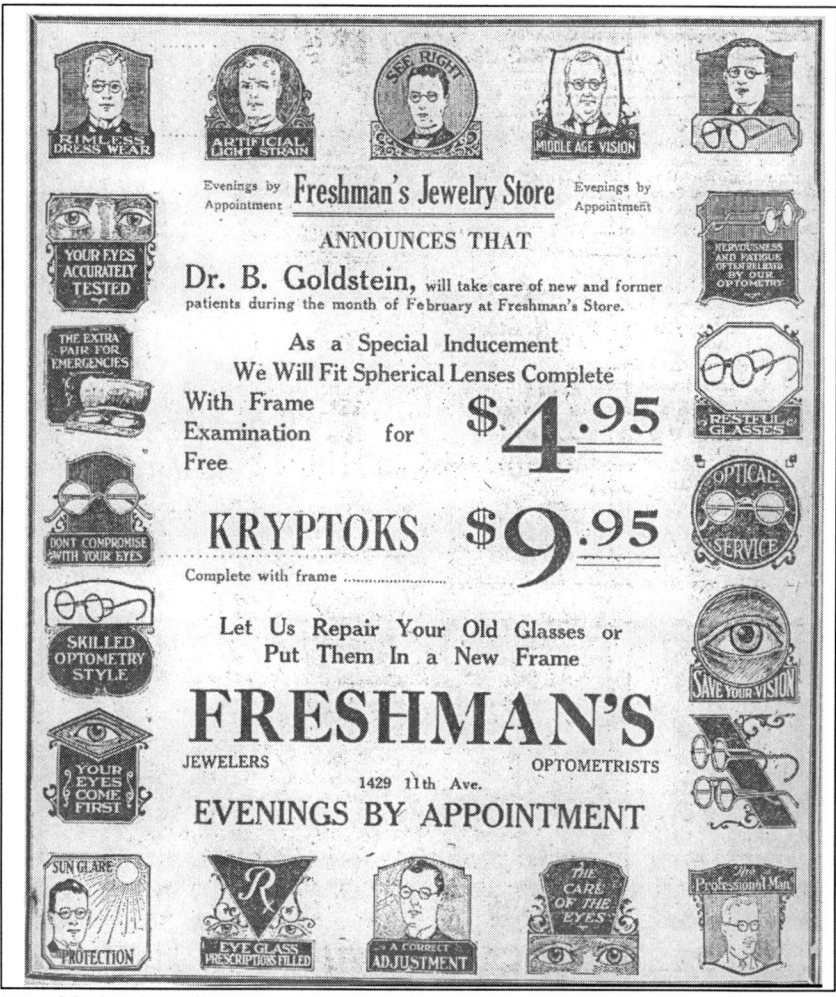

Harold Lloyd's influence on this particular optometry concern is obvious — this newspaper ad is from the *Altoona Mirror*, February 1, 1928.
COURTESY MARK JOHNSON.

postage stamps could be expanded into caricatures. And, there was no better practitioner of that art form than the late Al Hirschfeld. In the late 1980s, Hirschfeld submitted a proposal for 25 different stamps, each with a different caricature. On August 29, 1991, the first five of the Hirschfeld stamps were released, in a 29¢ series called "Comedians." In this series were Laurel and Hardy, Edgar Bergen and Charlie McCarthy, Jack Benny, Abbott and Costello, and Fanny Brice. Interestingly, originally slated to be in that quintet were Chaplin, Keaton, and Lloyd.

In 1923, a delightful fox trot was written by Lee S. Roberts and issued by the Aeolian Company, entitled "Oh! Harold." The song was frequently used by Lloyd silent film accompanyists, particularly the legendary organist Gaylord Carter. COURTESY RICHARD FINEGAN.

The rumor, as to why this did not materialize, was that Chaplin and Keaton were, at that time, deemed too *politically incorrect* for the Government's tastes (and, as fans of the film *Miracle on 34th Street* know, the US Postal Service is a branch of the Federal Government!). Harold, at first, was still in contention, until it was determined that the stamp series was too "male," and that a comedienne was needed: exit Harold, enter Fanny.

A new series brewed, though it could not include such already stamped legends as D.W. Griffith (10¢ stamp, issued in 1975), Will Rogers and W.C. Fields (both 15¢, 1979), the Barrymores (20¢, 1982), or Douglas Fairbanks (20¢, 1984).

Then came April 27, 1994, when the "Stars of the Silent Screen" series was released. This format took ten stamps and placed them into four "panes," comprising a "window" of forty stamps, available in a full pane (40 stamps) or half pane (20 stamps). The original group of ten, as planned, differed from the ten that were, ultimately, in the series. Cut from the series were Mary Pickford (licensing problems with her estate) and Pola Negri (who died in 1987, and was deemed ineligible by the "10-Year-Rule," which says that individuals cannot be immortalized on stamps until dead ten or more years — unless you were a U.S. President). Thus, with the cuts of Pickford and Negri came the additions of Chaney and Gilbert — they were the last two added. Through it all, with people cut and added, the one constant was Harold Lloyd, who remained on the list of inclusions from the very beginning of the caricature stamp concept to the very release of these stamps. That fact surely receives the stamp of approval for fans of Harold Lloyd.

THE HAROLD LLOYD COMEDY COLLECTION — HE FINALLY MADE IT TO DVD.

Fans of Harold Lloyd were anticipating this for years — and with the November 15, 2005 release of *The Harold Lloyd Comedy Collection*, the wait ended. *Finally*, a set was released that had the official sanction of the Harold Lloyd Estate and Film Trust. As any aficionado will attest to, this set is a treasure trove — the ideal introduction to the man and his films, and the perfect upgrade for seasoned video and film collectors. Your author served as a consultant to both the producing and distributing companies, hosted two featurettes, provided the Lloyd filmography, and contributed audio commentary on three films — thus, I'm kind of fond of this box set.

This seven-disc wonder — named 2005 Box Set of the Year by *The New York Times* — includes 15 feature films, 13 shorts, and a bonus disc which houses a bevy of interviews, home movies, featurettes, radio shows, photo galleries, and stereo images shot by Lloyd himself (3-D glasses are included in the box set). Five of the films contain alternate audio commentary tracks, designed to help viewers glean greater behind-the-scenes insight (we wanted to do more, but ran out of both time and budget), and three of the films feature alternate organ scores by the late Gaylord Carter.

Of course, there have been both prior and subsequent VHS and DVD collections of Harold Lloyd's films — thankfully — but with the stamp of approval by the family comes the access to the rare materials that only this set affords. The release of this set, truly, was a gift to all who appreciate quality silent film comedy of the most legendary sort.

A Mentor and an Inspiration, Still.

Little did Lloyd know the depth of his impact, both in his lifetime and beyond. His work and his example continue to live on, both in the characters his screen persona inspired, and the professionals who were touched by his influence.

"Harold was always available," noted actor Robert Wagner, who first met Lloyd through his daughter Gloria in the 1940s. "He encouraged me to pursue a career in the movies, just as he did with other young actors like Tab Hunter and Debbie Reynolds."

Another who was supported by Lloyd was the late actor Jack Lemmon. In fact, when asked who could best portray him in a bio-pic, Lloyd immediately cited Lemmon. However, this daunted the young performer: "The onus of trying to recapture someone like Harold Lloyd, who was famous because he was unique, would have been too great for me to have enjoyed the experience." Unquestionably, Lemmon would have supported the current renaissance of the Lloyd pictures. "His films should be seen, not just for their historical value, but for their sheer pleasure."

In 1969, Orson Welles noted that Lloyd was the "most under-rated comedian of them all," yet before and since that time, Lloyd's Glass Character inspired highly rated onscreen performances and even the gags performed. But one great example of this is Cary Grant playing Egyptologist David Huxley in *Bringing Up Baby* (1938). Director Howard Hawks urged Grant to pattern Huxley after Harold Lloyd. Behind the scenes, Lloyd mentored Grant. From the character's high-energy determination right down to the horn-rimmed glasses, Grant perfectly crafted a role that Lloyd himself would have handled beautifully. Interestingly, a few months after *Bringing Up Baby* debuted, Lloyd released *Professor Beware* in which he played—you guessed it—an Egyptologist.

HL and his friends certainly had a sense of fun — just like his fans do to this day. This party favor, from April 24, 1934, features the autograph of Walt Disney, as well as proof that Prisoner 1046 doesn't know, has eyes, won't talk, *and* had his right thumb print forged.

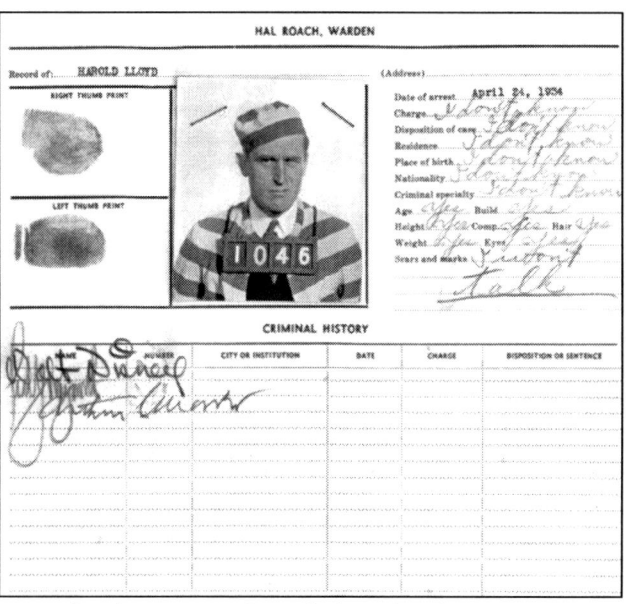

Also ponder some further examples of the Lloyd touch: Jackie Chan's 1983 film *Project A* features several stunts inspired by the Lloyd films, including one where he hangs on to, and eventually falls off from, the hands of a clock tower; similar clock references are found in *Back to the Future* (1985), including a tiny figurine clock which had Harold hanging from the hands; the charming *Man of the Century* (1999) boasts a main character named Johnny Twennies, who resembles Harold Lloyd in a stunning number of ways; a 2001 television episode of *Futurama* called "That's Lobstertainment!" was a tribute to Harold, featuring an alien version of him, named Harold Zoid; the clock reference again appears in the Jackie Chan feature *Shanghai Knights* (2003); a 2007 episode of *The Simpsons*, "The Wife Aquatic," has a bespectacled man hanging from clock hands in Ned Flanders' film, and the 2008 animated feature *Wall-E* was inspired by silent comedy in general, and Harold Lloyd in particular.

"I remember as a child watching Harold Lloyd, Buster Keaton and Charlie Chaplin," notes actor Jude Law. "I just remember loving them and never missing them. And I suppose that related somewhat to what I was doing at school at the age of seven or eight, wanting to put on plays, and make people laugh and fall over."

The legend and influence promise to live on, even further. Harold Lloyd can only remain a viable and important figure within the cinema world if *we*, the fans, continue to share his films with current and future generations. For too long, he was just a footnote, a passing reference, a mere name. Now, with the knowledge of how very important he was to the history of cinema, with the awareness of how the numerous turning points in his life changed him and his industry, and with a heightened availability of his body of work, Harold Lloyd becomes so much more.

This is not my first book on the man . . . and it probably won't be my last . . . but it is my hope that the contemporary sightings of Harold Lloyd — each a turning point in his legacy — will continue long after I type my last word on him. It is my dream that this literary effort will inspire some teenager — possibly reading these very words — to expand upon the work that has already been done, improve it, and keep it going: just like I did when I first saw him at the tender age of 17.

Now that *you've* gotten to know him, get out there and learn more about him — *and share it.* What greater gift can we give to a man who came from the humblest of roots, specialized, worked hard, and evolved right before the eyes of weekly audiences, to become one of the most respected and influential filmmakers in film history? A gifted actor who changed his character from film to film, reflected a diversity of audiences, and revolutionized the comedy of the everyman — all with no comedy hall or vaudeville training. A man whose example of courage, aptitude and fortitude, both on *and* off the screen, can help anyone who thinks he can't bust an obstacle and reach a goal.

In many ways, Harold Lloyd remains that undiscovered country, but his gifts and contributions are ripe for reawakening for new generations. Yet, for those who knew him, who learned from him, and who continue to admire him, his influence lingers . . .

"The most important quality that Harold Lloyd brought to the screen was hope," concludes Wagner, "and I think we all need that. So his hope and his positiveness mark him out as a person to identify with in this time and forever."

Daughter Gloria Lloyd: "He loved life, and he loved the joyous part of it — when you enjoy life, you feel good." [G]

THE COMPLETE CHRONOLOGICAL FILMOGRAPHY OF HAROLD LLOYD

He Leads, Other Follow . . .
"It's Been a Real Pleasure."

"I do want to say working in comedy, and having them presented to, more or less, people all over the world, fortunately, that it has been a great satisfaction, because I think when you can give people a little rest from their ordinary everyday complexities, there's a certain satisfaction about it. So, it's been a real pleasure. And I think that if I were able to start over again, that I would still be very happy to choose the vocation that I have chosen. As I say, it's been a real pleasure." [A]

The following is a cinematic inventory that has taken me nearly two decades to refine. For years, incorrect lists of his film appearances were perpetuated, passed down amongst generations of authors, necessitating your author to undertake scrutinous archaeology to fill in gaping holes, and give titles their proper place, or take away their improper place, within what I call The Complete Chronological Filmography of Harold Lloyd.

This list is presented by title, in the order released within the United States. An asterisk (*) after the film's release date signifies that the film is not known to survive. In addition, for those short films produced under Hal Roach and the Rolin Film Company, the Production Code Number will precede the film title. These numbers, within the P series (1915-1916), the A series (1916-1917), and the two L series (the first for Glass Character one-reelers, the next for Glass Character multiple-reel shorts), reflect the order in which the films were *produced*, not necessarily released. Note that you will find no A13 or an L13 in the Glass Character one-reel list: those boys *were* superstitious.

	The Old Monk's Tale — February 15, 1913
	The Twelfth Juror — April 19, 1913*
	Hulda of Holland — April 21, 1913*
	Rory o' the Bogs — December 22, 1913*
	Samson — April 30, 1914*
	The Sandhill Lovers — June 15, 1914*
	The Patchwork Girl of Oz — September 28, 1914
	Willie Runs the Park — January 2, 1915*
	Hogan's Romance Upset — February 13, 1915
	Just Nuts — April 19, 1915
	Love, Loot and Crash — April 24, 1915
	Their Social Splash — April 26, 1915
	Miss Fatty's Seaside Lovers — May 15, 1915
	From Italy's Shores — May 19, 1915*
	Into the Light — June 17, 1915*
	Courthouse Crooks — July 5, 1915
P1	*Spitball Sadie* — July 26, 1915*
P2	*Terribly Stuck Up* — August 28, 1915*
P4	*A Mixup for Mazie* — September 6, 1915*
P5	*Some Baby* — September 20, 1915*
P6	*Fresh From the Farm* — October 4, 1915*
P9	*Giving Them Fits* — November 1, 1915
P13	*Bughouse Bellhops* — November 8, 1915*
P10	*Tinkering With Trouble* — November 17, 1915*
P8	*Great While It Lasted* — November 24, 1915*
	A Submarine Pirate — November 24, 1915
P14	*Ragtime Snap Shots* — December 1, 1915*
P7	*A Foozle at the Tee Party* — December 8, 1915*
P3	*Ruses, Rhymes and Roughnecks* — December 15, 1915*
P11	*Peculiar Patients' Pranks* — December 22, 1915
P12	*Lonesome Luke, Social Gangster* — December 29, 1915*
P16	*Lonesome Luke Leans to the Literary* — January 5, 1916*
P15	*Luke Lugs Luggage* — January 12, 1916*
P17	*Luke Lolls in Luxury* — January 19, 1916*
P19	*Luke the Candy Cut Up* — January 31, 1916
P18	*Luke Foils the Villain* — February 14, 1916*
P20	*Luke and the Rural Roughnecks* — March 1, 1916
P21	*Luke Pipes the Pippins* — March 15, 1916*

P24	*Lonesome Luke, Circus King* —	March 29, 1916*
P23	*Luke's Double* —	April 12, 1916*
P22	*Them Was the Happy Days!* —	April 26, 1916*
P26	*Luke and the Bomb Throwers* —	May 8, 1916*
P25	*Luke's Late Lunchers* —	May 22, 1916*
P27	*Luke Laughs Last* —	June 5, 1916*
P28	*Luke's Fatal Flivver* —	June 19, 1916*
P29	*Luke's Society MixUp* —	June 26, 1916*
P30	*Luke's Washful Waiting* —	July 3, 1916*
A1	*Luke Rides Roughshod* —	July 10, 1916*
A2	*Luke, Crystal Gazer* —	July 24, 1916
A3	*Luke's Lost Lamb* —	August 7, 1916*
A4	*Luke Does the Midway* —	August 21, 1916*
A6	*Luke Joins the Navy* —	September 4, 1916
A7	*Luke and the Mermaids* —	September 18, 1916*
A8	*Luke's Speedy Club Life* —	October 1, 1916*
A5	*Luke and the Bangtails* —	October 15, 1916
A9	*Luke the Chauffeur* —	October 29, 1916*
A10	*Luke's Preparedness Preparations* —	November 5, 1916*
A11	*Luke the Gladiator* —	November 12, 1916*
A12	*Luke the Patient Provider* —	November 19, 1916*
A14	*Luke's Newsie Knockout* —	November 26, 1916*
A15	*Luke's Movie Muddle* —	December 3, 1916
A16	*Luke, Rank Impersonator* —	December 10, 1916*
A17	*Luke's Fireworks Fizzle* —	December 17, 1916*
A18	*Luke Locates the Loot* —	December 24, 1916
A19	*Luke's Shattered Sleep* —	December 31, 1916
A20	*Luke's Lost Liberty* —	January 7, 1917*
A21	*Luke's Busy Day* —	January 21, 1917*
A22	*Luke's Trolley Troubles* —	February 4, 1917*
A23	*Lonesome Luke, Lawyer* —	February 18, 1917*
A24	*Luke Wins Ye Ladye Faire* —	February 25, 1917*
A25	*Lonesome Luke's Lively Life* —	March 18, 1917*
A31	*Lonesome Luke on Tin Can Alley* —	April 15, 1917
A27	*Lonesome Luke's Honeymoon* —	May 20, 1917*
A28	*Lonesome Luke, Plumber* —	June 17, 1917*
A29	*Stop! Luke! Listen!* —	July 15, 1917*
A34	*Lonesome Luke, Messenger* —	August 5, 1917

A26	*Lonesome Luke, Mechanic* — August 19, 1917*
A30	*Lonesome Luke's Wild Women* — September 2, 1917
L1	*Over the Fence* — September 9, 1917
A32	*Lonesome Luke Loses Patients* — September 16, 1917*
L2	*Pinched* — September 23, 1917
L3	*By the Sad Sea Waves* — September 30, 1917
A36	*Lonesome Luke in Birds of a Feather* — October 7, 1917*
L5	*Bliss* — October 14, 1917
A35	*Lonesome Luke in From London to Laramie* — October 21, 1917*
L4	*Rainbow Island* — October 28, 1917
A33	*Lonesome Luke in Love, Laughs and Lather* — November 4, 1917*
L6	*The Flirt* — November 11, 1917
A37	*Lonesome Luke in When Clubs Are Trump* — November 18, 1917
L7	*All Aboard* — November 25, 1917
A38	*Lonesome Luke in We Never Sleep* — December 2, 1917*
L8	*Move On* — December 9, 1917
L10	*Bashful* — December 23, 1917
L11	*Step Lively* — December 30, 1917*
L9	*The Tip* — January 6, 1918*
L12	*The Big Idea* — January 20, 1918
L14	*The Lamb* — February 3, 1918*
L18	*Hit Him Again* — February 17, 1918*
L16	*Beat It* — February 24, 1918*
L17	*A Gasoline Wedding* — March 3, 1918
L19	*Look Pleasant, Please* — March 10, 1918
L20	*Here Come the Girls* — March 17, 1918
L15	*Let's Go* — March 24, 1918
L21	*On the Jump* — March 31, 1918
L25	*Follow the Crowd* — April 7, 1918*
L27	*Pipe the Whiskers* — April 14, 1918
L26	*It's a Wild Life* — April 21, 1918
L22	*Hey There!* — April 28, 1918
L23	*Kicked Out* — May 5, 1918
L24	*The NonStop Kid* — May 12, 1918
L29	*Two Gun Gussie* — May 19, 1918

L31	*Fireman, Save My Child* —	May 26, 1918
L32	*The City Slicker* —	June 2, 1918
L28	*Sic 'Em Towser* —	June 9, 1918*
L33	*Somewhere in Turkey* —	June 16, 1918
L34	*Are Crooks Dishonest?* —	June 23, 1918
L35	*An Ozark Romance* —	July 7, 1918
L39	*Kicking the Germ Out of Germany* —	July 21, 1918*
L36	*That's Him* —	August 4, 1918*
L37	*Bride and Gloom* —	August 18, 1918*
L38	*Two Scrambled* —	September 1, 1918*
L40	*Bees In His Bonnet* —	September 15, 1918*
L41	*Swing Your Partners* —	September 29, 1918
L44	*Why Pick on Me?* —	October 13, 1918
L43	*Nothing But Trouble* —	October 27, 1918
L42	*Hear 'Em Rave* —	December 1, 1918
L45	*Take a Chance* —	December 15, 1918
L47	*She Loves Me Not* —	December 29, 1918*
L48	*Wanted $5000* —	January 12, 1919*
L46	*Going! Going! Gone!* —	January 26, 1919*
L50	*Ask Father* —	February 9, 1919
L51	*On the Fire* —	February 23, 1919
L49	*I'm On My Way* —	March 9, 1919
L52	*Look Out Below* —	March 16, 1919
L53	*The Dutiful Dub* —	March 23, 1919
L54	*Next Aisle Over* —	March 30, 1919
L73	*A Sammy in Siberia* —	April 6, 1919
L56	*Just Dropped In* —	April 13, 1919
L57	*Crack Your Heels* —	April 20, 1919
L55	*Ring Up the Curtain* —	April 27, 1919
L58	*Young Mr. Jazz* —	May 4, 1919
L59	*Si Senor* —	May 11, 1919*
L60	*Before Breakfast* —	May 18, 1919
L61	*The Marathon* —	May 25, 1919
L62	*Back to the Woods* —	June 1, 1919
L63	*Pistols for Breakfast* —	June 8, 1919
L64	*Swat the Crook* —	June 15, 1919
L65	*Off the Trolley* —	June 22, 1919
L82	*Spring Fever* —	June 29, 1919

1919

will be a good year—
for those who show

Harold Lloyd

in the best one reel
comedies made!

Ask the man who shows them!

Produced by Rolin

PATHÉ
DISTRIBUTORS

L69 *Billy Blazes, Esq.* — July 6, 1919
L83 *Just Neighbors* — July 13, 1919
L66 *At the Old Stage Door* — July 20, 1919
L68 *Never Touched Me* — July 27, 1919
L67 *A Jazzed Honeymoon* — August 3, 1919
L70 *Count Your Change* — August 10, 1919
L71 *Chop Suey & Company* — August 17, 1919
L72 *Heap Big Chief* — August 24, 1919
L74 *Don't Shove* — August 31, 1919

L75   *Be My Wife* — September 7, 1919*
L76   *The Rajah* — September 14, 1919*
L77   *He Leads, Others Follow* — September 21, 1919*
L78   *Soft Money* — September 28, 1919*
L79   *Count the Votes* — October 5, 1919*
L80   *Pay Your Dues* — October 12, 1919
L81   *His Only Father* — October 19, 1919*
L1   *Bumping Into Broadway* — November 2, 1919
L2   *Captain Kidd's Kids* — November 30, 1919
L3   *From Hand to Mouth* — December 28, 1919
L4   *His Royal Slyness* — February 8, 1920
L5   *Haunted Spooks* — March 31, 1920
L6   *An Eastern Westerner* — May 2, 1920
L7   *High and Dizzy* — July 11, 1920
L8   *Get Out and Get Under* — September 12, 1920
L9   *Number, Please?* — December 26, 1920
L10   *Now or Never* — May 5, 1921
L11   *Among Those Present* — July 3, 1921
L12   *I Do* — September 11, 1921
L13   *Never Weaken* — October 22, 1921
      A Sailor Made Man — December 25, 1921
      Grandma's Boy — September 3, 1922
      Dr. Jack — December 19, 1922
      Safety Last! — April 1, 1923
      Dogs of War — July 1, 1923
      Why Worry? — September 16, 1923
      Girl Shy — April 20, 1924
      Hot Water — November 2, 1924
      The Freshman — September 20, 1925
      For Heaven's Sake — April 5, 1926
      The Kid Brother — January 22, 1927
      Carter DeHaven in Character Studies — 1927
      Speedy — April 7, 1928
      Welcome Danger — October 12, 1929
      Feet First — November 8, 1930
      Movie Crazy — September 23, 1932
      The Cat's Paw — August 7, 1934
      The Milky Way — February 7, 1936

Professor Beware — July 29, 1938
A Girl, a Guy, and a Gob — March 14, 1941 (HL Produced)
My Favorite Spy — June 12, 1942 (HL Produced)
The Sin of Harold Diddlebock — April 4, 1947/*Mad Wednesday* — October 28, 1950
Harold Lloyd's World of Comedy — June 4, 1962
Harold Lloyd's Funny Side of Life — November 9, 1966

BIBLIOGRAPHY

This bibliography includes works that were used as reference tools for this work: citations of books by and about Harold Lloyd, books with significant mention of Lloyd, vital works of depth from magazines, and newspaper articles. Books are listed alphabetically by author; magazine and newspaper articles are listed chronologically. Also included are major interviews, oral histories, and miscellaneous documents.

BOOKS

BY AND ABOUT HAROLD LLOYD

Bowser, Eileen. *Harold Lloyd's Short Comedies.* New York: Department of Film, The Museum of Modern Art, 1974.

Cahn, William. *Harold Lloyd's World of Comedy.* New York: Duell, Sloan and Pearce, 1964.

D'Agostino, Annette M. *Harold Lloyd: A Bio-Bibliography.* Westport, CT: Greenwood Press, 1994.

D'Agostino Lloyd, Annette. *The Harold Lloyd Encyclopedia.* Jefferson, NC: McFarland & Company, Publishers, 2003.

Dardis, Tom. Harold Lloyd: *The Man on the Clock.* New York: Penguin Books, 1983.

Lloyd, Harold. *An American Comedy: Acted by Harold Lloyd, Directed by Wesley W. Stout.* New York: Longmans, Green & Co., 1928.

McCaffrey, Donald W. *Three Classic Silent Screen Comedies Starring Harold Lloyd.* Rutherford, NJ: Fairleigh Dickinson University Press, 1976.

Reilly, Adam. *Harold Lloyd: The King of Daredevil Comedy.* New York: The Macmillan Company, 1977.

Schickel, Richard. *Harold Lloyd: The Shape of Laughter.* New York: New York Graphic Society, 1974.

WITH SUBSTANTIAL MENTIONS OF HAROLD LLOYD

Agee, James. *Agee on Film.* vol. 1. New York: McDowell, Obolensky, 1958.

Allgood, Jill. *Bebe and Ben.* London: Robert Hale & Company, 1975.

Arconada, Cesar Munoz. *Tres Comicos del Cine.* Madrid: M. Castellote, 1974.

Bardéche, Maurice, and Brasillach, Robert. *The History of Motion Pictures.* Trans. and ed. by Iris Barry. New York: W.W. Norton and Company, Inc., 1938.

Bawden, Liz-Anne, ed. *The Oxford Companion to Film.* New York: Oxford University Press, 1976.

Beck, Jerry and Friedwald, Will. *Looney Tunes and Merrie Melodies.* New York: Henry Holt and Company, 1989.

Blum, Daniel. *A Pictoral History of the Silent Screen.* New York: Perigee Books, 1953.

Brownlow, Kevin. *The Parade's Gone By*. Berkeley & Los Angeles, CA: University of California Press, 1968.

Brownlow, Kevin. *Hollywood: The Pioneers.* New York: Alfred A. Knopf; London: Secker & Warburg, 1979.

Byron, Stuart and Weis, Elisabeth, eds. *The National Society of Film Critics on Movie Comedy*. New York: Grossman Publishers, 1977.

Cahn, William. *The Laugh Makers*. New York: G.P. Putnam's Sons, 1957.

Cobb, Sally Wright, and Willems, Mark. *The Brown Derby Restaurant*. New York: Rizzoli International Publications, Inc., 1996.

Cowie, Peter. *Seventy Years of Cinema.* South Brunswick and New York: A.S. Barnes and Company; London: Thomas Yoseloff Ltd., 1969.

Edelson, Edward. *Funny Men of the Movies*. Garden City, NY: Doubleday & Company, Inc., 1976.

Endres, Stacey, and Cushman, Robert. *Hollywood at Your Feet*. Los Angeles and London: Pomegranate Press, Ltd., 1992.

Everson, William K. *American Silent Film*. New York: Oxford University Press, 1978.

Everson, William K. *The Films of Laurel and Hardy.* New York: The Citadel Press, 1967.

Farber, Manny. *Negative Space: Manny Farber on the Movies.* New York and Washington: Praeger Publications, 1971.

Fashions in Foods in Beverly Hills. Beverly Hills, CA: Beverly Hills Woman's Club, 1931.

Ferguson, Otis. *The Film Criticism of Otis Ferguson.* Ed. by Robert Wilson. Philadelphia: Temple University Press, 1971.

Fowler, Gene. *Father Goose.* New York: Covici-Freide, 1934.

Franklin, Joe. *Classics of the Silent Screen.* Secaucus, NJ: The Citadel Press, 1959.

Gehring, Wes D. *Screwball Comedy: A Genre of Madcap Romance.* Westport, CT: Greenwood Press, 1986.

Gilliatt, Penelope. *Unholy Fools: Wits, Comics, Disturbers of the Peace: Film & Theater.* New York: Viking Press, 1973.

Griffith, Richard, and Mayer, Arthur. *The Movies.* 1957. New York: Simon & Schuster, Inc., 1970.

Halliwell, Leslie. *Filmgoer's Companion.* 9th ed. New York: Scribner's, 1988.

Higham, Charles. *The Art of the American Film 1900-1971.* Garden City, NY: Doubleday & Company, Inc., 1973.

Hirschfeld, Al. *Hirschfeld: Art and Recollections From Eight Decades.* New York: Charles Scribner's Sons, 1991.

Houseman, Victoria. *Made in Heaven.* Chicago, IL: Bonus Books, 1991.

Ike, Leslie, ed. *The Silent Picture.* New York: Arno Press, 1977.

Jacobs, Diane. *Christmas in July: The Life and Art of Preston Sturges.* Berkeley and Los Angeles, CA; Oxford, England: University of California Press, 1992.

Katz, Ephraim. *The Film Encyclopedia.* New York: Crowell, 1979.

Kerr, Walter. *The Silent Clowns.* New York: Alfred A. Knopf, 1975.

Knight, Arthur. *The Liveliest Art.* New York: The Macmillan Company, 1957.

Koszarski, Richard. *Hollywood Directors: 1914-1940.* New York: Oxford University Press, 1976.

Koszarski, Richard. *An Evening's Entertainment: The Age of the Silent Feature Picture, 1915-1928.* New York: Scribner; Toronto: Collier Macmillan Canada; New York: Maxwell Macmillan International, 1990.

Lahue, Kalton C., and Brewer, Terry. *Kops and Custards: The Legend of Keystone Films.* Norman, Oklahoma: University of Oklahoma Press, 1968.

Lahue, Kalton C., and Brewer, Terry. *World of Laughter: The Motion Picture Comedy Short, 1910-1930.* Norman, Oklahoma: University of Oklahoma Press, 1966.

Lamparski, Richard. *Whatever Became Of . . . ?* 2nd series. New York: Crown Publishers, 1968.

Leyda, Jay, ed. *Voices of Film Experience.* New York: The Macmillan Company, 1977.

Life With the Lyons: The Autobiography of Bebe Daniels and Ben Lyon. London: Odhams Press Limited, 1953.

Maltin, Leonard. *The Disney Films.* New York: Crown Publishers, 1984.

Maltin, Leonard. *Great Movie Comedians.* New York: Crown Publishers, 1978.

Maltin, Leonard, and Bann, Richard W. *Our Gang: The Life and Times of the Little Rascals.* New York: Crown Publishers, Inc., 1992.

Manchel, Frank. *Yesterday's Clowns: The Rise of Film Comedy.* New York: Franklin Watts, Inc., 1973.

Mast, Gerald. *The Comic Mind: Comedy and the Movies.* 2nd ed. Chicago: The University of Chicago Press, 1979.

McCaffrey, Donald. *Four Great Comedians: Chaplin, Lloyd, Keaton, Langdon.* London: A. Zwemmer; New York: A.S. Barnes, 1968.

McCaffrey, Donald. *The Golden Age of Sound Comedy: Comic Films and Comedians of the Thirties.* New York: A.S. Barnes and Co.; London: The Tantivy Press, 1973.

Moholy-Nagy, L. *Vision in Motion.* Chicago: Paul Theobald, 1947.

Morgan, Willard D., and Lester, Henry M. *Stereo Realist Manual.* New York: Morgan and Lester Publishers, 1954.

Morino, Marianne. *The Hollywood Walk of Fame.* Berkeley, CA: Ten Speed Press, 1987.

Parish, James Robert, and Leonard, William T. *The Funsters.* New Rochelle, NY: Arlington House Publishers, 1979.

Peary, Danny, ed. *Close-Ups: The Movie Star Book.* New York, London, Toronto, Sydney, Tokyo: Simon & Schuster, Inc., 1978.

Pratt, George C. *Spellbound in Darkness: A History of the Silent Film.* Greenwich, CT: New York Graphic Society, 1973.

Quinlan, David. *Quinlan's Illustrated Registry of Film Stars.* New York: Henry Holt and Company, 1991.

Quinlan, David. *Quinlan's Illustrated Directory of Film Comedy Actors.* New York: Henry Holt and Company, 1992.

Ragan, David. *Who's Who in Hollywood.* New York: Facts on File, Inc., 1993.

Rebello, Stephen, and Allen, Richard. *Reel Art.* New York: Abbeville Press, 1988.

Rosenberg, Bernard, and Silverstein, Harry. *The Real Tinsel.* New York: The Macmillan Company, 1970.

Rotha, Paul. *The Film Till Now: A Survey of World Cinema.* New York: Funk & Wagnalls Company, 1949.

Sadoul, Georges. *Dictionary of Films.* Berkeley & Los Angeles: University of California Press, 1965.

Sadoul, Georges. *Dictionary of Filmmakers.* Berkeley & Los Angeles: University of California Press, 1972.

St. Johns, Adela Rogers. *Love, Laughter and Tears: My Hollywood Story.* Garden City, NY: Doubleday and Company, Inc., 1978.

Sarris, Andrew. *The Primal Screen.* New York: Simon & Schuster, 1973.

Schickel, Richard. *Schickel on Film.* New York: William Morrow and Company, Inc., 1989.

Seldes, Gilbert. *The Seven Lively Arts.* New York: Harper & Brothers, 1924.

Sennett, Mack. *King of Comedy.* New York: Doubleday, 1954.

Sennett, Ted. *Great Hollywood Movies.* New York: Harry N. Abrams, Inc., Publishers, 1986.

Sherwood, Robert E. *The Best Moving Pictures of 1922-1923.* New York: Small, Maynard and Company, 1923.

Shipman, David. *The Great Movie Stars: The Golden Years.* New York: Bonanza Books, 1970.

Shipman, David. *The Story of Cinema.* New York: St. Martin's Press, 1982.

Skretvedt, Randy. *Laurel and Hardy: The Magic Behind the Movies.* Beverly Hills, CA: Moonstone Press, 1987.

Slide, Anthony. *Early American Cinema.* New York: A.S. Barnes, 1970.

Stewart, John. *Filmarama.* vol. 1 & 2. Metuchen, NJ: Scarecrow Press, 1975 (vol. 1), 1977 (vol. 2).

Thomas, Tony. *Hollywood and the American Image.* Westport, CT: Arlington House, 1981.

Thomson, David. *A Biographical Dictionary of Film.* 2nd ed. New York: Wm. Morrow & Co., 1981.

Tibbetts, John C., ed., and Black, Gregory D., assoc. ed. *Introduction to the Photoplay: 1929, A Contemporary Account of the Transition to Sound in Film.* Shawnee Mission, Kansas: National Film Society, 1977.

Truitt, Evelyn Mack. *Who Was Who On Screen.* New York: Bowker, 1977.

Umphlett, Wiley Lee. *The Movies Go To College.* Rutherford, Madison, Teaneck, NJ: Fairleigh Dickinson University Press; London and Toronto: Associated University Presses, 1984.

United States Copyright Office. *Catalogue of Copyright Entries, Cumulative Series, Motion Pictures 1912-1939.* Washington, DC: Library of Congress, 1951.

Van Deventer, Fred. *Parade to Glory.* New York: William Morrow & Co., 1959.

Wagenknecht, Edward. *Stars of the Silents.* Metuchen, NJ: Scarecrow Press, 1987.

Walker, Alexander. *The Shattered Silents: How the Talkies Came to Stay.* London: Elm Tree Books, 1978; New York: William Morrow and Company, 1979.

Wallace, Irving. *Special People, Special Times.* New York: Pinnacle Books, 1981.

Welles, Orson, and Bogdanovich, Peter. *This Is Orson Welles.* New York: DaCapo Press, 1998.

MAGAZINES

CONTEMPORARY TRADE JOURNALS

Exhibitor's Trade Review
The Film Daily
The Film Spectator
Hollywood Reporter
Motion Picture Almanac
Motion Picture Classic
Motion Picture Herald
Motion Picture Magazine
Motion Picture News
Motion Picture Story Magazine
Motography
Movie Weekly
Moving Picture Stories
The Moving Picture World
The New York Dramatic Mirror
The Review
Variety
Wid's Daily

Articles by Harold Lloyd

Lloyd, Harold. "My Ideal Girl." *Motion Picture Magazine.* July 1918, pp 33, 113.

Lloyd, Harold, as told to Marcel H. Wallenstein. "For the People, By the People." *Filmplay Journal.* April 1922, pp 12, 52.

"The Autobiography of Harold Lloyd." *Photoplay.* May 1924, pp. 32-34, 116-119; June 1924, pp 42-44, 107-111; July 1924, pp 56-57, 113-116.

Lloyd, Harold. "What Is Love?" *Photoplay.* February 1925, p. 36.

"Harold Lloyd Tells the Most Dramatic Moments of his Life." *Motion Picture.* December 1925, p. 40.

Lloyd, Harold. "Hardships of Fun-Making." *Ladies Home Journal.* May 1926, pp 32, 50, 234.

Lloyd, Harold. "When They Gave Me the Air." *Ladies Home Journal.* February 1928, pp 19, 45.

Lloyd, Harold, as told to Louis Hochman. "My Adventures in Stereo." *Photography.* April 1954, pp. 52, 55, 122-125.

Articles about Harold Lloyd or of General Interest

Sheridan, Marguerite. "A Modern Harlequin and Columbine." *Picture Play.* December 1918, pp 216-219.

"How Harold Lloyd Joined the 'In-Bad Club'." *Photoplay.* December 1918, page unknown.

Granger, Frank. "Five Hundred a Laugh: Harold Lloyd Believes One Good Chuckle Deserves That Amount." *Motion Picture.* June 1919, pp 48-49, 92.

Laurel, Marie. "Harold Lloyd — the Happy Comedian." *Motion Picture Classic*. October 1919, pp 34, 76-7.

Leigh, Anabel. "Specs Without Glass." *Photoplay*. January 1920, p. 68.

Fredericks, James. "Lloyd: Laughsmith." *Motion Picture*. April/May 1920, p. 38.

Furman, Bess. "Alias Desperate Jack Dalton." *Motion Picture*. August 1921, pp 34, 89-90.

"Harold Lloyd's New Home." *Photoplay*. July 1922, pp 68-9.

Hall, Gladys, and Fletcher, Adele Whitely. "We Interview 'The Boy.'" *Motion Picture*. July 1922, p. 20.

Mullett, Mary B. "A Movie Star Who Knows What Makes You Laugh." *American Magazine*. July 1922, pp 36-39.

St. Johns, Adela Rogers. "What About Harold Lloyd?" *Photoplay*. August 1922, pp 21, 112.

Gebhart, Myrtle. "Mildred's Ambitions." *Picture Play*. October 1922, pp 96-97.

Howe, Herbert. "Out of His Shell." *Motion Picture Classic*. October 1922, pp 46-7, 90.

Carr, Harry. "Chaplin -vs- Lloyd." *Motion Picture*. November 1922, p. 55.

Smith, Agnes. "What a Famous Fan Thinks." *Picture Play*. November 1922, pp 27, 103.

Sands, Ethel. "A Fan's Adventures in Hollywood." *Picture Play*. December 1922, pp 56-8, 86.

"Married!" *Photoplay*. April 1923, p. 34.

Greenwood, Grace. "Why Harold Lloyd Married Mildred Davis." *Movie Weekly*. April 7, 1923, pp 21, 29.

Perlman, Phyllis. "The Boyhood of Harold Lloyd by Harold Lloyd's Mother." *Motion Picture*. July 1923, pp 38-40, 88-89.

St. Johns, Adela Rogers. "How Lloyd Made Safety Last." *Photoplay*. July 1923, pp 33, 117.

Winship, Mary. "Gag Men." *Photoplay*. July 1923, pp 44-5, 106.

"Mirrors of Hollywood. No. 2. Just a Nice Boy. Harold Lloyd is the One White Crow in the Hollywood Colony: He's Not Conceited." *Sunset*. August 1923, p. 15.

"Their Pet Aversions." *Photoplay*. June 1924, p. 74.

deRevere, F. Vance. "Faces of the Film Stars." *Motion Picture*. February 1925, p. 40.

Calhoun, Dorothy Donnell. "Harold Tells on Himself." *Motion Picture*. May 1925, p. 59.

"A House Built to Live In." *Photoplay*. September 1925, pp 56-7.

Taylor, Sam. "Directing Harold Lloyd." *Motion Picture Director*. November 1925, pp 13-14, 50.

Sherwood, Robert E. "The Perennial Freshman (Harold Lloyd)." *The New Yorker*. January 30, 1926, pp 15-16.

Howe, Milton. "Behind Harold's Spectacles." *Motion Picture*. May 1927, p. 24.

Kennedy, John B. "It Pays to Be Sappy." *Collier's*. June 11, 1927, pp 12, 28.

Donnell, Dorothy. "This is the Story of Harold the Hustler." *Motion Picture*. September 1927, p. 18.

Stevens, Jane. "7,000,000 Extras Can Be Right (as told by Roy Brooks)." *Motion Picture*. February 1928, p. 67.

Stout, Wesley W., ed. "An American Comedy." *Saturday Evening Post*. March 24, 1928, pp 6-7; March 31, pp 18-19; April 7, p. 27; April 14, p. 29; April 21, pp 26-27; April 28, p. 38.

Thomajan, P.K. "The Lafograph." *American Cinematographer*. April 1928, pp. 36-37.

Ludlam, Helen. "Harold Lloyd's New Home: Laugh That Off!" *Screenland*. September 1928, pp 48-9, 90-1.

Peterson, Elmer T. "Harold Lloyd in His Garden." *Better Homes and Gardens*. September 1928, pp 20-1, 66-7.

"Fame and Fortune From a Pair of Goggles." *Literary Digest*. October 6, 1928, pp 34-38.

"Harold Lloyd Stages a Tournament for the Professionals." *Golfers Magazine*. February 1929, p. 16.

"The Palace of a Laugh King." *Photoplay*. May 1930, pp 34-5.

Hall, Gladys. "Discoveries About Myself." *Motion Picture*. October 1930, p. 58.

"Mr. Harold Lloyd's Italian Villa in Beverly Hills." *California Arts and Architecture*. December 1930.

Hall, Gladys. "Thrift in a Palace." *Photoplay*. September 1932, pp 58-59, 104-105.

"The Return of a Comedian — Harold Lloyd." *Vanity Fair*. October 1932, pp 38-9.

Kelland, Clarence Budington. "The Cat's-Paw." *The Saturday Evening Post.* August 26, 1933, pp 5-7, 49-50, 52-53, 55. September 2, 1933, pp 20-21, 35, 39, 41-42. September 9, 1933, pp 20-21, 91-96, 98, 100. September 16, 1933, pp 20-21, 93-96, 98, 100. September 23, 1933, pp 26, 28-29, 91-92, 94, 96. September 30, 1933, pp 26, 28, 82-84, 86, 88.

Hall, Gladys. "Looking at the World Through Horn-Rimmed Specs." *Motion Picture.* September 1933, pp 40, 64.

"Portrait." *Newsweek.* August 25, 1934, p. 24.

Brundidge, Harry T. "Who'll Wear These Glasses: Harold Lloyd Wants to Know!" *Motion Picture.* November 1934, pp 45, 66.

Ganley, Frank. "Up Through the Years with Harold Lloyd." *Motion Picture Magazine.* February 1936, pp 40, 74.

Camp, Dan. "The Black Widow's Love Life (Not a Movie Star) -- Discovered by Harold Lloyd." *Motion Picture Magazine.* December 1937, pp 26, 66-67.

"Without Spectacles." *The New Yorker.* July 30, 1938, p. 8.

"Hollywood's Finest Estate Belongs to Harold Lloyd." *Life.* August 1, 1938, p. 28.

"Harold Lloyd's Hobbyhorse." *Life.* March 4, 1940, pp 68-9.

Crowther, Bosley. "Cavalcade of Movie Comics." *The New York Times Magazine.* October 20, 1940, pp 6-7.

"Lloydian Laughs by Proxy." *Newsweek.* March 17, 1941, p. 62.

Marshall, J. "Back to the Mines." *Collier's.* June 1, 1946, p. 58+.

"Harold Lloyd Comes Back." *Look.* July 23, 1946, p. 45.

Proctor, Kay. "Up to His Old Tricks." *Movieland*. October 1946, pp 62, 94-5.

"A Funny Guy with Glasses Comes Back." *Cue*. June 25, 1949, p. 18.

"Shriner." *The New Yorker*. July 2, 1949, p. 18.

"Shriners Invade City With Oriental Pageantry." *This Week in Chicago*. July 16, 1949, pp 14-18.

"Cinema: Vintage." *Time*. July 18, 1949, p. 76.

"World of Hiram Abif." *Time*. July 25, 1949, pp 13-16.

Agee, James. "Boy." *Life*. September 5, 1949, pp 78-79.

"Movie of the Week: Mad Wednesday." *Life*. November 6, 1950, pp 85,86,88.

"It's Tremendous." *Time*. January 19, 1953, p. 64.

Peck, Seymour. "Then and Now." *The New York Times Magazine*. May 10, 1953, p. 78.

Grafton, S. "Harold Lloyd." *Good Housekeeping*. May 1955, pp 54-57, 182+.

"Film Pioneers' Roll of Their Living Immortals." *Life*. January 23, 1956, p. 118.

MacGowan, Kenneth. "When the Talkies Came to Hollywood." *The Quarterly of Film, Television and Radio*. Spring 1956, pp. 288-301.

"Meeting with Harold Lloyd." *Sight & Sound*. Winter 1958-1959, pp 4-5.

"Scenes From a Side-Splitting Sampler." *Show Business Illustrated.* April 1962.

"Speedy." *The New Yorker.* May 26, 1962, pp 29-30.

Zunser, Jesse. "Comedy Is No Laughing Matter." *Cue.* June 2, 1962, p. 10.

"All-American Fall Guy." *Newsweek.* June 4, 1962, p. 98.

Garringer, Nelson. "Harold Lloyd Made a Fortune by Combining Comedy and Thrills." *Films in Review.* August/September 1962, pp 407-422.

"He Still Lives in a Star's Home." *The Philadelphia Enquirer Magazine.* December 30, 1962, pp 18-19.

"Just an Ordinary Millionaire: Harold Lloyd." *Sound Stage.* May 1965, p. 25.

"Harold Lloyd, Hal Roach: Old Chums and Litigants." *Variety.* July 21, 1965, pp 2, 70.

McCaffrey, Donald. "The Mutual Approval of Keaton and Lloyd." *Cinema Journal.* 1966-1967, pp 8-15.

"Harold Lloyd: The Serious Business of Being Funny." *Film Comment.* Fall 1969, pp 46-57.

Zimmerman, Paul D. "The Comic Merriwell." *Newsweek.* March 22, 1971, pp 110-111.

"Harold Lloyd: In Memoriam 1893-1971." *American Film Institute Report.* April 1971, p. 1.

Lipton, Norman C. "Harold Lloyd." *Popular Photography.* August 1971, pp 50, 153.

Slide, Anthony. "Harold Lloyd." *The Silent Picture.* Summer/Autumn 1971, pp 5-8.

Flinn, Tom. "Out of the Past." *Velvet Light Trap.* Winter 1971/1972, p. 6.

Kaminsky, Stuart. "Harold Lloyd: A Reassessment of His Film Comedy." *Silent Picture.* Autumn 1972, pp 21-29.

Leonard, William T., and Fulbright, Thomas. "Woody Wise Finds His Shangri-La." *Classic Film Collector.* Summer 1973, pp 8-9.

Fox, Charles. "The Harold Lloyd Estate: A Monument to Filmland." *Entertainment Magazine.* Fall 1973, pp 16-7.

"The House That Laughs Built . . ." *TV Guide.* October 20, 1973, pp 12-14.

"A Harold Lloyd Scrapbook." *Classic Film Collector.* Summer 1974, p. 48; Fall 1974, p. x2.

Kendall, Robert. "Make Way for Laughter — Here Comes Harold Lloyd." *Hollywood Studio Magazine.* October/November 1974, pp 4-12+.

Pratt, George C. "Mind Over Matter: Harold Lloyd Reminisces." *Image.* September 1976, pp 1-8.

"Time-Life Releases Lloyd Features." *Classic Film Collector.* Fall 1976, p. 1.

Reilly, Adam. "Films on Filmmaking: The Films of Harold Lloyd." *Filmmakers Newsletter.* April 1977, p. 53.

Sarris, Andrew. "Harold Lloyd: A Rediscovery." *American Film.* September 1977, pp 26-32, 49-51.

Goldstein, Ruth M. "The Feature Film in 16mm: 9 Harold Lloyd Programs." *Film News.* November/December 1978, pp 34-35.

Wilch, John. "Harold Lloyd: The All-American Boy." *Blackhawk Film Digest.* March 1979, p. 4.

Squarini, Peter. "The Enormous Popularity of Harold Lloyd." *Classic Images.* January 1980, p. 70.

Berglund, Bo. "Harold Lloyd at Keystone." *Classic Images.* September 1981, p. 16.

Fernett, Gene. "A Retrospective: Harold Lloyd." *Classic Images.* March 1983, pp 37-38.

Gordon, Herb. "Speaking of Silents: The Boy with the Glasses." *Classic Images.* May 1984, pp 51-52.

Braunstein, Bill. "The Hollywood Clowns." *New Orleans.* February 1986, pp 13-14.

"Form Harold Lloyd Endowment As Benefit To AFI Programs." *Variety.* March 9, 1988, p. 29.

Squarini, Peter. "Harold Lloyd: Box Office King." *Classic Images.* April 1988, p. 48.

Firstenberg, Jean Picker. "Passing the Baton." *American Film.* June 1988, p. 57.

deCroix, Rick. "Fighting for Reappraisal." *Classic Images.* November 1988, pp. 48-50; December 1988, pp. C8-C9; January 1989, pp. 26, 28-29; February 1989, pp. 44-45.

Brownlow, Kevin. "Harold Lloyd: A Renaissance Palace for One of the Silent Era's Great Comic Pioneers." *Architectural Digest.* April 1990, pp 160-165.

Santilli, Ernie. "Harold Lloyd: The Overlooked Overachiever." *Filmfax.* April/May 1992, pp. 70-78.

Brownlow, Kevin. "Preserved in Amber." *Film Comment.* March-April 1993, pp. 26-34.

Lyden, Pierce. "Nebraskans and Harold Lloyd." *Classic Images.* April 1993, p. 43.

"Flashback." *Vanity Fair.* April 1993, p. 93.

Rivers, Scott. "Harold Lloyd: The Third Genius." *Classic Images.* September 1993, pp C2, C4.

Newman, Byron Y. "Harold Lloyd, The Man Who Popularized Eyeglasses in America." *Journal of the American Optometric Association.* Volume 66, No. 5 (1995), pp 310-311.

D'Agostino, Annette M. "Silent Film Comedy, As Redefined by Harold Lloyd." *Films of the Golden Age.* Winter 1997/98, pp 74-79.

"Harold Lloyd: A Comic Genius Ahead of His Time." *Special Advertising Supplement of Variety, Inc.* November 1, 2005.

Robinson, Ben. "Al Flosso: An American Original Revisited at 100, 1895-1976." *The Linking Ring.* May 2006, pp 55-59.

NEWSPAPERS

"Reel Bomb Is a Real One." *The Los Angeles Times*, August 25, 1919, part 2: 5.

"Harold Lloyd Writes Describing His Accident." *Manitoba Free Press, Winnipeg*, October 18, 1919: 46.

"Harold Lloyd Weds Mildred Davis." *New York Times* 11 Feb 1923: 17.

"Form New Cinema Group." *New York Times* 23 Feb 1923: 16.

Lloyd, Harold. "Working in a Laugh Factory." *New York Times* 16 Dec 1923, sec. 9: 5.

"Harold Lloyd a Father." *New York Times* 23 May 1924: 2.

"Harold Lloyd Took a Chance." *New York Times* 20 Sept 1925, sec. 8: 5.

"Gorgeous Fairyland Playground Being Created by Landscape Architect for Harold Lloyd Home." *Los Angeles Sunday Times* 29 Nov 1925, sec. 3: 24.

"Harold Lloyd Unbosoms His Likes and Dislikes." *New York Times* 21 Mar 1926, sec. 8: 5.

Lloyd, Harold. "The Public Is The Doctor." *New York Times* 23 May 1926, sec. 8: 2.

"Lloyd a 'Frothblower.'" *New York Times* 1 Mar 1927: 30.

"Mr. Lloyd's Dogs." *New York Times* 20 Mar 1927, sec. 8: 7.

"Rain Balks Harold Lloyd." *New York Times* 28 Aug 1927, sec. 7: 3.

"Harold Lloyd's 'Specs.'" *New York Times* 6 Nov 1927, sec. 9: 5.

"Witwer Sues Lloyd for 'Freshman' Film." *New York Times* 12 Apr 1929: 8.

"Mr. Lloyd as a Talker." *New York Times* 20 Oct 1929, sec. 9: 8.

"Guard Daughters of Harold Lloyd." *New York Times* 18 Nov 1930: 2.

"Harold Lloyd Has a Son." *New York Times* 27 Jan 1931: 20.

"Who's Who This Week in Pictures." *New York Times* 18 Sept 1932, sec. 9: 4.

"Harold Lloyd Returns." *New York Times* 23 Feb 1933: 20.

"Drop Witwer-Lloyd Suit." *New York Times* 29 Aug 1933: 20.

"Modern Art Library Gets Famous Films." *New York Times* 9 Oct 1935: 27.

Churchill, Douglas W. "The Rebound of Harold Lloyd." *New York Times* 30 Jan 1938, sec. 10: 5.

Jones, Idwal. "Survivor of the Custard Pie Age." *New York Times* 3 July 1938, sec. 9: 4.

Crisler, B.R. "Of Harold Al Raschid." *New York Times* 31 July 1938, sec. 9: 3.

"Harold Lloyd Loses Tax Plea." *New York Times* 3 Aug 1940: 9.

"Mrs. Lloyd, Mother of Movie Comedian." *New York Times* 18 Aug 1941: 4.

"Harold Lloyd Saved from Fire by Wife." *New York Times* 6 Aug 1943: 17.

"Mr. Lloyd Emerges from Retirement." *New York Times* 12 Nov 1944, sec. 2: 7.

Gould, Jack. "Of Sundry Matters." *New York Times* 26 Nov 1944, sec. 2: 7.

"Lloyd Back on Screen." *New York Times* 24 June 1945: 22.

Parsons, Louella O. "Louella O. Parsons In Hollywood: Frances Ramsden and Harold Lloyd." *New York Journal-American* 2 Dec 1945: 15.

DuBois, William. "A Freshman Returns." *New York Times* 17 Mar 1946, sec. 2: 3.

"J. Darsie Lloyd, Father of Screen Actor." *New York Times* 18 Dec 1947: 29.

"Shrine Headquarters to Move to Chicago." *New York Times* 21 July 1949: 32.

"Harold Lloyd's Daughter Wed." *New York Times* 18 Sept 1950: 19.

Ludlow, Carter. "Lloyd's Daughter, Producer Mate Part." *Los Angeles Examiner* 8 Mar 1953, sec. 1: 15.

Pryor, Thomas M. "Republic is Adding Four Sound Stages." *New York Times* 16 June 1953: 24.

"Harold Lloyd's Daughter Gets Divorce Here." *Los Angeles Examiner and Express* 16 Nov 1956: A7.

Pryor, Thomas M. "Suit for $750,000 Settled by Lloyd." *New York Times* 19 Jan 1957: 13.

Crosby, John. "Twenty Years of Harold Lloyd." *New York Herald-Tribune* 2 Aug 1959: 9-10.

Ross, Don. "Freshman Now Post-Graduate." *New York Herald-Tribune* 9 July 1961, sec. 4: 4.

"Cannes Fete Cheers Harold Lloyd Film." *New York Times* 14 May 1962: 36.

Pryor, Thomas M. "670 Toss Nostalgic Nosegay to Mary Pickford, Harold Lloyd." *Variety* 8 Jan 1963: 1.

"Harold Lloyd Honored at Masquers Banquet." *Los Angeles Times* 19 Jan 1963: 8.

Schumach, Murray. "End of Era Nears for Small Studio." *New York Times* 5 July 1963: 13.

Canby, Vincent. "Young and Busy: Harold Lloyd, 73." *New York Times* 10 Nov 1966: 64.

"Mildred Davis, Wife of Harold Lloyd, 68." *New York Times* 20 Aug 1969: 47.

Otterburn-Hall, William. "Harold Lloyd: Still Hanging Around." *Louisville, Ky. Courier-Journal & Times* 8 Nov 1970: 1,3.

"Harold Lloyd, Screen Comedian, Dead." *New York Times* 9 Mar 1971: 1.

Main, Dick. "Harold Lloyd, Bespectacled Film Comic, Dies of Cancer at 77." *Los Angeles Times* 9 Mar 1971: 1, 12.

Illson, Murray. "Horn-Rims His Trademark." *New York Times* 9 Mar 1971: 1.

"Lloyd Gift to Build Film Museum." *San Diego Union* 13 Mar 1971: A-8.

Perry, George. "Harold Lloyd." *The Times (London)* 16 Mar 1971: 17.

Sarris, Andrew. "Harold Lloyd 1893-1971." *New York Times* 21 Mar 1971, sec. 2: 13.

"Harold Lloyd, Jr. Dies: Actor, Son of Comedy Star." *New York Times* 10 June 1971: 46.

Ward, Leslie. "Harold Lloyd Estate Going on the Block." *New York Times* 22 July 1975: 33.

"Harold Lloyd's Estate Brings a Top Bid of $1.6-Million." *New York Times* 28 July 1975: 24.

"See Little Chance of Saving Lloyd Estate." *Variety* 30 July 1975: 2, 62.

"Lloyd Estate Sold to Iranian." *New York Times* 31 July 1975: 33.

"Harold Lloyd Home Sale is Finalized." *Variety* 6 August 1975: 22.

Alexander, Max. "To the Rescue of America's Silent Films." *New York Times* 12 Nov 1989, sec. 2: 33.

Goodman, Walter. "Harold Lloyd: The Third Genius, on PBS." *New York Times* 15 Nov 1989, sec. 3: 26.

Grimes, William. "Hal Roach Recalls His First Century." *New York Times* 23 Jan 1992: 15.

Allan, Tom. "Weekend to Honor Silent Film Star." *Omaha World-Herald* 3 Jan 1993: 6-B.

Sterritt, David. "Chaplin, Keaton - and Lloyd." *Christian Science Monitor* 4 May 1993: 13.

Champlin, Charles. "Silent Film's Third Genius." *Los Angeles Times* 31 Mar 1993: F1.

Canby, Vincent. "Gaffes and Gags of a Shy Dimwit." *New York Times* 30 Apr 1993: pp C1, C20-21.

Allan, Tom. "Lloyd Event Is Anything But Silent." *Omaha World-Herald* 26 April 1993: pp 9-10.

INTERVIEW / ORAL HISTORY

Friedman, Arthur. "Interview with Harold Lloyd." Conducted in 1955. Transcribed in *Film Quarterly*. Summer 1962, pp 7-13.

"Oral History Project." Series III, Volume V, Pg. 76. Conducted January 1959 with Robert and Joan Franklin. Powell Library, Columbia University.

Cohen, Hubert I. "The Serious Business of Being Funny." November 1966, University of Michigan, Ann Arbor. Transcribed in *Film Comment*, V. 5, No. 3, Fall 1969, pp 46-57.

"The American Film Institute Seminar with Harold Lloyd." Held September 23, 1969. Beverly Hills, CA: Center for Advanced Film Studies, The American Film Institute, 1978.

MISCELLANEOUS DOCUMENTS

Case Papers: Harold Lloyd Corporation et al. v. Witwer, 65 F.2d 1, 1933 U.S. App., No. 6398, Circuit Court of Appeals, Ninth Circuit, dated April 10, 1933.

The FBI File (No. 9-2031) on Harold Lloyd.

The Last Will and Testament of Harold Lloyd, dated March 2, 1971.

The Hal Roach Collection. University of Southern California, Cinema-Television Library, Special Collections.

The Harold Lloyd Collection. Academy of Motion Picture Arts and Sciences, Margaret Herrick Library: containing telegrams, letters, internal communiqués relating to the Lloyd films.

E-mail communications with Richard Correll, 1995-present.

Interviews conducted for *The Lloyd Herald*, 1995-1999 and for *Variety* special issue, 2005.

Press Books: *Get Out and Get Under, Number, Please?, Now or Never, Never Weaken, Grandma's Boy, Doctor Jack, Safety Last!, Why Worry?, Girl Shy, Hot Water, The Freshman, For Heaven's Sake, The Kid Brother, Speedy, Welcome Danger, Feet First, Movie Crazy, The Cat's Paw, The Milky Way, Professor Beware, The Sin of Harold Diddlebock/Mad Wednesday, Harold Lloyd's World of Comedy.*

INDEX

Page numbers in *italics* refer to photographs, and can also contain text regarding the citation.

20th Century Fox. *See* Fox Film Corporation
3-D Hollywood, 29, 298
Abbott and Costello, 361
Academy Award, 18, 26, 247, *338*, *339*, 340; negative aspects of Lloyd's, 340-345
Academy of Motion Picture Arts and Sciences, *337*, *338*, *339*; *See also* Academy Award
Afshani, Nasrollah, 237
Albertan, The, 107
All Aboard, 91, 115
All Quiet on the Western Front, 216
All Wrong, 184
Altoona Mirror, The, 361
American Comedy, An, 23, 33, 253-254, *255*, 256-258
American Film Institute, The, 18, 28, 33, 328, 337
Among Those Present, 112, *122*, 138
Amos n' Andy, 131
Amsterdam, Morey, 354
Ancient Arabic Order of the Nobles of the Mystic Shrine. *See* Shriners, The
Anderson, Jimmy, *264*
Angus, Howard, 223
Arbuckle, Roscoe, 104-105, 133
Armour, Tommy, 307

Arnaz, Desi, *174*
Armstrong, Robert, 173
Ask Father, *99*, 157
Babe Comes Home, 247
Back to the Future, 365
Ball, Lucille, 173, *174*
Banks, Eulalie M., 234
Bara, Theda, 360
Barbier, George, 274, *278*
Bardwell, Anderson "Bard," *264*
Barthelmess, Richard, 212, *335*, *338*
Bashful, 92
Ben-Hur (1925), 176, 182
Benny, Jack, 311, 361
Bergen, Edgar, 361
Berle, Milton, 354
Best, Willie, 169
Beverly Hills, 15, 17, 18, 19, 112, 224, 228, 231, 235, 239, 292, 354
Beyond His Fondest Hopes, 72
Billy Blazes, Esq., 104, *105*, 213
Boland, Eddie, 216
Borzage, Frank, *62*, *63*, 215
Boston Herald, The, 212
Boston Red Sox, 247
Bow, Clara, 335, 360
Bowling, 308, *309*; *See also* Lloyd, Harold: hobbies
Brackett, Charles, 339

Bradbury Mansion, *90*
Brice, Fanny, 361
Bringing Up Baby, 364
Britton, Patty Lee, 336
Brooks, Roy, *14, 120*, 172, *207, 302, 303*
Brooks, Sammy, 96, *99, 103*
Brownlow, Kevin, 282, 320, 358
Bruckman, Clyde, 142
Brunet, Paul, *103*, 104, *106*, 115, 128, 133, 135, *136*, 185
Bumping Into Broadway, 22, 40, *116*, 118, 120-121, 123, 132, 302
Burkle, Ron, 237, 238
Burwood Stock Company, The, 46, 48
Bushman, Francis X., 333
Cabanne, Christy, 63
Cahn, William, 33
Cameraman, The, 215
Camp, Dan, 300
Canine Breeding, 304, *305*; *See also* Lloyd, Harold: hobbies
Captain Kidd's Kids, 22, *117*
Card, James, 335
Cartwright, Peggy, *4*, 133
Catalina Island, 214
Cat's-Paw, The, 24, *251*, 271, 272, *273, 275, 276*, 277, *278*, 279, *280*; strengths, 274
Chan, Jackie, 365
Chaney, Lon, 360
Chaplin, Charles, 8, 13, 65, 74, 75, 77, 80, 81, 82, 83, 123, 141, 143, 150, 172, 175, 335, 340-343, 345, 358, 360, 361, 362, 365
Chase, Charley, 95, 170
Chevalier, Maurice, 335
Chicago (monkey), 216, *217*, 218
Christy, Ann, 243, *249*
City Slicker, The, 96, 213
Close-Cropped Clippings, 72

Cobb, Bob, 342
Cohen, George W., 337
Cohen, Hubert I., 33, 258
Coin Flip, 13, 51-52, 54, 193, 273; early results of, 53; reason for, 51
Colman, Ronald, 335
Color Research, *289, 292*; *See also* Lloyd, Harold: hobbies
Coney Island, 241, 242, 243, 244, *249*
Conlin, Jimmy, *315*
Connor School of Expression, *45*, 48, 54, 55
Connor, John Lane, 13, 19, 20, 25, 43, 44-45, *46, 47,* 48-50, 51, 53; importance of, 48; initial meeting, 44
Coogan, Jackie, 143
Cooper, Gary, 335
Cooper, Merian C., 339
Corden, Henry, 357
Correll, Charles, 131, 326
Correll, Richard, 131, 282-283, 284, 285-286, 326, 354, 358
Coulter, Jim, 336, 342
Count the Votes, 106, 277, 332
Crawford, Joan, 335
Crizer, Thomas J., 142, 146, *178*
Cruikshank, Bobby, 307
Cummings, Constance, 278
D'Agostino, Annette M. *See* Lloyd, Annette D'Agostino
Dana, Viola, 184
Daniels, Virginia "Bebe," 20, 22, 26, 28, 61, *77, 78, 79, 80*, 97, *99*, 100, *101*, 102, *103*, 104, *105, 106*, 108, *117, 118*, 125, 133, 143, 183, *184*, 185, 186, 336, 351-352, 355
Dardis, Tom, 29
David White Company, 294
Davidson, George, 188
Davis, Caroline, 188, 242
Davis, John H. "Jack," 299, 300,

352, 353
Davis, Mildred, *14*, 15, 17, 19, 20, 22, 28, *111*, *120*, 125, 132-133, *147*, 167, 172, 184-185, *186*, 187-188, *189*, 190-191, *192*, *194*, *226*, 293, 317, 324, 326-327, 336, 351; marriage to Harold Lloyd, 186; on Harold Lloyd, 191
Day, Ned, 308
DeMille, Cecil B., 183, 185, 234, 333
Dinehart, Alan, *273*
Disney, Walt, 365
Doane, Warren, *178*
Dorgan, Tad, 80
Down Memory Lane, 346
Doyle, Diana, 188
Dr. Jack, 22, 138, 146
Dressler, Marie, 173
Dyer, Russ, 294
Eastern Westerner, An, 144, 213
Edison Film Company, 13, 55, 58
Edwards, Ralph, 336
Einstein, Albert, 355
Exhibitor's Trade Review, 91, 92, 93, 95
Fairbanks, Douglas, 123, 172, 293, 334, 338, 340, 362
Falkenburg, Jinx, 32
Famous Players-Lasky, 183
Feet First, 24, 152, *153*, *154*, 157, 271, 277; comparison with *Safety Last!*, 168
Fickett, Mary, 33
Fields, Ted, 237
Fields, W.C., 362
Fitzgerald, James "Slim Jim," 96, *99*
Flosso, Al, 304
For Heaven's Sake, 112, 114, 241, 259, 351
Forbidden Games, 339
Fox Film Corporation, 280, 346
Francis, Olin, *213*

Franklin, Robert and Joan, 33
Fraser, William R., 171, 201, 225
"Freckles and His Friends," *142*, *168*
Fresh From the Farm, 44
Freshman, The, 23, 24, 83, 112, 113-114, 141, 145, 175-176, 177, 195, *196*, 197-198, *199*, *201*, *202*, *203*, *204*, 205, 241, 246, *255*, 313, 317, 322, 339, 340, 345, 349, 350; comedy of embarrassment, 200; infringement lawsuit, 201; strengths, 197; use in *The Sin of Harold Diddlebock*, 314
Friedman, Arthur, 32
From Hand to Mouth, *4*, 22
Fun Facts, 39, 42, 49, 53, 58, 64, 72, 81, 89, 112, 123, 133, 143, 149, 167, 179, 191, 200, 209, 219, 239, 246, 256, 265, 277, 283, 311, 317, 329, 342, 349, 353
Futurama, 365
Garbo, Greta, 335
Garland, Judy, 311
Gaynor, Janet, 335
George Eastman House, 26, 27, 335
Gerstad, Harry, 166
Get Out and Get Under, 110
Gilbert, John, 254, 360
Gill, David, 358
Gillespie, William, 95, *161*
Gilmore, Helen, *96*, 98
Girl Shy, 9, 23, 113, 172, 175-179, *180*, *182*, 215, 285, 339; strengths, 181
Girl, a Guy and a Gob, A, 25, 173, *174*
Gish, Lillian, 335, 340
Glass Character, 13, 15, 21, 22, 23, 24, 73, 74, 79, 84-85, *86*, 91-93, 100, 105, 106, 115, 120, 140, 167, 205, 260, 268, 272, 279, 281, 312, 341, 364, 367; believability of romance, 84, 88, 99-100, 276-278; characteristics, 86; dawn of, 85; development of,

84; different from film-to-film, 61, 83, 88, 90-91, 150, 182, 343; early concept, 84; growth in multiple reels, 121; importance of, 90-91; most important one-reelers, 94-108; strengths, 87; surviving and lost films, 283; the glasses, 84, 87, 93; unhappy film endings, 102
Go West, 216
Gold Rush, The, 141
Golden, Robert A. "Red," 167, 171, *178*
Goldwyn, Sam, 14, 128, 337
Golf, *307*, See also Lloyd, Harold: hobbies
Gorman, Joseph G., Jr., 187
Graduate, The, 179, 180
Grandma's Boy, 22, 83, 88, 138, 144, 145, 146, *147*, *148*, 149, 150-151, 175, 204, 213, 252, *255*, 328, 339; strengths, 147
Grant, Cary, 364
Grauman, Sid, 333
Grauman's Chinese Theatre, 18, 23, *333*, 334
Great Train Robbery, The, 39
Great While It Lasted, 125
Green, Howard, 142
Greenacres, 15, 16, 19, 24, 25, 29, 33, 188, 191, 192, 194, *207*, 224, *225*, *226*, *227*, *228*, *229*, *230*, *231*, *232*, 235, *236*, 238, 239, 282, *284*, 297, 299, 306, 307, 308, 310, 324, *325*, 326, *327*, 328, 353; as film location, 237; auction of, 237; exterior features, 227; initial purchase of land, 225; interior features, 230; Rogues' Gallery, 234, subdivision, *226*
Gregg, O.M., 308
Grey, John, 142, 246
Grey, Thomas J., 142, 172
Griffin, Carlton, 177

Griffith, David Wark, 71, 143, 215, 340, 362
Griffith, Richard, 258
Guasti, William Orcutt, 26, 324
Guiol, Fred, *106*, 166
Guldin, Jere, 270
Hall, Gladys, 238, 271
Handball, 306, See also Lloyd, Harold: hobbies
Harold Lloyd: A Bio-Bibliography, 6, 30
Harold Lloyd: Master Comedian, 30
Harold Lloyd: The King of Daredevil Comedy, 29
Harold Lloyd: The Man on the Clock, 29
Harold Lloyd: The Shape of Laughter, 29
Harold Lloyd: The Third Genius, 29, 358
Harold Lloyd Comedy Collection, The, 11, 30, 274, 328, 356, 363
Harold Lloyd Comedy Theatre, The, 312, 313, *321*
Harold Lloyd Corporation, 22, 23, 24, 170, 171, 172, 174, 175, *176*, *178*, 179, 182, 200, 202, 205, 246, 303; example of mail envelope, *171*
Harold Lloyd Encyclopedia, The, 6, 30
Harold Lloyd Estate and Film Trust, The, 11, 327, 328, 329, 330, 363
Harold Lloyd Foundation, 327, See also Harold Lloyd Estate and Film Trust
Harold Lloyd's Funny Side of Life, 28, 349
Harold Lloyd's Hollywood Nudes in 3D!, 30
Harold Lloyd's Laugh Parade, 346
Harold Lloyd's World of Comedy (book), 28, 33
Harold Lloyd's World of Comedy (film), 27, 32, 346, 347, 348, 349, 350
Harold Lloyd's World of Comedy (TV series), 9, 29, 356, 357
Harrington, Joseph, *201*
Harron, Bobby, 71

Haunted Spooks, 21, 22, 125, 132, 134, 135, 136
Havez, Jean, 142, 146
Hawks, Howard, 364
Hayes, Christopher Lloyd, 29, *330*
Hayes, Jacqueline Gates, 29, *330*
Hayseed, The, 105
Heap Big Chief, 132, 170
Hear 'Em Rave, 98, 259
Herrin, Paul, 301, 302
Hey There!, 61
Hi-Fi Stereo, 298, See also Lloyd, Harold: hobbies
High and Dizzy, 100, 125, 144, 152, 157
His Royal Slyness, 22, 75, 123, 277
Holcher, Jerry, 294
Hollywood Brown Derby, 336, 342
Hollywood Filmograph, 269
Hollywood Hobby Horse, *310*, 311; See also Lloyd, Harold: hobbies
Hollywood Hobby Horse Company, Inc., 311
Hollywood Productions, 172
Hollywood Walk of Fame, 27, 28, 334-335
Holman, Russell, 246
Holt, Jack, 338
Hope, Bob, 339
Hoppe, Linda Hayward, 187
Horton, Edward Everett, 173
Hot Water, 23, 113, *172*, 357
Howe, Jay A., 142, 216
Howe, Wallace, 99, 172, *264*
Hughes, Howard, 313, 320
Hunter, Tab, 364
I Do, 110, *111*, 113, 138
I'm On My Way, 100, 105
International Bank Building, 163, *164*, 165
Intolerance, 215
It's a Wild Life, 97

Jacobs, Jake, *264*
Jamison, Bud, *95*, *99*
Joncas, Henry, 298, 299
Journal of the American Optometric Association, 87
Just Neighbors, 21, 94, 104, 105, *106*, 144
Just Nuts, 20, 64, 65, *67*, 69, 70, 72; strengths of, 67
Keaton, Buster, 8, 215, 216, 244, 335, 340, 343, 358, 360, 361, 362, 365
Kelland, Clarence Budington, 272
Kelvin, Charley, *178*
Kent, Barbara, 260, 262, *264*
Kerrigan, J. Warren, 62, *63*, 64
Keystone Film Company, 13, 20, 70, 71, 73, 135, 360; Lloyd's departure, 70
Kicking the Germ Out of Germany, 97, *98*
Kid Brother, The, 16, 23, 83, 112, 114, 145, 176, 212, *213*, *214*, 215, 216, *217*, *218*, 219, *220*, *222*, 223, 247, 277, 339, 351; strengths, 214; surprise element, 221
King of Kings (1927), 333
King, Henry, 212
KMPC (Los Angeles radio), 25
Knight, Fuzzy, *275*
Kornman, Gene, *156*, 172
Kyser, Kay, 173
Lamb, The, 93
Lampton, Dee, *99*
Langdon, Harry, 174-175
Laurel & Hardy, 8, 9, 170, 199, 361
Law, Jude, 365
Lebret, Robert Favre, 349
Lee, W. Douglas, 308
Lemmon, Jack, 364
Leonard, Gus, 96
Lesser, Sol, 175
Life (magazine), 311
Limelight, 341

Linkletter, Art, 235
Linkletter, Jack, 33
Linthecum, Dan, 64
Lloyd, Annette D'Agostino, *3*, 30, *330*
Lloyd, Elizabeth Fraser, 12, 17, 19, 20, 23, 24, 25, 34, 35, *38*, 51, 184, 190, 225, 341
Lloyd, Gaylord, 12, 17, 19, 20, 21, 25, 34, *38*, 40, 53, 56, *75*, 81, 123, 132, 171, 188, *214*, 285, 358, 363
Lloyd, Gloria, 15, 17, 23, 24, 26, 31, 33, *190*, 225, *226*, 228, 229, 242, 293, *307*, 311, 324, 336, 364, 366; interview source, 33; quotes by, 190, 191, 192, 193, 194, 226, 227, 231, 233, 234, 287, 288, 298, 355, 366
Lloyd, Harold, *3*, 4, 8, *10*, *14*, 36, *37*, *38*, *41*, *45*, *56*, *62*, *63*, *67*, *71*, *75*, *76*, *77*, *78*, *79*, *80*, *86*, *92*, *95*, *96*, *98*, *99*, *101*, *102*, *103*, *105*, *106*, *111*, *116*, *117*, *119*, *120*, *121*, *122*, *129*, *136*, *140*, *141*, *142*, *147*, *148*, *153*, *154*, *155*, *156*, *158*, *161*, *164*, *168*, *172*, *174*, *176*, *178*, *180*, *184*, *189*, *192*, *194*, *196*, *199*, *201*, *202*, *203*, *204*, *207*, *208*, *210*, *213*, *214*, *217*, *218*, *220*, *222*, *225*, *226*, *241*, *243*, *245*, *249*, *255*, *261*, *263*, *264*, *267*, *273*, *275*, *276*, *278*, *280*, *284*, *289*, *292*, *293*, *295*, *296*, *297*, *300*, *302*, *305*, *307*, *309*, *313*, *315*, *316*, *319*, *321*, *325*, *327*, *338*, *342*, *352*, *355*, *359*, *365*; admission of turning points, 6, 51, 123; anonymity afforded by glasses, 93; as a parent, 190, 193; as an inspiration for others, 364; as director of his films, 88, 89, 144, 262; autograph, 179; becomes a father, 188; biographical facts, 17; biographical sketch, 12; birth, 12, 17, 34, 358; bomb accident, 13, 14, 15, 21, 51, 125, 126-128, 129, 131, 132, 134, 135, 136, 137, 140, 144, 153, 169, 179, 209, 248, 256, 306, 334, discussion of, 126-127, impacts of, 132, on eye and hand injury, 129, 130-131, prosthesis, 128-129; break with Roach, 170; breakthrough contract, 120, 121, 132, *136*, 138; cancer diagnosis, 351; career turning points, 7, 55, 59, 65, 73, 83, 109, 115, 138, 145, 152, 170, 195, 212, 240, 259, 271, 281, 312, 345; centennial, 11, 19, 29, 34, 237, 358, 360; childhood jobs, 38, 39; chronological filmography, 367; chronology, 19; debut silent film, 55; debut sound film, 259; death, 16, 19, 28, 354; early salary dispute, 69; film debut, 55, *56*; filmmaking technique, 139; films most affected by previews, 110; final public appearance, 16, 28, 351, *352*, *355*; hobbies, 15, 26, 38, 39, 287, 288, *289*, 290, 293, 298, 299, 301, 304, 306, 307, 308, 310, 311, 312; hobbies' motivations, 288; honors, 18, 29, 30, 328, *333*, *338*, *342*, 360, 363; importance of his fans, 5, 356, 360, 366; interview sources, 32, 33; last will and testament, 28, 187, 188, 237, 327; life turning points, 34, 40, 44, 51, 125, 183, 206, 224, 253, 287, 324, 332, 351, 356; loss of films in fires, 24, 25, 281, 282, 283, *284*; marriage to Mildred Davis, 186; on radio, 25, 312; *321*; on television, 7, 8, 9, 11, 25, 26, 27, 29, 33, 235, 237, 328, 334, 336, 343, 346, 356, 360, 365; oral histories, 26, 27, 28, 32, 33; popularity, 7, 15, 76, 186, 188, 198, 200, 257, 349; quotes by, 6, 12, 31, 34, 36, 39, 40,

41, 42, 44, 46, 48, 49, 50, 52, 53, 54, 55, 56, 58, 59, 61, 62, 63, 64, 65, 69, 70, 71, 73, 75, 76, 79, 80, 82, 83, 84, 85, 86, 87, 88, 90, 91, 93, 108, 109, 110, 112, 113, 114, 118, 123, 124, 126, 127, 132, 135, 136, 138, 139, 140, 141, 142, 144, 145, 146, 150, 151, 152, 158, 159, 160, 163, 165, 166, 167, 170, 171, 172, 173, 175, 178, 185, 187, 195, 197, 198, 199, 207, 208, 209, 211, 212, 221, 223, 224, 226, 233, 240, 241, 244, 245, 247, 253, 254, 256, 257, 259, 260, 261, 262, 264, 266, 272, 273, 281, 283, 285, 287, 288, 291, 301, 302, 306, 312, 314, 317, 318, 320, 321, 322, 332, 337, 345, 346, 348, 349, 350, 356, 367; residences, 12, 21, 23, 34, 35, 56, *57, 129*, 188, 225, 227, *See also* Greenacres; salary, 14, 21, 22, 69-70, 134, 135, 186, 224; satisfaction with career, 367; stage debut, 41; stage work, 20, 41, 43, 46, 48; thrill comedies, 152; transition from shorts to features, 138, 144; transition from silent to sound, 260; use of gag men, 142-144; use of previews, 109, 221, 259, 348

Lloyd, Harold, Jr., 15, 18, 19, 24, 27, 28, *190*, 293, 336

Lloyd, James Darsie "Foxy," 12, 13, 17, 19, 20, 21, 24, 25, 34, 35, *38*, 51, 53, 56, 89, *129*, 171, *176*, 179, 188

Lloyd, Marjorie Elizabeth "Peggy," 15, 17, 18, 24, 25, 26, 27, 29, *190*, 336

Lloyd, Suzanne, 26, 29, 30, 31, 33, 131, 209, 235, 298, 324, *327*, 328, *330*, 331, 353, 358; interview source, 33; quotes by, 235, 238, 239, 288, 293, 298, 299, 324-325, 326-327, 328, 329, 330-331, 348, 351, 353; written into Lloyd's will, 326-327

Loeb, Edwin, 337

Lonesome Luke, 13, 20, 21, 73, *76, 77, 79*, 81, 83, 85, 91, 94, 98, 106, 109, 132, 195, 268, 272, 281; characteristics, 74, 76; importance of, 79-80; Lloyd's dissatisfaction with, 75, 79; surviving and lost films, 80, 283

Lonesome Luke, Lawyer, 277

Look Out Below, 21, 100, 101, 152, 157

Look Pleasant, Please, 95

Loos, Eddie, 307

Los Angeles Examiner, The, 139

Los Angeles Times, The, 127

Luke's Double, 75, 123, 335

Luke's Washful Waiting, 78

Lundin, Walter, 101, 166, 171, 176, 215, 216, 242, *264*

Lyon, Ben, 351, 355

Macdonald, J. Farrell, 274, *278*

MacKenzie, J.B., 308

Mad Wednesday, *319*, 321, 322; *See also Sin of Harold Diddlebock, The*

Magic, 301, *302*; *See also* Lloyd, Harold: hobbies

Mamoulian, Rouben, 335

Man of the Century, 365

March, Fredric, 335

Marino, Hank, 308

Marsh, Mae, 335

Marshall, Helen, 24

Marx, Groucho, 336

Mayer, Louis B., 337

McAllister, Mary, 260

McCaffrey, Donald W., 29

McCrary, Tex, 32

McGuire, L.J., 305

Mercer, Gordon, 298

Meredith, John, 297

Merkel, Una, 276, 279

Metzger, Frances, 137

Michelson, Harold, 267
Microscopy, 299, *300*; See also Lloyd, Harold: hobbies
Milestone, Lewis, 216, 247
Milky Way, The, 24, 175, 303, 312
Mitchell, George Alfred, 339
Mohan, Earl, *80*, 167
Mosquini, Marie, 99, 133
Motion Picture, 143, 271, 300
Motion Picture Classic, 267
Motion Picture News, 97, 105, 106
Movie Crazy, 24, 271, 274, 278, 303, 345, 350
Movie Weekly, 191
Moving Picture World, The, 143, 171, 212, 241, 250
Murphy, George, 173
Murphy, John L., 171, 250, *269*, 306
Museum of Modern Art (MoMA), 258, 349
My Favorite Spy, 25, 173
Nagel, Conrad, 338, 339
National Register of Historic Places, 18, 29, 30, 34, 228
Neal, Lex, 142, 216, 246
Negri, Pola, 363
Never Weaken, 22, 100, *119*, 134, 138, 152, *155*, 157, 302
New York, 23, 33, 51, 52, 55, 76, 93, 109, 114, 118, 132, 135, 188, 212, 227, 240, 241, 242, *243*, 244, *245*, 247, 248, *249*, 250, 252, 254, 270, 303, 304, 328, 335, 339, 349, 363
New York American, The, 149
New York Dramatic Mirror, The, 76
New York Herald Tribune, The, 212
New York Times, The, 109, 113, 114, 328, 363
New York Yankees, 247
Newmeyer, Fred, *105*, *141*, 142, 171, 203
Niblo, Fred, 176, 182

Nichols, Mike, 179
Nitrate Film, 25, 80, 282, 283, 284
Normand, Mabel, 8, 133, 173
Norris, Ed, 166
Novak, Jane, 65, *66*, 70
Novarro, Ramon, 335
Now or Never, 22, 112, 138
Nowell, David, 282
Nugent, Jean, 320
Number, Please?, 102, 110, *120*, 121
O'Brien, Edmond, 173
O'Byrne, Patsy, 95
Oh! Harold (fox trot), *362*
Old Gold Comedy Theatre, 25; See also Lloyd, Harold: on radio
Old Monk's Tale, The, 20, 55, *56*, 58
O'Neil, Jamie, *330*
Optical Products Corporation, 87
Orpheum Building (Los Angeles), 154
Ouimet, Léo-Ernest, 130
Our Gang, 8, 9, 170
Over the Fence, 21, 89, 94, *95*, 144, 278
Ozark Romance, An, 97, 213
Pacific Ocean Park, 120
Painting, *289*, *290*, *291*, *293*; See also Lloyd, Harold: hobbies
Paramount Pictures, 23, 118, 125, 172, 184, 237, 241, 242, *263*, 265, 303, 315, 336, 346
Parrott, James, 95, *99*
Parry, Harvey, *154*
Patchwork Girl of Oz, The, 63
Pathé, Charles, *136*
Pathé Distributors, 21, 24, 65, 69, 77, 78, 81, 82, 83, 85, 104, 115, 120, 123, 124, 125, 128, 132, 133, 135, 136, 138, 143, 184, 185, 186, 281, 282, 346; rooster, 78
Patten, Robert, 27
Pay Your Dues, 106, 115
Payne, Clyde, 311

Pelswick, Rose, 149
Pendleton, Nat, *273*
Pepperdine University, 328
Pete the Pedal Polisher, 72
Photography (magazine), 294; *See also* Stereo Photography
Photoplay (magazine), 238, 293
Phunphilms, *74*
Pickford, Mary, 123, 172, 184, 225, 293, 334, 335, 338, 340, 363
Picture Play (magazine), 14, 114
Pinched, 94
Pipe the Whiskers, 96
Pitts, ZaSu, 360
Playboy (magazine), 39
Pollard, Harry "Snub," 19, 22, 27, *79, 80*, 89, 90, 94, *95*, *99*, 100, *101*, *102*, *103*, *106*, *107*, 132, 134, 135, 170; on Harold Lloyd, 107
Popular Magazine, 202
Powell, William, 335
Pratt, George C., 33
Prevost, Marie, 293
Professor Beware, 24, 94, 287, 312, 364
Project A, 365
Queensboro Bridge, 245
Ragan, Hugh, *330*
Ralston, Jobyna, 20, 22, 23, 28, *172, 176, 177*, 181, 189, *199, 213*, 279
Ramsden, Frances, 278, 320
Reasoner, Harry, 33
Reddy, Joseph P., 172, 299
Reid, Wallace, 143
Reilly, Adam, 29
Reynolds, Debbie, 364
Reynolds, Vera, 133
Ring Up the Curtain, *101*, 102
Roach, Hal, 13, 19, 20, 29, 59, *60*, *62*, 63, 64, 65, 69, 70, 71, 73, 74, *80*, 82, 85, 101, 102, *103*, 104, 110, 115, 116, 128, 132, 133, 135, *136*, 146, 159, 160, 163, 170, 171, 174, 175, 185, 187, 212, 281, 306, 336, 340, 365, 367; initial meeting with Lloyd, 61
Robson, May, 53
Rogers, Charles "Buddy," 354
Rogers, Howard Emmett, 142, 246
Rogers, Will, 170, 362
Rolin Film Company, 13, 20, 21, 64, 65, 69, 70, 72, 73, *80*, 89, 90, 92, *98*, 102, 115, 116, 120, 133, 135, 184, 367
Romanoff, Constantine, 215, 216, *218, 220, 222*, 223, *280*
Rory o' the Bogs, *63*, 64
Rose Bowl (Pasadena, CA), 198, 204
Ross, Almon Bartlett, 25, 26
Ross, David Lloyd, 26
Rubber Limb Company of New York, The, 128
Ruth, George Herman "Babe," 247
Safety Last!, 8, 22, 83, 100, 129, 145, 151, 152, *156*, 157, *158*, *161*, *164*, 165-167, 175, 187, 197, 204, *255*, 302, 322, 339, 358; comparison with *Feet First*, 168; initial concept, 159; strengths, 160; technical details, 163-166
Sailor-Made Man, A, 15, 22, 112, 138, 139, *140, 141*, 144, 145, 147, 187
St. Clair, Malcolm, *264*
Sammy in Siberia, A, 101, *102*, 104
Samson, *62*, 63
Sands, Ethel, *14*, 15
Saturday Evening Post, The, 123, 257, 272, 276
Saunders, George M., 354
Schenck, Joseph M., 339, 340
Schickel, Richard, 29, 280
School for Visual Arts, 349
Seawright, Roy, Jr., 126

Sennett, Mack, 26, 70, 71, 175, 336, 340
Seventh Heaven, 215
Shanghai Knights, 365
Shearer, Norma, 334, 335
Shriners, The, 23, 24, 26, 206, *208*, *210*, 211, 237, 336, 340, 341, 346, 354; as Imperial Potentate, 207-208; importance of, 209
Shriners' Hospitals for Children, 209, 340
Sight and Sound (magazine), 167
Silch, Fred, 311
Silent Screen Stars Postage Stamps, 360
Sills, Milton, 338
Simonton, Richard, 284, 285; interview source, 33
Simpsons, The, 365
Sin of Harold Diddlebock, The, 25, 278, 312, *313*; 314, *315*; *316*, 319, 336; lawsuit, 322; Lloyd's dissatisfaction with, 318; Lloyd's idea for, 317
Singer Sewing Machine Company, 13, 51
Skelton, Red, 354
Solomon, Bernard, 237
Spaulding, Sumner Maurice, 225
Speedy, 18, 23, 93, 113, 197, 198, 199, 200, 201, 205, 227, *241*, *243*, 244, *245*, 246, 247, 248, *249*, 250, *251*, 252, 254, *255*, 259, 270, *276*, 340; locations filmed, 242; strengths, 240
Spitball Sadie, 21, 81
Spring Fever, 103, 144
Start Something, 132
Staunton, Field, Jr., 225
Stereo Photography, 293, *294*, *295*, *296*, *297*; See also Lloyd, Harold: hobbies
Stereo Realist Manual, The, 295
Sterling, Ford, 70, 175
Stevenson, Charles, *80*, 172, *178*, 302

Stewart, Roy, 64, 65, *68*, 70, 135
Stout, Wesley Winans, 33, 253
Strother, Bill, 159, 160, *164*
Sturges, Preston, 312, *316*, 317
Summer, John, *302*, 303
Sunday Bulletin, The, 134
Sutherland, Dick, 147
Swanson, Gloria, 335
Sylmar Earthquake, 353
Talmadge, Norma, 143, 334, 335
Taylor, Sam, 142, 146, 171, *178*
Tearle, Conway, 8
Terry, Frank, 125, *127*, 144
Thirty Days to a More Powerful Vocabulary, 191
Thompson, Jane, 188
Three Classic Silent Screen Comedies Starring Harold Lloyd, 29
Time (magazine), 276, 290
TimeLife Films, 356
Todd, Margaret Joslyn, 100
Tol'able David, 212
Trugman, Linda, *330*
Turning Point, defined, 6-7, 11, 137
Twist, Dolly, 80
Two-Gun Gussie, 213
UCLA, 26, 32, 270
Universal Film Manufacturing Company, 13, 59, 61, 63, 64, 278, 336
University of Southern California, 19, 29, 206, 328
Uplifters Club, 126, 133
Valentino, Rudolph, 360
Van Elm, George, 307
Vance, Jeffrey, 30
Variety, 274
Vernon Athletic Association, 89
Ville de Paris, 157
Vitch, Eddie, 342
Wagner, Rob (journalist), 150
Wagner, Robert (actor), 237, 364, 366

Walker, Harley M. "Beanie," 95, *139*
Wall-E, 365
Walt Disney World, 330
Warner, Jack L., 133, 307, 354
Washburn, Bryant, 184, 185
Washington Park, 89
Waterman, Thomas, 187
We Never Sleep, 21, 34, 81, 91
Weaver of Dreams, The, 184
Welcome Danger, 24, 252, 259, *261*, 262, 263, *264*, 265, 266, *267*, 268, 270, 278; change to sound format, 260; downside of sound, 263-266; initial life as a silent, 259-260
Welles, Orson, 167, 304, 364
West, Bobbie, 133
West, Mae, 173
Westmore, Wally, 303, 314, 336
Westwood Location Ranch, 23, 250, *251*, *276*, 304, 306
Whelan, Tim, 142, 171
Whiting, Dwight, *80*, 89

Why Worry?, *10*, 23, 51, 113, 142, 151, 170, 187, 189, 204, *255*, 347
Wilde, Ted, 93, 142, 171, 216, 246, 247, 248
Willie Runs the Park, 20, 72
Willie Work, 13, 20, *67*, 68, *71*, 74; characteristics, 65, 73; importance of, 65, 67; surviving and lost films, 67, 72
Willis, Leo, *213*
Wing, Paul, *330*
Witwer, H.C., 24, 200, 201, 202, 203, 205
Witzel Photographers, 14
Wrigley Field (Los Angeles), 89
Wyman, Jane, 173
Yankee Stadium, 242, 247
Yearsley, Ralph, 213
Young Mr. Jazz, 103
Young, Elmer, 112
Young, Noah, *99*, 103, 104, *105*, 266
Zeiss, Carl, 299

About the Author

ANNETTE D'AGOSTINO LLOYD has been the leading chronicler of the life and career of Harold Lloyd since the early 1990s. She is the author of four books on Lloyd, including *The Harold Lloyd Encyclopedia* (McFarland & Co., 2003), founded the world's first web site on Lloyd (www.haroldlloyd.us) in 1995, and served as a consultant/talent on the 2005 DVD box set, *The Harold Lloyd Comedy Collection*. She spent five years as the Production Coordinator and Celebrity Biographer at the historic Hollywood Forever Cemetery. She has written articles and books for *Variety* and the Motion Picture and Television Fund, has compiled two indexes on *The Moving Picture World* magazine, and has appeared in documentaries on such varied topics as Rudolph Valentino and Daytime TV Soap Operas. A native of Staten Island, New York, she now resides in Rumford, Rhode Island with her husband and son.

Here's a small sampling of a few more books published by BearManor Media.

Simply go online for details about these and other terrific titles.

www.BearManorMedia.com